From
the Field

From the Field

A Collection of Writings from

NATIONAL GEOGRAPHIC

Edited by Charles McCarry

NATIONAL
GEOGRAPHIC
SOCIETY

Grateful acknowledgment is made to all the authors who gave permission for their articles to be reprinted in this anthology.

"They Came to Stay" by Maya Angelou was originally published in *I Dream a World: Portraits of Black Women Who Changed America* by Brian Lanker. Copyright ©1989 Brian Lanker. It is reprinted with the permission of Maya Angelou.

"In Praise of Squirrels" by Diane Ackerman was originally published in NATIONAL GEOGRAPHIC and subsequently republished as part of *A Slender Thread* by Diane Ackerman. Copyright ©1996 by Diane Ackerman. It is reprinted with the permission of Random House, Inc.

Library of Congress Cataloging-in-Publication Data

From the field : a collection of writings from National Geographic /
        edited by Charles McCarry.
                p.   cm.
        Includes bibliographical references.
        ISBN 0-7922-7012-6 (hardcover)
        1. Geography. 2. National Geographic.   I. McCarry, Charles.
    G58.F   1997   97-14217
    910—dc21   CIP

TO JAMES CERRUTI
1918 - 1997

The writer's friend.

CONTENTS

FOREWORD

Gray Matter
    Charles McCarry...1

I. ORIGINS

Three Men Who Made the Magazine
    Charles McCarry...10

II. THE BACK OF BEYOND

The Land of the Yellow Lama
    Joseph F. Rock...30
Shocking the Shilluk
    Robert Caputo...37
Yankee Know-how at Machu Picchu
    Hiram Bingham...39
Preventive Measures
    Owen Lattimore...45
Mountaintop War in Remote Ladakh
    W. E. Garrett..47
A Word to the Wise
    John McCarry..55
Wild Man and Wild Beast in Africa
    Theodore Roosevelt...56
Beautification in Bali
    Donna K. and Gilbert M. Grosvenor..64
A Scidmore Sampler
    Eliza Ruhamah Scidmore
        Tsunami...65
        Morning in Benares..68
        Climbing the Gigantic Mushroom...70
"Let Me Kill, Let Me Kill"
    Loren McIntyre...72
The Celestial Horse's Mouth
    Jere Van Dyk..74
Heart of Africa
    Joseph Conrad...79

III. DESTINATIONS

A Season in the Minors
  David Lamb..82
Tough Love in the Outback
  Erla Zwingle..92
The Hard Ride of Route 93
  Michael Parfit..93
Into the Blue
  Not So Fast!
    Alexander Graham Bell...101
  Lost Over Mexico
    Charles A. Lindbergh..102
  Almost Like Someone Singing
    Anne Morrow Lindbergh..103
  My Beautiful Air-tight Cabin
    Auguste Piccard..106
  Preparing for the Worst
    Amelia Earhart..108
The Underground Railroad
  Charles L. Blockson..111
They Came to Stay
  Maya Angelou..119
Down the Zambezi
  Paul Theroux..121
Swift Justice in Swat
  William O. Douglas..130

IV. THE ANIMALS

Yesterday's Lion
  Shana Alexander...132
Dangerous Prey
  Geoffrey C. Ward 143
In Praise of Squirrels
  Diane Ackerman 145
Teaching a Dog to Speak
  Alexander Graham Bell..154
Tarantulas
  Richard Conniff 156
Outwitting a Three-toed Sloth
  David Attenborough 165
"I THINK SHE'S GOT IT!"
  Right in Among the Apes
    Jane Goodall..167

Learning the Language
    Dian Fossey..169
"Sir, the Tiger!"
    M. D. Chaturvedi..172
"Grizz"—Of Men and the Great Bear
    Douglas H. Chadwick...173
Counting Beavers
    Peter Newman...184

V. INTO THE PAST

Dinosaurs of the Gobi
    Donovan Webster...186
The Grave Beneath St. Peter's
    James Fallows...196
The Reader of Bones
    Rick Gore...200
I Found the Bones of the *Bounty*
    Luis Marden...203
The Field Itself
    Shelby Foote 219
Who Did He Think He Was?
    Willie Morris..220
Agents of Capitalism
    Nicole Duplaix...223

VI. DARK AND BLOODY GROUND

Moscow: The New Revolution
    David Remnick..226
Unretouched Photographs
    Jon Thompson...233
A Different Code
    Ross Terrill 236
Mujahidin
    Debra Denker..240
Living With the Monster—Chornobyl
    Mike Edwards..242
"Nichevo"
    Tad Szulc...248
Corregidor Revisited
    William Graves 249
Fire Fight in the Solomons
    2nd Lt. David Douglas Duncan, USMCR.......................................256

Something Great, Something American
  Arthur Zich...257
The Road of Hope
  William S. Ellis..264
Hue: My City, Myself
  Tran Van Dinh...266
"Some Missed Their Chance"
  Maynard Owen Williams 272
A Minyan
  Małgorzata Niezabitowska..273
To Heal a Nation
  Joel L. Swerdlow..275
Until the Stolen Children Die
  John J. Putman...287

VII. Nature Itself

War and Peace in a Coral Kingdom
  Peter Benchley..290
Sharks
  Feeding Frenzy
    Valerie Taylor...302
  White Death
    Richard Ellis..303
The Pole at Last?
  "Mine at Last!"
    Robert E. Peary 306
  "I Will Bank on Peary"
    Theodore Roosevelt 309
  "I Do Not Suppose That We Can Swear. . . ."
    Wally Herbert...309
Nothing Above Us
  Sir Edmund Hillary as related to Beverley M. Bowie 311
Critique
  Beverley M. Bowie..315
Frostbite
  Barry Bishop..317
Avalanche!
  Bart McDowell..319
St. Helens: Mountain With a Death Wish
  Rowe Findley..327
The Other Oregon
  William Least Heat-Moon 337
Islands at the Edge
  Jennifer Ackerman...339

Old-time Talk We Still de Talkem Here!
  Patricia Jones-Jackson 348
Monsoons
  Priit J. Vesilind 350
The Rain in Spain
  Mark W. Harrington 364

VIII. VALUE JUDGMENTS

The Peales: America's First Family of Art
  Otto Friedrich 366
Saturday to Monday
  Mark Girouard 380
The Incredible Potato
  Robert E. Rhoades 382
Il Trionfo di Gola
  Howard La Fay 390
Those Proper and Other Bostonians
  Joseph Judge 392
A Well-swept Walk
  Deborah Fallows 402
California Desert
  Barry Lopez 403
A Lean Year
  Robert M. Poole 416
How Mrs. K. Got That Way
  Boyd Gibbons 418
All That Glisters
  Peter T. White 422
The Business of Chic
  Nina Hyde 424
The Thrush on the Island of Barra
  Archibald MacLeish 430
Small-town America
  Griffin Smith, Jr. 431
Two Heartbeats
  Cathy Newman 436

IX. AFTERWORD

Oh! Susanna!
  Roy Blount, Jr. 440
A Barking Snake
  Mark B. Kerr 443

GRAY MATTER

CHARLES McCARRY

When I left NATIONAL GEOGRAPHIC in 1990, some of the picture editors who had been among my most enthusiastic allies in welcoming new writers and new kinds of writing to the magazine presented me with a mock, all-text cover as a farewell gift. It read in part: "In commemoration of all those pictures worth a thousand words you threw out of the magazine to make room for an extra 1,000 words." There was a touch of *Rashomon* in this. Though I may have coveted it, I had no power to throw a picture out of the magazine. I did sometimes oppose the inclusion, at the last minute, of yet another beautiful photograph when the only way to make room for it was to kill 50 or 60 lines of text. It was words that lived in danger at layout time, and as the editor in charge of freelance writers I took the position that text should be regarded as something more than a gray border designed to make the Kodachrome look brighter.

In time, that revolutionary thought began to make some sense to nearly everyone except, maybe, photographers, so my friends on the illustrations staff will not be surprised to discover that this book contains no pictures at all. It is 100 percent words—an example of Shelley's thousand combinations of thought as composed by the writers who have provided the magazine with its gray matter ever since the first issue appeared in 1888. Some of these writers are famous; many more are obscure. One or two were geniuses; most were talented. Although the overwhelming personality of the GEOGRAPHIC (not to mention its hypnotic illustrations) tended to obscure this fact, each wrote in his own natural voice. Somehow—and this is the point—the combination of these many different voices produced, over the 109-year history of the magazine, the singular, unmistakable voice of NATIONAL GEOGRAPHIC.

In the opening chapter of this book, an historical sketch of the GEOGRAPHIC, the reader will meet Gilbert H. Grosvenor, the brilliant amateur who transformed a tiny newsletter for geographers into a popular national magazine with an eventual readership of 40 million. Although he made the photograph queen of the magazine, GHG, as he is always called at Headquarters, started out as a writer, and all his life he remained a writer by temperament—a word man, in GEOGRAPHIC lingo. He was also, like most writers, a lover of pictures, for what is a writer if he is not an artist who attempts to capture in black ink on a white page images that only the mind's eye can see?

However, with the advent of color photography in the early 20th century, Grosvenor understood that something irreversible was happening to the business of publishing. Under the urging of his father-in-law, Alexander Graham Bell (also president of the National Geographic Society), GHG put aside his literary instincts and flooded the magazine with pictures. First with black-and-white photographs, then with hand-tinted ones, then with the muted tones of early color film, and finally with the garish hues of Kodachrome, Grosvenor and his successors transformed the magazine into a sort of monthly handheld Lascaux cave. It became, like the cave itself, a place filled with dramatically rendered images that converted familiar life-forms—exotic landscapes, rare flora, primitive peoples (especially nubile females), and above all, wild animals—into objects of myth. Alas for GHG, the lover of words, color photography turned out to be such a powerful substitute for experience that it made everything else—not just the culture of writing that dominated the 19th century, but nature itself—seem not really worth looking at. Gradually pictures, which had been inserted into a magazine for serious readers as a means of attracting subscribers from the hoi polloi, took possession of its pages. Circulation soared.

There is, of course, the aroma of a Faustian bargain in all this. But the soul of a great magazine is a hardy and resourceful creature, and the soul of the GEOGRAPHIC had millions of protectors—its subscribers. There is something deeply ironic about this. Famously, readers of NATIONAL GEOGRAPHIC never throw it away. Other magazines go into the trash bin as soon as the next issue comes out. GEOGRAPHICs go into the attic. Why? The answer, I think, is conscience. Most people subscribe to the magazine in the belief that it is educational in a particularly wholesome way—helpful in homework assignments, good for the entire family gathered around the fireplace. In reality, many members look at the pictures in each month's issue, glance at the legends (as GEOGRAPHIC picture captions are called), unfold the maps, and promise themselves to read the articles later. Not everyone actually gets around to doing so. Most Americans are too busy with their daily lives to keep ahead of the unstoppable avalanche of mind-improving information that the magazine empties into some nine million mailboxes every single month. My own mother, an indefatigable reader who inherited her older sister's collection, left me 99 years of back issues (1888-1987), which she had fully intended to read, but never did despite living to the age of 97. Conversely, neither she nor any other member of my family ever left a single line of the weekly *Saturday Evening Post* unread: In those days the only distractions from the text were not-very-funny black-and-white cartoons that could be appreciated and forgotten in a matter of seconds.

The GEOGRAPHIC's readers were right to keep the faith. While pictures heedlessly multiplied inside GHG's cave, storytellers continued to mutter away in the outer darkness, storing up in the pages of the magazine the detailed record of the actual: that which had been observed by the human eye, heard by the ear, and registered on the memory without the intervention of technology. Then as now, words drove the magazine. In most cases the assignment of a writer was the first order of business. Every story began as text—a proposal reducing the idea for an article to words, a manuscript purchased and held, sometimes for years in the hope that a suitable set of pictures would turn up and make publication possible. (Photos withered too fast to be saved for future use; they were usually rushed into print.)

If writers were valued and encouraged by GHG even after he put them on the back burner, they were less important to some later Editors—one of whom, it is said, never read a manuscript. They came to the fore again in the 1980s under the most gifted of the old man's successors, W. E. Garrett, commonly regarded as the magazine's best picture man ever. Garrett's stated objective was "to make the text as strong as the pictures," a purpose he largely attained by approving freelance assignments to an entirely new combination of famous authors, established professionals, and promising youngsters—and by bravely giving free rein to their talents.

Whatever the editorial climate, several generations of GEOGRAPHIC writers doggedly continued to turn out prose that was mostly literate and entertaining. Often it was brilliant, and rediscovering the excellence of this work has been, for me, the chief pleasure of compiling this anthology. As a youth growing up on a lonely farm in Massachusetts, I did read the GEOGRAPHIC—not because I was more virtuous than my elders but because I was a compulsive reader who, like a character in one of my novels, would read the label in her umbrella if nothing else was available on a rainy day. Lately, in the bound volumes of the magazines, I have met again the amiable companions of my youth—writers whose wonderful dispatches from the back of beyond entered my imagination in a chilly farmhouse attic during the Great Depression and continue to emerge from it decades later as the godparents of works of my own imagination. If these writers did not exactly teach me to write (only writing can do that), they taught me to want to write by suggesting what a thrilling process it was to gather the raw material of literature.

Costumed in riding breeches, puttees, and pith helmets, they were always marching—like Spencer Tracy in *Stanley and Livingstone*—toward some exotic destination where everything—absolutely everything—would be interesting. They did not bring the creatures they encountered back alive, caged and snarling like Frank Buck's tigers and gorillas. Instead, they memorized the worlds they encountered and brought them back to life on the printed page. Despite the general impression, deriving no doubt from its name, that the GEOGRAPHIC is a magazine about places, its writing is and always has been about people—strange people, naked people, quaint people, brave people, eloquent people. "I want people stories!" cried GHG's exuberant son Melville, his heir as Editor, President, and Chairman of the Board. He would have got them whether he wanted them or not. Humanity, vastly interested in itself, is the writer's only proper subject.

In my opinion, the best pure NATIONAL GEOGRAPHIC writer the magazine ever had was one of the very first—Eliza Ruhamah Scidmore. Her dispatches from Japan, from Manchuria, from one forbidden Asian vastness after another, fascinated me. She was a meticulous reporter, a fluently confident writer. A ripple of amusement ran across the crystalline surface of her prose; the essential mystery of life on Earth stirred in its depths. Her style was the expression of her personality, which was that of an independent, educated, late-Victorian woman of principle whose visible passions were those of the mind. She reminded me of my maternal aunts—schoolteachers, travelers, suffragettes, teetotalers all. Reading one of her stories was like reading a letter from my Aunt Carolyn, a teacher of geography who, every summer, set off for some interesting foreign destination aboard a tramp steamer. One could almost see Eliza's handwriting peeping through the typeface, dashing endstrokes connecting one headlong sentence to another.

Many years later, as a GEOGRAPHIC editor, I would tell blocked writers (that is to say, roughly two out of three) to compose their stories as a letter to an intelligent aunt with zero tolerance for cant or cliché. Almost always this advice worked, and when it did I usually thanked Eliza Scidmore's spirit—aloud. One day my secretary, a no-nonsense Scot who found the ways of writers very strange, popped her head through my door and asked, "Who is this Eliza you're always thanking?" Like many of the magazine's early stars, Scidmore (she would have liked that genderless modern locution, I'm sure) was a photographer as well as a writer. She was as good at the one craft as at the other, as though the two hemispheres of her brain, like the sexes in the world she desired to live in, worked in effortless harmony as absolute equals.

Quite different from wry, light-traveling, American Eliza was ponderous Joseph A. Rock, a self-dramatizing Central European who arrived in the middle of nowhere expedition-style, accompanied by platoons of coolies to carry his extensive baggage. He met royal personages on a basis of equality— with Rock condescending slightly to the monarch in order to bridge the difference between them. The double-threat man still exists in the person of Robert Caputo, a writer and photographer who traveled the length of the Nile and the Zaire and penetrated many another region of the globe little touched by civilization—most recently the Kingdom of Mustang. (That's in Nepal, of course.) Loren McIntyre spent some 40 years exploring the interior of South America, and in 1971, while on assignment for NATIONAL GEOGRAPHIC, discovered the ultimate source of the Amazon River—a pond in the Peruvian Andes afterward named Laguna McIntyre by the Inter American Geodetic Survey.

The most colorful and longest lasting of these ambidextrous types must certainly be Luis Marden, former chief of the Foreign Editorial Staff. Marden, discoverer of the bones of His Majesty's Armed Vessel *Bounty* among other wonders, has been everywhere, seen everything, known everyone—often aboard his private sailboat. The late Joseph Judge, a star among staff writers, claimed that a hermit in the far north of Alaska refused to grant him an interview because he was "saving my story for Luis Marden." In New Zealand, an airplane pilot—scarred and burned from many crashes—whom I hired to fly me into an active volcano remarked that he had flown Luis over Pitcairn Island—low. "Crazy bastard," said the pilot admiringly. A Buddhist monk in Kyoto whom I questioned about the many varieties of bamboo in the garden of his temple wondered why I was quizzing him when I might have saved myself a journey by consulting my colleague, Luis Marden, who was a renowned expert on the subject. "In Japan," said the monk, "we call Marden-san Doctor Bamboo."

For all their accomplishments, none of these people found writing for the GEOGRAPHIC easy. Nobody does. While writing any of the several articles I published in the magazine, I invariably pleaded with my wife never to let me accept another such impossible assignment. Of course, I almost always did— the satisfaction of reaching the summit makes up for the lack of oxygen, the frostbite, and the blind fear involved in the climb. To put it mildly, the magazine article is a difficult form, marrying the techniques of fiction—situation, character, conflict, dialogue—with a kind of reporting that is deeper and more textured, and longer lived, than newspaper journalism. Not everyone can master the form, and as an editor I saw some very gifted and famous writers indeed driven to despair by it. Although GEOGRAPHIC stories are sometimes longer (most of the pieces in this collection have been shortened, though not otherwise changed from their original form), the natural length of a magazine article is about 5,000 words. To describe an entire country in such a limited amount of space is a daunting undertaking. Because GEOGRAPHIC writers remain a long time in the field, the problem of sitting down to write is always the same: too much material. Nowadays a writer on a "country story" will spend about six weeks gathering material, down considerably from the two years or so that Joseph Rock lingered in China's Yunnan Province in the 1920s, but still long enough to generate enough quotes, anecdotes, and background material to write a book.

Writers who cannot cope by themselves with this embarrassment of riches ("How can I leave any of this great stuff out?") must sometimes fall back on an editor. If they couldn't write the story as a letter to a fictitious aunt, then they would be advised to just write at any length they pleased. If the reporting is there ("good writing" in the absence of solid facts is never enough), 30 excellent "greens," as the narrow, formerly emerald 186-word pages of an edited manuscript were called, can almost always be extracted from the 150-page "final" draft the writer thinks is just about the right length. No matter how radically rearranged, every word printed in the GEOGRAPHIC should be the author's; the magazine insists on printing the words it has paid for. In a typical year, the GEOGRAPHIC publishes some 70 articles. Scores of writers (and blissfully self-confident nonwriters) vie for these assignments; some staffers have produced only a handful in the course of a whole career; others, including freelancers possessed of the magic touch, may eventually take up a whole page in the Index.

Some ink-stained wretches contribute more than they get credit for. Until 1990, most adventure stories and many natural-history articles were ghostwritten. That is why there are so few of them in this anthology: It is reserved for the real thing. One real writer, William Graves, who retired in 1994 as the seventh Editor of the GEOGRAPHIC, is the actual author of most first-person tales about expeditions and adventures published in the last quarter of a century. Bart McDowell, known in the corridors as the "holy ghost," wrote many of the stories signed by Editors Melville B. and Gilbert M. Grosvenor, who were father and son. The celebrities whose stories are reprinted here—Charles Lindbergh and his wife Anne Morrow Lindbergh, Theodore Roosevelt, and others—generally wrote their own stuff, though most were trimmed to fit like everyone else.

A great pencil man, James Cerruti, the fatherly curmudgeon who was the first truly professional editor to handle "outside writers," used to claim that there were, at any given time, no more than a dozen writers alive who could write for the GEOGRAPHIC. Fortunately, new ones are born every day—to which Cerruti might growl, "Yeah, but most of them are smart enough do something easier for a living." Writers know better than anyone (better, especially, than many editors do) that writing is very difficult work. When James H. Webb, Jr., novelist, screenwriter and essayist, was Secretary of the Navy, I asked him which was more difficult, writing a novel or running the Navy and the Marine Corps. Webb replied, "Are you kidding? Nothing is as hard as writing!" Or, as Cerruti put it in a memorandum to management: "At first there is nothing but a pile of research, then weeks of running in the field filling notebooks, then sorting of material while the mind consciously and unconsciously begins to create from this Chaos a Form and finally, the Word! All we can say when it is done—with humility before the Mysterious—is 'Thank the Lord!' "

This anthology, then, is the product of 109 years of . . . admirable persistence and arduous endeavor in the face of unbeatable competition? Yes.

But more than that, of ardor. Of honest minds and honest workmanship. It is a record of how Americans saw the world—every last inch and corner of it—in the American century. Read all about it. And then, if you wish, America, throw away all those old GEOGRAPHICs, because in good conscience there will be little reason to keep them after you have read the best parts. It is even possible that those billions of back issues might still be put to good use. On the 100th anniversary of the magazine in 1988, one of the editors calculated that if all the copies ever printed were glued together end to end they would bridge the distance between Headquarters and the Moon.

As they say at the GEOGRAPHIC, What a picture!

ORIGINS

THREE MEN WHO MADE THE MAGAZINE

CHARLES MCCARRY

O n May 8, 1902, the volcano Pelee erupted on the Caribbean island of Martinique, releasing a pall of superheated ash and steam that killed nearly every man, woman, and child in the French colonial city of St. Pierre. A convict who happened to be confined in a dungeon and two or three others survived, but at least 30,000 lives were lost.

When news of the disaster reached Washington, Gilbert Hovey Grosvenor, the youthful Managing Editor of the monthly magazine of the National Geographic Society, telegraphed the Society's President, who was vacationing in Nova Scotia, to ask if he would approve spending $1,000 to send a two-man scientific expedition to the scene of the eruption. Grosvenor received the following wire in reply:

> Go yourself to Martinique in interests of Magazine and I will pay your
> expenses.... This is the opportunity of a lifetime seize it. Start within
> 24 hours and let the world hear from you as our representative. Leave Science
> to...others and give us details of living interest beautifully illustrated by
> photographs.
>
> —ALEXANDER GRAHAM BELL

Bell's telegram was the first true charter of the magazine, and every Editor since Grosvenor has been guided by Bell's masterly instructions.

When Bell became the second President of the National Geographic Society in January 1898, it had only about a thousand members, most of them in the District of Columbia, and debts of nearly $2,000.

Bell did not want the job. He was not a geographer, and he was occupied with his inventions—among innumerable other projects, he was attempting to invent the airplane through experiments with tetrahedral kites.

As he later wrote in his diary, he became President of the Society only "in order to save it." Family feeling was involved also: The Society's first President, who died in 1897, was Bell's father-in-law, the lawyer and entrepreneur Gardiner Greene Hubbard.

Bell saw THE NATIONAL GEOGRAPHIC MAGAZINE as the means of building a great organization that would permit anyone who was interested in the world to participate, as a member of the Society, in its exploration and discovery. Hitherto the privilege of supporting the great private expeditions that fascinated the 19th-century public with reports of strange peoples, inaccessible places, and great ordeals had belonged to a few scientists and men of wealth.

But Bell understood, as Gilbert Grosvenor remarked many years later, that "the simplest man takes pride in supporting research." Bell himself loved reading encyclopedias—"articles not too long, constant change in the subjects of thought, always learning something I have not known before." Though he may not have thought of his plan in exactly this way, he set out to turn the magazine into the perpetual encyclopedia of current knowledge that it has since become.

Other members of the Board of Managers strenuously opposed opening membership to men and women who had no qualification for it other than an intelligent interest in the world and all that was in it, but Bell prevailed.

"I can well remember . . . how the idea was laughed at that we should ever reach a membership of ten thousand," Bell said at the National Geographic banquet in 1912. "Why, it was ridiculous!" Yet by 1912 the Society had increased its membership more than a hundredfold, to 107,000. Prudent management of the Society's funds was providing an annual surplus of $43,000 to be devoted to the promotion of geographic science.

All this, Bell said, was primarily due to one man, Gilbert Grosvenor, who in less than 13 years had transformed the NATIONAL GEOGRAPHIC into "the greatest educational journal of the world." Grosvenor was an unlikely candidate for such striking success. When Bell hired him on April Fools' Day 1899, he was a slender, energetic 23-year-old preparatory-school teacher who had made an outstanding academic record and been a varsity tennis player at Amherst College in Massachusetts but had not a single day of experience in the magazine business.

Bell had offered the opportunity to apply for the job to Grosvenor and his identical twin brother. Edwin, the younger twin by about an hour, planned a career as a lawyer, but Bert was deeply interested in Bell's offer. He was already in love with the Bells' comely young daughter, Elsie May, whom he had gotten to know when her parents invited the twins to visit them in Nova Scotia in the summer of 1897. It was Elsie Bell who had suggested to her father that Bert might be the promising young man he had been looking for.

Bell hired Grosvenor at $100 a month, giving him the title of Assistant Editor and the mission of breathing new life into the GEOGRAPHIC. He also offered to put up $87,000 in capital—the same amount Bell and Gardiner Greene Hubbard had lost in an unsuccessful effort to popularize another magazine, *Science*, before selling their interest for $25. Grosvenor refused, protesting that he lacked the experience to handle such a vast sum (the equivalent of more than one million dollars in today's currency). He said that he believed that new ideas and hard work, rather than an infusion of money, were the answers to the magazine's problems.

The unpaid Editor was English-born John Hyde, a Department of Agriculture statistician. Young Grosvenor thought that Hyde and a staff of 12 associate editors, also unpaid, were producing a magazine filled with "cold geographic fact, expressed in hieroglyphic terms which the layman could not understand." In fact, Hyde's magazine contained some colorful, even controversial writing. Hyde was no fainthearted editor where photographs were concerned, either. He published in November 1896 the first photograph of a bare-breasted woman to appear in these pages.

Despite Bell's plan to change the style of the magazine, Grosvenor had no authority to do so. Nonetheless he went at his new job with a will, nominating his father, his twin brother, and his older brother, Asa, for membership, and pestering his father, Bell, and other eminent men to nominate their friends. The annual membership fee was then two dollars (worth about $28 in today's money), and by November 1899 he had signed up 750 new members. In his efforts to brighten the magazine's pages, Grosvenor importuned his father to approach his old friend, Gen. Lew Wallace, the author of *Ben Hur*, to contribute an article.

Then as later, Bert seemed to act on the principle that any problem could be solved by a combination of hard work, frank conversation, and good connections. In January 1904 Bell cabled Bert from Gibraltar asking that he arrange a "national reception" for the remains of James Smithson, which Bell was bringing from Genoa for reburial. The 28-year-old Grosvenor asked

President Theodore Roosevelt for an American warship to transport Smithson's remains from New York to Washington. Roosevelt detailed the U.S.S. *Dolphin* for this mission. Grosvenor then persuaded the War Department to provide a military escort to accompany the casket of the benefactor of the Smithsonian Institution through the streets of Washington.

Inevitably Bert Grosvenor's youthful brashness and energy brought him into conflict with the anti-Bell faction—some of whom, Bert noted, had "long white beards."

"I do not intend to get out of their way, as they plainly hint they want me to," he wrote to Bell on August 6, 1900. A week earlier he had written these words to his father: "Mr. Hyde is bent on remaining editor and knows that if I stay in, he will go out. . . . Outwardly I am very respectful and submissive, though it makes me boil."

It was a hot summer in Washington, with more than fifty days when the temperature went up to 90 degrees. Grosvenor sought relief from the heat by going out onto the fire escape of the Corcoran Building, where the Society's two-room headquarters was located, and listening to the jolly tunes of a hurdy-gurdy playing in 15th Street below. He found surcease from his battles with Hyde and the whitebeards by describing them in heartfelt letters to Elsie Bell, who was traveling in Europe with her parents.

His tales of intrigue, treachery, and insult had their effect. On August 30, 1900, Grosvenor received a letter from Elsie in which she promised to marry him. "I've got her at last and she won't get away—and won't try to, either," a triumphant Bert wrote his mother.

"I doubt whether Elsie would have been as sure of her own mind," Mrs. Bell wrote to Mrs. Grosvenor, "if all her love and sympathy had not been aroused by her indignation at the attacks upon him."

The turning point came when Bert was threatened with dismissal. Bell returned posthaste from Europe "to see what I can do for my boy." At a meeting of the full Board of Managers on September 14, Grosvenor was given an $800 raise and the title of Managing Editor.

The infighting that marked this situation left a lasting residue of resentment. Sixty-two years later, in an interview with Assistant Editor Allan C. Fisher, Jr., Grosvenor described his opponents as "real stinkers."

S. S. McClure, the famous editor of *McClure's Magazine*, had recommended that the NATIONAL GEOGRAPHIC change its name, move to New York, abandon the membership idea in favor of newsstand sales, and avoid all mention of the National Geographic Society on grounds that geography was an uninteresting subject. Grosvenor had opposed all these ideas.

When he and Elsie returned from their honeymoon, they learned that the Executive Committee had arranged to have the magazine printed in New York. Grosvenor canceled the printing contract on his authority as Managing Editor without consulting anyone and brought the magazine home to Washington, where he had it printed at half the cost.

This resolute action completed the rout of the opposition. In February 1903 Grosvenor was made the Editor of the magazine and Director of the Society. At the age of 27, Bert Grosvenor was in charge of everything. Thereafter very few people outside the family, and almost no one at the GEOGRAPHIC, ever called him "Bert." Dr. Melvin M. Payne, who came to the GEOGRAPHIC as a secretary in 1932 and rose to be Chairman of the Board of Trustees, says that he never heard anyone but Rear Adm. Richard E. Byrd and John Oliver La Gorce, the first member of the staff hired by Grosvenor, address him by his nickname. "Oh, he was it, the boss in every respect, no questions about that," says Dr. Payne.

Every editor who came after Grosvenor has been, as he was and believed the Editor must be, an absolute monarch whose opinions, judgment, and word are final in everything having to do with the magazine.

Although Bell retired as President in 1903, the year after Hubbard Memorial Hall was donated by the family of Gardiner Greene Hubbard as the Society's first real headquarters, his interest in the magazine did not flag. Bell frequently sent his son-in-law story ideas, as well as packages of photographs, clippings, and advice on the technique of editing. Grosvenor did not always find Bell's suggestions practical. "Mr. Bell was always anxious to be an editor," he dryly observed to Allan Fisher in 1962.

Bell kept on urging Grosvenor to travel for the magazine. "Alec won't be content until Bert goes somewhere," Mrs. Bell wrote in 1902. "This time it is to the wilds of Newfoundland to ascertain the truth . . . of a mysterious valley shut in among mountains with a still more mysterious river that disappears into the face of a perpendicular cliff 1,500 ft. high and goes—no one knows whither."

In 1907, responding to a request from Elsie Bell Grosvenor for his thoughts on the magazine, Bell wrote, "The features of most interest are the illustrations. . . . The disappointing feature of the Magazine is that there is so little in the text about the pictures. . . . It seems to me that one notable line for improvement would be either to adapt the pictures to the text *or the text to the pictures.* Why not the latter?"

In these four sentences, Bell predicted, if he did not invent, the whole future development of NATIONAL GEOGRAPHIC. With his brilliant gift for perceiving the obvious, he saw that the photograph could be turned into a narrative device that was, for journalistic purposes, more dramatic, more enticing, and more interesting than words.

Grosvenor, who in the early years spoke of improving the GEOGRAPHIC almost exclusively in terms of creating a more readable text, steadily guided the magazine in the direction Bell indicated. This may well have been because Grosvenor had already perceived that if he wished to make something new, he must use what was new—photography. He had published 11 pages of photographs of Lhasa, Tibet, from the Imperial Russian Geographical Society in the January 1905 issue, an editorial decision so unprecedented—and so expensive—that he expected to be fired for it. Instead readers stopped him in the street to congratulate him.

Grosvenor had printed the Lhasa pictures primarily to fill up empty pages, but when he saw the stir they created, he repeated the experiment, running 32 consecutive pages of photographs of the Philippines in April 1905. No editor, as he often said, had ever before printed so many pictures (138) on one subject in a single issue, and he regarded this feature as a turning point in the life of the magazine. Membership grew in 1905 from 3,400 to more than 11,000, and increased revenues permitted the Society to relieve Bell, after nearly six years, of the necessity of paying the first $1,200 of Grosvenor's annual salary out of his own pocket.

Thereafter Grosvenor was continually on the lookout for beautiful and unusual pictures, and by 1908 more than half the magazine's pages were devoted to photographs. In a letter from Kyoto, Japan, in 1912 Eliza R. Scidmore, an adventurous writer and photographer who may have been the first American professional geographer of her sex and was certainly the first woman to be elected to the Society's Board of Managers, gently tweaked Grosvenor's nose over his enthusiasm for photographs.

"Herewith 31 pictures of Japanese 'Women and Children,' mostly children, as you see," Miss Scidmore wrote. "I have had them made uniform in size and strongly colored, so that you can cover yourself all over with glory with another number in color and thereby catch a few thousand more subscribers."

This was a reference to Grosvenor's triumph in printing, in the November 1910 issue, 24 pages of hand-tinted photographs of scenes in Korea and China. These were black-and-white photographs that had been colored by a Japanese artist according to the instructions of the photographer, William W. Chapin. The response was so overwhelming that Grosvenor inserted a color feature in every subsequent November issue of the magazine. "November," he explained, "is the big renewal number."

When true color photography was perfected, he crowded the pages of the magazine with images captured by each new process. Some thought that he overdid it, or did it with too little method. In Grosvenor's time modern ideas of page design had scarcely been thought about. Although GEOGRAPHIC editors provided layouts to show the printer where the words and pictures should go, photographs often appeared in the middle of articles that bore no relation to them whatever.

"It is not against color that my soul rebels. It is against the artificial massing of color, the lily-painting," wrote bluff Maynard Owen Williams later. Williams, the far-ranging Chief of the Foreign Editorial Staff who contributed 70 articles and more than 2,200 photographs to the magazine, described himself as "a rough-neck and a camera-coolie."

Grosvenor pressed on. He had, wrote Frank Luther Mott in *A History of American Magazines*, "transformed the GEOGRAPHIC into a kind of periodical never before known."

Although it was clear very early that pictures were responsible for this success, Grosvenor continued to take pride in the progress of GEOGRAPHIC writing toward his goal of realistic reportage and simple, clear exposition, and with some reason. Joseph F. Rock, the most famous and probably the most eccentric of the free-lance explorer-photographer-writers, distilled the style that made the GEOGRAPHIC into this paragraph:

> "All was quiet and hushed, as I lay on my camp cot facing the tomb of the
> buddha whose room I occupied. Outside, the glacier stream roared, the thun-
> der rolled, and Dordjelutru staged an electrical display in this weird canyon.
> I shivered. Here, all alone, in the presence of a sacred mummy in a hoary
> lamasery, I listened to the tempest breaking over the icy peak of Minya
> Konka. . . . Had time been set back a thousand years? Did I dream, or was
> it all reality?"

Rock and the others traveled by steamship across the oceans and by camel, mule, and litter across the land. Threatened by Chinese bandits, Rock and his coolies escaped with his trunks of cameras and film across a river on inflated goatskins. Correspondents sometimes vanished for a year or two at a time, returning with half a dozen stories and a motion picture.

Grosvenor did not restrict subject matter. "When I hear of a story that will interest our members," he said, "I do not ask if it is about geography."

The excavation and mapping of the lost Inca city, Machu Picchu, by Hiram Bingham in 1912, was essentially archaeological—so much so that Grosvenor told Bingham at first that the work might not be "sufficiently geographic" to justify a grant of money. Bingham's findings, supported in part by a $10,000 GEOGRAPHIC grant, produced 186 pages of photographs, text, drawings, and maps for the April 1913 issue of the magazine. The lesson was a valuable one, and after that the Society covered every sort of expedition, flight, voyage, and excavation that promised to produce new knowledge—and interesting reading.

Grosvenor was keenly interested in what interested people. He studied other magazines for ideas, and at National Geographic lectures, which commonly attracted 3,000 people in the afternoon and another 3,000 in the evening, he watched both screen and audience to determine which pictures the people liked the most. He found that even well-brought-up young ladies preferred the dramatic ones and were not shocked by the most explicit material. The result was a dazzling, and sometimes dizzying, array of stories about everything from backyard insects (Grosvenor's brother-in-law, David Fairchild, built a camera 12 feet long, making novel images of grasshoppers, flies, and ants many times larger than the creatures themselves) to royal tombs in Egypt to "The Acorn, a Possibly Neglected Source of Food" to the magnificently illustrated "Fifty Common Birds of Farm and Orchard."

Grosvenor let his writers describe things as they saw them, and they sometimes expressed opinions that would make a modern editor blanch. ("From the sounds that blind street musicians in China produced on their strange, discordant instruments," wrote Chapin in 1910, "we thought it would be much to their own advantage to be deaf also.")

Grosvenor tried to turn his writers into photographers, providing them with the best cameras available and all the film they needed.

Some resisted. Grosvenor explained the principle to Maynard Owen Williams: "The illustration made the NATIONAL GEOGRAPHIC magazine and the magazine's life depends on getting better and better pictures.

The professional writer always *patronizes* the photographer. All right, let him, but pay no attention to him, but go ahead and *get pictures.*"

He continually warned Franklin L. Fisher, the conscientious Chief of the Illustrations Division, against penny-pinching. "Please note that I do not care whether he gets $50 or $100 or $200 worth more photographic material than he can use," he wrote in regard to Rock, a profligate user of film. *"The point to insure is that he get material to work on."*

As Williams told Assistant Editor Jesse R. Hildebrand, "Nothing lies as badly as a photograph that is not up-to-date."

More and more, Grosvenor came to regard text stories as an opportunity for photography. Often he would buy a manuscript, file it away, and wait for years for the photographs that might make it publishable. "There was quite a store of articles to be pulled out in case the subjects became newsworthy," recalls Frederick G. ("Ted") Vosburgh, a professional journalist who in 1967 became the first word man to be appointed Editor of the magazine [William Graves (1990-1994), was the other one.] "That meant you had to update an article that had been lying in the files for maybe ten years.

"Travel funds went mainly to the double threats, fellows like Maynard Owen Williams and that other great field man, Bob Moore, who could bring back the story in words and pictures," says Vosburgh. "Most of us had to write on our own time on subjects close to home to get stories into the magazine."

Grosvenor made himself into a first-rate photographer, and he was a student and teacher of the craft. Some of his pictures, particularly the luminously affectionate candid portraits that he made of his wife and children in the company of the Bells and other relations at their summer place at Baddeck, Nova Scotia, rank among the best ever taken by a GEOGRAPHIC photographer.

Grosvenor, the descendant of seven generations of New England gentry (the first Grosvenor to come to America was killed in 1691 by the blow of an Indian's tomahawk at Roxbury, Massachusetts), was a formal man who called his colleagues and most other people Mr. or Mrs. or Miss; the staff referred to him as "Chief." There is a certain endearing stiffness to the many photographs of the solemn Grosvenor that were published in the magazine over the years, as if his affectionate wife had placed his aviator's cap on his head or propped him up against a redwood just before the photographer exposed the film. Yet he was a gregarious man—he loved big ceremonial occasions and was never so happy as on an outing with his wife and children—who seems to have understood the value of humor.

"Father never minded all the jokes about the GEOGRAPHIC," says his daughter, Dr. Mabel Grosvenor, a pediatrician. "He said they made people sit up and think about the GEOGRAPHIC."

Grosvenor had a keen sense of public relations. Remembering a dinner that he had inveigled his second cousin, William Howard Taft, who became the 27th President and the tenth Chief Justice of the United States, into attending, he said, "Mr. Taft came, and we got a lot of publicity for the magazine we needed." Other Presidents, including Calvin Coolidge, who had played handball with Grosvenor at Amherst, visited the GEOGRAPHIC, especially to award the Society's Hubbard Medal to such noted explorers as Richard E. Byrd and Charles A. Lindbergh.

Volkmar K. Wentzel, a member of the Foreign Editorial Staff, was reprimanded by the business office for spending $400 to buy a surplus army ambulance on assignment in India and emblazoning it with the American and Society flags and the GEOGRAPHIC legend *National Geographic Photo Survey of India*. "I was so depressed I was ready to jump into the Ganges," Wentzel recalls. "However, a couple of days later I got a telegram from Dr. Grosvenor saying, 'Congratulations acquisition NATIONAL GEOGRAPHIC Photo Survey Car.' He understood, you see."

When the *New Yorker* magazine ran a three-part profile of Grosvenor in 1943, some believed that the author, Geoffrey T. Hellman, had had a bit too much fun with the Chief's eccentricities, especially his passion for bird-watching and for inserting pictures of birds in the magazine at every opportunity. But Grosvenor liked the portrait, admired Hellman's writing and reporting, and wrote *New Yorker* Editor Harold Ross a courtly letter of thanks for "the honor you have done me and the NATIONAL GEOGRAPHIC magazine."

A somewhat stunned Ross wrote back: "The NATIONAL GEOGRAPHIC was my father's favorite magazine. . . . If he were alive, I'd show him your letter and impress him as I never was able to impress him during his lifetime."

Grosvenor's patrician manner probably encouraged the legend that the editorial offices of the GEOGRAPHIC were in his time a sort of gentlemen's club, but in fact Grosvenor often was one of the few certifiable gentlemen on the premises. He hired people for what he thought they could do for the magazine, not for their social or educational credentials. Many early stars belonged to that class of self-taught American go-getters that flourished in the 19th and early 20th centuries. Charles Martin, the inventive head of the photo lab, had been an Army enlisted man whom Dean Worcester, then a government official, had borrowed to make photographs for the article on the Philippines. Joseph Rock was the son of an Austrian manservant. John Oliver La Gorce, Grosvenor's right-hand man for half a century and the third Editor of the magazine, was a charming and gregarious person who made friends with some of the most famous people in the world, but he had only a high-school education.

Some were newspapermen or footloose youths who simply walked in off the street and captured Grosvenor's fancy. Luis Marden, a photographer, writer, and Renaissance man who discovered the wreck of the *Bounty* among many other feats and became one of the greatest stars in the history of the magazine, overheard another man on an elevator saying that the GEOGRAPHIC was looking for an unmarried man to work as a photographer. He applied for the job and, somewhat to his own surprise, got it.

The place became so militantly unpatrician, in fact, that Grosvenor felt that he must warn Franklin Fisher. "I wish you would rid yourself of your grudge against Boston Harvard men," he wrote in 1934. "Our job on the NATIONAL GEOGRAPHIC magazine is to get the best material, regardless of whether we like or dislike the speech or manners of the man who has it."

Grosvenor was proud of having been among the first employers in Washington to hire female secretaries and clerks and thought that they were far better than men at such work. His longtime Director of Personnel, Mabel Strider, is still remembered as one of the most powerful figures in the annals of the Society. It is clear from Grosvenor's correspondence with Eliza Scidmore and many others that he liked women and wrote to them in the same tone that he used to address male correspondents. In the 1930s and 1940s he urged his editors to find more female writers, noting in 1938 that many best-sellers of that year were written by women.

"I am sure there must be some hidden talent," he wrote to Hildebrand in 1949. "Men are more forward . . . than women; perhaps that is one reason why the ladies . . . have not received as many assignments."

Yet he insisted that male and female employees eat in separate dining rooms. Carolyn Bennett Patterson, who became Senior Assistant Editor in charge of the caption-writing staff, recalls that she was scolded by Miss Strider for "walking too fast down the hall."

The practice of printing photographs of women in what a GEOGRAPHIC caption writer described as "true native dress" may seem questionable. While it can hardly be denied that these pictures played a role in the dramatic growth of membership, Grosvenor regarded the decision to publish them as a victory over prudery.

"That sort of picture at that time was quite novel—why, people were afraid to print anything showing a woman's breasts," he told Allan Fisher. Then, breaking off to examine an illustration dating from 1910, he exclaimed, "There you see a suckling child and its mother. They're beautiful!"

On the other hand he instructed his first Director of Advertising, John Oliver La Gorce, never to accept advertisements for alcohol, tobacco, or patent medicines. Grosvenor reported in his article on Russia in 1914 that the tsar's wartime ban on vodka had proved so popular with the people that they wished their sovereign to make prohibition permanent.

Grosvenor was overjoyed in his earliest days when someone overheard two workingmen discussing the GEOGRAPHIC. Those were the readers he wanted in their millions. "Please remember always to make your text as simple and natural as you can—so simple that a child of ten can understand it," he wrote to Williams, a former missionary who sometimes wrote like an ecstatic preacher.

Grosvenor could be brusque with a subordinate who displeased him or who strayed from the principles of accuracy, fairness, and high-quality production that he had laid down. After detecting an error in a story about Chicago, he blistered long-suffering, and in this case quite innocent, Assistant Editor William Joseph Showalter: "The cornerstone of the success of the NATIONAL GEOGRAPHIC is fidelity to truth; once lose our reputation for accuracy, and the GEOGRAPHIC is doomed." At the bottom of this memo he scrawled, "Please do not talk to me about this matter."

Yet when Luis Marden, then a junior member of the staff, was married, Grosvenor heard about the event and sent him a two-volume bird guide and a touching note of congratulations. "Now that you are married," he wrote, "you will realize what unfortunate people bachelors are."

In 1926 Grosvenor sent this terse memorandum to Assistant Editor Ralph Graves: "Never accept anything from Magoffin. His ways are not our ways." What exactly the ways of Magoffin might have been and why they alienated Grosvenor are not recorded in the files.

Gradually the staff and Gilbert Grosvenor grew old together. Joseph

Rock, the friend of the king of Muli (who dined in the same room with the gilded mummy of his royal uncle, and whose body wastes were "molded into pills, gilded, and dispensed among the peasants to prevent illness"), continued to send back his marvelous photographs and his long, convoluted manuscripts from the remotest parts of Asia. In 1948, after 29 years of service, Maynard Owen Williams wrote to Grosvenor: "Never grieve for me if it is my good fortune to die with my boots on. That's what I most hope for."

The magazine settled into a long afternoon, repeating the successes of an earlier day, living by methods of an earlier time. After decades on the job, the staff Grosvenor had assembled knew, perhaps too well, what the Chief wanted, and they kept giving it to him.

In the late 1930s the guard began to change. Andrew H. Brown, a fluent young writer who greatly pleased Grosvenor with the popularity of his articles, was hired in 1936. After World War II Beverley Bowie, a former intelligence officer and Harvard man, introduced a note of poetry into the text before dying young of cancer in 1958.

George W. Long, the only GEOGRAPHIC staffer ever to lose his life in the line of duty (his aircraft vanished over the Atlantic in 1958), and a skillful editor named Robert Conly began handling the copy of the veterans. John Scofield, a future Associate Editor, joined the staff in 1953, after his free-lance articles impressed Ted Vosburgh. New men sometimes found older ones out-of-date and chafed under the system that kept editorial experimentation to the minimum.

"Nothing I can do in the name of God, grammar, or friendship will prevail upon Williams to write a simple declarative sentence," wrote Hildebrand to Grosvenor.

"I am going home," Williams retorted in a countermemo. "(Declarative sentence.)"

Gilbert Hovey Grosvenor remained on the job for 55 years, and when he retired in 1954 at the age of 78, the Society's membership exceeded two million. He had outlived 65 of the 88 persons who had served during his tenure as members of the Board.

In his letter of resignation as Editor, Grosvenor referred to "the presence of a strong son beside me" that he had enjoyed for 30 years, but he recommended John Oliver La Gorce as his successor. The son, Melville Bell Grosvenor, who had been waiting quietly for his opportunity since 1924, became Associate Editor and Vice President.

Melville, born in 1901, was the first of Gilbert and Elsie Grosvenor's two sons and five daughters and is remembered by nearly everyone who ever knew him for his joyful nature, his good-hearted impulsiveness, and his love of life.

"He had the enthusiasm of several 12-year-olds," recalls Melvin Payne. "I don't often use this word, but there was a certain sweetness about Melville. It was unusual in a man as big and strong as he was. But it was there." Apparently it was there from the beginning. "You never saw such a fascinating baby," wrote Melville's Grandmother Bell in 1902. "I don't know how I live without him from day to day."

Melville and Grandfather Bell were all but inseparable. "My first conscious memory was sitting on the lap of a jolly man with a snow-white Santa Claus beard and sparkling black eyes," Melville wrote after he grew up. "He'd say, 'Pull my nose, Melville.' I'd reach up and tweak his nose and he'd go 'bow-wow-wow....' 'Now my beard.' Then he'd bellow an awful growl."

Melville rode on the back of Bell's beautiful coach horse, Champ (and later learned to ride standing up on the back of a galloping horse of his own), did his homework in his grandfather's study while the inventor did his own work, made a toy steamboat with an egg and a candle under the old gentleman's direction, went to the movies with him—and stopped on the way home at the bakeshop at Wisconsin Avenue and P Street for apple pie. Sweets were forbidden to Bell, a diabetic, and he would warn, "Don't you say a word to your grandmother."

Grandfather and grandson spent a whole winter planning a Robinson Crusoe experiment in Nova Scotia, and when summer came, roughed it together in Bell's beached houseboat in an uninhabited cove of Bras d'Or Lake with the idea of living off berries and roots. "They lasted about a day," Dr. Mabel Grosvenor recalls.

"My brother Mel was very like my Grandfather Bell," says Dr. Mabel. "I don't know whether he inherited it or not, but he had the same enthusiasm and curiosity. They were very, very much alike. Mel was much more like Grampy than like Father."

Melville graduated from the United States Naval Academy in 1923. He resigned his commission and joined the staff of NATIONAL GEOGRAPHIC the following year, beginning a wait for leadership that in its length, and in the patience of the heir apparent, rivaled that of Queen Victoria's son,

Edward VII, who was 59 when he became king of Great Britain and Ireland. Melville was almost 56 when at last he was appointed Editor and President in January 1957. He had risen slowly through the ranks, performing nearly every job on the masthead dealing with both words and pictures.

He was a fine picture editor and an excellent judge of text, even though he was a miserable speller (his father advised him to write faster and look up troublesome words in a 50-cent dictionary afterward). He was such an impatient reader that Senior Assistant Editor Bart McDowell, who ghosted many of the articles that Melville signed, once suggested that manuscripts should be lopped off at the point where the Editor stopped reading, since his attention span was perfectly calibrated to that of the average reader.

The Magazine's distinctive first-person style has been an uncomfortable one for many writers. When Melville's son, Gilbert M. Grosvenor, and Allan Fisher proposed a poll of the members to see if they would accept a change, Melville told them to go ahead, but predicted that 80 percent would want GEOGRAPHIC writers to continue using "I" and "me."

"He was off by 2 percentage points," says Fisher. "Eighty-two percent of those polled favored keeping the old familiar first person."

But Melville's greatest quality, by common consent, was his talent for leadership. He recognized good people when he found them, and when he found them, he hired them.

Few remember him by any but his given name, and few would differ with Senior Assistant Editor Howard E. Paine, who says, six years after his old chief's death and 21 years after his retirement as Editor, "I miss Melville every day."

Like his Grandfather Bell, Melville retained the boundless curiosity of boyhood well into old age. "Oh, boy, this is going to be wonderful!" he would cry, setting out for a sail on Bras d'Or Lake, waters he had navigated thousands of times before. Once under way he would be captain, guide, storyteller, and chief cook all in one, making pancakes in the shape of letters of the alphabet to match the names of any youngsters who happened to be aboard. His style as Editor was not so very different.

This miraculous capacity to be interested in everything brought him through his long apprenticeship with his spirits not only intact but also glowing in anticipation of the fun that lay before him. Although it is likely that Melville's gift for enthusiasm was a factor in the length of that apprenticeship, his father was pleased by the results his son achieved as Editor.

"Melville realizes, as I have tried to, that as the years pass, a different . . . method of expression is necessary," Gilbert Grosvenor said, five years after the changeover.

Even before he took the helm, Melville was working toward methods that would break down the orthodoxy that had settled onto the magazine as the staff grew older and more set in its ways. There had been signs of rigidity for many years. When Maynard Owen Williams tried out a Rolleiflex camera in the 1930s, he was told to "junk it" because the pictures he sent back were square, whereas only rectangular pictures, vertical or horizontal, were permitted in NATIONAL GEOGRAPHIC layouts.

Although the Rolleiflex eventually became standard equipment, a prejudice against candid cameras ran deep and lasted long. Even after the smaller cameras were adopted, they were often used to make the same static pictures produced by older cameras mounted on tripods. By the time Melville took over in 1957, of course, the magazine was half-filled with the slightly overbright, nervous hues of Kodachrome, a film that made it possible, in conjunction with new cameras and lenses, to photograph fast-moving objects in color and to make enlargements of any size that would be absolutely faithful to the colors of the tiny original.

The flexibility and artistic license that this new technology bestowed on photographers and picture editors opened up the possibility of a magazine as new, in its way, as the one that Melville's father had created.

New technology made possible an expansion, both in circulation and in the horizons of coverage, that the elder Grosvenor could only dream about—although La Gorce had foreseen the need for new printing methods if the magazine were to grow. By the early 1960s Melville had moved the printing of the magazine to Chicago, where high-speed presses made it possible not only to print many times the 2.3 million copies that could be produced on the old presses in Washington, but to print every illustration in color.

Melville wanted a staff that would understand this opportunity and one with the talent and daring to take advantage of it. Even before La Gorce retired, he started hiring. In this, as in everything else, he acted decisively on instinct, offering jobs to virtual strangers on the basis of brief interviews. Behind his seeming impulsiveness lay a clear purpose and a firm plan.

Senior Assistant Editor Mary Griswold Smith, one of the first new people brought aboard by Melville, was hired as a picture editor in June 1956. She was 21 years old. "I had very little education, and my only qualifications were that Melville had been introduced to my father and I was crazy about photographs," Mrs. Smith says. "Melville hired me on the spot. He said, 'I'm going to be Editor and I need young people around me.'"

"Melville transformed the GEOGRAPHIC from a Victorian to a 20th-century organization," says Mary's husband, Tom Smith, who rose to be Illustrations Editor, then Associate Editor. Like most others of his generation who worked with Melville, Smith remembers the experience as the happiest and most fulfilling of his life. "He was like a father to us—a wonderfully unorthodox father, and that was very stimulating to young people," Smith says. "When you'd done something he liked, he'd put that big paw of a hand on your shoulder, and with a huge smile he'd let you know that he liked you and liked your work. You treasured those moments."

Peter T. White, a staff writer who was fiercely protective of his copy, remembers returning from Laos to find that deep changes had been made in one of his stories. He stormed into the Editor's office. White was so upset over the violence that had been done to his prose that he actually shouted at Melville.

"Peter, you're not well!" Melville cried in shocked tones. "You have worms! Somebody else came back from a trip and talked to me like this, and *he* had worms." After calling White's friend and colleague, W. E. Garrett (a future Editor of the magazine) into the room to calm White, who by now was misty-eyed with loyal affection, Melville picked up the telephone and dialed a number. "I'm going to send you over to my own doctor right this minute!" he said.

Merle Severy and Howard Paine took the dummy of a 436-page book about ships to the Editor's home on a Saturday morning, expecting to spend about an hour going over the material. "We stayed for lunch, dinner, and many mint juleps—somebody had sent Melville 23 kinds of mint," Paine recalls. "When he saw what the dummy was, 'Wow! The ship book! I've been waiting for it!' So we crawled around on the floor of Melville's study until ten that night, changing the layout around. Time flew."

Predictably, this sort of management released creativity. The whole aspect of the magazine changed; the staff felt itself involved as members of a family. It was impossible to lose interest because the head of the family insisted on living in an atmosphere of new ideas and boundless optimism. Old constrictions fell away. Gone were the acorns, the rigid rules about the size of pictures and the way in which pictures might be trimmed, cropped, and laid out on the page. Photographers, exposing thousands of frames of Kodachrome in order to capture the one instant in the life of an image that would speak directly to the reader, achieved pictures the like of which had never before been seen. Writers roamed the world as freely as photographers in search of equally telling words. The magazine was, as it had been in Gilbert Grosvenor's heyday, wholly at ease with its times. Membership had more than doubled, to 5.6 million by the time Melville Grosvenor retired as President and Editor in 1967—to be succeeded first by Ted Vosburgh, and then by his son, Gilbert M. Grosvenor.

Melville Bell Grosvenor was Editor of NATIONAL GEOGRAPHIC for only ten years. But in a sense, because the young people he chose and inspired more than 30 years ago are now producing the magazine he re-created, Melville is still the spiritual Editor of NATIONAL GEOGRAPHIC, just as Alexander Graham Bell remains its inventor and Gilbert Hovey Grosvenor its architect.

Their GEOGRAPHIC was born out of change, and it has continually reinvented itself in order to keep up with the changing world that is its inexhaustible subject matter. Yet at the end of its first century the magazine remains unmistakably its original self, constant to the principles of accuracy, fairness, optimism, and experimentation on which it was founded. It is, in short, a monument to the three singular men who made it—and to their truly revolutionary idea that this journal belongs to the millions who read it, not as mere subscribers, but as members of an unending expedition to explore the earth and everything that exists upon it and beyond it.

SEPTEMBER 1988

THE BACK OF BEYOND

THE LAND OF
THE YELLOW LAMA

Joseph F. Rock

My caravan finally arrived. I donned my best and sallied forth to meet the king. The prime minister, or lord treasurer, and the king's secretary, who spoke Chinese excellently, accompanied me to the palace—a large stone structure on the lower edge of Muli, built 60 years ago.

The gateway to the palace was imposing. At either side of it two large bundles of whips were displayed to impress the villagers.

We ascended a broad, steep stairway in utter darkness. The steps were close and narrow and the railing was so low to the ground as to be useless. I had to feel my way. Two flights up and we stood before a greasy curtain, black from the marks of buttered fingers. A Hsifan servant drew it aside and we passed through an antechamber, then a large, bright room, and we were in the presence of the king.

I had great difficulty in distinguishing my host's features, as he sat with his back to the light coming from an open bay window, while he watched every muscle of my face.

The king stood 6 feet 2 inches, in high embroidered Tibetan boots of velvet. He was 36 years old, of powerful frame; his head was large, with high cheekbones and low forehead. His muscles were weak, as he neither exercises nor works. His manner was dignified and kind, his laugh gentle, his gestures graceful.

He wore a red, togalike garment, which left one arm bare. Below the tunic was a gold and silver brocaded vest and on his left wrist a rosary.

I spoke first, saying that I had heard much of the splendors of Muli and of the king's beneficence, and that I had long wished to meet him. He replied that Muli was a very poor place, and that he felt honored by my visit, coming, as I had, from so distant a country as America, whence no other man had ever come to Muli.

I doubt whether until that time he had known of the discovery of America. He did not have the slightest idea of the existence of an ocean, and thought all land to be contiguous, for he asked if he could ride horseback from Muli to Washington, and if the latter was near Germany.

Then, the king suddenly held forth his hand, asked me to feel his pulse and tell him how long he was to live! From this he jumped to field glasses, asking if I had a pair with me which would enable him to see through mountains.

He then whispered some orders to a lama, who, with great reverence and hands folded in prayer, said, "Lhaso, Lhaso," a term of humble acquiescence, and, walking backward, retired.

The prime minister soon returned with a stereopticon and some faded photographs. The king evidently thought this a splendid opportunity to satisfy his curiosity. The pictures were handed me one by one, and I had to explain what they represented, from the captions in English on the cardboard. The first was the dining room of the White House, in Washington; the others ranged from Windsor Castle to Norwegian fjords, and wound up with a jolly pre-war crowd in a German beer garden.

After the lecture, the king urged me to partake of Muli delicacies. There was gray-colored buttered tea in a porcelain cup set in exquisite silver filigree with a coral-studded silver cover. On a golden plate was what I thought to be, forgetting where I was, Turkish delight, but it proved to be ancient mottled yak cheese, interspersed with hair. There were cakes like pretzels, heavy as rocks.

It was an embarrassing situation, but, in order not to offend His Majesty, I took a sip of tea, which was like liquid salted mud. I then requested the privilege of taking photographs in Muli, and, if he would permit, some of His Majesty himself; whereupon he smiled in acquiescence. The hour was set for the next morning after prayers.

While we were talking about photography, the king issued an order to the lamas. They rushed out and returned in a few minutes with two huge boxes tied in skins, from which, to my astonishment, they took two cameras of French make, with fine portrait lenses; also an Eastman kodak, boxes with plates, rolls of printing paper, and spools of film—all of which had been opened and examined in broad daylight!

When I explained that all the plates and films and papers had been ruined, they laughed in unison and momentarily His Majesty's presence was forgotten. The king explained that the outfit was a present from a rich Chinese trader who once passed through his kingdom.

There were chemicals sufficient to start a photographic shop, but none of the court knew what they were. They watched me in awe, as I read the labels, and the king, without asking my permission, detailed a trembling lama to come to my house that very afternoon and learn all about photography within an hour!

After two lamas brought trays filled with mandarins and pretzels, I bowed and left His Majesty, who accompanied me to the greasy curtain, which he raised to let me pass.

All afternoon there droned forth from the sword temple, near the palace, the mournful sound of trumpets, gongs, and conch shells, occasionally accompanied by brass cymbals and the beating of a drum. In the evening, the king's soldiers played the bugles and drums in military fashion; a shot was fired at 8 p.m. and a bugler sounded taps.

When I had opportunity to decipher the king's calling card I learned that though his name is, briefly, Chote Chaba, his full appellation is "Hsiang tz'u Ch'eng cha Pa, by appointment self-existent Buddha, Min Chi Hutuktu, or Living Buddha, possessor of the first grade of the Order of the Striped Tiger; former leader of the Buddhist Church in the office of the occupation commissioner, actual investigation officer in matters relating to the affairs of the barbarous tribes; honorary major general of the army, and hereditary civil governor of Muli. Honorific: Opening of Mercy."

The ruler's knowledge of Tibetan was very poor, and of Chinese he knew next to nothing. He used to reside in Kulu before he became king, and was the Living Buddha of its monastery.

Early next morning the trumpeters were busy and the drummers, too. About 10 a.m. we made our way to Muli proper, within the walls, to take photographs of the temples, buildings, prayer wheels, and other things of note. The king was attending prayers.

The massive palace had window frames painted an ultramarine blue, and decorated ends of beams bearing the Buddhist colors of red and yellow. In the windows were wooden shutters made like doors. The windows may now have glass, for I suggested to the king that he have the photographic plates washed and used as windowpanes, since they were useless for making pictures.

The prime minister guided us through Muli, even to the great sanctuary, called Churah, surrounded by a special wall. A rude monk was about to slam the big gate in my face, when he spied the prime minister, and humbly, with out-sticking tongue [a sign of humility], threw it wide open.

The king spied me from his window, beckoned me upstairs, and received me kindly. Soon I had made preparations to take his first photograph.

I selected a spot against the wall, under the fat-bellied God of Luck. The monks flew in all directions, and brought numerous well-wrapped bundles containing beautiful carpets, tiger skins, gold brocade, and yellow embroidered silks and shawls. The throne was placed on the spot selected, and the carpets, cushions, and hangings arranged satisfactorily.

After a kneeling lama had taken off the king's boots, he stepped nimbly to the throne and sat cross-legged, his merry, boyish face assuming a solemn expression. A yellow and white silk cloak was placed over his shoulders and a yellow hood upon his head.

The king's dogs—three King Charles spaniels—jumped on his lap, where they usually repose. With a display of great affection, the royal pets were finally sent away, at my orders.

Then the king sat motionless for nearly 20 minutes, while I took many poses. When all was finished, he stepped gleefully from the throne—a different man.

After luncheon I was escorted to the palace square, where the king's officers and soldiers, his private guard, were assembled. Two lama officers, in spotless red garments and jackets of gold brocade, were the military chiefs of Muli. One was a stout, powerfully built man, with short mustache; the other was lean and almost lost in the folds of his uniform.

The soldiers were splendidly arrayed in red woolen cloth trimmed with leopard fur. They also wore tall red turbans, Tibetan boots of black cloth trimmed with red leather, and in their sashes short swords in silver sheaths.

While I was photographing this colorful military array, the king looked down upon the scene from the palace window. Presently he sent word that he wished me to photograph his charger fully caparisoned; but to this I demurred unless the king should come down and ride the horse. He declined, saying there were too many people about, and that he did not wish to be seen. He would, however, send down the Living Buddha of the monastery. This pleased me more, as the latter had not yet come before the camera.

When the horse was fully arrayed, the Living Buddha came through the somber palace gate. He was a boy of 18 years, fairly handsome, with rosy cheeks glowing from behind an unsuccessful wash. He wore the regulation lama robe of red, with gold brocade, and from his shoulders flowed a silken mantle with embroidered disks and borders. Then appeared the lord high treasurer with a hat of solid gold, wherewith the boy was crowned.

It was a splendid scene, worthy to be recorded on an autochrome plate, but, unfortunately, I could preserve it only in black and white.

The king's temple, with wide curtains twisted around its pillars, made a splendid background. When the Living Buddha appeared, all natives of low degree vanished like the smoke from the incense-offering chimneys in front of the palace. The sky grew dark-gray, and presently snow began to fall. I had to hurry to make the photographs.

This young Living Buddha, who now wore a golden hat and a silken mantle, was the son of a Tibetan beggar family living in a hamlet to the north. When the former Living Buddha of Muli died, he gave directions as to where his reincarnation might be found. The lamas sallied forth to seek his soul in some infant born about the hour of the late Buddha's demise. They took with them certain of the latter's possessions.

Having found a baby born at the specified time, they displayed the objects. When the child reached for a rosary, this was deemed conclusive proof that the true Living Buddha had been discovered. Thereupon the baby was carried with great pomp to the lamasery, to be worshiped thenceforth by all Muli, even the king.

What joy came to that beggar family! His mother now dwells in comfort in a house outside of Muli, while his father has passed on. The boy's title being "Hutuktu," he lives forever.

The next afternoon I took dinner with the king. The meal was served in the reception room, on separate tables, before the window, while lamas, including the king's brother, held prayer service in his bedroom.

A steaming iron pot inlaid with silver contained a great array of meats vertically arranged in slices, below which were vegetables of every kind. Rice and several other dishes were served, besides buttered tea gray as mud and of the consistency of soup.

Dessert consisted of a bowl of solid cream. Neither spoons, forks, nor chopsticks were placed beside the bowl. Not knowing Muli table manners, I waited for the king to make the first move. He raised the bowl to his mouth and took one smacking lick. I followed suit. It was the best dish served that day, but, as my tongue was not so agile nor of the proper length, I had to leave a good deal in my bowl.

The lama's secretary, who acted as interpreter, sat humbly on the floor and was not offered any delicacies. He had only buttered tea served in a wooden bowl, while ours were of gold.

After informing me that there would be a great procession of the lamas in front of my house later in the evening, the king arose and remarked that the next day he would go out to pray among the hills, but I was to see him late that evening to say farewell.

Our last day in Muli was a glorious one, during which I took photographs of the town's prayer wheels. One long row of cylindrical yak-hide wheels stood on the south side of the palace and were let into its wall. They contained miles of paper, tightly wound and covered with prayers of "Om Mani Padme Hum." All monks when passing gave each wheel a turn—a most convenient way of saying millions of prayers.

At 5 o'clock that afternoon I called upon the king to thank him for his kindness and hospitality. He graciously received me and seemed loath to have me go, saying he hoped I would come again. I was about to leave, when the lord high treasurer entered with a large tray loaded with gifts. Of these I prize most a golden bowl, two Buddhas, and a leopard skin.

His Majesty accompanied me this time not only to the door, but to the stairway, on which had gathered many curious slaves, who flew headlong in fear down the steps at the king's approach.

At the palace gate were assembled the church dignitaries, who escorted me to the big gate of Muli, lined up, and bowed me out.

We left Muli before sunrise, but took one last ride through the gates of this lama stronghold past the palace. We were met by the lama officials, among them the magistrate and judge, as well as our friend the military chief. They bowed, and we passed out through the south gate into the Muli Valley.

We were soon overtaken by the king's secretary, mounted and accompanied by a Hsifan servant. Despite his poverty, he presented me with two large brass ladles as souvenirs. Then he rode with us as far as Sili, on the other side of the Muli Valley. There he emptied a bag full of mandarins and walnuts, a parting gift from the Muli king.

We proceeded through the wilderness. The mountains were sharply outlined against the sky. In the north was one vast sea of ranges, pink and yellow, with black slopes indicating fir forest interspersed with brown meadows.

Higher and higher we ascended through silent forests. The deep valleys were lined on both sides with snow-capped crags. A peculiar loneliness stole into my heart as I rode through the firs draped with long yellowish lichens. I thought of the kindly, primitive friends whom I had just left, living secluded from the world, buried among the mountains, untouched by and ignorant of Western life.

Passing through quiet forests of pine and oak, which gave place to spruce and rhododendron higher up, I reached my first camping ground, Agù, at 12,000 feet elevation, in the midst of a fir forest. The king had ordered eight men to go out the day before and prepare camp for us. This kindness was repeated every night while we were in his domain. The balsam fir boughs were so arranged as to form a lovely compound, the fragrant branches covering the frozen ground.

There we pitched our tents and there I let my dreams take me back once more to Muli, that weird fairyland of the mountains, where its gold and riches of the Middle Ages contrast with butter lamps and pine-chip torches.

APRIL 1925

SHOCKING THE SHILLUK

R O B E R T   C A P U T O

T he Shilluk live in a frieze of villages on the west bank of the Nile, north of the Sudd, the great swamp that blocked river traffic and exploration until the mid-1800s. There they grow sorghum and graze cattle. Their *reth*, or divine king, is believed to be the incarnation of Nyikang, mythical ancestor of the tribe. The person of the king must be flawless. If even a tooth is broken, or if he is ill, he is no good, for his well-being symbolizes that of the entire tribe.

The 33rd reth, Ayang Anei Kur, graciously received me in the royal village, made up of a large courtyard surrounded by several small huts for the people and one large one for the cattle, about three miles from the Nile. While I waited for the audience, I joined a group of royal advisers in one of the huts. They wore traditional pink togas, and their brows were marked with a row of beadlike scars, symbol of the Shilluk. One of the king's many wives served us *atabobo*, the local sorghum beer, in a clay pot that was passed around the circle of men. Though a bit nervous about drinking water from the Nile, I could not show it, for the advisers watched curiously for my reaction.

The king sat in an open courtyard, cross-legged on a small platform draped with leopard skin. He held a fly whisk in one hand and his staff in the other. Petitioners approached, crouching, touching the ground with their fingertips. On the ground near him were arranged a large tape deck, a litter of cassettes, and a spittoon. Like nearly all Shilluk men, the king uses snuff, but it is taboo for his spittle to touch the ground.

Over the blare of Afro-rock music on his tape deck, the king spoke to me with grave dignity. "You have come from a long way off and have seen many things, but not the Shilluk," he said. "You must stay." I remained for several days, overwhelmed by kindness—sorghum beer at dawn, hippo stew, and much conversation. One day, as I sat on the ground next to the king, he confided a problem. "We are suffering here," he said. "We have to bring water from the river, and it's very heavy. We wish that America could help us, to make wells in our villages."

The king's secretary explained that this was a gentle hint to use my car to bring water from the river. Happy to be able to help, I unloaded equipment and filled the car with young warriors who joyfully climbed in, leaving spears and shields behind. At the Nile, watchful for hippos and crocodiles, they leapt in for a swim. We made two boisterous trips between river and village, passing women of the tribe who had walked to the water's edge to fill their own cans and carry them home—a twice-daily task.

The Shilluk take their cattle to the river every day and then drive them back to the villages. Innocently, I suggested that they could lash the water cans onto the backs of the cattle. The tribesmen were shocked. "Women have always brought water," the king's secretary explained. "Cattle are our wealth. It would be a very bad thing to make them work—it would be *torture*."

FROM "JOURNEY UP THE NILE," MAY 1985

YANKEE KNOW-HOW AT MACHU PICCHU

HIRAM BINGHAM

We decided to make a thorough hunt for places of burial and to collect as much osteological and ethnological material as could be found. Our task was not an easy one.

The engineers of the 1911 expedition—H. L. Tucker and P. B. Lanius—who had spent three weeks here making a preliminary map, had been unable to use the trail by which I had first visited Machu Picchu, and reported that the trail which they used was so bad as to make it impossible to carry heavy loads over it.

We knew that mule transportation was absolutely impracticable under these conditions, and that it was simply a question of making a foot-path over which Indian bearers could carry reasonably good-sized packs.

The first problem was the construction of a bridge over the Urubamba River to reach the foot of the easier of the two possible trails.

The little foot-bridge of four logs that I had used when visiting Machu Picchu for the first time, in July, 1911, was so badly treated by the early floods of the rainy season that when Mr. Tucker went to Machu Picchu at my request, two months later, to make the reconnaissance map, he found only one log left, and was obliged to use a difficult and more dangerous trail on the other side of the ridge.

Knowing that probably even this log had gone with the later floods, it was with some apprehension that I started Assistant Topographer Heald out from Cuzco early in July, 1912, with instructions to construct a bridge across the Urubamba River opposite Machu Picchu, and make a good trail from the river to the ruins—a trail sufficiently good for Indian bearers to use in carrying our 60-pound food-boxes up to the camp and, later, our 90-pound boxes of potsherds and specimens down to the mule trail near the river.

At the most feasible point for building a foot-bridge, the Urubamba is some 80 feet wide. The roaring rapids are divided into four streams by large boulders in the river at this point. The first reach is 8 feet long, the next nearly 40 feet, the next about 22 feet, and the final one 15 feet.

For material in the construction of the bridge Mr. Heald had hardwood timber growing on the bank of the stream; for tools he had axes, machetes, and picks—all made in Hartford—and a coil of manila rope. For workmen he had 10 unwilling Indians, who had been forced to accompany him by the governor of the nearest town. For "guide, counsellor, and friend" he had an excellent Peruvian soldier, who could be counted on to see to it that the Indians kept faithfully at their task. In describing his work, Mr. Heald says:

"The first step was the felling of the timber for the first two reaches. That was quickly done and the short 8-foot space put in place. Then came the task of getting a stringer to the rock forming the next pier. My first scheme was to lay a log in the water, parallel to the bank and upstream from the bridge, and, fastening the lower end, to let the current swing the upper end around until it lodged on the central boulder. On trying this the timber proved to be so heavy that it sank and was lost.

"We next tried building out over the water as far as we could. Two heavy logs were put in place, with their butts on the shore and their outer ends projecting some 10 feet beyond the first span. The shore ends were weighted with rocks and cross-pieces were lashed on with lianas (sinewy vines), making the bridge about 4½ feet wide, as far as it went. Then a forked upright 10 feet high was lashed and wedged into place at the end of the first pier.

"A long, light stringer was now pushed out on the completed part and the end thrust out over the water toward rock No. 2, the end being held up by a rope fastened around it and passing through the fork of the upright.

"This method proved successful, the timber's end being laid on the rock which formed our second pier. Two more light timbers were put across this way, and then a heavy one was tried, part of its weight being borne by the pieces already across by means of a yoke locked in the end. This and another piece were successfully passed over, and after that there was little trouble, cross-pieces being used to form the next and shorter span. . . .

"On the second day of work we finished the bridge about noon and started making a trail up the hill under the guidance of a half-breed who lived in the vicinity. After the first quarter mile the going was very slow. Not only did the steepness of the slope and the tangled condition of the cane jungle retard us, but the men were very much afraid of snakes, a fear which proved itselfjustified, for one of them was very nearly bitten by a little gray snake about 12 inches long.

"The second day's work on the trail took us to the city. The path was still far from being finished, though. There were many places which were almost vertical, in which we had to cut steps. Up these places we now made zigzags, so that there was comparatively little difficulty in climbing.

"On the first day I had set fire to the cane in order to clear the trail. This fire did not clear much, however. On the second day I was about a quarter of a mile behind the workmen, or rather above them, when suddenly Tomás (the Peruvian soldier mentioned above), who was with me, said: 'Look, they have fired the cane.' Sure enough, they had started it, and in a minute it had gained headway and was roaring up toward us, the flames reaching 15 or 20 feet into the air.

"There was nothing for us but to run, and we did that, tearing through the jungle down hill in an effort to get around the side of the fire. Suddenly, on one of my jumps, I didn't stop when I expected to, but kept right on through the air. The brush had masked a nice little 8-foot jump-off, and I got beautifully bumped. In a minute there came a thump, and Tomás landed beside me. It amused me so much to watch him that I forgot all about my own jolted bones. There was nothing broken, however, and we made our way without much more trouble around the fire and fell upon the peons, who were gathered in a bunch, speculating as to where we might be."

Three days later I reached Machu Picchu in company with Dr. Eaton, our osteologist, and Mr. Erdis, who, as archeological engineer, was to have charge of the general work of clearing and excavating the ruins.

Mr. Heald was at once relieved from further duty at Machu Picchu, where he had just begun the work of clearing, and was asked to see whether he could get to the top of the neighboring peak, called "Huayna Picchu," and investigate the story that there were magnificent ruins upon its summit. The same Indian who had originally told me about the ruins at Machu Picchu had repeatedly declared that those on Huayna Picchu were only slightly inferior. Mr. Heald's report of his work on Huayna Picchu runs in part as follows:

"Huayna Picchu, lying to the north of Machu Picchu, and connected with it by a narrow neck, rises some 2,500 feet above the Urubamba River, which runs around its base. On one side, the south, this elevation is reached by what is practically one complete precipice. On the other, while there are sheer ascents, there are also slopes, and, according to the account of one Arteaga, who claims to have explored the forests which cover a good deal of it, was once cultivated, the slopes being converted into level fields by low earth terraces.

"This mountain is, like Machu Picchu, cut from medium-grained gray to red granite, which accounts in part for its sharp, craggy outlines. The lower slopes, where there are any, are covered with forest growths of large trees. A peculiar thing in this connection is one solitary palm tree, which rises above the other vegetation. Near the top the large trees give place to cane and mesquite, while many slopes have nothing but grass. This last is due more to steepness and lack of soil than to any peculiarity of elevation or location, however. . . .

"My first trip to reach the summit of Huayna Picchu and to ascertain what ruins, if any, were on it, ended in failure. The only man who had been up (Arteaga), who lives at Mandor Pampa, was drunk, and refused to go with me; so I decided to try to find a way without his help. I knew where his bridge crossed the Urubamba River and where he had started up when he went the year before. With these two things to help me, I thought that I could very likely find as much as he had. Accordingly, I started with four peons and Tomás Cobines, the soldier, to have a look.

"The river was passed easily on the rather shaky four-pole bridge, and we started up the slope, cutting steps as we went, for it was almost vertical. About 30 feet up it moderated, however, and, after that, while it was steep, we seldom had to cut steps for more than 20 to 30 feet on a stretch. The greatest hindrance was the cane and long grass, through which it was hard to cut a way with the machetes.

"Our progress, slow at first, got absolutely snail-like as the men got tired; so, getting impatient, I resolved to push on alone, telling them to follow the marks of my machete, and charging Tomás to see that they made a good trail and did not loaf.

"I pushed on up the hill, clearing my way with the machete, or down on all fours, following a bear trail (of which there were many), stopping occasionally to open my shirt at the throat and cool off, as it was terribly hot. The brush through which I made my way was in great part mesquite, terribly tough and with heavy, strong thorns. If a branch was not cut through at one blow, it was pretty sure to come whipping back and drive half a dozen spikes into hands, arms, and body. Luckily I had had enough practice to learn how to strike with a heavy shoulder blow, and for the most part made clean strokes, but I didn't get away untouched by any means.

"Finally, about 3 p. m., I had almost gained the top of the lowest part of the ridge, which runs along like the back-plates of some spined dinosaur. The trees had given way to grass or bare rock, the face of the rock being practically vertical. A cliff some 200 feet high stood in my way. By going out to the end of the ridge I thought I could look almost straight down to the river, which looked more like a trout-brook than a river at that distance, though its roar in the rapids came up distinctly.

"I was just climbing out on the top of the lowest 'back-plate' when the grass and soil under my feet let go, and I dropped. For about 20 feet there was a slope of about 70 degrees, and then a jump of about 200 feet, after which it would be bump and repeat down to the river.

"As I shot down the sloping surface I reached out and with my right hand grasped a mesquite bush that was growing in a crack about 5 feet above the jump-off. I was going so fast that it jerked my arm up, and, as my body was turning, pulled me from my side to my face; also, the jerk broke the ligaments holding the outer ends of the clavicle and scapula together. The strength left the arm with the tearing loose of the ligaments, but I had checked enough to give me a chance to get hold of a branch with my left hand.

"After hanging for a moment or two, so as to look everything over, and be sure that I did nothing wrong, I started to work back up. The hardest part was to get my feet on the trunk of the little tree to which I was holding on. The fact that I was wearing moccasins instead of boots helped a great deal here, as they would take hold of the rock. It was distressingly slow work, but after about half an hour I had gotten back to comparatively safe footing. As my right arm was almost useless, I at once made my way down, getting back to camp about 5:30, taking the workmen with me as I went.

"On this trip I saw no sign of Inca work, except one small ruined wall."

Five days later Mr. Heald judged that his arm was in sufficiently good shape so that he could continue the work, and he very pluckily made another attempt to reach the top of Huayna Picchu. This likewise ended in failure; but on the following day he returned to the attack, followed his old trail up some 1,700 feet, and, guided by the same half-breed who had told us about the ruins, eventually reached the top. His men were obliged to cut steps in the steep slope for a part of the distance, until they came to some of stone stairs, which led them practically to the summit.

The top consisted of a jumbled mass of granite boulders about 2,500 feet above the river. There were no houses, though there were several flights of steps and three little caves. No family could have wished to live there. It might have been a signal station.

FROM "IN THE WONDERLAND OF PERU," APRIL 1913

PREVENTIVE MEASURES

O W E N   L A T T I M O R E

One night I stayed at the hut of a Chinese trader. These were his winter quarters; in summer he followed the Mongols in camp, trading for wool and pelts. A good enough life, he said, but too many fleas. All summer there was a pest of fleas that lived in the grass; nothing to do about it but scratch until the weather got cold. I wondered if it might not be these fleas that convey the dreaded Manchurian plague from marmots to human beings.

I slept on the same *ka ng*, or heated brick bed, with the trader, a Chinese officer, and a couple of soldiers, and reflected that the cold weather might also have its little disadvantages. Sure enough, before the trader turned in, he inspected his shirt and the waistband of his trousers. Only one or two. He grunted with satisfaction and picked up his opium pipe, which lay ready prepared, so that he could smoke rolled up in his bedding.

"Better have a puff," he said to me affably; "it certainly does keep down the lice." I almost laughed aloud. It was exactly like a man saying, "Have a shot of whiskey. Keep you from catching cold." Any excuse will do for a smoker as for a drinker. Nevertheless, it is very generally believed in those parts, and may quite possibly be true, that opium keeps down the vermin, unless they become addicts, too!

Many bandits had served as mercenaries in Chinese armies. At the tumble-down but comical inn called the Golden Horn, where I stayed, living on beef, cabbage, bread, and thin Russian beer, was a decrepit billiard table. Russians, Chinese, and Mongols played pool there all day. Among them was a Russian who was remarkably skillful, in spite of the fact that on each hand he had only the thumb and little finger, the other fingers having been chopped off. This, I was told, was because he had been a soldier in a Chinese army. In the course of a civil war it was not uncommon, when any of the dreaded Russian mercenaries were taken prisoner by the other side, to cut off their fingers in this way to make sure that they would never handle a rifle again.

FROM "BYROADS AND BACKWOODS OF MANCHURIA," JULY 1932

MOUNTAINTOP WAR IN REMOTE LADAKH

W. E. GARRETT

On my first night in Ladakh, it had been minus 30°F. in these high passes, but now we stood in the warming midday sun. Maj. C. S. Tanwar, of the Indian Army's northwest frontier forces, was telling me of his part in the recent battle at Chushul airstrip.

"Chinese loud-speakers had been telling us we were on their land and must leave peacefully. They didn't want trouble, they said. They wanted to be our friends. Then, during a blizzard at 3 a.m. on the 18th of November, they started shelling us—about 600 mortar rounds altogether. By 3:30 several hundred Chinese were closing in."

The major made a gesture of fumbling with a bolt-action rifle. "Our hands were so cold we could get off only five shots a minute. We had to fall back. The company on our right was surrounded. Their area fell by 6:30, but we heard some firing until 8:00. Their commanding officer was a good friend of mine. Six of his men got out, all wounded; he didn't. There had been 130 men there."

Major Tanwar's cold frankness about his defeat was embarrassing at first. But as I began to understand the odds he had faced here, the loss of only one ridge seemed a victory.

His men, like the rest of the Indian Army, were equipped with World War I Enfield rifles. They were trained for peace with China. They had been attacked by an army toughened by action in Korea and Tibet, firing the latest automatic weapons. Now a cease-fire proclaimed by the Chinese had stopped the fighting as suddenly as it had started.

What had brought about this Sino-Indian collision? Back in New Delhi, India's Prime Minister Nehru, still clutching at neutrality, had told me sadly: "We were betrayed."

Betrayed? Perhaps. But certainly not surprised. Even before 1954, Chinese maps were claiming all of Ladakh north of the Indus, and repeated border clashes led to accusations that fill eight volumes of white papers.

Much of Ladakh's border is poorly defined and has never been surveyed. The part now occupied by India covers 27,000 square miles, which corresponds to the size of West Virginia. The inhabitants number 80,000. Pakistan occupies a large area in the northwest.

For at least six years the Chinese have maintained outposts in northeastern Ladakh, in an 8,000-square-mile area called Aksai Chin. They built a road there, to connect their Sinkiang Province with their strong points in Tibet. An Indian patrol, sent to investigate in 1958, was captured.

Last October Prime Minister Nehru told his soldiers to free Indian territory of Chinese intruders. Fighting followed, and on November 18 the Chinese launched a major attack. They captured another 2,000 square miles of Ladakh before the cease-fire.

Now the Indians had dug into new positions, and new weapons were arriving from Britain and the United States. I had landed at Leh, Ladakh's capital, with an arms shipment delivered by the U.S. Air Force, and traveled 65 miles to the front by helicopter.

As I talked with Major Tanwar an Indian correspondent from the plains huddled behind our jeep, suffering from altitude sickness. Our New Delhi briefing on Ladakh had warned us: "Newcomers will experience difficulty in breathing, sleeplessness, and loss of capacity for sustained mental effort." Nobody had mentioned nausea, which was to afflict several of our party.

The major voiced sympathy. "The altitude bothers everybody the first few days. During the battle two of my men died of heart failure."

Here the heart could not always be as strong as the mind's will to fight. The thin air of this rocky roof of the world starves the heart and lungs of the fighting man. Ladakh's lowest valley lies more than a mile above sea level. Its highest mountain, K2, rises to 28,250 feet—only 778 lower than the summit of Everest.

Alternate heating and freezing pulverizes the bare rock slopes into a fine granite dust that seems lighter than air. Wind sweeps the dust into Sahara-like dunes, and flings it back in thin layers on the rocks. Dust billows behind every footstep and moving wheel, and mixes with the blowing snow.

The Indian Government has restricted travel to Ladakh, but throughout history the most forbidding deterrent has been the terrain. It was 1631 before the first Westerners reached Leh, in its mountain-locked valley near the Indus River.

The first automobile road from the outside world was opened three years ago, but it is closed by winter weather. Several months in the year Ladakh can be supplied only by air.

Many stories have grown up around the Ladakhis' reaction to airplanes. According to one, when the first plane landed in 1948, they brought hay to feed it.

Another story tells of a father pointing to the jeeps being unloaded from a plane and telling his son that these babies would grow up, sprout wings, and fly like their mother.

The big U.S. Air Force C-130 that had brought me to the airstrip near Leh was unloaded quickly. Soon it circled up and out of the valley heading back to New Delhi for another load before a sudden winter storm could close the field. I tossed my bedroll into a jeep and rode up to Leh, which snuggles against a cleft in the mountains 500 feet above the airstrip.

On my first walk through the 11,550-foot-high capital, the mental vagueness of hypoxia—oxygen shortage—made it easy for me to imagine myself a traveler in some earlier century.

It snowed gently, the tiny flakes falling so slowly that they seemed suspended in the air. The snow-filtered light softened the ugliness of Leh's wide dirt main street and the two-story buildings of stone and clay. Little Asian ponies with top-heavy loads were led by short, heavily robed Tibetan-looking men. I side-stepped slow-moving dzos, animals half yak and half cow that provide the Ladakhis with milk, meat, and transportation.

Soldiers from south India, racially almost as novel to these people as I who had come from the other side of the world, strolled among them.

Occasionally I greeted a native with the one word I knew in their Tibetan-Burmese dialect: "*Jooley.*" It means "Good morning," "Good day," or "How are you?" and it always brought a friendly "Jooley" in return.

But one of my "Jooleys" brought a surprising "Hello" from an elderly, well-dressed man. We introduced ourselves.

Mr. Het Ram was a shopkeeper, the president of the local merchants association and, like most of Leh's businessmen, he was not a Ladakhi but an Indian from the plains. For 42 years he had traded in silks and spices between India and China, through the 18,290-foot Karakoram Pass. He had led many of his caravans himself.

On my boyhood bookshelves the Oriental caravans had seemed immeasurably far away, and deep in the romantic past of Marco Polo and the Chinese bandits. But here was a man who had recently lived this life.

"We carried wool, cotton, dyes, spices, and general merchandise to Yarkand and Kashgar in China," Mr. Het Ram told me. "We brought back silk, tea, and carpets. Sometimes we had a hundred animals but usually about 30. We used horses, camels, yaks, and even sheep."

I asked, "Did bandits bother you?"

"Never."

Sensing my surprise, he went on: "Say that one year we would have 90 loads and only 30 animals. We would make three trips to the pass in the fall and leave the goods up there. In spring, when the passes opened, we would make three trips down into Sinkiang. Sometimes we left our merchandise at the pass for a whole year. Nobody bothered it.

"Then last year the Chinese soldiers turned back one of our caravans. The trade was slow anyway, but now we won't be going there at all."

Leh had long been a meeting place for caravans. Now the town was drab and quiet, but another shopkeeper told me of summers past when Leh was colorful and crowded. "We used to have Tibetans, Chinese, Afghans, even a few Russians here. Business was better then."

Even so, Ladakh has always been poor. Its sole industry is agriculture, but only one acre in ten can be farmed. The main crop is a loose-grained barley called *grim*—an unintentional comment on the land. The harvests barely suffice to feed all the villagers and the lamas. Without the traditional income from supplying the caravans, the country has become even poorer.

The second evening in Leh my two roommates and I tried to fortify ourselves against another cold night in the government resthouse. We stoked the stove with precious firewood and latched the doors and windows.

In the middle of the night I awoke. The stove was cold, and I had a pounding headache. In the small room, three men and a stove apparently had used up what little oxygen the air could offer. I slipped out of my sleeping bag, pulled on my stiff boots, unlatched the door, and went outside.

Without benefit of countdown or rocket trip I had stepped into a lunar scene. Never had I heard such silence. The subzero cold seemed to quiet my own pulsebeat. The dust underfoot silenced my footfalls as if I were walking on talcum powder.

I looked down five hundred feet to the frozen and lifeless Indus Valley and up thousands of feet to the peaks of granite and snow. No moon was in sight, but the barren landscape was not dark; it lay in a diffused gray-blue light, and what by day had been rocky textures now seemed soft and remote.

By contrast, the stars had never been etched so sharply. In the thin, unclouded atmosphere they looked down untwinkling, making me feel as if I were part of them and not of the planet Earth.

The cold soon drove me back to my sleeping bag, my headache gone. Now I understood why the Buddhists of Ladakh imagine hell as a place of bitter cold. Cold threatens them most of the year, and their houses of stone and mud offer little protection. Rarely is there enough dung, straw, and scrub wood even for cooking. Fortunately germs do not thrive in the cold. The most common ailment is eye trouble, caused by dust and by the acrid smoke from the open cook fires in the villagers' one-room homes.

The next morning I had to thaw my tube of toothpaste before I could squeeze it. I sympathized with Ladakh's villagers, who are among the world's least-washed people. I found it convenient to abide by the local custom and forego a bath—at least until summer. A 1962 government pamphlet reveals plans for a civic improvement in Leh: "There is also a proposal to set up two Public Bath Rooms at suitable places in the town—one for ladies and the other for gents." I hope they will be heated.

Warmed by breakfast and hot tea, six Indian correspondents and I climbed into two Jeeps. We carried emergency oxygen because we were off to visit army outposts along one of the highest roads in the world. Narrow, twisting, snow-covered, and hair-raising, it crosses the 18,370-foot-high Chang Pass.

This was the trail the caravans, such as Mr. Het Ram's, had followed from Leh into Tibet and China for centuries. Now the only caravans carried army supplies. Every curve revealed a new and more exciting view of the valleys and the peaks.

When we reached Zingral, at 17,000 feet, we had cups of hot chocolate around the stove in the middle of a round army tent. A local commander, Brigadier E. Sen, had heard I was from the NATIONAL GEOGRAPHIC, and he had sought me out.

"You described how people in Outer Mongolia build their *gers*, or tents," said the brigadier, referring to a recent issue of the magazine. "Well, I had a tent built according to your pictures. It's perfect for the cold of Ladakh. Now the design is standard in this area."

After this trip I had enough of jeeping in the Himalayas, at least for a while. When I was offered a chance to go from Leh to the front at Chushul, I was glad that I could ride over the Ladakh Range in a Russian-made helicopter.

The peaks rose higher as we flew east through desolate and unforgettably rugged passes, beside snow-covered peaks that slanted 1,000 feet above us. I asked the pilot, Flight Officer M. D. Lalvani, what our helicopter's maximum altitude was.

He replied: "The Russians' specifications say about 18,500 feet."

But the rugged thrust of mountains made flying unsafe below 20,000 feet. How could he get that much more out of this machine?

"At first we simply had to do it," he said. "On one day alone we had to take out 76 casualties. Mostly frostbite. I could see the bones sticking out of some of the men's feet. We couldn't just leave them there."

Our helicopter carried four passengers plus Lalvani and the copilot—it would have been a full load even at a lower altitude. Lalvani said: "We took out nine or ten on each trip."

Lalvani had three days' growth of beard and he looked tired, but he still had a combat pilot's cockiness.

"A Russian test pilot came to see how we were using their choppers. When he saw, he refused to ride with us. He said, 'Either you are mad or you don't care for your lives.' I think their safety factor is too high."

Half an hour later we landed near Chushul, where Major Tanwar and the men of his regiment had dug in after their disastrous encounter with the Chinese. Chushul, at 14,235 feet, had been India's highest airfield. Now it was a no man's land.

At our urging, the major drove us to the middle of the field for a closer look at the outposts of the Chinese.

"See the little pimple on that edge of the ridge?" he said, pointing to the hills on the other side of the field. "That's one of their new positions. It's about two miles away."

The distance seemed a lot less to me. The major explained: "That's because of the thin, clear atmosphere." I said no, it was because of my distrust of the Chinese.

"They don't bother us now," he said. "But we don't go too close. The only casualties have been some wild horses—killed out there by our mines after the cease-fire."

How much longer, I wondered, before men would be blown up here once more? Certainly the Chinese were both observant and touchy. That night Radio Peking complained that our quick visit to the airfield had endangered the cease-fire.

After returning to Leh, I visited the religious center of Ladakh—the Himis Monastery, in a canyon 22 miles south of the capital. Mr. Tundup Sonem, a Ladakhi information officer, volunteered to be my guide. The army solved our transportation problem by lending us a jeep.

We set out along the dirt road that follows the banks of the half-frozen Indus, and soon passed the monasteries of She, Tikse, and Stakna, each a huge stone structure on a hilltop overlooking its village. Near each monastery we saw *manis*, or prayer walls, some half a mile long. These walls of unmortared field stones were about 20 feet wide and six feet high.

"The villagers built them out of religious devotion," said Mr. Sonem. "Every stone on top of the wall has a prayer carved on it. The lamas carve these stones and sell them to the people. Each stone constantly offers a prayer for the one who donated it."

We stopped the jeep at the next wall and investigated. It was true. As far as we could see, the crude wall was covered with stones of many sizes, all beautifully inscribed with the words *Om Mani Padme Hum*—the basic prayer of Tibetan Buddhism. I estimated one stone per square foot, which would mean 100,000 prayers per mile.

We also saw many prayer wheels—small ones held by men as they walked, large ones mounted along the roads. The wheels contain many prayers—sometimes thousands—and each is wafted heavenward with every revolution of the wheel. The Buddhists of Ladakh believe that the more prayers one offers in a lifetime, the better are one's chances for a desirable reincarnation, and—ultimately—for nirvana, a complete escape from the cares of living.

In June thousands of pilgrims from all over Ladakh, and some from Tibet, jam Himis for the annual summer festival and devil dances. But on this cold December day only a few lamas scurried from one building to another, wrapped tightly in red robes.

We followed Mr. Sonem into the main temple, having taken off our shoes before entering. Behind the carved wooden doors young lamas sat on the cold stone floor, beating a ponderous rhythm on double-sided hanging drums. Older lamas chanted from ancient Tibetan prayer books. My feet felt as cold as if I had been skating barefoot on the frozen Indus River.

We couldn't meet the Skushuk, or head lama, of Himis. The Ladakhi equivalent of the Dalai Lama went to Lhasa to study and is now a prisoner of the Chinese.

"We hope that his next reincarnation will be found in Ladakh, so that Himis will have its Skushuk back," Mr. Sonem said. "But he is still young, and his next incarnation may be many years away."

Ladakh is often called Little Tibet or Western Tibet, because of its many centuries of religious and cultural ties to Tibet. Skushuk Bakula of Pituk Monastery is now the leading lama in Ladakh, and one evening we had an audience with him. After an exhausting climb to the entrance of his monastery, we again removed our shoes and entered a small chamber lighted by kerosene lanterns. From the rafters hung religious paintings on scrolls, called *tankas*. In the center of the room was a gilded Buddha.

We were offered cushions on the floor, at the foot of the serious, slightly built Skushuk, who sat on a low platform. He signaled to two of his lamas who brought English tea and cookies. An interpreter told us that the Skushuk traced his reincarnations back to a contemporary of Buddha. He also holds the title of Minister of State for Ladakh Affairs in the cabinet of the Indian State of Kashmir.

More lamas entered and prostrated themselves three times as they must do whenever they come into the Skushuk's presence. They began playing drums and long trumpets.

Outside there was an explosion. The monastery shook. Was this the end of the cease-fire? Were the Chinese attacking the nearby airfield of Leh?

We rushed to the single window. In the last light of day we saw a black cloud of smoke and dust on the plain far below. When the interpreter could make himself heard in the confusion, we had the explanation: The army was blasting alongside the 900-year-old monastery, to extend the runway.

MAY 1963

A WORD TO THE WISE

John McCarry

The musicians begin—a beating of drums, and then the hollow plaint of a flute. After a crowd-pleasing sword dance, a small man with wild eyes and tangled black hair darts out from behind the musicians; the children cry out excitedly. He is the *bitan*, or shaman, and he has come to learn the future from the fairies who live on the mountaintops. He leaps and canters in a circle. An assistant puts a long colorful silk coat on him; another hands him the severed head of a goat.

The tourists gasp. Camera shutters snick as the bitan resumes his dance, holding the goat's dripping head to his mouth to drink the blood. He stops for a moment to inhale the fumes of burning *gal*, or juniper, which grows only on those mountaintops where fairies dwell, and begins to sing in a whining, high-pitched voice.

The old man sitting next to me interprets: "This bitan says that the people of Hunza are blessed because the Aga Khan will come soon to see them, and when he does, he will build them a hospital." The bitan inhales more gal and makes more predictions, but the old man beside me advises me not to believe him.

"This bitan is a fake," he says. "He is making these things up as he goes along so the tourists will give him big tips." How can you tell? I ask him. He points to one musician. "He's playing a *tutek*, a flute you hold vertically from your lips," he says. "If he were the real thing, the musician would be playing a *gabi*, which is a flute you play horizontally from your lips and which is the only flute fairies can hear."

FROM "HIGH ROAD TO HUNZA," MARCH 1994

WILD MAN AND WILD BEAST IN AFRICA

THEODORE ROOSEVELT

South of the desert region lies Africa proper—the Africa of zoologists, the recently unknown Africa, the Africa that has become open to white explorers, merchants, missionaries, and scientists only within the last half century. Our expedition landed on the east coast of Africa a little south of the equator, went right across the belt of fever-haunted lowland, the fever-haunted coast region, on to the high, broad, healthful uplands of equatorial East Africa, crossed it, went to the great central lakes of Africa, the great Nyanza lakes—Victoria Nyanza and Albert Nyanza—and then went down the Nile, traveling from south almost due north, and came out at Khartum, in the Sudan.

There were no real hardships connected with the trip. There is, of course, a mild amount of danger in chasing the wild beasts, and there is a good deal more danger from disease; but we were fortunate enough not to lose a single white man on the expedition. We had casualties to two of our native attendants from wild beasts. One man was mauled by a leopard and one man was tossed by a rhino. A very few died from dysentery and fever, because it is almost impossible to make them take care of themselves. For instance, we could always get the white men to boil their water before drinking, but we could not make our porters do this. They looked upon it as a superstition upon our part—as one of the queer vagaries of the white people, the strangers from over the seas, which had no foundation in reason.

Most of the higher land of British East Africa, in the regions where we were, reminded me rather of the eastern portions of Wyoming and Colorado, and of parts of New Mexico and Arizona, than of what we are accustomed to think of as the tropics. Of course, there was an infinite difference in detail, but the general effect was the same. It was a region of light rainfall, and that rainfall came in the shape of a violent rainy season, so that there were periods when the rivers would run as boiling torrents, and then long periods when the rivers would be totally dry or consist merely of strings of shallow pools. Over most of the plains there were scattered thorn trees and huge euphobias. Elsewhere they were mere seas of withered grass. Out of these barren plains rise great mountains, right under the equator, with snow-peaks.

I spent several months in this East African region, going north, where the table-land sank lower and lower until we got to the dry, hot desert country of the Guaso Nyero, an equatorial river. Then we went across Victoria Nyanza into the low-lying very fertile and very unhealthy central African region, Uganda. In East Africa the natives were pure savages, ranging from the mere hunter-tribe type, the so-called 'Ndorobo of the mountain forests, to pastoral and agricultural tribes who live out in the plains or on the forest border. There were wide differences among these tribes, some of them very significant. The purely negro tribes, the tribes of pronounced negro type, throughout East Africa, were for the most part agriculturalists. Whenever we came upon a region where the people lived in beehive huts and tilled the ground, we were certain to find a nearly pure negro type; but there has been all through that country for ages an infiltration of northern races, many of whom have clear-cut, aquiline features; and those men you never find living in beehive huts. They live in queer square huts placed in a ring, making what we would call in the West a big corral—a big ring fence in which their cattle are kept. The pastoral tribes which we met north of the Guaso Nyero had camels, and north of these are tribes which own horses. But the Nandi, Masai, and other tribes south of them have neither camels nor horses; they own large herds of cattle, with donkeys, goats, and hairy sheep. They do not till the soil; they live exclusively on meat, blood, and milk. I hate to shock the vegetarians, but I am bound to say that those people, who never eat anything but meat, blood, and milk, are as hearty and strong a set of people as I have ever seen in my life. Many of the Masai and Nandi are particularly fine looking.

I shall always keep in my mind the memory of one evening when I had killed a lioness. The porters with me were, as they always are, very much excited over the killing of a lion, for the lions are often man-eaters, and kill many of the natives, so that the natives like to reciprocate and see the lions killed. I had killed this lioness quite late in the evening, and the men asked permission to carry it in whole to camp. I did not think they could do it, but I let them try. They started carrying the lioness in relays. It was a very heavy load. After a while they found that it was heavier than they had thought. We were about ten miles from camp, and we had gone only about a mile when darkness set in. There was an element of interest in going through that part of Africa at night, because then all the wild beasts were abroad. On the occasion in question we were accompanied on one side by a lion for one-half an hour. I do not think he could quite make us out. He could smell the dead lioness and he also smelt us; but I do not think he knew quite what had happened; and so he walked alongside us for a couple of miles, moaning or yawning as he went. Of course we had to keep a lookout for him. I had another white man with me, and either he would go ahead and I behind, or vice versa, so as to keep the porters closed up; because, in a case like that, if a lion does attack a party of travelers, he is most likely to seize the one behind. We still had the lion on one side of us when suddenly on the other side there was a succession of snorts like a steam-engine blowing off steam. It was a rhinoceros, I think two rhinoceroses, up on that side.

While a rhinoceros's short suit is brains, his long suit is courage, and he is a particularly exasperating creature to deal with, because he has not sense enough to know that you can harm him, and he has enough bad temper to want to harm you, so that there is often no way of keeping rid of him except by killing him. Of course we did not want to kill anything we did not use—and we still more strongly objected to being killed ourselves. It was almost pitch dark and there was no moon, although there was star-light. We would hear this rhinoceros snort, and then we would run forward and kneel down or lay down on the ground and try to catch the loom of the rhinoceros against the skyline, so that we would have a chance to shoot him if he came on. I sometimes had to adjure the porters—I use a mild word when I say "adjure"—in order that they might not break and scatter, when one or more would probably have been killed.

Finally we left both the lion and the rhino and came to a Masai corral, which was about three miles from our camp. The men carrying the lioness were very tired and I thought it best to stop and skin her. So we called to the people inside of the corral to let us come inside and skin the lioness. The Masai replied that we could not come in, because the smell of the lioness would make the cattle stampede. I think they were a little suspicious of us. My companion offered to give them his rifle to hold as a proof of our good intentions; but they said no; that they didn't want that. They handed us torches; we started a fire. They finally became convinced that we were peaceable, and then they came out to witness the skinning. The porters crouched near the blazing fire, and our gun-bearers started to skin the lioness. Masai warriors and girls came out and, forming a circle around the porters, chaffed and jested with them. There was one man, evidently the wit of the Masai camp, who described how the Swaheli would go out with the white man to hunt lions; how the Swaheli would find the lion, and then the lion would seize him and bite him, whereupon he would cry and call for his mother. Loud laughter greeted this sally, and the gun-bearers retorted with jest about the lions at the expense of the Masai.

As the Masai stood there, the fire lighting up their faces, they reminded me strongly of the pictures of the soldiers of Thothmes and Rameses by the Egyptian sculptors . . . as if they were blood kin to the Egyptian soldiers who 4,000 years ago made the great Egyptian Empire that extended from the upper Nile to the Euphrates.

Another thing about these natives of East Africa: their clothing was very scanty. In one tribe, the Kavirondo, the men and women literally wore nothing. The curious thing was that those people had extremely good manners. They were very courteous and perfectly at ease—at least the chiefs and the gentle folk—but they did not have any clothes—not a stitch.

When we struck Uganda we found an entirely different and a very curious little semi-civilization. Right in the midst of this huge sea of black savagery there had sprung up this island of progress, representing the beginning of a very primitive civilization. Many of the chiefs are distinctly semi-civilized, and some of them write English well. Two or three have kept up quite a correspondence with me since I left. One of them sent me a gift of four hippopotamus tusks and a leopard's skin, together with a letter of condolence on account of the death of King Edward! This particular chief had done everything he could for me while I was at Lake Albert Nyanza. I had little to give him, as I had exhausted about all my presents. However, I still had a watch with the hands and the figures of the face picked out with radium, so that one could tell the time at night. I gave him this watch, and he and all his companions spent the entire night looking at it. Since then he has been one of the most grateful people I have ever known, and has written me twice. I try to think of something in this country sufficiently interesting to him to write him, but it is a hard matter to do so.

Of course, to a hunter or a naturalist, one of the absorbingly interesting features of the part of Africa that I visited is the enormous and wonderfully variegated fauna. It is literally as if the fauna of the Pleistocene had come to life again. [And] right on top of this Pleistocene has been imposed the twentieth century civilization.

Nairobi is a town of perhaps 5,000 or 6,000 people. The wild beasts come right up to the edge of the town. A friend, Mr. McMillan, lent us the use of his house in town while we were staying there, and a leopard came up to the piazza one night after one of the dogs. On two evenings in succession I dined at houses. The dinner was much as it would be in Washington, London, or anywhere else, the ladies in pretty soft dresses and the men in the usual evening garb of civilization. The houses were about a quarter of a mile apart, and a few days previous a young lady, in the early evening, while bicycling from one to the other to take part in a rehearsal of "Trial by Jury," was knocked off her bicycle by a stampede of zebras, and was really quite hurt and had to give up the rehearsal.

There was one incident to which really only Mark Twain could have done justice. We all know—any of us who have had any dealings with government offices—the type of bureaucrat who upholds to the letter the rules of his office, even if the heavens fall. Among the "rules" out in East Africa are some excellent game regulations. The head of the reclamation service, a British army officer, Captain Smith, was trying to raise flowers and vegetables, and was much bothered because the zebra and antelope would come in and eat them. One night he heard some zebras in the garden and he sent out the gardener, a wild Masai, with instructions to drive the zebra out. The gardener killed a zebra; whereupon an upright judge *fined the gardener for killing game without a license!* I do not think that the most sensitive soul could object to my calling *that* judge fossilized.

The largest terrestrial mammal, next to the elephant, is the white rhinoceros. It was formerly found in South Africa, where it is practically exterminated. It was not supposed to exist anywhere else; but within the last few years it has again been discovered, along the headwaters of the Nile in mid-Africa. This is much as if the bison had only been known in Canada; had become exterminated there, and had finally been found again in Guatemala. There is just as wide a space of territory in between from which the species had totally disappeared. We obtained a full series of skins and skeletons of these huge beasts.

The two beasts that are the most interesting to my mind, as indeed they are to most hunters, are the elephant and the lion. A really successful effort is being made to preserve the elephant in East Africa. The bulls are only allowed to be shot after they have reached a certain point in the development of their tusks, and the cows and young stock are not allowed to be killed at all. The result is that, while of course there has been a diminution in the number of elephants, I think that they are now holding their own in many parts of East and Central Africa. Elephants are always interesting. It is rather exciting to study them in their haunts, because you have to watch them carefully, and there is some risk if you are discovered. I do not myself think that an elephant is quite as dangerous as a buffalo, and I think it considerably less dangerous than a lion. Still, many of them are wicked, and they kill a good many people. When you get close to them and watch them for a time you will note that they are perpetually in motion. I have never seen an elephant entirely still. He will flap one ear; then he will suddenly put up his trunk and curl it and try to see if he can smell anything; then he will shift from one foot to another. They never seem to stand entirely still. When we were camping in the Lado, hunting white rhinoceroses, there were a good many elephants around. We had obtained our elephant series and did not want to molest them. Once, when walking about a mile and a half from camp, we suddenly saw a herd of 50 or 60 elephants accompanied by a flock of a couple of hundred white cow herons. When we first saw the elephants they were in an open flat, where the long grass had been burned. As the elephants walked through the short grass the herons marched alongside, catching the grasshoppers put up. As soon as they came to long grass all the herons flew up and lit on the backs of the elephants. There was one little pink elephant calf and two herons perched on its back. The elephants evidently did not mind the birds; otherwise they could have removed them with their trunks. Those elephants were quite indifferent to our presence if we did not come too near. While looking at them we heard Dr. Mearns shooting birds around camp; but it did not disturb the elephants. They stayed two days in the neighborhood, and we got as close a look at them as we wished.

The most interesting thing I saw in Africa was a feat that was infinitely greater than anything we performed with our rifles, although not greater than a feat that was recently performed in the same region by three American plainsmen, Buffalo Jones, Loveless, and Mearns, who roped a lion, a giraffe, and a rhino, and have got moving photographs of them.

It was one of the really most notable feats I have ever known to be performed in hunting.

We saw the Nandi spearmen kill a lion with their spears. These people are a northern branch of the Masai. They are a splendid race physically—tall, sinewy fellows. The warriors carry ox-hide shields and very heavy spears, seven or eight feet long, the long-bladed head of soft iron kept with a razor edge and the iron of the rear half of the spear ending in a spike, the only wood that is bare being just about enough to give a grip for the hand. The brightly burnished head is about four feet in length. These Nandi came over on purpose to show me how they killed a lion with their spears.

Several of us went out with them on horseback to round up a lion for them. We traveled three or four hours—half a dozen horsemen and 30 or 40 stalwart naked savages with ox-hide shields and spears. Then we roused a big lion with a fine mane, and, after running a mile or two, rounded him up under a bush, and the spearmen came trotting up. It was as fine a sight as I ever saw. The first spearman that came up halted about 60 yards from the lion. (We were watching him with our rifles to see that he did not attack the first spearman.) Then this man knelt down with his ox-hide shield in front of him, looking over the shield at the lion; and, as man after man came up, they formed a ring around the lion, all kneeling. The lion stood under the bush. As they closed in on him he began to grow more and more angry, roaring, and looking first to one side and then to the other and lashing his tail furiously. It was a fine sight to see these men make the ring, with their spears and their eager, intent faces, and the great, murderous, man-eating beast in the middle, ever growing more and more angry. As soon as the ring was completed they all got up and started to close in. The lion charged straight for the weakest part of the ring. The man in front braced himself; we could see his muscles all stand out as if he were a bronze statue. There were five or six men who took part in the fight. From each side the two or three nearest men sprang in to see if they could not get the lion as he came straight on toward the man in his immediate front. When he was about not more than six feet from him the man lobbed the spear; that is, he did not take his arm back and throw it, but simply cast it loose with a little motion of the wrist and trusted to the weight of the spear to go in.

As the lion came forward the spear struck him on the left shoulder, and came out diagonally through him in front of his right hip. The lion reared like a rearing horse and bore the shield down, burying his teeth and claws in the man. At the same moment another man leaped in on one side and threw his spear; the spear-head glimmered like white fire in the sunlight, and, entering transversely, came out through the lion on the hither side. The lion turned on that man, but could not bite him, only clawing him a little. Another spear struck the lion, and he went down; he took one spear in his mouth and bit it, twisting it so that it looked like a horseshoe; the next moment the men were on him and it was all over. I do not suppose the thing lasted ten seconds, but it was as remarkable a spectacle for those ten seconds as any human being could wish to see. I had one funny after-experience in connection with it. The two men were pretty well mauled, and when we were putting disinfectant into the wounds it hurt them a little, and I thought it would cheer them up to tell them, through the interpreter, that I would give each of them a heifer. It cheered up those two all right, but all the other men were very angry! They thought that these men had got their share of honors already, and that it was a most unjustifiable thing for me to give them heifers in addition.

JANUARY 1911

BEAUTIFICATION IN BALI

Donna K. and Gilbert M. Grosvenor

"The gods must be smiling on you," our Balinese guide, Njoman, told us. "There will be a tooth-filing ceremony at the family compound of the village chief. The head of that family is an old friend, and I will introduce you."

Centuries ago, teeth were filed mainly to enhance the appearance of boys and girls at puberty. But after Hinduism came to Bali some nine centuries ago, the ritual acquired more religious significance.

"We must ward off *sadripu*, or the evil qualities of the human nature, like greed and conceit," said Njoman. "No Balinese should be cremated until his teeth are filed; otherwise the gods might mistake him for a fanged demon."

A typical thatch-topped, mud-brick wall surrounded the compound. From beyond the courtyard floated the excited young voices of boys and girls preparing for the ceremony. Screened partitions had isolated them for the past 24 hours.

The girls, clutching small mirrors, scrutinized every detail as they were dressed by elders in layers of yellow cloth and sashes of silver and gold. Fragile gold leaves crowned black hair glistening with beeswax lacquer and ornamented with frangipani blossoms.

Gamelan rhythm blended with chanting voices. The air grew sweet with burning incense. Each participant was carried to the pavilion, then placed on a couch before a lay priest. The priest traced magic symbols with a gold ring upon the forehead, lips, and upper six front teeth of a girl. Assistants steadied her hands and feet. The priest raised his long, slender file.

Back and forth, back and forth he scraped, filing the front teeth flat and even. The file screeched like a hundred fingernails scratching on a blackboard. Pearly enamel yielded to grinding metal. Intermittently the girl spat tooth dust into a coconut shell. Later the filings would be buried in the compound; to Balinese, a portion of the soul dwells even in the teeth.

FROM "BALI BY THE BACK ROADS," NOVEMBER 1969

A SCIDMORE SAMPLER

Eliza Ruhamah Scidmore

TSUNAMI

On the evening of June 15, 1896, the northeast coast of Hondo, the main island of Japan, was struck by a great earthquake wave (*tsunami*), which was more destructive of life and property than any earthquake convulsion of this century in that empire. The whole coastline of the San-Riku, the three provinces of Rikuzen, Rikuchu, and Rikuoku, from the island of Kinkwazan, 38° 20' north, northward for 175 miles, was laid waste by a great wave moving from the east and south, that struck the San-Riku coast and in a trice obliterated towns and villages, killed 26,975 people out of the original population, and grievously wounded the 5,390 survivors. It washed away and wrecked 9,313 houses, stranded some 300 larger craft—steamers, schooners, and junks—and crushed or carried away 10,000 fishing boats, destroying property to the value of six million yen. Offshore rocks were broken, overturned, or moved hundreds of yards, shallows and bars were formed, and in some localities the entire shoreline was changed.

A high mountain range bars communication with the trunk railway line of the island, and this picturesque, fiord-cut coast is so remote and so isolated that only two foreigners had been seen in the region in ten years, with the exception of the French mission priest, Father Raspail, who lost his life in the flood. With telegraph offices, instruments, and operators carried away, word came slowly to Tokyo, and with 50 to 100 miles of mountain roads between the nearest railway station and the seacoast, aid was long in reaching the wretched survivors. The first to reach the scene of the disaster was an American missionary, the Rev. Rothesay Miller, who made the usual three days' trip over the mountains in less than a day and a half on his American bicycle.

There were old traditions of such earthquake waves on this coast but the barometer gave no warning, no indication of any unusual conditions on June 15, and the occurrence of thirteen light earthquake shocks during the day excited no comment. The villagers on that remote coast adhered to the old calendar in observing their local fêtes and holidays, and on that fifth day of the fifth moon had been celebrating the Girls' Festival. Rain had driven them indoors with the darkness, and nearly all were in their houses at eight o'clock, when, with a rumbling as of heavy cannonading out at sea, a roar, and the crash and crackling of timbers, they were suddenly engulfed in the swirling waters. Only a few survivors on all that length of coast saw the advancing wave, one of them telling that the water first receded some 600 yards from ghastly white sands and then the Wave stood like a black wall 80 feet in height, with phosphorescent lights gleaming along its crest. Others, hearing a distant roar, saw a dark shadow seaward and ran to high ground, crying *"Tsunami! tsunami!"* Some who ran to the upper stories of their houses for safety were drowned, crushed, or imprisoned there, only a few breaking through the roofs or escaping after the water subsided.

Shallow water and outlying islands broke the force of the wave in some places, and in long, narrow inlets or fiords the giant roller was broken into two, three, and even six waves, that crashed upon the shore in succession. Ships and junks were carried one and two miles inland, left on hilltops, tree-tops, and in the midst of fields uninjured or mixed up with the ruins of houses, the rest engulfed or swept seaward. Many survivors, swept away by the waters, were cast ashore on outlying islands or seized bits of wreckage and kept afloat. On the open coast the wave came and withdrew within five minutes, while in long inlets the waters boiled and surged for nearly a half hour before subsiding. The best swimmers were helpless in the first swirl of water, and nearly all the bodies recovered were frightfully battered and mutilated, rolled over and driven against rocks, struck by and crushed between timbers. The force of the wave cut down groves of large pine trees to short stumps, snapped thick granite posts of temple gates and carried the stone cross-beams 300 yards away. Many people were lost through running back to save others or to save their valuables.

One loyal schoolmaster carried the emperor's portrait to a place of safety before seeking out his own family. A half-demented soldier, retired since the late war and continually brooding on a possible attack by the enemy, became convinced that the first cannonading sound was from a hostile fleet, and, seizing his sword, ran down to the beach to meet the foe. One village officer, mistaking the sound of crashing timbers for crackling flames, ran to high ground to see where the fire was, and thus saved his life. Another village officer, living on the edge of a hill, heard the crash and slid his screens open to look upon foaming waters nearly level with his veranda. In a moment the waters disappeared, leaving a black, empty level where the populous village had been a few minutes before.

Four women clung to one man, seeking to escape to high ground, and their combined weight resisting the force of the receding wave, they were all saved. The only survivors of another village were eight men who had been playing the game of "go" in a hillside temple. Eight children floated away and left on high ground were believed to be the only survivors of one village, until one hundred people were found who had been borne across and stranded on the opposite shores of their bay. One hundred and fifty people were found cast away on one island offshore. From two large villages on one bay only thirty young men survived, hardy, muscular young fishermen and powerful swimmers, yet in other places the strongest perished, and the aged and infirm, cripples, and tiny children were miraculously preserved. The wave flooded the cells of Okachi prison and the jailers broke the bolts and let the 195 convicts free. Only two convicts attempted to escape, the others waiting in good order until marched to high ground by their keepers.

Japanese men-of-war cruised for a week off Kamaishi, recovering bodies daily. The Japanese system of census enumeration is so complete and minute that the name of every person who lost his life was soon known, and the *Official Gazette* was able to state that out of a population of 6,529 at Kamaishi [alone] 4,985 were lost and 500 injured, while 953 dwellings and 867 warehouses and other structures were destroyed or carried away, and 176 ships carried inland or swept out and lost.

The survivors were so stunned with the appalling disaster that few could do anything for themselves or others. With houses, nets, and fishing-boats carried away and the fish retreating to further and deeper waters, starvation faced them, and, the great heat continuing while so many bodies were strewn along shore and imprisoned in ruins, the atmosphere fast became poisonous. The north-coast people are opposed to cremation and insisted on earth burial, which delayed the disposal of the dead and augmented the danger of pestilence. Disinfectants were sent in quantity, and the work of recovery and burial was so pressing that soldiers were put to it after all available coolies had been impressed. The Red Cross Society, with its hospitals and nurses, had difficulty in caring for all the wounded, the greater number of whom, besides requiring surgical aid, were suffering from pneumonia and internal inflammations consequent upon their long exposure in wet clothing without shelter and from the brine, fish oil, and sand breathed in and swallowed while in the first tumult of waters.

The plainest inference has been that the great wave was the result of an eruption, explosion, or other disturbance in the bed of the sea, 500 or 600 miles off the San-Riku coast. The most popular theory is that it resulted from the caving-in of some part of the wall or bed of the great "Tuscarora Deep," one of the greatest depressions of the ocean bed in the world, discovered in 1874 by the present Rear-Admiral Belknap, U.S.N., while in command of the U.S.S. *Tuscarora*, engaged in deep-sea surveys.

The "Tuscarora Deep" is nearly five and one-third statute miles in depth. That disturbances were taking place in this tremendous abyss was again suggested at six o'clock on the morning of July 4, when the Canadian Pacific Railway Company's mail steamer *Empress of Japan*, sailing directly over it in a smooth sea, was shaken as if a propeller blade had been lost or the ship had struck an obstruction. Every one was roused by the peculiar shock, but no visible explanation was furnished. The destructive wave and this incident together should stimulate further investigation of this dangerous, bottomless pit of the Pacific Ocean, which owes its discovery to United States explorers by deep-sea soundings.

FROM "THE RECENT EARTHQUAKE WAVE ON THE COAST OF JAPAN," SEPTEMBER 1896

MORNING IN BENARES

Benares stretches for three miles along the left, or west, bank of the Ganges, that there turns northward, and all the city's extent is sacred ground. Who dies there on the left bank is sure of exalted estate hereafter; while the right bank is desolate and accursed, and whoever dies on that stretch of Ganges shore becomes a donkey in the next incarnation, without hope forever. No one dies [there] if mortal effort can prevent. The dying are bundled into boats in panic haste, for it is as good to give the death rattle on Mother Ganges' breast as on the Benares shore.

Sight-seeing begins at Benares before daybreak, and one drives through the two miles of uninteresting streets in the starlight and gray gloaming, across to the boats at the river bank. In mid-winter, the "cold-weather" months of Indian travel, it is bitterly cold at that hour—hoar frost on the ground, blue and lilac frost haze in the air. Every one at that hour was hurrying in the one direction, and when we had raced down the great steps and the houseboat was poled off from the bank, all the river front was before us like a theater stage lighted by the rising sun striking full upon it.

As the sun shone red, orange, and yellow through the thick frost haze, a great murmur of voices rose from the length of the ghats, the tens of thousands of fervent worshipers, standing on platforms built over the water and standing waist deep in the water, repeating in muttered chant the ancient Vedic hymn. They dipped themselves beneath the swirling mud flood; they lifted the water in jars and poured it over their heads; they lifted it in their hands and let it trickle through their fingers or run down their arms, and they dipped tufts of sacred grass in the water and sprinkled themselves; they pressed their nostrils, they twisted their fingers, and did all manner of motions as they chanted and muttered to themselves, each one rapt, intent, absorbed entirely in the long religious recitals. They paid no heed to us, nor to any happenings, for the Hindu ritual is so elaborate and exacting that if they should make a slip or omission, they would have to begin all over again. For the priests and high-caste Brahmans, the daily prayers are of two hours' duration by the water side, and continue all day; but the ordinary man of Benares' bazars gets his morning ceremony done in far less time, wades back to shore and dry garments, spots and stripes himself with fresh caste marks for the day. He fills a brass jar with water and strolls along the ghats with the crowd, stops for a prayer or two, salaams to a cow or two, pours his water offering over some greasy black image, and his religious work is done.

The sun transforms the scene when it conquers the haze and throws clear yellow beams upon the solid and fantastic buildings and the white-robed company. The air mellows, and one basks in the sun thankfully, as do the beggars and fakirs, who shake off their wrappings of mat and sacking, and creep like numb flies to the side of sunny walls.

The boats are rowed along, close in-shore, barely avoiding the most devout ones, who wade farthest out, and all the way there is the same spectacle of religious zeal and spiritual exaltation. At the Woman's Ghat every woman carries a brass lota, or water jar, or a still larger and heavier jar of red pottery, and the unending procession of gracefully-draped figures going up and down the broad ghat is an unending delight. Swathed head and all in their winding *saris*, they wade into the river and pray, one is sure, to every Hindu deity which the ten fingers represent to let them come into the world again in some human form less ignoble than a woman's.

FROM "THE BATHING AND BURNING GHATS AT BENARES,"
FEBRUARY 1907

CLIMBING THE GIGANTIC MUSHROOM

And we had brashly said, from Kandy to Dambool, that we were going to Sigiri! "And climb the Rock?" other tourists asked. Of course. Silence for a little longer would have been as gold or radium in our pockets, for we were as the most microscopic of ants about to climb the stem of a gigantic mushroom, and to crawl up over its curving, umbrella edge.

The name of Lion Rock for long had no especial significance, until on this guard-house terrace the archæologists descried three claws and the dew-claw of the feet of the gigantic lion, whose head, moulded on to the rock front, gave the name *Sinha-giri*, lion rock. The lion's claws measured four and five feet across, and passing between them was the original staircase of glittering quartz, and then a long, iron ladder laid against the wall, as ladders are generally laid. The wind blew fresh from northeast and eddied up from underneath, as we mounted the rungs and looked down on dizzy vistas of far green jungle space. Then the ladder ran at right angles out in the air, parallel with the face of the rock, the gas pipe rungs driven into sockets drilled in the rock. Lizards *chuck-chucked* and ran derisively away as we advanced, the very flies kicked their heels in scorn as we clung with death grips to rails and stanchions. As we stopped to rest, and to look upward only, there were perpendicular hand rails and iron loops of steps driven in the perpendicular rock, as on the side of a ship's hold or mast. A Zermatt climber might have reveled in the prospect, but not I. On foot and knee, on all fours fairly, a solid rock slope was negotiated; and then came the gymnast's feat up the straight steps, lifting one's weight by main force, and the worst was over. We had rounded the mushroom's lip and had only to tread in the grooves in a long, smooth rock slope, with a comforting hand rail on the side of dizzy space, as we followed around the curving rim to a final long, quartz staircase that reached the summit.

There is a space of level terraces up there quite three acres in extent, and the trees that look like saplings from below, mere tufts, few and scant as the hairs on Bismarck's head, are spreading banyans that give grateful shade from the too radiant sun. Walls and walls, lines of stone foundations and lines of crumbling bricks ran here and there, with quartz and carved stone steps in short flights, and platforms happening everywhere. The whole ground-floor plan of the king's palace has been scraped down to bed rock, hard and clean. There are wells and cisterns, and a bathing tank, thirty feet square, cut from the living rock; and a square throne or divan hewn on the eastern rim, where the king could lounge in the afternoon shade and survey his populous domains below. There are sockets in the rock showing where the supports of a wooden pavilion roof, or the staffs for a silk canopy were set, and the seat for the umbrella-bearer behind the king's cushion is also intact. The coarse rock glitters with garnet crystals and is a natural "Jeweled Throne" that any jeweled personage of the East might envy.

When the descent began and one looked down and off into vistas of space and diminishing perspectives over each boot tip, all sense of exhilaration was gone. The little Tamil horse boy sat on his heels flicking the noonday flies from the ponies when we reached the level lowland and its steaming, greenhouse atmosphere. He grinned at us, and we knew the black imp had seen our abject crawling on the Sigiri heights.

"Did he go up?" and the coachman answered, "Yes; and it was very nice, he says, but the get-downing was awful. He has prayered and been saved."

FROM "ARCHAEOLOGY IN THE AIR," MARCH 1907

"LET ME KILL, LET ME KILL"

Loren McIntyre

They avoid eye contact during serious pow-wows, a practice I've seen in other Amazon tribes. This time the subject could not have been more serious: to kill or not to kill the strangers in their midst. The naked warrior with necklaces of boars' tusks, Canindé, and the headman in the red shirt, Djauí, chant in ritual argument. Djauí repeats over and over in the Urueu-Wau-Wau tongue something that sings like this: "They offer knives and axes, and clothes for bitter nights. They chase away the miners. The strangers are *catú*—they are good." The strangers he approves of are *sertanistas*, or frontiersmen, of FUNAI, Brazil's National Foundation for the Indian, who have come to prepare these natives of Rondônia for the unwanted arrival of civilization.

Canindé's contrapuntal reply is a single repeated phrase: "Let me kill. Let me kill."

The sertanistas see Canindé as an archetypal rain forest warrior. He carries a .38-caliber bullet embedded in his left arm and shotgun pellets in his back. He has slain numerous invaders and would kill another if he could corner Alfredão, the rubber tapper who kidnapped his mother and little sister a decade ago. Alfredão kept Canindé's sister to serve him; she became his unwed wife and bore his children.

The powwow is taking place outside the blue plastic visitors tent at Alta Lídia, a Brazilian government outpost in the central highlands of Rondônia. Well before Canindé's arrival, the sertanistas had come to regard as friends the warriors who hung around camp. But one morning three bowmen shot at Bahiano Maia, the frontiersman in charge. An arrow pierced Bahiano's lung.

Everyone began to wear sidearms after the incident. Every sertanista kept a flashlight near his hammock and a tin can as a urinal, because no one was allowed to venture outside after dark. "The Urueu-Wau-Wau love to make necklaces of primate teeth," cautioned Apoena Meirelles, who quickly took command of the camp. Apoena is a famous sertanista, as was his father, Francisco.

One day a lookout in a tree called *"Urueu vêm! Urueu vêm!*—They're coming!" It was Canindé and his warriors. Djauí walked out to meet him, and it was clear that Djauí had prevailed. Indian employees at Alta Lídia were soon dancing and exchanging gifts with Canindé's warriors. That night Canindé's young men tried to set fire to the camp, but the thatch was wet.

Somewhere in the forest Canindé sharpens hardwood arrow points, while somewhere else a rubber tapper jokes nervously about fastening rearview mirrors to his hat. Canindé slings his hammock in one of several lean-tos strategically hidden within 7,000 square miles of primeval forest reserved for his small and scattered tribe. Perhaps fewer than 350 Urueu-Wau-Wau survive.

FROM "LAST DAYS OF EDEN," DECEMBER 1988

THE CELESTIAL HORSE'S MOUTH

JERE VAN DYK

We rode west toward the source of the river Tibetans call the Zangbo. High white peaks rose around us. We passed herds of yak and sheep, black wool tents, and solitary horsemen whose long hair blew in the wind.

Tibetan eagles were silhouetted against high peaks; furry marmots, hares, and foxes bounded up hills or sat still in the sun; giant Himalayan ravens soared above us; antelope stared; and elegant kiangs, wild asses with black manes, tan-and-white bodies, heads and necks held high, ran in herds for miles across the plains. We lived at 15,000 feet and crossed passes of 17,500, where our Tibetan companions shouted "Victory to the gods" in greeting to the beings that protect these places.

Weeks before in Kathmandu, I met photographer Galen Rowell and Ted Worcester, a Tibetan-speaking American who would be our guide. We made final preparations to depart, purchasing gear and food, when word came from Lhasa that our trip was canceled. We decided to try anyway. With our crew of three, Pema, Gompo, and Targye, Tibetans who had fled to Nepal, we made our way to 2.2-mile-high Lhasa, where we heard new reports of fighting between China and India on the Tibetan border.

"You cannot travel beyond Zetang," said Mr. Chen, a soft-spoken officer in the Chinese Army. We could not go near the gorges at the eastern edge of the Himalaya, through which the Zangbo crashes down into India. "You can, however, go west to Mount Kailas." We did not mention our destination, the source of the Zangbo, and were grateful for the permits that he issued us.

On the second day out from Lhasa we came upon a truck stuck in a stream. "Where are you going?" Gompo asked the travelers.

"To Nyalam. It is our home."

"How far is it?"

They smiled. "Who knows?"

One night we shared tea with three pilgrims. The next night they were at our camp again. "They rode in the back of our truck," Pema said. "They are going to Kailas. They will bring us good luck." We would gain merit, Pema explained, by protecting pilgrims.

Our goal, and my assignment, was to find the true source of the Zangbo, where no Westerner had been in more than a hundred years. I was to follow the river from the Chemayungdung Mountains, where it rises, 700 miles across Tibet down into India, where it becomes the Brahmaputra, and then through Bangladesh to the Bay of Bengal, 1,800 miles away, where, at a maximum rate of 2.3 million cubic feet of water a second, it joins the sea.

On the 16th day two women and four children appeared, gathering yak dung for the fire. Ted smiled. "They must have sneaked on at Paryang." Pema came over. "This woman is from Amdo. Her husband died, and she and her children and sister are going to Kailas. She waited 20 days in Paryang." Beyond Gurla Mandhata, 25,355 feet, near the borders of Tibet, Nepal, and India, there were more pilgrims, old women with heavy packs, young men together, always smiling, always trying to hitch a ride. We were now 20—six members of the expedition and 14 pilgrims—and had no more room.

We reached Lake Manasarowar, at 14,950 feet, 54 miles around. It was turquoise and sparkled in the sun. From there we saw Mount Kailas, 22,028 feet high, the center of the universe for Hindus, Buddhists, and Jains, and the Tibetans clapped and shouted for joy. Tamchok Khambab, "the river coming out of the horse's mouth," spilled from a glacier in the Chemayungdung Mountains. The water was cold, the sands were composed of cat's eyes and emeralds, and those who drank from the newborn stream became as strong as horses. This was the source we sought.

"One walk around Kailas," Ted explained, "washes away the sins of a life; 108 (an auspicious number to Tibetan Buddhists) and you achieve nirvana in this life."

At a lake below Dolma La, 18,100 feet on our altimeter, Targye and Gompo sought a new vision as they looked into the water. A large pile of clothes lay where pilgrims had cast off the old life and pricked their fingers to shed old blood.

On the far side three Tibetans in their twenties, two men and a woman, sat by a rock with their faces glowing. "We are from Litang, and we have run away from our Chinese school to become monks. She will become a nun. Our parents do not know where we are. We have neither papers nor money, but when we finish here, we want to go see the Dalai Lama in India."

They would take three weeks to prostrate themselves around the holy mountain, walking one step, raising their hands in prayer, lying down on the ground, their arms in front. Their merit would be great; the Marxism vigorously taught in school could not compete against the spiritual force of Buddhism that appealed to their young and ardent souls.

Near Togqen we stopped at an adobe compound, hoping to find a guide. The wind whipped our clothes and burned our faces, and we shivered in the hot sun. Inside we were introduced to a man with a deeply lined face. His ears were pierced. A knife and a flint for making fire hung from his belt.

"Do you know the Chemayungdung?"

"I was born there," he said.

"Would you show us where it is?"

He looked us over slowly. "Yes."

His name was Tsewang Norbu, but we would call him Abu, which means "big brother" in his Horpa dialect. He was a nomad, or *drokpa*, with 50 yaks, 300 sheep, and 6 horses. "My wife and sons are up in the hills," he said, "but I came to build a house."

"A home?"

"No, a place to store barley and wool. I could not live in a house. It is better to be with animals in the open." Pema nodded in agreement.

With Abu we traveled across prairies, streams, valleys, ridges. Abu pointed the way. We passed a little girl watching a thousand sheep. Animals stretched out for a mile. Abu pointed to a tent. "My sister lives there." They touched heads in familiar greeting, and she invited us in. Her name was Sonam Zangmo; she poured yak cow's yogurt from a sheep belly, and we gulped it down. It was thick and sweet and the best I had ever eaten.

"We came down through the Mayum La. Later this summer we'll move the animals across the Yarlung Zangbo," she said.

We continued on and came to a mile-long lake with white-capped waves two feet high. "It must be Tamulung Lake," Galen said. "This must be the Angsi River." We had our maps spread out. No one was certain. Abu pointed south. The vehicles could not go any farther.

Saying we would return in four days, but not certain we would be able to do so, Targye, Abu, Galen, and I started walking south. The vehicles turned and disappeared over a ridge. We came to a stream and waded in above our knees. We reached another wider stream and believed it was the Angsi. We walked south-southwest into the wind.

We camped in a hollow by a lake, and Targye made hot mutton soup. On the far ridge a herd of kiangs moved in single file toward the lake. A burst of wind, and they were gone.

The next morning we crossed soft tundra. Water flowed beneath thin ice that cracked as the sun grew warm. We reached a glacier valley floor a mile wide. The Zangbo flowed by in front of us, bright emerald green. The legend was true. It was silent here, with no people, no birds, no trails.

"We are here," said Abu, resting his pack against a rock. "The beginning is up there."

We made camp an hour's hike farther up, and with six hours of sunlight left, kept going. Galen consulted a guidebook written for pilgrims by Swami Pranavananda in 1949. "There should be a *chorten*, a shrine of holy relics, a place of offering. The swami saw it in 1937. From there it is not far to the source."

"I do not know this chorten," said Abu.

An hour passed. "There it is," Galen cried. We approached a solitary gray monument with tattered prayer flags and Buddha figurines inside, and two stones deeply indented in the center. These were the Buddha's footprints, to show us the way. We came to a gully; the Zangbo now flowed under ice.

"Look, look—drongs!" Galen cried. Wild yaks at the source. There were 20 of them, like a line of poetry against the mountains, a few newborn. They stood still for a moment, then ran back up onto an ice lake. Galen grabbed his camera. "Wait here," he said.

An hour passed. Targye drew a mandala in the sand. We curled up like dogs out of the wind and slept. In another hour Galen returned. "I chased them as far as the source."

"The source?"

"It's a ways up there. My altimeter said 16,800 where the glacier began." We walked back to camp, and I climbed into my sleeping bag and fell asleep.

The next morning I set out alone. We had all been together 24 hours a day, and I welcomed the solitude. The only sound was the water rushing beneath the ice and the wind by my ears. Two jagged mountain ranges rose on either side. I walked up across an ice lake, and then a ravine, and onto another lake, half a mile across. The ice was four or five feet thick, except where the stream cut through.

A crack as loud as a cannon shattered the silence as a chunk of ice broke. I followed the stream up another ravine and onto a third lake where—I stopped dead—20 drongs watched from a hundred yards away. They were thin, each the size of a large cow, with thick, long, black hair and horns that came out from the sides of their heads and then turned up. They were bunched together and stared at me with big dark eyes. In the north of Tibet, I had heard, these wild yaks can grow to be 6 feet high and 12 feet long. I walked slowly toward them and pondered Abu's warning: "A herd is safe, but a single drong will attack."

I got within 75 yards, but the animals turned quickly and ran across the lake and, with the babies behind, bounded up a ridge. I crossed the lake, and at the far end there was a glacier, the source. A trickle flowed from the ice. As Galen had said, the altitude was 16,800 feet. I named the ice on which I stood Drong Lake.

I slowly climbed the glacier. The two jagged ridges continued back. They were, I thought, the two ears of the horse, and the glacier was its mouth. *Tamchok* means "celestial horse," and *khambab* means "coming out of the mouth of." Thus, the Tamchok Khambab.

I was standing at the beginning of the river.

I climbed until I twice sank up to my waist in snow. The drongs were disappearing over the top of the ridge. The glacier continued, and another mountain range rose beyond it. The sun would set in a few hours. I looked once more at the drongs—the last baby had caught up with its mother—and started back down.

FROM "LONG JOURNEY OF THE BRAHMAPUTRA," NOVEMBER 1988

HEART OF AFRICA

JOSEPH CONRAD

One day, putting my finger on a spot in the very middle of [a map of] the then white heart of Africa, I declared that some day I would go there. My chums' chaffing was perfectly justifiable. I myself was ashamed of having been betrayed into mere vaporing. Nothing was further from my wildest hopes. Yet it is a fact that, about eighteen years afterwards, a wretched little stern-wheel steamboat I commanded lay moored to the bank of an African river.

Everything was dark under the stars. Every other white man on board was asleep. I was glad to be alone on deck, smoking the pipe of peace after an anxious day. The subdued thundering mutter of the Stanley Falls hung in the heavy night air of the last navigable reach of the Upper Congo, while no more than ten miles away, in Reshid's camp, just above the falls, the yet unbroken power of the Congo Arabs slumbered uneasily. Their day was over.

Away in the middle of the stream, on a little island nestling all dark in the foam of the broken water, a solitary little light glimmered feebly, and I said to myself with awe, "This is the very spot of my boyish boast."

A great melancholy descended on me. Yes; this was the very spot. But there was no shadowy friend to stand by my side in the night of the enormous wilderness, no great haunting memory, but only the unholy recollection of a prosaic newspaper stunt and the distasteful knowledge of the vilest scramble for loot that ever disfigured the history of human conscience and geographical exploration. What an end to the idealized realities of a boy's daydreams!

I wondered what I was doing there, for indeed it was only an unforeseen episode, hard to believe in now, in my seaman's life. Still the fact remains that I have smoked a pipe of peace at midnight in the very heart of the African Continent, and felt very lonely there.

FROM "GEOGRAPHY AND SOME EXPLORERS," MARCH 1924

DESTINATIONS

A SEASON IN THE MINORS

DAVID LAMB

I t was an hour to game time. Evening shadows crept over the wooded hollow and bathed the infield in twilight. George Fanning, the Bluefield, West Virginia, Orioles' 81-year-old general manager, ambled out of his tiny office, fiddling with a key that would open the padlock on Bowen Field's sole gate. Fanning had completed his trip to the bakery to buy its supply of surplus buns—three dozen for a dollar, which enabled him to sell hot dogs for 75 cents each—and now, with the first fans already in line at his wife's ticket booth, he settled onto a bench by the gate, his baseball cap pulled low over his brow, palms on his spread knees.

Down the dirt road, the lights of a few houses shone through the trees, and Fanning could see kids riding their bicycles toward the ballpark. Bowen Field feels as timeless as a summer memory from our youth, and somehow that's how it should be. For here in the low-rent district of professional baseball, in these hamlets of the Appalachian League and in other minor-league towns across the nation, is the face of Norman Rockwell's vanishing America—a place where, for hundreds of young men, the journey to the major leagues begins and, more often than not, ends.

Fanning exchanged evening greetings with the fans passing his bench and seemed to know most of them by their first names. "People tell me I'm crazy not to do promotions," said Fanning, a retired high school chemistry teacher who has run the team for nearly four decades, "but I know I'm not. If I promote, the damn federal government's just going to take that much more money anyway. I get people to keep coming back because I don't rob 'em. I don't promise anything but a good evening of baseball. And I don't charge but two bucks for admission. If someone doesn't have any money, heck, I let 'em in for free."

The 3,000-seat park filled quickly. Entire families came, sometimes three generations in a group. There were old men in suspenders who chewed tobacco and miners' widows who brought padded cushions to soften the bite of concrete bleachers. Teenage boys with slicked-back hair and freshly ironed shirts came too, leading girlfriends by the hand to the semiprivacy of the uppermost row.

From the steps of the first-base dugout, Bluefield's rookie pitching coach, Chet Nichols, watched the fans stream in. He had white hair and a paunch and, just shy of 60, was old enough to be the starting pitcher's grandfather. Back in the early fifties, when I was growing up in Boston, I had seen Nichols pitch in Braves Field, and, not having heard of him in all those years, I asked what he had been doing since he left the majors.

"Banking, for 29 years," he said. "I ended up as the bank's vice president. But you know, I got tired of the pressure. Then a couple of months ago an old friend calls and asks if I'd be interested in going back to the minors. 'Damn right!' I said." So now Nichols was living at a cheap motel and loving every precious moment of his second childhood, working with young athletes whose dreams of reaching the majors ignored the basic truth of the under-paid, overworked life they lived: Only one in fourteen would ever make it to the major leagues.

Bluefield gave the visiting Pulaski Braves a pasting that night. Pulaski's 18-year-old Tab Brown, making his first professional appearance, gave up seven runs in three innings and left the mound looking as though he were about to burst into tears. The catcher kept rising out of his crouch, thwarting a succession of pitchers. Manager Fred Koenig, a veteran of 37 years in baseball, including ten as a major-league coach, jotted himself a note. "Shoot the catcher," it said.

I had started my journey nearly three months earlier, on the opening day of baseball season, with the Stockton, California, Ports, self-proclaimed descendants of the Mudville Nine, starring Mighty Casey, immortalized by Ernest Lawrence Thayer in his poem of 1888. The Ports had won more games in the 1980s than any other team in minor-league baseball.

For their first home game the team hired a band—"Mudville's Finest: Available for Intimate Bashes, Wakes, and Fancy Balls"—and three female sky divers, who made a perfect landing on the infield just before the first pitch. In the press box the public-address announcer, Buddy Meacham, sang "The Star-Spangled Banner," unaccompanied, and the crowd applauded generously as his final words swept over the field.

Ahead of me on that April evening lay a sport I had loved as a child and a country I had lost touch with during eight years as a foreign correspondent for the *Los Angeles Times* in Africa and the Middle East. I feared that perhaps professional baseball had changed more than the nation had. Salary disputes—the average major-league salary is now about $600,000, with .250 hitters routinely earning a million dollars or more—and labor strikes and lockouts had disillusioned me. In the minors I hoped I would find the people and values that had not yet been corrupted by fame or fortune.

There was a time when, for most American towns, particularly those in the still isolated West, having a minor-league team was tantamount to being part of the nation's growth and progressive spirit. "Salt Lake City has for a number of years fostered the game of baseball," said the *Salt Lake Daily Tribune* in 1887. "In fact, our city would not be up to modern ideas did she not do so. In these times baseball clubs are almost an imperative necessity."

For a long time the minor leagues were sovereign entities, competing for fans with the National and American Leagues. Some players spent their entire career of 20 years or more in the minors. Then, in 1919, Branch Rickey became manager of the St. Louis Cardinals, a team so poor they wore shoddy mended uniforms for spring training—held it that year in St. Louis instead of Florida. Rickey decided that since the Cardinals couldn't afford to buy players, they would have to raise their own. Over the next 20 years he got control of 32 minor-league teams, and the minors became what they are today—a farm system, subsidized by major-league teams needing a pool of young talent to compete in an industry that has room at the top for only 650 men. If a minor-leaguer's career goes as planned, he ascends through the four levels of the farm system—Rookie, Single-A, Double-A, and Triple-A—and in a few years reaches the majors, "the show." Figuring in the players who fail to complete the journey, the cost of developing a major-leaguer is upwards of two million dollars.

The Ports' starting pitcher, Steve Monson, was built like a concrete block on which someone had painted a blond flattop. He glowered and mumbled wisecracks through clenched teeth, cultivating the image of a tough guy and trying to camouflage a heart that was as soft as a teddy bear's. Like his peers, Monson earned less than $1,000 a month, plus $11-a-day meal money on road trips, and pursued his baseball dream with missionary zeal. He worked the graveyard shift at a convenience store in the off-season so he could train during the day, and to keep his legs in condition he ran before games until sweat poured off him.

This was Monson's fifth season in pro ball and his second at Stockton with the Ports, a team he remained with after his pitching arm became sore during spring training. He spoke of "turning my life around for baseball," of the need for a pension plan in the minors, of the fear of debilitating injuries, and of a book he'd like to write titled *Highs and Lows: My Life in Baseball.* Those were things one might expect to hear from an older man. Monson was 22.

"You watch me pitch," Monson said. "I'm aggressive. I like to intimidate, like I'm coming after you, so what are you going to do? You won't see me smile. I do that for atmosphere. I want batters to think, 'This guy doesn't fool around. He doesn't take bull from anyone.' "

I left Stockton after two weeks and followed the backroads through the Arizona desert, poking along toward Texas. Whenever I found a minor-league team, I stopped and lingered in that town until my feet again grew restless. In those little ballparks, I found moments of shared summer leisure and time to dream—of the days when I was young and all great feats seemed possible. The world around me had changed, yet everything about baseball was exactly as I had remembered it—the game's rules, the language of the fans, the rituals on the field, even the soft glow of June nights.

By the second inning El Paso's cheerleaders, the Diamond Girls, were dancing on the roof of the Diablos' dugout. P. A. announcer Paul Strelzin was playing "Charge!" on his kazoo and waving a green flag out the window of his booth. Shon "the Avenger" Ashley obliged with a three-run triple, and moments later 2,000 fans were on their feet, waving white tissues they had been given at the gate as the Arkansas Travelers' starting pitcher plodded off the mound.

Sitting next to me in Section CC was Mitch Malott, nearly 80, a gentlemanly fellow who from time to time would surprise me by emitting a terrible bellow—"Aw, come on, ump! That was a strike when I played." Malott wore white suspenders, blue sneakers, and a baseball cap. He sat with his feet draped over the seat in front of him, his hands folded between his knees like a boy. Every year he took a road trip with the Diablos, and one year, when he didn't have the money to follow the team from San Antonio to Wichita, the players offered to cover his expenses. He said no, he couldn't accept, because they had less money than he did.

Talking to Malott, I lost track of the game and hardly saw the ball Sandy Guerrero banged over the right-field fence and into the El Paso Zoo.

Suddenly Malott was on his feet, hurrying down the aisle while reaching for his wallet. Guerrero circled the bases, then slowly made his way along the infield wall, where Malott and 70 or so other fans waited, each holding out a dollar bill. Guerrero cheerfully piled the crumpled bills into his helmet, one by one, chatting, shaking hands, signing autographs. The ritual, dating back to barnstorming days when underpaid players counted on contributions to survive, is celebrated after every Diablos home run.

Minor-league baseball—like the El Paso franchise itself—seemed moribund in 1974 when a Vietnam veteran, Jim Paul, bought into the Diablos with a thousand dollars he had borrowed. Against all odds, Paul's original investment is now worth several million dollars. Owning a minor-league club became the trendy business of the 1980s, and into its ranks came a host of celebrities: actors Bill Murray and Robert Wagner, athletes Don Drysdale and Roman Gabriel, singers Jimmy Buffett and Conway Twitty. It was a strange investment because they didn't own the stadiums (the municipalities did) and couldn't depreciate the players. Even the balls and bats were the property of the big-league teams. All the owners really owned, besides a few typewriters and maybe a Cub tractor to drag the infield, were the territorial rights to do business in the most American of industries.

"Ten years ago you didn't hear anything in ballparks but organs, and organs are for funerals," Paul said. "We play rock and roll. We dance in the aisles. We have a promotion every night. We give away trucks and pizzas. We have Bart Simpson look-alike contests and fireworks nights. We make it fun again to come out to the park."

On the infield below, just as the fifth inning ended, a Diablos employee dressed in a chicken costume took up position on second base. A little girl chosen from the stands was stationed nearby, midway between first and second. If the girl, running, could beat the chicken, walking, she would win ten dollars.

"Move the kid up," a fan yelled from the stands.

"Like hell," Paul shot back. "You ain't paying the ten bucks. She stays where she is." The crowd roared as the girl, her tiny legs churning like the blades of an eggbeater, rounded second, closed the gap at third, and flew down the stretch. Diablos catcher Tim Torricelli intercepted the chicken with a hip block inches from victory, and the girl crossed home plate to thunderous applause.

"Don't you love it?" Paul laughed, slapping his knee in delight. "Isn't this wonderful?"

The purists shuddered at first, complaining that Paul's circus-like antics were overshadowing the game. But Paul started filling up his park, night after night. Attendance nearly doubled his first year in El Paso and set a franchise record the next. Before long even the stodgiest owners had become P. T. Barnums with nightly promotions, discounted tickets, and distinctly nonbaseball food that ranged from smoked-turkey drumsticks at Sec Taylor Stadium in Des Moines to stuffed potatoes at Derks Field in Salt Lake City. By 1990 attendance had climbed above 25 million—a 39-year high—and one of the 171 minor-league teams, the Buffalo Bisons, was outdrawing three major-league clubs.

In one park in the South I knocked on a green door that said "Unauthorized Visitors Not Allowed," and the young umpire who answered, Brian York, was rubbing a stack of baseballs with mud, a ritual umpires performed before every game. Good "working mud" takes the gloss off a ball so it doesn't slip from a pitcher's grip. The mud must have just a touch of grit, though not enough to scar or discolor, and should be sufficiently slimy to spread easily. Sometimes it is mixed with tobacco juice, spit, or other ingredients that umpires fuss over like chefs, each believing he has created the finest recipe, lightly garnished with Copenhagen or Bull Durham.

"Some nights I go back to my room, and I can still hear the yelling and booing. That bothers me," York said. "Then, when I think about it, I realize what's really bothering me is that I didn't have a very good game. So you replay the game in your head; you analyze your mistakes and try to learn from them. That's the only way you're going to get to the majors, a step at a time."

York and his partner, Bryan Wilber, both recent college graduates, pursued their dream through the Midwest League in a battered '77 station wagon missing two hubcaps. They traveled at night to elude the heat, avoided bars and motels frequented by players whose performance they had to judge, and lived a Spartan existence, spending virtually every moment together from the first pitch of the season to the last. Each earned $1,900 a month, paid by the individual minor league; each man was expected to pay all his road expenses from that salary.

York stuffed the game balls into his pockets, and Wilber flicked some lint off his jacket. "It's seven of," he said. "Time to go." Shoulders straight and heads back, they moved together down the concourse and with deliberate strides walked onto the field to a chorus of boos.

Some of the old parks are joys to behold. They are full of nooks and crannies and odd angles, squeezed into downtown blocks, their size determined by existing buildings. In Durham, North Carolina, just behind the Bulls' right-field fence is the brick wall of an old tobacco warehouse. In Great Falls, Montana, Legion Park sits in the shadow of grain elevators, beneath a western sky that seems to stretch clear to the Pacific.

In Birmingham, Alabama, the Barons' new suburban home—12-million-dollar Hoover Metropolitan Stadium—offers sky boxes at $17,500 a season, and everything has the whiff of major-league quality. But it was the home the Barons abandoned after the 1987 season that I found compelling. "I wouldn't be leaving your van on the street if I was you," the man from the recreation department said as he unlocked the gate to Rickwood Field. "Better to park inside where it'll be safe. Then I'll lock up behind you."

Rickwood Field was low and airy with a single deck and a wooden outfield fence. I parked in the shade of a dark concourse, next to a wall with nine painted flags, each marking one of the Barons' league championships. Outside, weeds crawled across the diamond, though the city still clipped the infield grass every two weeks, as if the Barons were only away on a road trip. I wandered into the home-team clubhouse and found a light that worked. Bare lockers lined the wall like skeletons. A cardboard box full of athletic tape and cans of shaving cream and a discarded baseball shoe sat on the trainer's table. By the light switch was a note from manager Rico Petrocelli [ss-3b, Boston Red Sox, 1963-76] saying batting practice would be held at 5 p.m.

For a long time I sat alone in the bleachers, thunderclouds swirling overhead, and the ghosts came floating back. The stands filled, and I could see blurry faces in the crumbling press box across the field. Lumbering Walt Dropo stood between home and first, watching his soaring drive clear the clock deep in left field. . . . There was Babe Ruth, in an exhibition game of touring major-leaguers, rounding second with mincing steps, his ball settling on a moving freight train that did not stop until it got to Nashville, 200 miles away. It was said to be the longest home run ever hit. . . . And Norm Zauchin chasing down a foul ball. He crashed over the railing at first and landed in the lap of a fan named Janet Mooney, whom he would marry two years later.

During my travels, only one thing never changed—the ballplayers. Knowing neither fame nor fortune, they were trusting and approachable and without pretense. They didn't wear earrings or have long hair or dress out-landishly. They were gracious with writers and fans. And they had passion for their work, a pride in excelling, a trait that seems all too rare in today's society. What their lives were really about, I decided, was the acceptance of defeat, because in baseball failure is the norm. Even the best teams lose one of every three games, the finest hitters fail seven times in ten. When failure comes, a player's mind begins to focus on what has gone wrong. In a game his nervous and muscular systems go through the sequence of past failure, reinforcing the likelihood of more failure and less confidence.

"My first reaction was, this can't be happening to me," said Durham's slump-ridden second baseman, David Butts. "Then I started thinking I just wasn't much of a ballplayer." His batting average kept slipping, down to a minuscule .080, and every time he came to the plate, his eye would be distracted by the movement of an umpire or would focus on an outfield sign he had never even seen when his concentration was working. His mind had taken control of his body. He looked for reinforcement, but his teammates became distant, not wanting to say anything to hurt him and not knowing what they could do to help him. A deathly hush fell over the crowd every time he came to bat.

One week Butts would show up at Durham Athletic Park early for extra batting practice, the next he would stay away as much as possible. Nothing helped. Pitches blurred by him. "It was like I'd lost my vision," he said. Then one of Atlanta's batting instructors, Willie Stargell, came to Durham. Butts was alone in the park, working out, and Stargell walked up to him and said, "Here, let me help you." For a long time the overweight black Hall of Famer with 21 years as a major-league player stood in his street clothes in front of the mound, patiently throwing slow pitches to the young, white infielder with the furrowed brow. "Bat back, level swing, drive the bat right through the ball," Stargell would say. "Thataway. That's good contact."

Whether Stargell's encouragement was responsible for breaking the spell is hard to say, but by the time I got to Durham, Butts had started to hit again. But he knew that, at age 25, his career was almost over.

"The hardest part of David's being released or however it ends will be going home, because they won't understand," his wife said one night as we watched the game in seats behind home plate. "What they won't understand is how far he's come and what a long, hard endurance test this is."

If I had gotten to Helena, Montana, and the Pioneer League at the beginning of the season, rather than in August, at the tail end of my 16,000-mile journey, I might have stayed all summer. Kindrick Legion Field was small—its seats extend only 13 rows back from the field—and felt as cozy as a village green. The stands look out toward Mount Helena, rising from a low chain of pine-clad mountains. Just beyond the outfield fence were a church, its steeple topped by a gold cross, and a row of small homes, on one of which was painted a huge yellow mitt as a target for hitters.

The crowd was sparse the night I got to Helena, only a few hundred, and the skies were heavy with the threat of rain. Many of the fans seemed to know one another, and I found the park an easy place not to be a stranger. Mary Gunstone was one of the first fans to arrive, a 40ish woman carrying 33 photograph albums—each a chronicle of the season—that she had put together. She had taken shots of players with their arms around one another's shoulders, of infielders scooping up grounders, of young men, bats cocked over their shoulders, their white uniforms pressed and spotless, each looking as proud as a newly commissioned Army officer. The albums were carefully wrapped in plastic, and each bore the name of one of the Brewers.

"Mary, why don't you just give them doughnuts?" the owner of the bakery where she worked had asked. "You could get them for free."

"No," she replied, "you can't take home doughnuts. I want them to have something they can keep, something to remember their season in Montana by."

She waited at the railing beyond the dugout, calling the Brewers aside one by one to make her presentations. The young men blushed, mumbled thanks, and seemed very pleased. "Come here, Emmett," she called. Emmett Reese, a retired California fire captain, was the clubhouse manager, and during the season he lived where he worked—in the clubhouse, on a rollaway bed stored by the washing machine. He walked over and quickly scanned the album she gave him.

"Oh, Mary," he said, giving her a hearty hug, "this is beautiful. Really beautiful."

Overhead thunder boomed, and, with one out in the fifth inning, the black skies opened and torrents of rain swept across the field. Fans dashed for cover.

The rain delay lasted two hours, and it was midnight before the Medicine Hat Blue Jays secured the last out to beat Helena, 5-2. Only 40 shivering fans remained to the end, among them eight-year-old Heidi Goettel, who used her allowance each week to buy snacks for her favorite player, Kevin Tannihill.

After an hour or so the players had showered and drifted away. Randy Bruce stood alone under the lights, pounding, raking, and poking at the infield, a solitary performer on an abandoned stage. Emmett Reese scurried from locker to locker, scooping up jerseys, socks, and jockstraps, which he stuffed into the washing machine, the first of 14 loads he would do before rolling into bed at dawn. He knocked on the door of a closet-size office, where manager Dusty Rhodes and pitching coach Ray Burris, twice a 15-game winner in the majors, were filling in game reports to be phoned to the parent club, the Milwaukee Brewers.

"Would you fellows drink a pot of coffee if I made one?" Emmett asked. They nodded.

The nights were cold now, and I warmed my hands on the mug of coffee. The season had dwindled down to its last few days. I stayed in the clubhouse, talking to Rhodes. He spoke about the pressure on his players to succeed, about how baseball was like war, preparing every day for a new battle, every skirmish producing a winner and a loser. Only the best survived.

After a while I went out into the darkened parking lot and started up Forty-Niner. I had intended to stay one more night in Montana, but for reasons I cannot explain, a compulsion overtook me and I started driving. California lay over the mountains and down the coast. A chilled breeze gusted through the Prickly Pear Valley. I turned on the radio and heard a recap of exhibition football games.

Summer was over, and it was time to go home.

APRIL 1991

TOUGH LOVE
IN THE OUTBACK

ERLA ZWINGLE

The wedding was off. By the time I rolled into Zanthus, Western Australia, that night on the Tea and Sugar Train, the preparatory celebrations had reached dangerous levels. In a fit of prenuptial nerves, aggravated by more than the usual quota of beer, the bride-to-be (or not-to-be) and her intended had come to blows. Rumors flew along with the fists: confused accounts of who had started it, how she had gotten her three or more brothers to hold her beloved down while she hit him, and who had gone after whom with the scissors.

It was clear to the guests (some of whom had driven 15 hours to see the couple joined in holy wedlock) and to the Reverend Henry Noack (who had come out on this run to do the joining) that a pastor's services would not be required. Mr. Noack, who has a long-standing professional interest in minimizing the unsanctified living arrangements of railway couples, covered his disappointment with a mixture of hard-bitten irony ("She's just given him a great thwack on the head, and then they're going to talk about love and honor?") and high evangelical hopes ("There's a good sermon in this"). But there was a bright side to it as well: The train crew believed that this meant we might reach Kalgoorlie a little ahead of schedule.

The cautiously pleased padre told me later that the couple had calmed down shortly after the train departed, drove into Kalgoorlie to the registry office, discovered the fee had risen beyond their means, and so, properly penitent, intercepted him on his return via another train. It is possible that they are, even now, still married.

FROM "THE TEA & SUGAR TRAIN," JUNE 1986

THE HARD RIDE OF ROUTE 93

Michael Parfit

"I drive Highway 93," the bumper sticker reads. "Pray for me." It was printed in the seventies, and, like the road, it's frayed. You see it on old cars, but you see more old cars on this road than on the broad, sterile interstates that float across the country hardly touching the land. This is Highway 93, a tough two-lane blacktop that runs 1,860 miles from a car wash and a liquor store in Phoenix, Arizona, to the Canadian National Railway yard in Jasper, Alberta—long, narrow, dangerous, magnificent; in hard contact with America all the way.

I drive 93. All the time. I live on it in Montana. I've lived on it in Idaho. I've worn out six cars on it. I fly up and down it in my old Cessna. I ride it in buses and in the odd vehicles that pass for buses around here. I've even gone down it in an ambulance, flat out on a gurney, hanging on for dear life to the hand of an emergency medical technician who turned out to be the woman who rents me movies.

In a country linked by interstates, that's Highway 93: the last hard road. On 93 you can still experience the buffet of large vehicles breaking the speed limit going the other way, be blinded by headlights bearing down on you, and know when trapped behind a combine that the next passing lane is 40 miles ahead. A rest stop is a gravel turnout with a picnic table, a pit toilet, and a garbage can with bullet holes in it. You don't have to pay to use Highway 93; the only toll is on your shock absorbers and your mind. Life on Highway 93 is close to the bone.

Farmer's Liquor. Weiss Guys Car Wash. Cinder-block motels, a machine shop, a liquor store turned into a boxing gym. Just beyond Surprise, I pass a line of skulls on a dirt turnout. It's a guy selling boiled longhorn skulls out of his Oldsmobile. "Funny about a road," a woman in Wikieup told me.

"There's a lot of ranchers on 93. And there's a lot of. . ." She searched for the word. "A lot of—*questionable* people on this road."

Yeah, I know. I love it.

Wickenburg, 52 miles out of Phoenix, celebrates them all: a Cowboy Poets Gathering, an autumn Bluegrass Festival, Gold Rush Days in February. From up and down 93 and all over the West people come to sing and rhyme about working hard and loving lonely.

One night in Wickenburg, at the Bluegrass Festival, I hung around an impromptu jam session in a little arena formed by three parked motor homes. Astroturf was thrown on the dust. Lanterns hissed. There were two fiddles, two mandolins, a banjo, one mournful steel guitar called a Dobro, and three guitars.

The Dobro player, Millie Vannoy, had two Shih Tzu dogs. The male wore a red cowboy bandanna, the female a stuffed heart on each ear. They barked.

"Let's sing one the dogs don't know," said itinerant guitarist Art Kershaw, who once lived in Kalispell. Millie was tentative on the Dobro. She didn't like making mistakes where all these experts could hear.

A banjo picker named Les gave advice I got to thinking about as I rolled up the road at two that morning: "Hey, Millie," he said, "you gotta hit them bad notes hard."

Highway 93 was once promoted as running all the way to Central America, but that was an exaggeration. It never even made it to Mexico, and lately it's been losing ground to bureaucracy. Signs still label it Arizona 93 from Phoenix to Wickenburg, but the state's abandoning the number. The federal designation begins just north of Wickenburg. I stop there on gravel that glitters with glass and talk to truckers on the CB. Where are you headed, and what do you have on?

"Come out of L.A.," one says. "Goin' to Texas. Windows."

"Outa Tucson. Vegas. Pipe."

"Going to Georgia. I got bodies."

I swear that's what it sounds like. Bodies? In a semi? Say again?

"Potties. Universal toilets."

Before I reach Wikieup, the road gets mean. A good two-lane is 34 feet wide; enough shoulder outside the white fog lines to duck from someone else's drift. Here the road's 24 feet narrow. Gamblers drive 93 back to Phoenix in the morning after all night at the casinos: "Drunk, tired, broke, and mad," a wrecker told me.

Help! There's a semi right on top of me. The buffeting air slams me. A wall of iron pipes booms past and is gone. I shiver, hot.

"This will be the best milk shake you have ever had on the planet, bar none." Whew. I'm ready. I've crept into the village of Wikieup to visit Paul Moss, proprietor of the Chili Factory. Paul has a ponytail, small red sunglasses, and a background teaching young doctors business management at the University of Utah Medical Center. We may look like hicks out here on 93 in our Levis and old trucks, but don't count on it.

"They call this Blood Alley," Paul says genially over the whir of the machine. He gestures broadly and slowly, all poise and presence, like an actor delivering Lincoln.

My truck chugs a quart of oil and rolls on. North of Kingman there's a hand-painted sign put up by someone angry about his loss to this road. "KILLER HIGHWAY," it reads, red on yellow. "CAUTION."

I come to Hoover Dam in the dark. From the air, at night, Highway 93 north of the dam is a boulevard of light—malls, convenience stores, fast-food joints, and gas stations—all the way to Las Vegas. It's a long spear of glitter shoved into the bonfire. I follow it straight through the blazing city and then out again, heading for Lincoln County, the one part of the highway where I always seem to get in trouble. I don't know if I remember the trouble more or the people who helped.

In 1974, my wife Debbie and I landed here in an ancient plane and a brake failed. We got help from Bill and Bob McCrosky's Texaco station, a towing service, and bar a mile from the airfield. A few years later I landed there, low on fuel, not knowing that the airport fuel pumps were empty. Dan Devlin, who worked at McCrosky's, gave me a ride to Pioche to pick up five gallons of high-octane car fuel. Then, just last winter, I flew up out of the warm South, intending to camp, but the temperature was only 10 above. There was Clyde Mecham at the airport with an old truck, worried that I might freeze. He drove me to McCrosky's, where the bartender, Cordelia "Cordy" Benezet, gave me a ride to a motel in Caliente in her old station wagon.

"The people here are friendly," she said. When I agreed with feeling, she modified it.

"I don't mean *outgoing* friendly," she said. "I mean they're generous with themselves."

Now when I get to Panaca, it's day again and there's somebody else in trouble. It's Reyes Martinez, who has been driving 93 all the way down from Twin Falls, Idaho, with his family, towing a broken Chevy pickup on a U-Haul trailer behind a big old yellow Dodge. Two hours back up the highway, where there's nobody, a trailer tire blew and ruined the wheel. Martinez managed to jam the Dodge's spare on the trailer and got to McCrosky's. Bill McCrosky finds him an old wheel and tire out back and puts it on. There's no charge.

"Got to give 'em credit," Bill says as they pull away. "Most people would have made us come get 'em. They figured out how to get it here. Saved us the trip."

Another day, another quart of oil. I'm off, past Pioche out into the vast spaces of the geologic province called Basin and Range: long valleys that drain only into themselves, bounded by austere mountains, populated by cows and coyotes. In the heart of this is Geyser Ranch, where I stopped late last year.

In the ranch house Kathy Baumeister was making good, thick boiled coffee. She reminded me of a cowboy poem heard in Wickenburg:

> She does what is needed
> And won't look for praise.
> Knowin' it comes as seldom
> As her eight-hour workdays.

Her husband, Luke, the ranch foreman, was talking to Sean Keele, who had brought a flatbed load of hay down 93 from Twin Falls. Turned out Sean was related to my friends Lynn and Ruby Keele, who lived up in Idaho near Debbie and me. They ran one of the smallest post offices in America, where they cacheted envelopes with a woodcut of a grouse. Lynn and Ruby are dead now too.

Luke showed Sean a piece of wrought silver. "Cowboy without silver," he said, "might as well work in Texas."

Another quart of oil, another hundred miles. Ely stands high and windy at a junction of valleys and highways, 93, 6, and Route 50—nicknamed "the loneliest highway in America." I drive past the junction thinking: In some places there might not be many cars on 93, but I would never call this highway lonely.

The road runs fast, but I stop and let slowness catch up with my life at the gas station, motel, bar, and café at Schellbourne Station, 40 miles out in the desert north of Ely.

Lyman Rosenlund, who owns Schellbourne Station, wears stained overalls, red Budweiser suspenders, a blue shirt, and a questionable hat. His talk is slow and quiet.

When I drop in for coffee, Lyman's reading the *Wall Street Journal*. At the bar George Murray, a trucker on his way down 93 out of Montana with a load of potatoes bound for Los Angeles, eats ham and eggs cooked by Charlcia "Charlie" Rosenlund, Lyman's wife.

Lyman points to a story in the *Journal* and says: "After another 30 years they'll prove this planet was not made for civilization."

"Great breakfast," says George.

Lyman and Charlie came here in 1953. Outdoor toilets, no well, no electricity. The power didn't get here until 1974.

"All we had was whiskey, shot glasses, and four kinds of cigarettes," he says. "Those miners was in here every night. It was so easy to make money."

We sit. George eats. Lyman reads. I sip. "Those days," he says at last, "if you couldn't get a job, you could cut cedar posts or Christmas trees, or sort ore. You could do lots of things. Today it's even difficult to acquire dynamite. Hell, we used to put it under the bed to keep it warm. Mom and I knew the United States of America at its best."

The road draws me on, away from beautiful deep sunlight of afternoon in the high desert out into low windy clouds and nightfall north of Twin Falls. I rise and fall as 93 crosses hills of lava, the lights of small towns showing occasionally in the distance. It feels exactly like sailing ten miles offshore. In fact, a lot of large yachts use this part of Highway 93: riding the swells of rock on their flatbed trucks to avoid overpasses on the interstate.

Once I came through here, past Craters of the Moon National Monument, in a snowstorm at 2 a.m., hurrying home to Debbie, and drove 93 for 20 minutes without headlights because I could see better through the snow. The whole 20 minutes I met no other car, but I saw two mule deer and a coyote.

I turn left at Arco and head for the magnificent mountains of the Big Lost River Valley and the village of Mackay. For me it's dangerous territory, close to the bone. Debbie and I moved to Mackay in 1971, when she was 21 and I was 24, and we left in 1976, but from where I stand today it looks like the best time of our lives.

I drive slowly, trying to catch the storm of memory that roars past somewhere overhead. It is elusive. I park the truck by a bad bridge over the creek and walk slowly home. It is an old log homesteader's cabin out in the sagebrush, with cottonwoods around it. We had happened upon Highway 93 by chance while wandering around the United States and had found the house by chance while wandering around this valley. I had no idea then how unusual both house and highway were, and how unlikely it would have been to find such a wild and beautiful place to live anywhere but on this anachronistic road.

Much of each winter, snowdrifts would block our dirt road, and we would have to walk a mile to the house. It seems now that it was always 40 below and the wind was always blowing. But she hung in with me, cooked our meals, heard out my heartache, and walked with me in the bitter wind. Across the open sagebrush slope we could hear home long before we got there: The wind blew in the bare cottonwoods and made the sound of the sea.

The door is not locked. It never was. The house was abandoned when we moved into it and is abandoned now. Some people lived in it for a while after we left, but they changed nothing. It is as if we left last week. Here's the pitcher pump that replaced trips to the spring; it's dry. The bay window I cut in the logs—chainsaw architecture—has lost a pane. And here's my ingenious door, with a latch hidden by a nail; it still works. On log posts and ceiling, my varnish shines.

But I didn't hang in with Debbie, and our marriage came apart in Montana in 1989. Man, I hit those bad notes hard. What I remember now is driving back to Montana through here in June of '91 in a motor home I'd rented because Debbie was too sick to ride in a car. Then, in July 1991 at her sister's home in California, with our two kids in the next room and her brother, her sister, and me by her bed, 20 years and 11 days after we were married, she died.

I touch a log. Suddenly I find myself desperate to fix the house up again the way it was. Prime the pump! Put flowers in a jar! Then I think: Why? As if I could capture those days with varnish. The varnish is still there, but the days aren't.

Mackay's gone. Challis passes. The canyon of the Salmon River rises on either side like the gates of a refuge, dry golden walls of rock and grass in late sunshine. At last in need of a voice—the more questionable the better—I stop along the river to visit "Dugout Dick" in one of the 16 caves he has built of stones, adobe, old lumber, car parts, and tires in a talus hillside. He plays me his guitar and talks about ghosts.

"Bonnie comes to visit me," he says, all scraggly gray beard and sincere eyes. "She was my common-law wife. She got beat to death by a drunk in a spud cellar in '63."

Dugout Dick is 76. His real name is Richard Zimmerman. He's lived here in a cave since 1948. To pay his bills, he rents spare caves for $15 to $50 a month, milks goats, and sells tourists religious poetry.

"I been out of the body several times," he says—no wild gestures, no rolling eyes. "Another time I floated to another planet."

I follow Lewis and Clark's route out of Salmon and cross Lost Trail Pass on 20-mile-an-hour switchbacks.

I drive slowly down into Montana, and the character of the land changes. The sagebrush is gone, the grasslands diminish, cowboy boots on the bar rail give way to logger boots. The rock ridges of the Bitterroot Range rise from cloaks of pine, Douglas fir, and tamarack. The cloaks are threadbare in patches, and I pass hundreds of acres of forest cut down and decked in rows in each town.

Missoula is busy in the night, kids cruising the strip of shops and fast-food joints near an intersection on 93 known as Malfunction Junction. I dash through and head north. Lot of traffic on this road: It's the main highway from Missoula to Glacier National Park. The state highway department has plans to widen it—to a full four lanes in many parts—but environmentalists are worried that a larger road will be a barrier for animals, because the forests that close in on 93 at a pass provide the only east-west crossing corridor for wild animals for almost a hundred miles in either direction. Wolves have crossed there, and a mountain lion using the corridor killed a child there in 1989.

In the solitude and mist of early morning I follow 93 past the wooded coves, the quiet villages, and the astonishingly calm waters of Flathead Lake. Past Cranbrook the Canadian Rockies grow huge on the northern horizon, vast but weightless in snow and alpenglow.

The village of Lake Louise, the gem in the heart of the Rockies, looks like the ultimate tourist town. The first time I called the famous Chateau Lake Louise, the public relations woman said, sounding snooty: "We don't think of ourselves as being on Highway 93."

Yeah, I wanted to say: You don't belong here either. All your money goes into old wine.

But the snootiness was a facade. These people are just as questionable as the rest of us on this road. Maybe it's because many of the 650 employees of the hotel are 20 years old, work for minimum wage, and love the mountains with a lunatic love that drives them out into the high country on skis in January. Maybe it's because isolation strikes here too.

My kids and I spent Christmas at Lake Louise, far from the memories of home. People had come from all over the world to the hotel, but it was still just another small town on Highway 93. Christmas Eve, as the lights in the rooms were going out, Erica, David, and I went to the lake and skated up and down holding hands, thinking lightly and without pain about friend and mother, Debbie. Skating, we sang every carol we knew, to the mountains, the moon, the sleeping hotel. As Christmas morning came, we were still singing.

I live on 93. Envy me.

DECEMBER 1992

INTO THE BLUE

NOT SO FAST!

ALEXANDER GRAHAM BELL

The Wright brothers' successful flying-machine travels at the rate of about thirty-seven miles an hour; and, judging from its great flying weight (nearly two pounds per square foot of supporting surface), it is unlikely that it could be maintained in the air if it had very much less velocity. But should an accident happen to a body propelled through the air with the velocity of a railroad train, how about the safety of the occupants? Accidents will happen, sooner or later, and the chances are largely in favor of the first accident being the last experiment. While, therefore, we may look forward with confidence to the ultimate possession of flying-machines exceeding in speed the fastest railroad trains, it might be the part of wisdom to begin our first experiments at gaining experience in the air with machines traveling at such moderate velocities as to reduce the chances of a fatal catastrophe to a minimum.

It might be advisable to begin, if possible, with such a moderate flying weight as to permit of the machine being flown as a kite. There would be little difficulty, then, in raising it into the air, and should an accident happen to the propelling machinery, the apparatus would descend gently to the ground; or the aviator could cast anchor, and his machine would continue flying, as a kite, if the wind should prove sufficient for its support. If it could fly, as a kite, in a ten-mile breeze, then a velocity of only ten miles an hour would be sufficient for its support as a flying-machine in calm air, while a less speed would suffice in heading into a moderate wind.

Such velocities would be consistent with safety in experiments, especially if the flights should be made over water instead of land, and at moderate elevations above the surface. Under such circumstances the inevitable accidents which are sure to happen during first experiments are hardly likely to be followed by more serious consequences than a ducking to the man and the immersion of the machine. If the man is able to swim and the machine to float upon water, little damage need be anticipated to either.

FROM "AËRIAL LOCOMOTION," JANUARY 1907

LOST OVER MEXICO
CHARLES A. LINDBERGH

The *Spirit of St. Louis* had covered only a little over thirty thousand miles at the end of its tour of the United States. The plane was practically new and its engine was capable of many more hours of flying.

I always had a desire to fly in the Tropics; also, I was particularly interested in the feasibility of Pan American airlines; consequently, when I received an invitation from the President of Mexico to visit his country, it required less than a week to complete my preparation for the flight.

The tail skid cut through the mud on Bolling Field for nearly 2,000 feet and the wheels ran along for another thousand before the *Spirit of St. Louis* lifted, hopped over the puddles and into the air. Thus, shortly after noon on December 13, 1927, began my flight from Washington to Mexico, to Central America, and home through South America and over the Caribbean. (As I have said, I do not believe it wise to make unnecessarily long flights in a single-motored plane over water. That was why, on this tour, I always reduced the water hops to a minimum.)

A thousand feet up [above Mexico] I got over the clouds, and less than two hours later had passed the first mountains. I crossed a railroad and a small town. It was at this point that I made an important error in navigation by mistaking my position as south of my course, whereas it was actually north. Consequently I changed course in the wrong direction and greatly increased my error.

My mistake soon became apparent, but I was not able to locate my position. The only maps of Mexico I had been able to obtain in the United States were inaccurate and showed few natural landmarks.

Occasionally I passed over a winding railroad, but upon consulting the map I could find none that were not straight.

After following one of these for a time, I arrived over a fair-sized village and flew low past the station to pick up the name from its signboard.

It did not, however, correspond with the names of any towns on the map. After several other similar attempts, I decided that there had been a disagreement somewhere, or that the towns had been renamed and I would have to locate myself by some other method.

I then climbed to an altitude of over 12,000 feet.

The rivers below were flowing toward the south, and far to the east was a high mountain peak towering above the others in its range. Directly underneath, the country was rough and uninhabited.

I located my position approximately by the direction of the rivers and headed east, toward the peak, which, from my map, appeared to be Mount Toluca.

About and hour later I came to the largest city I had passed over since leaving Tampico.

I again attempted to shoot the station, but without result. After circling three times over the city, however, I noticed a sign saying "Hotel Toluca," painted on one of the buildings near the station.

After locating Toluca on my map as being about thirty miles west of Mexico City, I headed east, and a few minutes later, after passing over a low ridge, the city itself appeared in the distance.

I had lost between two and three hours by my mistake and flown nearly far enough to have reached the Pacific Ocean and returned to Mexico City, had I followed such a course accurately.

I landed at the airport 27 hours and 15 minutes after taking off from Bolling Field, or one hour and 15 minutes over my estimated time.

FROM "TO BOGOTÁ AND BACK BY AIR," MAY 1928

ALMOST LIKE SOMEONE SINGING

ANNE MORROW LINDBERGH

We decided to try to take off [from Bathurst, the Gambia, British West Africa] at daybreak, the time of most wind, with all fuel tanks full, part of which we could unload if necessary and still have a safe reserve. The morning of December 3 we taxied out into the bay, the pontoons almost submerged under their heavy load, the plane heaving bulkily from side to side as we taxied across the wind and waves. After several hopeless attempts to take off—the spray sluiced down over the wings continually and we never got up on the step—we turned back to the mooring. Unloading our extra gasoline, we tried again. But the wind had dropped by then, and though this time we got up on the step we could not get off the water. We decided to go back and wait for a wind.

That night at midnight, we tried again with the moon just past full, lighting a path for us on the water. I watched the red light on the wing-tip glow, disappear, and glow again as the spray passed over it, and held my breath to lighten the load. It was no use; after several attempts we taxied back to the lights of the town.

"What was the matter, Colonel?" asked a friend who had kindly stayed to watch us.

"Overload, that's all," answered my husband. "We've taken off with that much before (in Greenland). But it's different down here in the Tropics; different air."

We drove home through the dark streets in silence and went to bed very tired after our long unsuccessful day.

"We still have a few tricks to try," said my husband.

I wondered what they were.

My husband spent the [next] day inside the plane, cutting out an unused gasoline tank, piece by piece, with tin snips. It was very hot with the sun beating down fiercely on the outside of the ship, and the fumes from the empty tank were suffocating. He was tired at the end of the day, but much more cheerful at the thought of the saved weight.

By the next evening we had cut out even more weight: some emergency chocolate (there was still enough food and water left for a month); the anchor; the rope; the tin bucket: a great many tools; the flying suits; the sleeping bag; all our clothes, except the ones we wore; our duffel bags, and many other things—a total of about 150 pounds.

The day seemed unusually calm, the tops of the palms hardly stirring. At sunset, when I walked out on the pier, there was not enough wind to lift a handkerchief. The moon rose about nine, reddish and grown lopsided since the night before.

"We could still take off at daybreak, couldn't we?" I asked my husband.

"No," he answered. "You see, the moon rises later every night—and it wouldn't be light enough when we reach the other side [Brazil] to land by."

There was never any wind at sunset; this seemed to be our last chance as far as Bathurst was concerned.

We left Government House at 10:30, local time, carrying only what we wore, some lunch, and two sun helmets. It took us a long time to get started after we reached the plane. First we pumped out the pontoons. They were loaded so heavily that the back ends had to be lifted out of the water by a rowboat under the tail. Next, we sealed up the anchor box in the pontoons with putty, to prevent water from leaking in during taxiing.

"There's about a five-mile wind right now," said my husband cheerfully to the Captain of the Port, who had come out to help us.

Our friend held up his hand. "You air folks must look at it differently," he replied.

"Why? What would you call it?" my husband queried.

"Almost dead calm."

We all laughed. My husband took off the lantern and the plane's mooring bridle and handed them to the Captain.

"If we come back we'll want these; otherwise"—he stopped for a moment and then—"we'll have another try, anyway"—and off we went.

I looked back in the tail to be sure that everything was securely lashed; sat on my extra shirt; stuffed the lunch into the map case; put the radio bag in the seat beside me, and fastened the belt. The lights of the town were on our left and, above them, the palms were outlined quite plainly in the moonlight. Out in the bay there was more wind. We turned, slowed up, throttled down. A pause for breath.

"All set?"

"Yes, all right."

Then the roar—the spray. I watched it over the wing and looked down at my watch. The spray stopped. We were spanking along—up on the step—a good deal faster than before. Sparks from the exhaust. We're going to get off! I thought in a flash of realization. But how long it takes! We're off? No— spank—spank—spank—but almost—.

I held my breath. We're off! No more spanks.

Yes, we're off—we're rising. The engine smoothed out into a long sigh, like a person breathing easily, almost like someone singing, ecstatically. We turned from the lights of the city. The plane seemed exultant, then, even arrogant. We did it—we did it! We're up above you—we were dependent on you, just now, River, asking you for favors, for wind and light. But now, we are free of you; we are up—we are off. We can toss you aside—you, River—there below us, a few lights in the great, dark, silent world that is ours—for we are above it.

From "Flying Around the North Atlantic," September 1934

MY BEAUTIFUL AIR-TIGHT CABIN
Auguste Piccard

There we were, bound for the stratosphere. This had been my dream for many years.

Thousands of people looked on from below as the balloon left the ground; but Kipfer and I saw nothing. The first thing I had to do was to close the last hole that linked the interior of our cabin with the outside world—just a tiny hole one inch in diameter. I had to get an electrostatic sounding instrument into this hole.

I exerted myself to place this sounding instrument, but the fall sustained by the cabin had slightly deformed it and my task seemed impossible.

During my hopeless efforts the balloon continued to rise. The exterior air became rarefied, and the air in the cabin escaped through the hole. Kipfer told me we were at 15,000 feet altitude, and that the interior altimeter marked the same height. There was my beautiful air-tight cabin, absolutely of no use. We would have been quite as well off in a gondola of wickerwork.

But we had to do something. Kipfer came to my rescue and by a vigorous effort finally succeeded in inserting the instrument, but at what a price! The tube of quartz forming an insulation was broken and the air of the cabin escaped, whistling. I had a reserve of liquid oxygen in insulated bottles. By pouring small quantities of this on the floor of the cabin, we caused evaporation of the oxygen, which compensated for the escaping gas, and the internal pressure dropped no more.

Luckily we had foreseen the possibility of an accident of this sort. I had carried a considerable quantity of a mixture of oakum and vaseline.

In great haste I smeared the mixture around the ailing instrument. The work was not easy. All this was taking place under a board in an almost inaccessible place. I said to Kipfer, "If we do not rapidly succeed in stopping up the hole, I shall be obliged to pull the valve and land."

It is lucky that I did not then know that I could not pull the valve and release some gas, and that it would be impossible to come down before nightfall; for, confident in that last resource to fall back upon in case all else failed to rescue us, I worked feverishly to fill the hole through which our air continued to escape with a whistling noise. Bit by bit I succeeded. The whistling decreased and finally I heard nothing more.

Ah, that wonderful silence, what a relief it was! Never have I felt so keenly the satisfaction that can come from perfect silence. We were now air-tight. I glanced at the watch; we had been in the air 28 minutes.

I glanced at the altimeter. We had risen to an altitude of 9.65 miles. This was an average speed of approximately 20 miles an hour. For an automobilist on the road that would not be much, but ascending straight into the air is quite different. We were right in the stratosphere. What a change! A half hour ago we were wondering if the ascension would be made. Now we were in a world absolutely new.

Now for a look through the portholes to see what the stratosphere was like.

From 10 miles above the earth I gazed around. First I looked up at my balloon that, at the take-off, had not been so beautiful, with all her folds. But now she was superb, a perfect sphere, illumined by the sun that was just rising.

Later on in the morning when we tried to pull the valve, the rope broke because of an oversight at the moment of taking off. So we were unable to descend then.

Slowly we were pushed toward the Bavarian Alps. We arrived there at 5 o'clock in the afternoon, at slow speed; luckily, because one of our chief dangers was the possibility of going over the sea. That day seemed very long.

What heat! What thirst! What uncertainty!

"The heat?" you will say. "Since the temperature of the stratosphere is some 60 degrees below zero, Fahrenheit, you could not be too hot."

But we *were* too hot. To protect myself against the cold, I had painted one side of the gondola black, so as to absorb the solar radiations and thus provide heat. The other side of the gondola was shiny. I had an arrangement for turning the gondola around, black to the sun if it grew too cold, and shiny side to the sun if it became too hot.

The black side absorbed the sun's rays perfectly; but when we wanted to turn the gondola, the mechanism provided for this purpose would not work, on account of a short circuit caused in the motor line when taking off. So the temperature in our gondola continued to rise.

Seventy-seven or 86 degrees, Fahrenheit, would have been pleasant, but 95 to 104 degrees, Fahrenheit, was too much. This torrid heat was rendered all the more painful, as our supply of drinking water was soon exhausted.

There was something else still graver: the excessive heat had deformed the rubber joints of the manholes, and these began to lose air, so that the internal pressure of the gondola was again slowly dropping. There was only one thing to do, and that was to wait. So we decided to wait and see what would happen.

In the afternoon the balloon started to descend about a hundred feet an hour. At that rate it would have taken us three weeks to get down to earth. But at sundown we knew the balloon would descend rapidly as the cooled gases contracted. At 8 o'clock we felt we were quite low. We were then seven and a half miles up. Here we remembered other aëronauts who had been to this height, some of whom survived, and this was comforting.

At 8:50 we were two and a half miles up, and there opened the manholes. We were above high mountains, but that made no difference. At least, the sea and asphyxiation had been avoided.

Happily luck was with us, for if we were ourselves unable to pick our landing place, the balloon appeared to have the power of avoiding the surrounding crevasses and peaks, and calmly settled down on a flat part of a glacier, the most suitable of all visible spots. We landed at an altitude of a mile and three-quarters, near Ober-Gurgl, in the Innsbruck region, and camped there that night in an improvised fashion, going down to Ober-Gurgl village next morning to resume our contact with mankind.

FROM "BALLOONING IN THE STRATOSPHERE," MARCH 1933

PREPARING FOR THE WORST

AMELIA EARHART

The night I found over the Pacific was a night of stars. They seemed to rise from the sea and hang outside my cockpit window, near enough to touch, until hours later they slipped away into the dawn.

But shortly before midnight I spied a star that differed from the others. It was too pink and it flashed as no star could. I realized I was seeing a ship, with its searchlights turned into the heavens as a lamppost to guide me on my way. I snapped on my landing lights, which are on the leading edge of the wings midway to their tips, and had them bravely blink a greeting to whoever might be watching.

I was wearing my radio earphones, and after a moment the spattering buckshot of code wiped out everything else on the air, as the radio operator on that ship broadcast to shore stations that I had been sighted. Though we could not converse directly, it was comforting to hear the crackle he produced and to realize that at least thus far I was on the course. Later I learned the vessel passed was the Matson ship *Maliko,* 900 miles from Honolulu.

An interesting data sheet in my "chart room" (a tiny space in the wing beside my shoulder, where reposed maps, tools, etc.) was a blueprint showing the position of every vessel on or near the course, and the exact time I should be over it, reckoned on an average flying speed and a predetermined hour of starting.

But before starting I thought it unlikely that I would sight a ship. The chance of two specks, one on the surface of a very large ocean, the other thousands of feet above it, passing near enough to see each other seemed slim.

I have said little about the precautions taken in case something went wrong.

Mine is a land plane, equipped with wheels. Occasionally such a one has come down safely on water, though the landing is generally dangerous.

There are a number of factors which affect the result. Among them are the roughness of the water, the buoyancy of the craft itself, and its position when it strikes. I had dump valves in the two largest fuselage tanks, which permitted almost instant evacuation of the contents. Empty, these alone had considerable buoyancy—added to that of any wing tanks from which fuel had been used. I felt there was every likelihood the plane would remain afloat for some time.

Paul Mantz, my technical adviser, who in his flying for motion pictures makes airplanes do unbelievable things, helped me plan the best way to bring a high-wing monoplane down on water without somersaulting. The feat has been accomplished and a craft of that type has been known to float for eight days before the crew were rescued. Of course, a steep dive into the sea would so damage any plane that it would tend to sink at once. Similarly, high waves would demolish either unfortunate land or water craft forced down on their merciless surface.

Over my warm flying clothes I wore an inflatable rubber vest, divided into two compartments. Each would blow up instantly when I released the compressed carbon dioxide contained in two little metal capsules at the waist.

Strung to my belt I had a hatchet and a sheath knife. Once down and out of the plane, I was to crawl back along the fuselage. Because of the weight of the motor, the tail surfaces presumably would be sticking out of the water. Immediately behind the gas tanks was a rubber raft. I was to hack my way through the light fabric-covered wood of the plane to reach it. It, too, was instantly inflatable from a carbon dioxide container. The sealed compartments of the raft held tomato juice, chocolate, malted-milk tablets, and a container of water.

For distress signals I carried a Very pistol which shot regulation red and green rockets. Small flares which burn on contact with water and several small balloons completed my attention-attracting equipment. The balloons were to be let up on stout fishline and bear aloft a very red silk flag.

The raft, once in action, was to be moored beside the plane, as long as the latter kept afloat. Then, as a last resource, I was to abandon ship.

FROM "MY FLIGHT FROM HAWAII," MAY 1935

THE UNDERGROUND RAILROAD

CHARLES L. BLOCKSON

Though forty years have passed, I remember as if it were yesterday the moment when the Underground Railroad in all its abiding mystery and hope and terror took possession of my imagination. It was a Sunday afternoon during World War II; I was a boy of ten, sitting on a box in the backyard of our home in Norristown, Pennsylvania, listening to my grandfather tell stories about our family.

"My father—your great-grandfather, James Blockson—was a slave over in Delaware," Grandfather said, "but as a teenager he ran away underground and escaped to Canada." Grandfather knew little more than these bare details about his father's flight to freedom, for James Blockson, like tens of thousands of other black slaves who fled north along its invisible rails and hid in its clandestine stations in the years before the Civil War, kept the secrets of the Underground Railroad locked in his heart until he died.

So did his cousin Jacob Blockson, who escaped to St. Catharines, Ontario, in 1858, two years after my great-grandfather's journey to the promised land, as runaway slaves sometimes called Canada. But Jacob told William Still, a famous black agent of the Underground Railroad in Philadelphia, the reasons for his escape: "My master was about to be sold out this Fall, and I made up my mind that I did not want to be sold like a horse. . . . I resolved to die sooner than I would be taken back."

Years after that backyard conversation with Grandfather, I read Jacob's words in Still's classic book, *The Underground Rail Road*, and saw the name of my great-grandfather written there too. I found accounts of the heroism of the fugitive slaves and that of the men and women, black and white, North and South, who helped them flee from bondage at the risk of their own lives, fortunes, and personal liberty. For the Underground Railroad was no actual railroad of steel and steam. It was a network of paths through the woods and fields, river crossings, boats and ships, trains and wagons, all haunted by the specter of recapture. Its stations were the houses and the churches of men and women—agents of the railroad—who refused to believe that human slavery and human decency could exist together in the same land.

No one knows how many fled from bondage along its invisible tracks: As many as 100,000 between 1830 and 1860? As few as 30,000? Probably no one will ever know. What we do know is a mere fragment of the whole, but it is enough. Ordeals may have gone unrecorded and names may have been forgotten, but such records as have survived in the memories of men like my grandfather and in the memoirs of those who risked all for freedom and brotherhood make it clear that the flight to freedom on the Underground Railroad was an epic of American heroism.

The flight to freedom actually began long before the Underground Railroad was known by that name. George Washington wrote in 1786 about fugitive slaves in Philadelphia "which a Society of Quakers in the city (formed for such purposes) have attempted to liberate." Washington, a slaveholder himself, was probably referring to the Pennsylvania Abolition Society, which included among its members at various times such non-Quakers as Benjamin Franklin, Thomas Paine, Dr. Benjamin Rush, and the Marquis de Lafayette.

Ottawa Indians led by Chief Kinjeino were among the earliest friends of fugitives in western Ohio. Portuguese fishermen are said to have conspired with members of the Shinnecock tribe to transport fugitive slaves from the north shore of Long Island into ports of freedom in Massachusetts, Connecticut, and Rhode Island. The Seminoles harbored escaped slaves and fought a continuing war with the United States to preserve their refuge in Florida. Most heroic of all were the slaves and free blacks who offered their churches and their homes to help the enslaved—and above all, the passengers themselves.

The vast Dismal Swamp on the Virginia-North Carolina border was a refuge for many slaves and a magnet for slave hunters who disabled their human quarry with bird shot, so as not to damage such valuable flesh with heavier ammunition. A runaway slave belonging to Augustus Holly of Bertie County, North Carolina, when finally recaptured in the swamp, was found to be wearing "a coat that was impervious to shot, it being thickly wadded with turkey feathers." Henry "Box" Brown, a "model slave" from Richmond, had himself nailed in a box with a bladder of water and a few biscuits and shipped to the Philadelphia Vigilance Committee. Though he traveled upside down part of the way, he arrived safely. But the white Virginian who helped him, Samuel A. Smith, was sentenced to prison for a subsequent attempt to freight slaves to freedom.

Most simply walked to freedom. "Guided by the north star alone," wrote the great rescuer William Still, "penniless, braving the perils of land and sea, eluding the keen scent of the blood-hound as well as the more dangerous pursuit of the savage slave-hunter.... [enduring] indescribable suffering from hunger and other privations."

Slaveholders, of course, looked upon the Underground Railroad as organized theft. Under the Constitution of the United States, it was. Slavery was lawful and slaves were property. The Fugitive Slave Law of 1850 gave slaveholders the right to organize a posse at any point in the United States to aid in recapturing runaway slaves. Courts and police everywhere in the United States were obligated to assist them.

Fugitives were plucked from churches in Ohio, from ships in Boston harbor, from the bosoms of free wives and husbands whom they had married in the North. The runaways were not safe anywhere in the nation. Those who aided them faced criminal penalties of six months in jail and a $1,000 fine in addition to a civil liability to the owner of $1,000 for each fugitive.

Some who helped the runaways were important figures in American history: Thaddeus Stevens, Frederick Douglass, Allan Pinkerton, Henry David Thoreau, Harriet Beecher Stowe, William Lloyd Garrison. One among them is a colossus: John Brown. Captain Brown, the Old Man, Osawatomie Brown, Brown of Kansas—called by whatever name, he was known to all. Among abolitionists, some of whom supported him with money, Brown was revered as a righteous warrior and martyr. Others, including the government, regarded him as a murderous insurgent.

Like his stationmaster father before him, Brown supported the Underground Railroad body and soul. In December 1858 he and his guerrilla fighters undertook one of the boldest adventures in the history of the Underground Railroad. With 11 slaves, including men, women, and children, the group set out in wagons on a journey of a thousand miles from Missouri to Windsor, Ontario, in the dead of winter. In Chicago they met the celebrated detective and Underground Railroad agent Allan Pinkerton.

Pinkerton helped the group on to Detroit, where they boarded a ferry to Canada.

Nestled in the woods on Hines Hill Road in Hudson, Ohio, is a house where John Brown once lived. Only the red chimney is visible from the road, and still existing somewhere under the barn floor is said to be a secret compartment where runaways hid.

Not far from there I came upon a surprising symbol of the Underground Railroad—an iron manikin of a young black groomsman, hand outstretched, which had been designed as an ornamental hitching post. Just such a lawn statue was used on the property of Federal Judge Benjamin Piatt, whose wife was an agent of the Underground Railroad, as a signal to fugitives and conductors. If the manikin held a flag, runaways were welcomed; if the flag was missing, the judge was at home and fugitives must pass on.

Invisible though it may have been, the railroad had many subsidiary routes and innumerable sidings and spurs. The great trunk routes led north from the slave states. The one my great-grandfather probably followed when he escaped from Seaford, Delaware, ran through Wilmington and Philadelphia to New York City and the Canadian border. Farther west, fugitives passed through Lancaster County and on up through central Pennsylvania to the Finger Lakes and Lake Ontario.

Eliza Harris, immortalized as a fictional character in Harriet Beecher Stowe's *Uncle Tom's Cabin*, is modeled on a real woman who crossed the ice of the Ohio River. Faced with the threat of being separated from her only child, Eliza planned to make her flight to freedom beyond the river. But when she reached its banks she discovered that the ice had broken up and was drifting in large cakes and floes. In desperation as her pursuers closed in, Eliza darted into the river, holding her child in her arms. Springing from one floe to another, she lost her shoes in the icy waters but struggled on with bleeding feet to the opposite shore and the safety of the Ohio underground. Before publishing *Uncle Tom's Cabin*, Stowe kept an underground station in Walnut Hills, near Cincinnati.

Although most runaways reached the protection of the Free States and the underground on their own, abolitionists did daring work even in the heart of the South. Virginian John Fairfield conducted dozens across the Ohio. The son of a slaveholder in New Bern, North Carolina, secreted slaves aboard ships hauling lumber to Philadelphia.

When the Seminoles were removed to Indian Territory starting in the early 1830s, 450 to 500 black members of the tribe, representing about 15 percent of its numbers, went with them. Some of these black Seminoles were formed into a special U.S. Army unit to fight the Comanches and Apaches. About 800 descendants of these fugitives, known as Seminole freedmen, now live in Seminole County, Oklahoma, as members of the tribe that harbored their ancestors.

To me, the most vivid of all figures connected with the Underground Railroad was Harriet Tubman, who lived on the Eastern Shore of Maryland, just across the Delmarva Peninsula from my great-grandfather. Born a slave, Harriet was one of ten or so children. As a woman in her 20s, she set off one dark summer night in 1849 from Bucktown, Maryland, to follow the North Star. From there the railroad route passed through country filled with fearful dangers: armed patrols on horseback, bloodhounds, placards advertising rewards for the capture of runaways posted at every tavern and crossroads. At length Harriet crossed the Mason-Dixon Line into free territory in Pennsylvania, penniless and "a stranger in a strange land," as she later remembered.

In Philadelphia she found employment and saved almost every penny she earned for the real work to come. Her own freedom was not enough for Harriet Tubman. Again and again she returned south through the nights, seeking passengers for her train, risking recapture and defying the wrath of slave hunters. The price on her head, by the time she conducted her final perilous journey as a liberator, reportedly reached $40,000. Among those Harriet brought north in her caravans were her parents, whom she conducted to Canada. Dark of skin, medium in height, with a full broad face topped often by a colorful kerchief, Harriet developed extraordinary physical endurance and muscular strength as well as mental fortitude. John Brown so admired Harriet's character and prowess that he nicknamed her "General Tubman."

One cannot travel very far along the Underground Railroad without encountering a Quaker. In the graveyard of Longwood Meetinghouse, not far from my present home in Pennsylvania, sleep great conductors of the railroad: Darlington, Mendenhall, Taylor. All were members of this progressive Quaker meeting that concealed fugitive slaves and spirited them away from the meetinghouse under the very eyes of proslavery spies and informers who knew of their activity but could not prove or prevent it. At Longwood Harriet Tubman, too, found sympathizers to welcome her into their homes in moments of danger.

The eloquent Frederick Douglass labored as a slave at Fells Point, but met a friendly sailor who provided false papers and so obtained his freedom. He wrote a powerful autobiography and became one of the greatest of the black antislavery orators as well as U.S. minister to Haiti. In his lifetime and beyond, the connection of the term "statesman" to his name seemed a natural thing. Douglass also served as a U.S. marshal for the District of Columbia, where, well into his manhood, manacled slaves had marched under the windows of the White House to the auction block at Decatur House on Lafayette Square, across Pennsylvania Avenue.

In Cambridge, Maryland, not far from Harriet Tubman's birthplace on the Edward Brodas plantation in Dorchester County, I encountered her kinswoman Addie Travers. Together we explored the crooked creeks of the Eastern Shore, where Harriet's route took her along the Choptank River and its many inlets.

This was perilous country, home ground of the slave hunter Patty Cannon and her merciless gang. A tall, striking woman whose salty language was her trademark, Mrs. Cannon ran her underground railroad in reverse. A letter to Philadelphia Mayor Joseph Watson in 1826 suggests that her gang was abducting blacks as far north as his city.

Sometimes she employed renegade blacks to entice fugitives into their homes as false station stops on the Underground Railroad. There the trusting runaways were entrapped by Patty's gang, who often tortured and murdered free blacks as well as escaped slaves and sold the survivors. My great-aunt Minerva Blockson, born only nine years after Appomattox, was terrified as a child growing up on the Delmarva Peninsula by tales of this villainess. "We children would hide behind chairs while the big folks told how evil old Patty Cannon would catch us and sell us to slavers down south," she told me in a voice hoarse with age. And in Aunt Minerva's bright face the old terror rekindled, though she was then 102 years of age. Finally captured and indicted for the murder of four fugitives—two of them children—Patty Cannon poisoned herself on May 11, 1829, in her prison cell at Georgetown, Delaware.

Through peril and wilderness, Harriet Tubman was a natural navigator. She did not keep a journal, but she described her various routes of escape to her biographer Sarah Bradford and others. Usually she followed the route from Cambridge along the Choptank toward Camden, Delaware. Harriet always carried a pistol to ward off pursuers. She didn't hesitate to raise it when slaves refused to travel on, crying, "You go or die." She carried tincture of opium to quiet crying babies and frightened and wounded fugitives.

My pilgrimage took me, finally, across the Canadian border to St. Catharines, an Ontario city that Harriet Tubman once called home. Here too James Blockson and his cousin Jacob had briefly lived. Nearby, the trembling suspension bridge over the Niagara River had been the passage between slavery and freedom.

William Lloyd Garrison reported that there were 25,000 fugitives in Canada in 1852. No fewer than 3,000 had arrived there within three months after the Fugitive Slave Law of 1850 was passed. The Reverend William Mitchell, a black Underground Railroad conductor and historian, estimated that at the end of the decade at least 1,200 refugees were reaching Canada every year.

Josiah Henson, on whom the character of Uncle Tom is partly based, settled in Dawn, not far from St. Catharines, after escaping from slavery in 1830. In 1841 Henson and a group of abolitionists purchased 200 acres and established a vocational school for fugitive slaves known as the British-American Institute. Henson made numerous trips on the Underground Railroad, leading fugitives to Canada. It is a supreme irony that the name of this activist's fictional counterpart should have become synonymous with servility in the usage of a later generation.

In nearby Chatham, before John Brown marched to his apotheosis along a forest route long used by fugitive slaves, he had plotted the new government he dreamed would follow his attack on the Harpers Ferry arsenal.

Walking through this hushed Canadian town, I remembered that other quiet town—Harpers Ferry. In both places John Brown's tumultuous spirit seemed to reside. I found myself humming "The Battle Hymn of the Republic," of which the tune, of course, is "John Brown's Body."

A little time before, while visiting Harriet Tubman's home in Auburn, New York, I had attended her old church and with a group of friends sang the coded spirituals of the Underground Railroad: "Steal Away to Jesus" and "Wade in the Water, Children," songs doubtless sung by Harriet Tubman during her journeys through that vanished South where men would have taken her life because she had taken her freedom.

These coded songs had double meanings: "Follow the Drinking Gourd," for example, was a metaphoric allusion to the Big Dipper and North Star. And, as Frederick Douglass once said, "A keen observer might have detected [Canada] in our repeated singing of:

'O Canaan, sweet Canaan,
I am bound for the land of Canaan.' "

We also sang the soulful "Amazing Grace," whose origins amaze with their power, for the hymn was written by a former English slave trader, John Newton, after he was seized by the Lord and exchanged his slave ship for the ministry.

The spirituals, filled with secrets that perhaps could only be told in song, have not lost their power to join one heart to many others and to explain mysteries. Standing beneath the tall evergreen that guards the grave of Harriet Tubman, I felt close to this woman who was called the Moses of our people, and to the ancestors, those of blood and those of spirit, black and white, who had trod these rights-of-way to freedom and kept the stations of the Underground Railroad and kept the faith in the oneness of mankind.

We held hands in a circle. Gladys Bryant, 77-year-old great-great-grandniece of Harriet Tubman, told us that "Harriet would be proud of the gathering assembled here today. She would have supported the causes that brought us together."

Saying good-bye, we tightened our hands one upon the other and sang "Swing Low, Sweet Chariot," the song, beloved by Harriet and by each of us, that Harriet's friends sang on March 10, 1913, the evening that she died.

JULY 1984

THEY CAME TO STAY

MAYA ANGELOU

Black women whose ancestors were brought to the United States beginning in 1619 have lived through conditions of cruelties so horrible, so bizarre, the women had to reinvent themselves. They had to find safety and sanctity inside themselves or they would not have been able to tolerate those torturous lives. They had to learn to be self-forgiving quickly, for often their exterior exploits were at odds with their interior beliefs. Still they had to survive as wholly and healthily as possible in an infectious and sick climate.

Lives lived in such caldrons are either obliterated or forged into impenetrable alloys. Thus, early on and consciously, black women as reality became possibilities only to themselves. To others they were mostly seen and described in the abstract, concrete in their labor but surreal in their humanness.

They knew the burden of feminine sensibilities suffocated by masculine responsibilities.

They wrestled with the inescapable horror of bearing pregnancies that could result only in issuing more chattels into the rapacious maw of slavery.

They knew the grief of enforced separations from mates who were not theirs to claim, for the men themselves did not have legal possession of their own bodies.

> And men, whose sole crime was their hue,
> The impress of their Maker's hand,
> And frail and shrinking children too,
> Were gathered in that mournful band.
> —FROM "THE SLAVE AUCTION,"
> FRANCES ELLEN WATKINS HARPER

The larger society, observing the women's outrageous persistence in holding on, staying alive, thought it had no choice save to dissolve the perversity of the black woman's life into a fabulous fiction of multiple personalities. They were seen as acquiescent, submissive Aunt Jemimas who showed grinning faces, plump laps, fat embracing arms, and brown jaws pouched in laughter. They were described as leering buxom wenches with round heels, open thighs, and insatiable sexual appetites. They were accused of being marauding matriarchs of stern demeanor, battering hands, unforgiving faces, and castrating behavior.

These women regard us, understand us, gaze through us into a beyond, alien to our most common view. Each seems to know something we have not known. The sameness of their gaze informs us that they will not be removed, that indeed although they are shaken, bruised, and uprooted, they are determined to remain. Their visages do not entertain hypocrisy. To those who would desire chicanery, the honesty of these women is terrifying.

The heartbreaking tenderness of black women *and* their majestic strength speak of the heroic survival of a people who were stolen into subjugation, denied chastity, and refused innocence.

These women have descended from grandmothers and great-grandmothers who knew the lash firsthand and to whom protection was a phantom known of but seldom experienced. Their faces are captured here for the ages to regard and wonder, but they are whole women. Their hands have brought children through blood to life, nursed the sick, and folded the winding cloths. Their wombs have held the promise of a race that has proved in each challenging century that despite threat and mayhem it has come to stay. Their feet have trod the shifting swampland of insecurity, yet they have tried to step neatly onto the footprints of mothers who went before. They are not apparitions; they are not superwomen. Despite their majestic struggle they are not larger than life. Their humanness is evident in their accessibility. We are able to enter the photographs and enter into the spirit of these women and rejoice in their courage and nearness.

Precious jewels all. Thanks to their persistence, art, sublime laughter, and love we may all yet survive our grotesque history.

August 1989

DOWN THE ZAMBEZI

PAUL THEROUX

In the extravagant African sunset the Zambezi River, like a vessel thick with blood, was deep red, reflecting the crimson sky. "This magnificent stream," David Livingstone exclaimed when he first traveled down its 1,633-mile length in 1855. More tellingly he called it "God's highway," an access route for the Christianity and commerce Livingstone imagined the river would bring to the interior of Africa. But 141 years later I saw a world little changed since Livingstone's day—clusters of mud huts and fishermen in dugout canoes. What could have been clumps of boulders scattered all over the river were pods of hippos, preparing to scramble up the banks for their nighttime grazing. And the small villages of thatched-roof huts glowed by the light of cooking fires and candles.

It was old eternal Africa. "We're off the map here," said Bernie Esterhuyse, and it was true—I never found this bend in the Zambezi, Ngulwana, on any map. Like many other South Africans, Bernie and Adrienne Esterhuyse had migrated north to the Zambezi Valley to start tourist businesses. They had a tent camp for fishermen who come here to battle the tiger fish, which can grow to 34 pounds.

"The Litunga gave us permission to build here," Adrienne said, referring to the king of the Lozi people, the dominant tribe in this corner of Zambia. "Most of this land is his."

We were driving through deep sand, towards the market town of Lukulu, two hours away. Strictly speaking there was no road, just a sandy floodplain stretching for miles along the river, like a beach that had become detached from an ocean.

At a cluster of huts under some deep-green mango trees I saw a group of women pounding corn in a mortar—taking turns with the loglike pestle. Like many other riverside villages, it was orderly and well stocked.

"We know we are lucky," one of the women said, acknowledging that they owed their lives to the river.

After we passed the time of day I wondered whether, in leaner times, anyone ate the rats we had seen skittering across the floodplain. The word for rat is *khoswe* in Chichewa, which I had learned as a Peace Corps volunteer in Malawi. "*Kodi ichi amadya?*" I asked. "Are they edible?"

"We Lozis don't eat them," another woman boasted. She understood me: Because of the wide dispersal of Malawians Chichewa was understood along almost the entire length of the Zambezi. "But the Luvale and Lunda people like them."

The Luvale and Lunda are the far-flung and poorer tribes of this immense area of the upper Zambezi, the Western Province of Zambia, once known as Barotseland, kingdom of the Lozis, who are still loyal to their king, the Litunga.

I could see the king's people out on the great river, men in dugouts, big and small, paddling slowly upriver. All the way to Lukulu we saw people in the distance crossing the sandy floodplain using ox-drawn sleighs, with heavy wooden wishbone-shaped runners plowing the sand. And sometimes—speaking of appropriate technology—a dugout canoe was pulled across the sand by a pair of oxen.

"My mother was from Malawi," said Petrus Ziwa, explaining why he, a Zambian, spoke Chichewa so well. We set off in a four-wheel drive vehicle through the Luena Flats, where the upper Zambezi drops south through Zambia. The floodplain was very hot, but it was beautiful—at this season a broad expanse of sand scattered with clumps of fine golden grass. Our destination was Mongu, a short distance from Lealui, where the Litunga had his royal compound. I wanted to meet this king, who rules a third of the river.

We drove downstream, bumping along the riverbank for hours in the sun, pausing in the middle of the plain at a place called Mbanga, just a small collection of buildings and mango trees. I asked a man, how far to Mongu?

"By foot it is ten hours," he said. "By vehicle I don't know."

Wishbone sleds were passing, one with a load of cassava, another carrying an elderly granny, the last with a sick person, all of them pulled by plodding oxen in the heat.

"This is all the Litunga's land," a herdsman named Vincent Libanga said to me along the way. Vincent said he walked 16 miles to the river to buy bream or dried ndombe, barbel.

Vincent spoke of his king with great respect, yet he had never seen the Litunga. The Litunga kept to himself in his compound at Lealui, a peaceful shady settlement of twittering birds, on the low level plain which is criss-crossed by canals. This royal compound, dating from the 1860s, is near the river, which plays a central role in the Litunga's rule and his rituals, the most elaborate being the annual royal progress, called the Kuomboka, from his summer to his winter quarters. At the end of the rains, when the river is in flood, the royal barge and the attendant canoes are paddled with great ceremony from one palace to the other, Lealui to Limulunga, through the system of canals.

The gateway to the king's palace was surrounded by a tall reed enclosure, like a stockade, with pointed stakes. Out of respect, no one ventured near the Litunga's compound, but his subjects and petitioners dozed under the trees, behind the royal storehouses and the council house. Some people had obviously been there for quite a while and had set up makeshift camps, where they were cooking and tending goats and looking after children.

Virtually the whole of the Western Province, an area the size of New England, once belonged to the Litunga; to his almost two million subjects today, it still does. As a consequence, this province of the Republic of Zambia pays for its monarchist sentiments by being neglected. The central government in Lusaka pays little attention, and the Litunga's roads are poor or nonexistent, the schools are substandard, and many of the hospitals are run by foreign doctors. It looked and felt to me precisely like the rural Africa I had first seen over 30 years ago—independent, self-sufficient, and, of course, underdeveloped.

A helpful young man showed me to a small compound where a tall man emerged from a mud hut with religious mottoes tacked to the wall. He introduced himself. "I am Maxwell Mututwa, the Litunga's prime minister." His title, Ngambela, was translated as "the king's chief counselor," and it was his task to interview me to determine whether I had a worthy motive in visiting the king. The chief counselor was fleshy and heavy, with the easy manner and the soulfulness of a blues singer.

"I am the Litunga's spokesman," the Ngambela said. "He is like a baby. I have to speak for him." He lamented the opportunism of elected politicians and assured me that a monarchy with a chiefly system is the ideal form of government.

"A monarchy is a family, you see," he said. "People love their chiefs more than they do their president. Because it is in their blood—the same blood. We are all related. We are one people." A chief is controlled by the people.

"Give me an example," I said.

"Chiefs have to listen. If a chief makes a mistake, he will be told by the people." He gestured to the door of his hut. "Look, out there in my compound."

I looked out the side door and saw 50 people.

"All of them want to speak to me," he laughed. "They want to see the Litunga, they need help, they need advice. I am their prisoner!"

The Ngambela approved my visit but said that I also had to be presented to the Kuta, which was the council of chiefs.

"If this is going to take time," I said, "I will have to make camp."

"You must ask the Kuta for permission to camp here."

It was late in the afternoon before I was granted an audience with the Kuta. This council was nine elderly men, the sentries of a threadbare monarchy, sitting on old creaking chairs propped on ceremonial straw mats, in an unswept stone building, the council house. I sat some distance away on a low chair and thanked them for their attention.

"What is your mission?"

I explained that I wished to see His Royal Highness, to discuss the Zambezi River.

For a long time, the chiefs debated my request, each chief and minister in turn, speaking at length, while roosters crowed outside. A skittering and squealing above the thin board of the ceiling was almost certainly a family of rats.

I sat, baffled by the progress of the debate, making notes to pass the time. After two hours my petition to camp in the royal village was granted, and so was my request to visit the Litunga in the royal compound. "Maybe tomorrow." It was sadly clear to me from his tone that "tomorrow" was a metaphor for "fairly soon."

But I had permission to stay, and so I pitched my tent near the Ngambela's compound and, after dinner, turned in. Through my mosquito net I could see only candle flames and lamplight. The laughter of children, the muttering of adults, even the barking dogs went silent soon after nine, and then there was darkness that was unrelieved by a small scrap of moon like an orange rind.

The royal drums sounded at 9:30 p.m. and midnight and 4 a.m., sometimes with chanting and the tripping notes of a marimba. At dawn as the sun rose over the 50 or so thatched roofs, there were cockcrows and the lowing of cattle and the children laughing again.

"We cannot find the king," one of the chiefs said to me. "We have looked everywhere."

Still no Litunga two days later. I spent the time bird-watching, writing my notes, and making inquiries. On the third day, seeing that the number of people waiting for an audience with the king had swelled, I made my excuses to the Ngambela and left. My not meeting the king was part of an old tradition. Travelers in Africa arrived at a remote royal compound, asked for an audience and waited for months. "One cannot get away quickly from these chiefs," Livingstone wrote in similar circumstances.

Following the Zambezi bank closely on a parallel road, Petrus and I drove southeast for the only ferry that was operating on the upper Zambezi that month, at Sitoti, south of Senanga.

"Usually we have no trouble with hippos, but one man was killed last month. He was cut in the stomach by a hippo," the ferryman, Ivan Mbandwe, told me, as he steered us across the river, near a pod of watching hippos.

Near the ferry landing, a pinkish buttocky hippo with a cavernous mouth and peglike teeth and tiny ears, blowing sour notes through the grommets of its nostrils, only looked goofy and lovable. But it could turn swift and deadly, a big bossy brute.

"A hippo can hold its breath and stay submerged for seven minutes," Petrus told me.

Not long after, while paddling an open canoe on the river, I saw some hippos ahead and, of course, gave them a wide berth. They snorted, they complained, they disappeared. I waited for seven minutes and then moved on through the smooth water.

Suddenly, very near to my boat, just feet away, I saw a mottled pinkish head emerging through swirling water. I dug my paddle into the water and thrust it, hearing the flap and blow of the hippo fussing astern. I kept going until I was well downstream.

"That was a mock charge," I was told later, by a river guide.

"How do you know?"

"Because he didn't get you."

Petrus and I followed the south bank of the Zambezi out of Zambia and into Namibia, where it flowed muddily past Katima Mulilo and Schuckmannsburg. Soon we were back in Zambia, and Petrus was saying good-bye and "Travel well," in his own language.

The many stamps in my passport—I got one every time I crossed the river—were the proof that the Zambezi is a frontier. The river flows through or forms the border with seven countries. We had traveled from Zambia, across the Caprivi Strip in Namibia, and farther on past Botswana, and back again to Zambia through Zimbabwe.

The Zimbabwean town of Victoria Falls is visibly more prosperous than its sister city, Livingstone, across the bridge in Zambia. But I found an older mellower Africa in Livingstone. Its Maramba market attracts people for miles around—Africans buying clothes and getting haircuts and stocking up on provisions, and tourists from over the border in search of bargains before heading off for whitewater rafting or bungee-jumping on the river.

That night I camped midstream, as near to Victoria Falls as it was possible to be, on Livingstone Island. The explorer stayed on this small mound of rock and palm he called Garden Island in November 1855, and afterward he wrote: "No one can imagine the beauty of the view from anything witnessed in England."

As the boat drew near, a low murmuring grew to a mighty roar, and at last an industrial bellow and an odd grinding sound that was unceasing. It is an ear-shattering engine of collapsing water with a rainbow suspended above it, arching from Zambia to Zimbabwe, and above that rainbow the rising vapor, *musi oa tunya*, the smoke that thunders.

Tourists who come to see the falls stay at sumptuous riverside safari lodges. They sip drinks under the trees and watch wildlife, as I did one sundown. Just across the river from the veranda of our lodge, a crowd of about 30 chacma baboons were doing the same, crouched at the river's edge, sipping and barking companionably.

Some carmine bee-eaters began to gather on a branch near the lodge. They roosted side by side, their number growing—now there were nine of them. People were counting excitedly. Now there were eleven.

"The record is twelve," the resident bird-watcher said.

And then I sneezed, and a cry of disappointment went up.

I left soon after and resumed paddling downriver at Kariba, a relatively new town in Zimbabwe, on Lake Kariba. Until the 1950s, this lake had been a deep gorge, where the Batonga people thrived. But a dam, finished in 1960, turned Kariba Gorge into a lake, with houseboats and ferries bobbing on its surface, and crocodiles—a notoriously dangerous number of them—gliding just beneath.

At dusk at a small sandy island, I drew my canoe out of the water and pitched my tent. In the morning the river level had dropped so much that my canoe was now 30 feet from the water's edge. During the night the dam had decreased its power output—possibly to conserve the water in the lake—and the reduced flow revealed mud banks where there had been water yesterday.

I dragged my boat out and paddled on, intrigued by commotion in the middle of the river—many heads and flapping ears. When the elephants came to a sandbar and clambered out and crossed it, I was able to count 40 of them. They were big and small, swimming from Zambia to Zimbabwe, enormous bulls up ahead and cows behind nudging the babies. The current was swift and the babies needed encouragement.

They were panting from the effort as they swam, taking little notice of me because they had a larger obstacle ahead, a steep muddy bank rising from deep water. It meant they had to climb, to maintain their balance for their exit, crowding near the bank to splash and struggle free of the river.

The Zambezi made the elephants more elephantine—blacker, bigger, the water streaming from their flanks making their hides shine, and their tusks were washed a brilliant white in the river. It was a procession of gleaming black hides and bone-white ivory, and something about their heavy breathing and the way they were winded from this crossing made them seem hardworking and vulnerable.

Not long after, I discovered just how vulnerable elephants can be.

"This is like a tour of carcasses," Mark Evans told me as he drove me in his Land Rover a quarter of a mile from a side channel of the river where a large elephant lay dead, its tusks hacked off. At first light we had heard 36 shots from poachers using what Mark guessed was an AK-47. By the time the rangers showed up, the poachers had killed the elephant, hacked one tusk away, cut off its head, and rolled it over to get at the second tusk. The corpse was covered with vultures, and for the next five days and nights it attracted wild dogs, hyenas and lions, and even crocs from the river which had gotten wind of it.

For over 500 years the elephants here have been dodging bullets. Muslim traders—Swahilis from Zanzibar—were well established here by the end of the 15th century, trading cloth and other goods for ivory. One tusk produced three billiard balls, two tusks a piano. "Every keyboard entailed one elephant killed and at least two slaves to carry the tusks," wrote Timothy Holmes in *Journey to Livingstone.*

"There were once rhinos here," Mark said. "There are now none at all. The world demand is great. The Chinese grind the horn and sell it as medicine. The Omanis use rhino horns for dagger handles."

He then added a sentiment that I heard often on the Zambezi: "Tourism discourages poaching. Rhinos feel safer near the camps and lodges where the poachers don't dare to go."

Lions padded to the river in the evening to drink and digest after feeding on the carcass of the elephant we had seen. I drank the river too. Though I was hesitant at first about drinking the Zambezi, only wetting my lips or sipping it, I eventually developed a taste for it on my long trip. On the hottest days I dipped my cup into the river and guzzled it, without ill effects.

The Zambezi flows for almost 500 miles in Mozambique, though for upwards of 30 years two guerrilla wars, one after the other, closed this hinterland. Millions of people were either killed or displaced, bridges blown up, communications shattered, roads closed, towns and villages depopulated by massacres. The interior of Mozambique was a heart of darkness.

With Alastair Macdonald, a Zimbabwean guide who knew the river well, I paddled down the Shire River from Nsanje in Malawi through the marshes and into the Zambezi. We were able to accomplish this only with the help of two Malawian paddlers, Karsten Nyachikadza and Domingo Mon, who guided in their dugout canoe. "Don't walk far," Domingo said, when he saw me heading into the bush to relieve myself. "There are bombs all over."

He meant land mines. The peace agreement had been signed, but thousands of land mines remain. Every bridge I saw in rural Mozambique had been blown up—some had been replaced with flimsier spans, others not at all. The entire north-south railway network that had crossed the Zambezi was a rusty ruin. I saw the roofless houses, the old scorched and windowless villas, the deserted farmhouses, the tipped-over locomotives. But the waterways were open.

"We go to the Zambezi all the time," Karsten Nyachikadza told me. There weren't many hippos, he said. The people had eaten most of them during the war. The crocs would not bother us. I was touched when he said, "The people are good."

"No problems, then?"

"The wind," he said. "Just the wind."

The wind came up each afternoon—the same prevailing easterly that I had cursed upriver, and this head wind slowed Karsten and Domingo's big dugout and turned my kayak into a clumsy weather vane at times.

"We're going to the Zambezi!" Karsten called out confidently to the people on shore or in dugouts, as he shoveled at the river with his lollipop-shaped paddle.

The people greeting us here were a community of marsh-dwelling Africans, perhaps 2,000 of them, the sprawling Sena nation, whose precarious settlements were not on any map. No road, no school, no church, betrayed the Sena's existence. When they wanted to sell fish or buy nets or cooking pots, they paddled upriver to the markets in Malawi; when they bartered their fish for bags of sugar, they loaded their flotilla of dugouts and rode down to Mozambique.

"We don't need passports, Father," Karsten told me, explaining how the locals pay little attention to borders.

We camped in villages of the Sena people who seem as remote today as they were in the time of Livingstone, the men fishing in the river to the cries of birds, and the women and girls grinding corn. That rhythmic thud of the pestle and mortar is like a heartbeat on the river, the same here as on the upper river.

After five days of heat and mosquitoes on the muddy, slow-moving Shire, I looked up one noon and saw the river turning a corner, entering the Zambezi—clearly the Zambezi, for it was half a mile wide and tumbling down from Tete on its way to the sea, a river of mythic power, endlessly pouring from the heart of Africa.

OCTOBER 1997

SWIFT JUSTICE IN SWAT

WILLIAM O. DOUGLAS

In most civil cases, the law of the Koran is the law of Swat. Should a case arise which cannot be settled by a mullah, or village religious leader, the aggrieved person may petition the Wali for permission to sue. In more serious criminal trials—such as those involving murder, rape, and adultery—the Wali himself sits in judgment.

In a recent murder case the following facts appeared: A married woman disappeared. Her mother grew suspicious and went to the police who found the wife's body in a well. Eventually the husband confessed that he had choked her during a fight.

The Wali, invoking tribal law, ordered the man executed. It is customary in Swat for the nearest relative of the condemned man to do the killing. But the man's children were all quite young, and the Wali thought it would be unwise to wait until they had reached maturity. So he allowed the brother of the wife to be the executioner.

The police tied the defendant hand and foot to a tree. Then the brother-in-law stepped off a dozen paces and, turning, shot the man with his rifle.

"How many lawyers do you have in Swat?" I asked the Wali.

"None," he said.

FROM "WEST FROM THE KHYBER PASS," JULY 1958

THE ANIMALS

YESTERDAY'S LION

SHANA ALEXANDER

In inky darkness, hyenas barked and laughed on the Serengeti Plain. Then the sun seeped over the horizon, turning the morning from lavender to pink to the flame blue of African daylight. Now thousands of moving beasts shimmered at the rim of the sky like a heat mirage—the multitude of wildebeests flowing westward at the end of the rainy season.

In a single sweep of the eye, one could see 5,000 living creatures. At my feet a family of spur fowl—red-masked, huge-footed—scurried across the track. Fat elephant dung, still steaming, lay on a papyrus-edged dam. In distant, pied tree shadow, giraffes fed.

Gazelles abounded. Serengeti has a quarter of a million of the most numerous species, Thomson's gazelle—the beloved little "Tommy" with ever flagging black tail—and many thousands of the larger Grant's gazelle, lilac fawn color with white backside. Kopjes, huge tree-tufted piles of boulders, rose like islands in the sea of grass. The nearest was overrun with rock hyraxes and bright orange-and-blue lizards. A pair of dik-dik antelopes, the size of tomcats, browsed nearby. Two female lions lay belly up on the flat topmost stone. One idly lifted her hind leg, revealing a third and fourth lioness. They were all looking in the same direction, and looking too, I saw him—a big male lion with black-tipped mane and tail, a kingly creature of habit on his morning stroll, cleaving the tawny savanna.

In a meadow of purple wildflowers plump zebras grazed among the wildebeests like glass beads on a black necklace. We came up from the rear on a herd of *Loxodonta africana*, 70 elephant rumps in baggy trousers. With trunks upraised, they moved off, trumpeting, the infant elephants barely visible in the great forest of legs. Two incandescent rainbows of birds—blue, green, orchid—whirred out of a bush to devour insects kicked up by the herds. In a yellow fever tree a vervet monkey was stealing eggs. Eight or nine

132

Fischer's lovebirds—small vivid jade parrots—darted into the tree. Beyond them a pair of large topis stood as if carved in wood, each atop its own termite mound to gain a better, slightly elevated view of the lion-haunted landscape. Rarely do Serengeti lions have topis for breakfast.

At high noon my binoculars strayed to a stout sausage tree. In a light-dappled fork 15 feet above the wildflowers lay a perfectly camouflaged leopard. Minutes passed before the big cat stretched its muscular neck down the trunk, extended a thick foreleg and paw, and slithered away like a great snake into the grass, raising a cloud of white-and-yellow butterflies.

In late afternoon two big, steely gray rainstorms moved in fast from the east. Seventy white-backed vultures and a pair of hideous pink-necked marabou storks roosted in a dead tree or huddled by the putrid puddle beneath. One hunched a scraggly neck down into lousy shoulders and turned his back, as if ashamed to face us with his filthy habits.

The rainstorms merged and produced a double rainbow, one inside the other. Seven lionesses and three young males rested together in the soft rain, beneath an iridescent halo of pearl pink and surrounded horizon-to-horizon by dark blue sky.

My thoughts turned to the cave paintings of Cro-Magnon man and his powerful dream sense of being surrounded by streams of running game. Here in Tanzania's Serengeti National Park the dream still lives. This vast wilderness of semiarid grassland and woodland, lying just south of the Equator, is the greatest natural wildlife spectacle on earth. Yet its preservation has resulted in an unnatural isolation from the rest of the continent. Today the only humans permitted inside the preserve are paying tourists, the Africans who work in and police the park, and a few resident scientists.

Roughly the size of Connecticut, the 5,700-square-mile park is part of the Serengeti-Mara ecosystem. The ecosystem is about twice the size of the park and is defined by the annual wildebeest migration. The triangular migration route extends from Kenya's Masai Mara reserve and the Serengeti woodlands of Tanzania in the north, southward to the Serengeti Plain as far as the spectacular volcanic highlands of the Ngorongoro Conservation Area, then westward to Lake Victoria.

Around the park perimeter to north and east dwell the nomadic Masai herdsmen with their cattle. They and other peoples who live and farm and hunt to the south and west coexist in an ecosystem so in balance that one can arrive on a scrubby, dry plain only weeks after a million animals have passed by in annual migration and find the hard ground absolutely free of droppings.

I was introduced to the Serengeti by Dr. Markus Borner, the Frankfurt Zoological Society's representative in the park. Borner, a compact, ruddy Swiss who wears a khaki flight suit and one gold earring, flew me down from Nairobi, over Kenya's Lake Magadi, covered with a crust of alkali, past Mount Lengai, the Masai's holy volcano. From the air I saw mud villages and the cattle of the Masai but little sign of agriculture and few roads.

It was a memorable flight—Markus prefers altitudes below 350 feet so that he can observe and count the animals in their unimaginable numbers and variety flowing beneath the wings of his Cessna. Animal census is Markus Borner's specialty. Later, as I sipped wine with him and his wife, Dr. Monica Borner, on the porch of their bungalow in the park, conversation turned inevitably to *Serengeti Shall Not Die*, a book by Dr. Bernhard Grzimek of the Frankfurt Zoological Society published in 1959. Activists have been discovering trouble in paradise ever since; many have prophesied the end of the Serengeti world. Markus Borner, as an expert on the park's animal populations, is more optimistic.

"I'm so tired of hearing that!" Borner burst out. "Basically, the Serengeti is thriving. Most animal populations in fact are stable or increasing." The wildebeest herd increased from 250,000 in 1960 to 1.5 million in 1978, and remains stable. Zebras remained stable at 200,000 from 1960 to 1980, probably kept so by the lions and other predators. African buffalo increased steadily through the early 1970s, though in the past decade there has been a marked decrease. Borner suspects the decline is due to meat poaching and a combination of drought and rinderpest. A great rinderpest epizootic decimated the wildebeests and nearly wiped out the Masai cattle in the early 1890s; immunization programs now aim to create a rinderpest-free zone around the Serengeti. Lions take cover in the brush and cannot be accurately counted from the air, but they are rapid, successful breeders, and specialists believe that they too are increasing and may number around 3,000. The giraffe population seems relatively stable.

The elephants, recently returned, are in danger. Thirty years ago the Serengeti had no elephants. Today it has perhaps 2,000, forced out of areas north and south of the park by increasing human activity. Recent poaching has been so severe in the northern Serengeti that the elephants have redistributed themselves, some moving south to mid-Serengeti, others up into the Mara. Elephants have been hunted for their ivory for centuries, and at last the old bull with great tusks is vanishing. Ivory poachers had slaughtered four elephants in the northern Serengeti the week before I arrived. In 1981, wardens found eight elephants slain for their tusks. They discovered 23 in 1982, three in 1983, and 64 in 1984. Authorities say many more were killed but not found. Today all appear spooked, every naturalist I talked to agreed. The elephants seem to know that they are being hunted.

The animal most endangered by poaching is the rhinoceros. In the early 1970s the park contained about 500 black rhinos. Today fewer than 20 survive. The animal is slaughtered for its horn, which is not a true horn but hard-packed hair and other fibrous keratin. In Asia powdered rhino horn is widely believed to possess medicinal value, and it is used as an aphrodisiac in parts of India. But the main market for the horn is North Yemen, where it is made into ornate, highly polished handles for the *jambiyya*, a curved dagger worn as a badge of manhood and class. Rhinos have a 16-month gestation period, a two-year lactation, and only a 30- or 35-year life span. The rhinos are on the brink of extinction, even though new young ones are being seen.

Impalas decreased in the northern Serengeti when fire and elephant damage destroyed much of the woodlands. But elsewhere they have flourished. Topis have also increased. The wild dog population may be on the rise after a recent decline, perhaps due to canine distemper coupled with a rise in the number of hyenas, intense competitors for food, especially during the dry season. "The Serengeti is a very complex ecosystem," says Borner. "We don't want to interfere—but we must hold down the poaching so that we can observe how nature really works."

But in a continent haunted by famine, it is difficult in some cases to view illicit harvesting as criminal. "It would not be correct to call killing an antelope or zebra or wildebeest to feed one's family meat poaching," says Borner. "Certainly it would be wrong to outlaw killing all wild animals for food—with millions of wildebeests, a few thousand animals is no big loss."

Although hunting is prohibited within the park, thousands of animals are killed every year by human beings. Most poachers are Wakuria tribesmen from the northern and western borderlands of the Serengeti. Almost all of those arrested are armed with bows and poison arrows and wire snares. These tribesmen once killed only for their own sustenance. But now a profitable commercial market has developed, and with it a new breed of modern, professional hunter has appeared, sometimes equipped with trucks to carry away his butchered carcasses.

An advance party sets pit traps for migrating wildebeests, and a follow-up gang herds the animals into them. All the poachers need is a hundred-yard-square patch of bush, far from the few roads and invisible from the air, in which to butcher and dry the meat. While the hunters and butchers continue to follow the moving animals, runners, moving in darkness and dodging from one staging post to another, carry the dried meat out of the park.

A further toll is exacted by the trophy poachers, using two-way radios and automatic weapons to slaughter elephants and rhinos, hacking away the prized tusks and horn, leaving the flesh to predators and putrefaction.

In 1978 Tanzania established a national antipoaching unit designed to be on call to all park rangers, but it has been unable to stop the slaughter. Tanzania cannot really afford to maintain its vast park system. In recent years the money budgeted for the Serengeti did not arrive in timely fashion, so that personnel went unpaid and property and equipment fell into disrepair. Although a fourth of the country is contained within parks and reserves that enjoy some sort of protection, and Tanzania spends one and a half times as much of its national budget on conservation as does the United States, the total (two million dollars) is tiny compared to the magnitude of the job to be done, and I heard many pleas for donations of funds and equipment from the outside world. The largest outside contribution currently comes from the Frankfurt Zoological Society—about $450,000 a year. The World Wildlife Fund, African Wildlife Foundation, and New York Zoological Society also have been longtime supporters.

Serengeti's chief warden commands 75 rangers distributed among nine outposts. They maintain continual patrols through the bush and over 150 miles of track. In theory each outpost has a four-wheel-drive vehicle and an airstrip, as well as "some tents, but not enough," arms and ammunition, and a working shortwave radio, thanks to solar-battery chargers donated by Frankfurt. But the park's one small airplane is not always airworthy, and fuel is always in short supply. The vehicles, shuttling continually between posts, have a short life expectancy.

A ranger post had been attacked with automatic weapons only days before I arrived. Military weapons and ammunition are readily available on the black market in this part of the world to anyone who can pay for them.

A ranger earns about $75 a month—sometimes risking his life for a wage that may be weeks late in coming.

The Serengeti's great acacia woodlands began disappearing in the early 1960s, when elephants were driven into the park and destroyed large trees. Subsequent fires also consumed large trees along with seedlings and saplings, creating a grassy plain where a forest had been before. Then wildebeests came through and ate the new grass. This reduced the fire hazard, and the trees began to grow back. Now there are many small borderline trees, but measurement of tree age is imprecise because older acacias are kept short by browsing giraffes.

Like royalty in another epoch, elephants are endearing even when they lay waste the land. If you were Noah, I thought, the first pair of animals you'd push overboard would be the elephants. They eat too much, excrete too much, destroy too much, take up too much space, and are generally hard to manage, especially in confined quarters. But then you would have to imagine a world without elephants.

Clare FitzGibbon, 22, a shy doctoral candidate from Cambridge University, studies gazelles and their predators, including the cheetah. She looks not unlike the cheetah—blond, slender, and finely made. Some cheetah males have territories, while others float, and she was studying the benefits of floating. The population ratio is three female cheetahs to two males. There are about 300 cheetahs on the plains, which constitute some 20 percent of the park.

Researchers such as Clare go into the bush alone and live in their vehicles. She spends a week at a time sitting behind the wheel of her long-wheel-base, 16-year-old Land-Rover hoping to see the cheetah, an animal that mostly sleeps. Clare usually waits two days to catch any action. Sometimes *she* falls asleep and misses it. Then she must watch for another two days. "A lot of waiting," she said, then smiled. For protection Clare is armed—only—with two fire extinguishers. She comes home to Seronera once a week, to bathe, and had recently discovered that a leopard uses her roof to catch hyraxes.

The presence of all these scientists and increasing numbers of tourists inevitably changes the behavior of the animals they are here to see. George Schaller reported that two out of three attempted lion kills do not succeed. Could it be that the presence of so many animal watchers, despite the scientists' best precautions, has something to do with this inefficiency factor?

On our way to Ngorongoro Conservation Area, we continued across the Serengeti, about 5,000 feet above sea level. Beyond Olduvai Gorge, in the far distance, the cloud-wisped Crater Highlands rose to 11,000 feet. In a muddy culvert 22 ragged ears, 11 hyenas, raised their ugly heads. One female, very pregnant, muddy belly hanging, got up and wallowed away from our car. "Probably newborn cubs in the culvert," said my companion, Finn Allan, the son of a former warden of Serengeti National Park. Four more heads popped up, faces spotted and muddy, like hideous teddy bears.

We watched seven young lions feed on a young wildebeest, their early morning kill. One lifted a red-dripping muzzle to stare at us before returning to the meal. Two other cats, already gorged, lay panting in the heat. "They will eat all but the tail and some skin and bones," said Finn. No sound but lion gurgle, and a strong smell. Overhead, a black-and-white Egyptian vulture circled patiently, watching, waiting. Out beyond the lions, jackals waited to scavenge the lions' leavings.

In the distance a lone young wildebeest, running fast, made a mad dash to rejoin the herd that grazed more than two miles away. The wildebeest— actually a species of antelope—is a ridiculous-looking animal with a horned, block-like head, long white beard, and a fondness for stampeding and bucking like crazy. This one would need to find a way to get past several gangs of lions. Dodging, angling wildly like a broken-field runner among the dry scrub, the calf got through the danger zone where seven lions watched from a tussock, then crossed the range of a second lion trio, and, near exhaustion, finally plunged across his goal line back into the herd. But the herd was over a thousand strong. It seemed unlikely he would find his mother. Another predator, another day, would almost certainly eat him.

The wildebeest is the plankton of this sea of grass. Its great annual migration across the Serengeti, insofar as the constant movement of a million and a half grazing animals can be said to have a beginning and an end, commences in the spring in the breeding grounds of the shortgrass region of the southeast. The herd moves west toward Lake Victoria across long-grass savanna, a hundred miles wide, to the woodlands, turns north to the Mara, and finally returns to the shortgrass. The whole journey amounts to a great circle of some 500 miles, with all the predators and scavengers of the plain following alongside.

In late May the rutting season was just beginning. In January or February, during the "long rains," the three-week calving season would occur. Nature has arranged it so that all the animals calve in the morning at approximately the same time and in the safest possible place—there is very little cover around here. Within minutes the newborn calf is able to follow its mother and move with the herd. Each calf imprints at birth on its own mother and must remain attached; otherwise it becomes almost certain meat for the waiting predators.

Several hours later, climbing now toward the Crater Highlands, we saw our first humans since leaving Clare: two stork-legged, elegant Masai herdsmen, red-cloaked, necklaced and earringed in bright-colored beads, each carrying an iron spear as tall as himself. Bells signaled herds of Masai cattle driven by boys. Smiling, shaven-headed women in bright clothes and beads climbed the mountain alongside our car. The smell of crushed herbs underfoot was almost overpowering.

The Masai live in huts of cow dung thickened with straw and plastered onto a framework of branches, clustered in a fenced compound called an *engang*. They move from one place to the next, seeking good grazing. But these wanderings are becoming more compressed as population increases (there are more than 300,000 Masai today as compared to 115,000 in 1958), due mostly to modern medicine for man and beast. Since Masai herds are growing and pastureland is increasingly limited, much overgrazing occurs.

To the Masai, cattle stealing is an ancient and honorable way of life, but not to pursuers, who sometimes set fires to mark their trail. These "hot fires" are more destructive to tree seedlings and saplings than the controlled fires set by park wardens in a careful, checkerboard pattern timed at the start of the dry season. It is windy in the dry season, and hot fires can travel 15 feet a second. Grass fires are valued by the Masai because they burn away the ticks that cause east coast fever and other bovine diseases. "It's a problem between two cultures," observed Markus Borner.

To avoid the trampled and barren areas around waterholes, Masai villages are nowhere near water. The women walk miles to get it—and use very little. Whenever possible they substitute urine. After a brief period of flirtation and fun with the warrior age-set above them, Masai girls endure circumcision, marry, and commence a life of water carrying, wood carrying, and house building. One wonders why the women smile.

Only in a theater operated by a crazed lighting designer or, of course, in a painting by J.M.W. Turner could one ever have seen so outrageously gorgeous a dawn as greeted us the next morning at Ngorongoro Lodge on the crater's rim. We stopped by ranger headquarters to pick up Martin Men'goriki, 42, the gentle, knowledgeable, powerfully made conservation officer who would be our escort.

When the Serengeti and the Ngorongoro Crater were gazetted—officially made part of the national park system—Masai lived throughout the area, and a conflict developed between their demands for grazing lands and the needs of wildlife. In 1957 a parliamentary commission was appointed to study the problem, and in 1959 the Ngorongoro Conservation Area was established as a multiple land-use project.

Martin, himself a Masai, told us that the Masai had "wanted to develop themselves, to live in modern houses, not dung huts." But such houses would, of course, spoil the crater, which is a pestilence-free heaven of animals. Were man to dwell among the animals, Eden would be spoiled. And so in 1974 the Tanzanian legislature decided to give the crater separate protection. The result: Masai out. The crater is a place where the Masai may still water their herds at gushing springs and visit the salt licks. But only wild animals may remain overnight.

At Lobo in the northern part of the park, Finn went off seeking gasoline. He returned with the news, overheard on shortwave radio at the fly-specked ranger post, that fierce fighting had taken place early this morning somewhere to the north. Lobo's park warden, Ernest Kapela, 34, acknowledged that there was frequent gunplay between rangers and poachers. And he confirmed that early this morning his men had shot and killed two poachers.

Rangers with binoculars had been watching an area where four elephants had been found dead the week before and spotted a suspicious-looking party of men. Two rangers accompanied by a pair of Tanzanian policemen went to investigate. Creeping up the hillside, they stumbled upon a large herd of elephants, at least 60, and had to retreat to avoid being trampled.

When the rangers and policemen were able to inch upward again, they saw the poachers—20 or 30 men—watching the ranger post across the valley through binoculars. A gun battle broke out, poachers began shooting and running in all directions, and the four-man reconnaissance detail retreated. They returned, after a rugged two-mile climb through dense forest, and found the two dead Wakuria. The others had escaped. Night was coming, and the four, fearing an ambush, covered one corpse with cloth, the other with branches, and returned to the post.

When warden Kapela arrived at the scene of the battle next day, much evidence had disappeared. Hyenas had eaten the dead poachers. Nevertheless Kapela was in good spirits, certain that his raid had foiled the poachers' original plan to drive the entire elephant herd to an even more remote region near the border, where they were unlikely to be seen, and there slaughter them all.

Some evidence survived—four small tusks stuffed with green grass and bundled in old rags. The tusks, from a female or young bull, weighed not more than eight or ten pounds each. Not fresh, they were probably the fruit of the previous week's kills. In the old days one could still find many big bulls carrying 60 or 70 pounds of ivory in each tusk. "Then it was *worth* it!" a ranger said.

The rangers had captured a well-oiled .404 rifle with a homemade sling of eland hide and a much used, old-model Mannlicher elephant gun. They had also seen and heard automatic weapons fire, possibly from a Soviet AK47 or a Belgian FN.

Left behind at the post were the poachers' remains—their gnawed bones—and their meager and sad belongings: some scraps of bloody cloth, a pound or so of butchered elephant meat, a small skin bag of maize meal, two battered cooking pots, and a worn leather quiver containing four poison arrows for hunting small game.

For the joy and purity and planetwide uniqueness of being in this part of Eden-Africa, the visitor overlooks all discomfort, or all but one: the odd glimpse of how Africans live—in mean, fly-infested rooms with a mattress on the floor as the only furniture for the entire family. Here dwell skinny children with fly-rimmed eyes and mothers who work like the one-eyed, water-wheel-driving donkeys of Egypt, round and round, dawn to dusk.

These are the people described in a study of human population pressure on the Serengeti ecosystem. About four million human beings live in the eastern Lake Victoria basin, with an average of 50 persons living on a square kilometer of land. Thirty years ago, a thinly settled buffer zone protected the ecosystem from the pressure of agricultural activity. But as people have pushed in and multiplied, grazing and cultivation have moved in some places onto the very border of the park.

Africans who share living space with wild animals are not usually sentimental about them. "Why should the rural African look after creatures that could potentially destroy him—eat his domestic animals' forage, drink his water, wreck his crops?" Finn asked.

As conservationist, as poacher, as competitor for space and food, man is part of nature and part of the Serengeti ecosystem. Like the elephant, he would be happier elsewhere, and he is responsible for a certain amount of damage. But is he more an enemy of the rest of nature than is the elephant? Like all the other creatures, the human being faces the problem of survival. In the management of this problem lies the answer to the question of whether the Serengeti as we know it shall or shall not die. And despite all the fears for its future, the park was recognizably itself after 17 years.

But I could not concentrate on facts and statistics, however comforting they might be. I found myself remembering the great black-maned lion, as pure of line as if he were carved on an Assyrian tomb, that I had watched along with the four lionesses on my first day on the plain. In my mind I had seen him again and again and given him a name: Yesterday's Lion.

Will he still be here as tomorrow's lion? Or will he too survive only in memory—like all the other hostages and casualties to the progress of civilization?

FROM "THE SERENGETI: THE GLORY OF LIFE," MAY 1986

DANGEROUS PREY

GEOFFREY C. WARD

It had been three weeks since the tigress killed 18-year-old Rajesh Kumar, but the earth where he had lain after he was dragged into the sugarcane was still stained with blood, and we could still hear the horror in his grandfather's voice.

I was on the outskirts of the village of Govindanagar, near Dudwa National Park in the northern part of the Kheri District of Uttar Pradesh. Listening with me to the man's tale were "Billy" Arjan Singh, a 75-year-old author and tiger expert who has lived in Kheri for almost half a century, and Kishan Chand, a forest official who headed the chronically undermanned local Tiger Watch, meant to monitor the activities of tigers.

It had been early morning, the old man said, and he had sent his grandson into the fields to shoo birds from the freshly planted wheat. When the boy failed to answer repeated calls to breakfast, he set out to look for him. At first he seemed simply to have vanished. Then the old man spotted his sandals and saw scuff marks leading into the tall, thickly planted cane.

He parted the thicket, bent forward, and peered inside. His grandson lay sprawled on his back. Crouching just behind the corpse was the tigress, growling steadily. The grandfather fled, and by the time he returned with several men from his village, the tigress had slipped away into the cane.

Had the tigress been seen since she had killed the boy? "No," a tall Sikh said, "but her big pugmarks and those of her two cubs have been seen several times, scattered through the fields." The whole village was frightened, a grizzled Muslim added. No one dared stir outside his hut after dark.

Everyone was very polite as Kishan Chand explained to the grieving old man how he should go about applying for compensation from the forest department for his loss. He was entitled to 10,000 rupees, or about $400 at the current exchange rate. (Had the boy been a minor, his loss would have brought only 5,000 rupees; a buffalo was worth 3,000, a cow just 800.)

As the conversation continues, a very old woman totters along the path toward us. Too ancient to be thought immodest if she lets herself be looked upon by strangers, she stops to listen.

Then, suddenly, she begins to shout in a strident, cracked voice from behind the corner of her sari: "Government cares nothing for us. It only cares about tigers. They should kill all the tigers before we are all killed."

The men look sheepish. Some smile. She has spoken out of turn, but she has also spoken for many of them.

In the old days when the villages were few and there were still substantial stands of forest, tigers were seen as the night watchmen of the fields, their steady threat a reliable deterrent to the deer and wild boars that now routinely devour the crops.

But now the forest has dwindled to nearly nothing. The ragged patch of trees from which the errant tigress and her cubs had evidently strayed was a mile or so away across the fields, and little larger than a neighborhood park in some American city.

To an outsider it seems small wonder that the villagers of northern Kheri increasingly take the law into their own hands. Nearly 40 of them have been killed by tigers since 1984 [as the number of India's wild tigers has doubled due to preservation efforts]. About the same number of people have been badly mauled. Over the past few years more than 20 tigers have been killed in and around Dudwa: Some were shot, others poisoned; still others had their heads blown off by bombs placed in their kills. After several dead tigers were found floating in canals and lying along railroad tracks, a local politician claimed that Kheri's tigers had, for unknown reasons, begun "committing suicide."

FROM "INDIA'S WILDLIFE DILEMMA," MAY 1992

IN PRAISE OF SQUIRRELS

DIANE ACKERMAN

One misty, rain-soaked April morning, I crank open a garden room window and call the squirrels as usual, warbling to them in a melodic two-note that starts high and slides lower: "Squirr-rels, squirr-rels, squirr-rels." Then I quickly scatter a mix of peanuts, hazelnuts, Brazil nuts, and almonds in a wide arc. The nuts are unroasted, unsalted, and still in their shells, just as squirrels would find nuts in nature.

Knowing this unseasonal bounty will soon be devoured, I sit back and survey the dawn. There's nothing like the fecund beauty of spring in upstate New York. Separate raindrops lie along the twigs of a maple branch—round, brilliant globules—trembling without falling. All the light of the morning seems trapped in their small worlds. You can smell the mixing fragrances of spring, bud-luscious and full of growth. But it's a hard time for animals. Roused from their winter stupors, they find food scarce and little yet in bloom.

Dark scufflings begin deep in the two acres of woods as squirrels leave the warmth of their leaf nests and rush down tree trunks, leap across brush and woodpiles, and run along telephone and electric wires toward the house, using their tails to balance tightrope-walker style. A drumroll across the roof grows louder and then stops. I feel something watching me, look up, and see the Pleader—a large muscular male gray squirrel—on the roof, examining me, the morning, and the sudden appearance of manna. Whiskers twitching, he leans over the edge and fixes me with dark shiny eyes.

"Breakfast?" I ask.

He coils up, raises and lowers his head rapidly, springs off his haunches, leaps eight feet to a slender hickory, is down its trunk in four strides and at the window in two more. It's not that the strewn nuts aren't appealing;

it's just that the Pleader prefers walnuts, and, as he knows by now, I keep those indoors.

Holding a walnut lightly between my thumb and forefinger, I offer it to him and feel the gentlest tug as he lifts it free. Then he swivels around fast, takes a watchful position on a rock, and turns the nut with his paws until he finds the exact spot to drill a hole. This he does with his chisel-shaped front teeth. He carries it like a bowling ball as he runs to a large hickory and scampers up its shaggy trunk to the first branch. From that lookout post he can see a mob of squirrels arriving, grabbing nuts, squabbling over status. He widens the hole in the walnut and attacks the meat, spitting out a plume of husk fragments.

"What a buzz saw," I say, smiling. He continues to watch me with a look of uneasy vigilance. When he finishes half of the nut, he holds the remainder like a bowlful of porridge and carefully lifts out the nutmeat.

Eastern gray squirrels are small mammals belonging to the order Rodentia, a word that derives from the Latin *rodere*, which means "to gnaw," one of their best known (if not best loved) skills. Their ancestors appeared in the fossil record about 35 million years ago, and they have hundreds of cousins around the world (flying squirrels, fox squirrels, red squirrels, Persian squirrels, pine squirrels, tassel-eared squirrels).

Grays usually reach a length of about 18 inches, half of which consists of bushy tail. A full-grown adult weighs between 12 and 26 ounces, and males and females look the same both in size and color. Social rank often depends on weight and age. They live in tangled pockets of leaves, twigs, moss, sticks, and whatever else opportunity provides—Kleenex, Christmas decorations, molted hair. The nest is roughly two feet in diameter, built in a tree hollow, perched on a branch, or wedged in the fork of a tree.

Females bear a litter between February and April, and sometimes another in midsummer. After a pregnancy of 40 to 44 days, mothers nurse three to five newborns for as long as ten weeks. Squirrels may live 15 or 20 years in captivity, but their life span in the wild is often only one year. They fall prey to disease, malnutrition, marauding red-tailed hawks, crows, weasels, owls, foxes, raccoons, dogs, cats, cars, and humans. Many homeowners regard squirrels as pests. In 1994 hunters in New York State reported killing 577,211 squirrels during a six-month hunting season.

All the same, squirrel-watching has become a national pastime and squirrel feeding a parkgoer's treat. Although I enjoy studying animals in the wild, I also relish the natural mysteries and dramas that surround us every day. I can only begin to list the many animals that inhabit the small patch of woods behind my house, from deer, raccoons, skunks, wild turkeys, and garter snakes down to spiders, moths, and swarming insects. I spend happy hours there watching nature bustle about its business. The animals all seem to be running intriguing errands, especially the squirrels, a changing assortment of which I observe throughout the year.

I especially enjoy the Pleader because of the way he finds me in my study or in the living room and gives me a look insistent as a placard. When he gets my attention, he runs to the glassed-in garden room, races up to the window, and stares. He stands up on his back feet, arms held to his chest, stretching to look in, face alert and expectant. Above all, the Pleader is daring—brave enough not to flee when I open the creaky window. Brave enough to take a large walnut from my hand. Brave enough to drive off competitors from his small pile of food. Often when I open the window, he comes up and puts his head inside, watching me as I reach into a half barrel of nuts. If I leave the window and nut barrel open, he will climb right in, help himself, and dart outside to eat. When the window is closed, he puts his eye up to it and peers in. A small irregularity on his left ear is his only marking, but I always know him by his unusual alertness, muscular shoulders, and eager, exploratory verve.

Mind you, this is nothing compared with the legendary chutzpah of squirrels. *Daylight Robbery!*, a British film about gray squirrels, reveals the high jinks of one that figured out how to break into a vending machine. The squirrel enters through the opening at the bottom, climbs up inside, and moments later returns with a Baby Ruth bar, which it calmly unwraps and eats. I've known of people setting obstacle courses for squirrels—the most ingenious one requiring them to climb a pole inside a clear plastic chimney, leap to a windmill, cross a chain studded with spinning disks, run through a canvas tunnel, grapple with a length of slippery rollers, fly across the yard in a red rocket ship, and, finally, leap eight feet to reach a pile of hazelnuts. It took the squirrels just over a month to master.

Myself, I put up a squirrel gymnasium, which includes a Ferris wheel of four corncobs, a tiny picnic table with a chair the squirrel must sit in if it wants to eat from a corncob, a Pandora's box filled with peanuts (the lid is too heavy for birds but perfect for a squirrel to lift to remove nuts one at a time), a seesaw with a corncob at either end, and a trapeze with a corncob in the middle. They figured out all five within half an hour and seem to enjoy the challenge each offers. It gives me a better chance to observe their stretchings, agility, and undersides.

It's hard to choose what I like best about squirrels. No other animal looks so much like eagerness incarnate as a squirrel standing up on its hind legs, sniffing, erecting its ears, hands at its chest, eyes wide and wet. "Did that human just drop something edible?" its whole body seems to say, as it watches me toss apple slivers and sunflower seeds onto the snow. Squirrels will stare right at you, seeming to hold your gaze with their large almond-shaped eyes.

A relaxed squirrel looks like a relaxed spaniel: sprawled out with all four legs splayed, tail on the ground, head lolling between its paws. But there seems little relaxation in the world of the squirrel. Rainstorms soak the fur, crows and raccoons steal the young, food must be found for both now and later. If chased, a squirrel often runs straight at a tree, then does a Fred Astaire move—leaps against the trunk and springs away. When squirrels get frightened, their palms sweat the way human palms do. After a long, aggressive standoff, as a squirrel moves aside, I've seen small paw prints on the flagstones.

My squirrels keep the same hours as hot-air balloonists—they are most active at dawn and sunset. Early in the summer all the squirrels seem to be swept up in mating chases, spinning around tree trunks, waltzing around the yard. In a hormonal frenzy, they'll chase around, across, and over most anything. Two biologist friends were astounded one day to find two squirrels leaping onto *them*, spiraling around their bodies, and leaping away in their distraction.

When the females go into estrus, they exude a fragrant hormone that scents the air. From a squirrel's perspective, the woodlands are drenched in the smell of sex. A male sniffs around the nether parts of a female. She coyly moves a step or two away. He follows and sniffs, she steps away. He sniffs even the grass where she sat. He sniffs her shadow. She bolts. He follows. She slows down. He gains on her. She waits. He grabs her around the middle, as if doing the Heimlich maneuver; she moves her tail to the side, and they mate. But only when she allows him to.

A female chooses her mate from a posse of ardent, fleet-footed suitors—it takes speed, agility, and persistence to win sexual favors. Some females choose males that have already ingratiated themselves and accompanied them while feeding. Or, to put it in human terms, I think they prefer friends. Of course, a gigolo male may cozy up to several females, so that when the mating chases begin, he'll be close at hand and familiar and thus unlikely to be rebuffed. After mating, the male leaves the female to fend for herself, while he chases others elsewhere. Only fertile for one day, the female turns her attention to nesting and collecting food.

Squirrels are excellent greengrocers, first-rate assayers. I often see them judging nuts by weighing one in each paw, testing for the most value but also for freshness. In addition to nuts, squirrels also enjoy fungi, buds, flower shoots, seeds, berries, apples, catkins, caterpillars, and other delicacies. In winter I've seen a squirrel peel the bark off a tree to lap the sweet sap underneath.

Young squirrels learn to recognize different kinds of nuts, full ones from empty ones, fresh ones from weevil-infested ones, by both odor and weight. This shouldn't surprise us. Blind for five weeks, nestlings depend on smell, hearing, and touch.

When they finally emerge from their leaf womb, they develop keen visual skills, but they can still smell their way along tree branches to find mother and food. All the mixing fragrances of the nest include the mother's unique fingerprint of odors and the educational smell of her meals. Returning to the nest with food, the mother partly chews it, and the youngster puts its face up to hers and sniffs what she's eating or actually takes food from her mouth. "Mom likes it, maybe I'll like it," the instinctive motto goes. We do much the same, of course, giving our children cut-up morsels as we dine.

Few things in nature are as marvelous as a squirrel's tail. Or as transformable. The tail is an all-purpose appendage: a balance pole, a scarf on cold days, a semaphore flag. Indeed, the name "squirrel" comes from the Greek for "shadow tail." When marking its neighborhood, a squirrel flicks its tail in an arpeggio of twitches, then moves a few feet up the tree trunk or along the branch and marks again. Sometimes, in strong winds, a squirrel's tail blows forward over its forehead, and it looks like a balding man who has combed his hair all to one side only to find it blown straight up in a breeze. It's amazing how a squirrel can clasp itself on the back with its tail, embrace and comfort itself. When it rains, squirrels fold their tails up over their heads as umbrellas. Tails are cozy as sweaters—squirrels can wrap up in them when cold or lay them aside when warm or wrap them around small offspring.

Squirrels prefer to carry their food up a tree to a low secure branch, arrange themselves with their tails curved in a question mark, and scout the ground below as they dine. When they eat, they hold a nut with both paws together like mittens. Squirrels have four long fingers on each hand, but they don't flex or bend them for eating. Fastidious about fruit skins, they carefully peel grapes and apples with their teeth while eating them. When they chew, their cheeks move a lot and their long whiskers twitch. Whiskers are sensing organs, so squirrels must feel the movement of air, snow, wind, and rain as they eat, which probably adds to the pleasure. On the ground, squirrels face upwind when they eat, so that their fur will be ironed shut by the wind.

Sometimes squirrels hang from their hind feet, stretching long down a tree trunk, their tummies pressed against the bark as they devour a nut held in their front paws. They look perfectly comfortable upside down, as bats do. Tendons in the feet, when stretched, automatically pull the toes closed. That's also how birds sleep securely on branches without falling off.

One blustery morning a dozen grays are breakfasting outside my garden room window. Four more grays, bounding in from a neighbor's yard, pause to make a sudden detour. Masters of circuitousness, sly indirection, the long way round, squirrels don't like to head straight for anything. For safety they may run past and sweep around from the side. And that's just what one husky gray does, running a circle around the others to see if there's room enough to squeeze in behind.

There isn't, so the only alternative is to challenge one of the others by running at it until it leaps straight up, jumping right over the challenger, launched by the trampoline of its fear and aggression. Husky takes a position at the nut feast I've strewn, and the others soon find new positions. They're a little too close together, so they all eat with their tails folded into pompadours high over their heads to make themselves look taller, like big, bad, hoodlum squirrels, and I guess it works.

Soon another intruder arrives, a medium-size gray with a brown chin strap, and it takes a spot close beside a plump female named Collops. With her personal space threatened, she faces her foe and sits still, but rapidly twitches her cheeks and, with them, her whiskers. It's a visual growl. Even though her mouth is busily chewing almonds, she makes small insistent harmonica-like noises. "Too close! Too close! Too close!" they warn. Chinstrap doesn't retreat, and Collops cheek-twitches while bending her tail right up and over her back and head into a warbonnet, while growling a syncopated terror whine that sounds like a swarm of insects. Still Chinstrap won't budge, so there's nothing left but to tussle, and tussle they do—first leaping high to kickbox, then shrieking while nipping at ears and flanks. The other squirrels watch and make elbowroom but continue eating.

In a moment it's all over—the lunging, the chasing, the scolding—and Chinstrap swiftly gives ground. Though there are no serious injuries, it seems to be a technical knockout. Collops picks up a peanut, rips the husk off, and settles down to eat, while keeping a steady eye on Chinstrap, who circles round the crowd and finds a less-than-ideal spot at the edge of the banquet.

A crow calls loudly, other birds join in, and the squirrels dash for the trees. Birds sometimes attack squirrels in the trees, but they don't like to battle sharp teeth and powerful jaws. Raccoons may raid the nests to steal babies, but they don't like to duel with the adults either.

The ground is a land of greater vulnerability, so at the first sign of danger squirrels climb. In the rain forest in Brazil I've seen golden lion tamarins move crabwise around a tree trunk when a hawk flies overhead. Squirrels do the same to keep out of sight when a bird snoops or threatens. The world of the squirrel is more vertical than horizontal, an Escher-like kingdom of pathways and labyrinths, signposted both visually and by smell.

Squirrels share their tree homes with untold numbers of insects, spiders, ticks, and mites. Gray squirrels give sanctuary to the squirrel flea, *Orchopeas howardi*, whose larvae sometimes swarm in the nest linings. Certain beetles visit the nest to feed on the fleas. The beetles appeal to other insects, and so it goes, until the nest becomes its own twitching ecosystem.

No one knows why, but a mother will at times laboriously carry her young to a new nest. Perhaps she is escaping the infestation of bugs. Perhaps she is trying to baffle predators. She carries the babies one by one in her mouth, her jaws gently around their bellies; they wrap their legs around her neck and become a squirming pink collar. Alert to her nestful of squealing young, she doesn't stray far to feed. So I see the same females daily at the feeder. Males, on the other hand, roam over a wider range (up to seven acres), tend to be loners, and may not show up for a week or more.

As deep summer arrives with its baggage of hot humid days, I discover a serious change in the squirrels. They come for nuts and sunflower seeds, as before, but they're much more aggressive, challenging one another, growling, and leaping ninja-like, flailing with claws and teeth. When I feed them now, I'm careful to scatter the seeds over six or eight feet, because they can't seem to resist warfare if another squirrel is within pouncing distance. Most have bite marks on their ears and claw scars on their coats. One squirrel's left ear is split in three—Fork Ear, I call him—and he is the fiercest, driving off the others with much savagery. Another has only half a tail and drags the stump behind him like a pirate with a wooden leg.

And where is the Pleader? I haven't seen him for days, and I fear he may be dead, a victim of battle. Or perhaps he fell from a tree. (This happens from time to time, especially if a squirrel is old or weak.) Are new Young Turks—plump, strong, with few visible scars—demoting and dashing the elders? Has there been a coup, with the Pleader and his kin driven off?

Once I watched, amazed, as an odd war drama unfolded in my backyard. Two armies of squirrels faced each other on the pool deck and then, at a signal I couldn't detect, suddenly charged in a pitched battle. One squirrel fell in the water and struggled to climb out, then shook itself and ran away; others were scratched, bitten, and chased up and out of trees. I've never before or since seen them fight formally like that.

At sundown one August day seven squirrels feed tolerantly outside the windows. Fork Ear clearly rules the territory. A shudder of leaves and bushes catches my eye, and I see a battered, frightened squirrel staring tentatively at the seeds. A large patch of fur is missing from his back and head, where raw skin shows. When I see his earmark my heart sinks and soars at the same time. It is the Pleader! But he's woefully subdued, all the spirit knocked out of him. I open the window, but he doesn't come. Later he returns, when all the others have gone, to feed by himself. It is painful to see him so broken and ill. Even if he builds up his strength on the nuts and seeds, will he dare the yard when others rule?

The next day the Pleader drags in again after most of the other squirrels have fed. I toss nuts out to him, and he eats a few, patiently, slowly, in a kind of trance. The others growl at him, one attacks, and he leaps onto a sapling. Then he returns, eats one nut, and leaves. The wound on his back reveals angry flesh, and his eyes are lusterless, not glossy and alert. The change in personality is startling. For a while there weren't enough nuts in the world to eat or store. He wanted all of them and could drive away any squirrel that bothered him. Now he seems lethargic and frail, with little appetite. Slowly he climbs up the large hickory and lies down on a branch, while the others feed below. A human in that condition we would call depressed.

After a few weeks he begins to heal—a recovery that seems miraculous—and he again chases and harangues the other squirrels. Once more he comes to the window and puts his head in for a walnut, which he takes with a delicate, tentative tug of his teeth or, occasionally, grasps with his paws. He may have been ousted from this territory, but he's fighting his way back in.

In time, though, the Pleader disappears for good, as do other favorites of mine. It's hard not to grow attached to them and mourn when they vanish. Collops continues to feed by hand and bring her new crop of perfectly miniature babies, whose faces she licks even after they're adolescents. Many of the squirrels take dust baths in the summer as a sort of flea powder. I am watching one now soothing itself in the staggering heat of the afternoon by lying with its belly exposed on the cool shaded flagstones.

Soon it will be autumn, the living larder of the year, when nuts are plentiful and the squirrels start thickening up their fur and growing small tufts behind each ear. Then winter, when the squirrels conserve energy by doing less. On harsh days, they may stay curled up in the nest. Venturing forth, they plow channels through the snow, and bury nuts in the drifts, and sometimes wash their faces with falling snowflakes.

When the snow melts, the yard will be coated in unburied nuts, which will make it clumsy underfoot for me and a real fright for the postman, meter reader, and visitors. They've known me to stand vigil over dying sphinx moths and bicycle for nearly a mile at the exact speed of a flock of finches flying overhead. Still, there's no explaining my squirrel mania to the unbesotted. But that's a small price to pay for a front-row seat at one of life's little operas.

NOVEMBER 1995

TEACHING A DOG TO SPEAK

Alexander Graham Bell

I was always much interested in my father's examinations of the mouths of his elocutionary pupils. They differed in an extraordinary degree in size and shape, and yet all these variations seemed to be quite consistent with perfect speech. I then began to wonder whether there was anything in the mouth of a dog to prevent it from speaking, and commenced to make experiments with an intelligent Skye terrier we possessed.

By the application of suitable doses of food material, the dog was soon taught to sit up on his hind legs and growl continuously while I manipulated his mouth, and stop growling when I took my hands away. I took his muzzle in my hands and opened and closed the jaws a number of times in succession. This resulted in the production of the syllables "ma-ma-ma-ma," etc., as in the case of the talking-machine.

The mouth proved to be too small to enable me to manipulate individual parts of the tongue, but upon pushing upward between the bones of the lower jaw, near the throat, I found it possible to completely close the passageway at the back of the mouth, and a succession of pushes of this character resulted in the syllables "ga-ga-ga-ga,"etc.

The simple growl was an approximation of the vowel "ah," and this, followed by a gradual constriction and "rounding" of the labial orifice by the hand, became converted into the diphthong "ow," as in the word "how" (ah-oo), and we soon obtained the final element by itself—an imperfect "oo." The dog's repertoire of sounds finally consisted of the vowels "ah" and "oo," the diphthong "ow," and the syllables "ma" and "ga."

We then proceeded to manufacture words and sentences composed of these elements, and the dog's final linguistic accomplishment consisted in the production of the sentence "Ow-ah-oo-gamama," which, by the exercise of a little imagination, readily passed muster for "How are you, grandmamma" ("Ow-ah-oo-ga-mama")?

The dog took quite a bread-and-butter interest in the experiments and often used to stand up on his hind legs and try to say this sentence by himself, but without manipulation was never able to do anything more than growl.

The fame of the dog soon spread among my father's friends, and people came from far and near to witness the performance. This is the only foundation for the newspaper stories that I had once succeeded in teaching a dog to speak.

FROM "PREHISTORIC TELEPHONE DAYS," MARCH 1922

TARANTULAS

RICHARD CONNIFF

Somewhere up the Amazon, a big pink river dolphin breaches the surface with a pneumatic venting of its blowhole, then glides off humpy and slow through the placid brown water. A flock of parrots brawls homeward overhead. The setting sun lights up the sheaves of tall grass on the riverbanks, into which we have nosed our boat for the night, and squadrons of mosquitoes wing down to join us for a drink.

Our expedition in search of tarantulas is traveling the upper Amazon on a long, thin bathtub-toy of a riverboat, painted ocher and green. An open-sided white cabin runs the length of the boat, and the ceiling is hung with clear plastic bags holding live snakes, lizards, scorpions, and, above all, large, hairy tarantulas. We make our bunks on the benches below. This is Peru, in the sort of terrain where an early adventurer, P. H. "Exploration" Fawcett, thrilled his readers with reports of a monstrous black tarantula that "low-ered itself down at night on the sleeper beneath, and its bite meant death." As it happened, Fawcett later vanished in the jungle. We somehow live to tell the tale.

Tarantulas are by and large timid creatures. Like almost all spiders they are venomous, but they rarely bite people, and the medical literature does not contain a single reliable report of a death from the venom. The fear of tarantulas is so wildly exaggerated that our guide, a highly regarded tarantula expert named Rick West, interrupts any discussion of his favorite subject with a slightly defensive assertion: "Tarantulas are kind of boring," he says.

We humans, on the other hand, are genuinely scary. Besides West, our gang consists of a writer, me, with an interest in animals humans commonly deem loathsome; a herpetologist whom we have learned to locate in the jungle at midnight by his habit of belching like a frog (the frog, he says with unabashed precision, would be *Hyla boans*); and an entomologist who aspires through study and personal Zen to achieve the worldview of an insect (walking one night under the green vault formed by a tangle of feathery ten-foot-high ferns, he exults, "I feel like a flea on a bird's back").

By coincidence, all four of us are large. We are bearded. We are hairy. On appearance alone we are capable of frightening strong men, sensible women, and small children. We can empathize with the spiders we have come here to study. When we visit a remote village seeking tarantulas, the effect, West observes, is about what it would be if a Viking horde were to descend on a North American backyard asking to see the earwigs.

But there is method to our madness: The Amazon rain forest is one of the richest habitats in the world for tarantula species, many of them unknown to science. When we play our flashlight beams up the tree trunks at night, we can spot them camouflaged as lichenous pink star bursts on the mottled bark, poised for some unsuspecting insect or amphibian to come in range. When we tread softly, we can find them waiting at the mouths of burrow holes all over the forest floor.

As a newcomer to the subject, I have a twofold interest in tarantulas. First is a question I contemplate as I lie in my berth with the spiders just overhead: Since tarantulas pose no plausible threat to humans, why does the merest glimpse of these creatures rile up so many primordial terrors? The question has immediacy because I am meanwhile killing a dozen little vampires every time I toss or turn. How is it that the mosquito can give us malaria and yellow fever and seem like a mere nuisance, while tarantulas give us nothing worse than the willies and yet get typecast, in the words of the 1957 film *The Incredible Shrinking Man*, as "every unknown terror in the world, every fear fused into one hideous night black horror?" Considering how well we have succeeded as a species, human beings can be plain dumb about recognizing real enemies in the natural world. It would be a question to sleep on, if anyone were getting much sleep.

Instead, we spend the night out in the rain forest pursuing the second question: What, in fact, is a tarantula, and how do these splendid creatures live in the wild? There are about 800 known tarantula species in the world, and they inhabit every continent except Antarctica. In this hemisphere they range from Argentina to Missouri and from remote rain forests to the deserts of the American Southwest.

The name tarantula comes from a cult in Taranto, Italy, where the bite of a spider served as pretext for Dionysian revels of frenzied dancing. The cult gave us a good dance, the tarantella, rooted in bad biology: Taranto has a kind of black widow spider, whose bite can be highly toxic. But the cult arose around a much larger wolf spider, which looks dangerous though its bite is harmless. In the popular mind, the term tarantula has since come to mean almost any big, hairy spider.

For researchers it now refers not to wolf spiders but to a separate family, the Theraphosidae, mostly big, always hairy, and often with grooves on the carapace arranged like spokes around a dimple at the center. They can be formidable spiders, living more than 20 years and growing to the size of a dinner plate.

If size is part of the tarantula's scary image, it may also be a blessing. Tarantulas are too big to stomp underfoot, the common human response to lesser spiders. I started the research for this story mildly disliking spiders. But watching tarantulas in Peru, and later in the American desert and at home, where I acquired a tarantula as a pet, I began to see that spiders can be lovely: the velveteen fur, the plush cat feet, the high, arched legs moving in delicate coordination, the subtle pink and brown and black colorations, the fingerlike weaving of the spinnerets laying silk.

One day I watched two tarantulas mating, and it had all the ferocity and passion of a tango. Gingerly their front legs touched; then she sidestepped, and he followed. With his pedipalps, the leglike appendages at his front end, he beat a tattoo on the ground, a declaration of interest. He began to caress her, drumming his pedipalps on her carapace. Gradually, face-to-face, they twined their front limbs together like the fingers of two hands in velvet gloves.

They pushed one another up in the reared-back position of both love and war. The male hooked his front legs over her fangs, and with his second set of legs bent her backward. Then he reached under to transfer the sperm from his pedipalps to the epigastric furrow at her midsection. The dance ended with the male scrambling safely out of reach. In moments of postcoital *tristesse*, a female will sometimes kill the male, a handy source of protein for her newly fertilized eggs.

No one looks more closely at tarantulas than Rick West, who keeps 2,000 of them alive in the basement of his home, plus another 3,000 preserved specimens. He has been studying them without pay for most of his 44 years. He is a pure enthusiast, earning his living as an inspector with the Society for the Prevention of Cruelty to Animals in Victoria, British Columbia. He holds no academic degree, but museums and government agencies routinely consult him. Tarantulas are a subject on which informed opinion is quite rare, and sooner or later all roads seem to lead to West.

Except that at the moment, no roads do. West is searching for burrows near the Río Yarapa, ankle deep on a soupy trail through the rain forest. "Pretty wet," he remarks dismally. He is pale and freckled, with close-set blue eyes, a red beard, a mournful manner, and a cracked, comical worldview.

On a high spot he finds a likely hole with a litter of desiccated insect parts nearby and starts to dig. Tarantulas are solitary creatures, and a single featherweight spider has dug this foot-deep burrow using only its mouthparts. West, who weighs 240 pounds, spends ten minutes hacking with his machete into the gluey red earth. He looks up, breathless and glowering. "It's abandoned," he announces. A toucan passes overhead, and the sight fills West with fond longings for civilization. "God," he sobs, "I miss my Froot Loops."

When West says tarantulas are boring, he means in part that they don't use any fancy tricks to get their food. A tarantula cannot leap 25 times its body length to seize its prey, as some spiders do. Nor can it construct elaborate webs or hurl a sticky droplet at the end of a silken thread to lasso a passing insect. Exploration Fawcett to the contrary, tarantulas never lower themselves from the ceiling on strands of silk. "They're sit-and-wait predators," says West. "They don't do much."

Their venomous fangs are located at the front of the carapace, at the ends of two furry, fingerlike mouthparts known as chelicerae. Most spiders bite with a pinching movement, like the grip of human thumb and forefinger. But tarantulas bite straight down, enabling them to take on larger prey. A large ground-dwelling spider can sometimes kill a small rattlesnake or a fer-de-lance, one of the deadliest South American snakes. But crickets, beetles, and other insects are more typical prey.

One rainy night West pointed out a tarantula just inside the mouth of its burrow in the undergrowth, a home that looked as cozy as Mole's House in *The Wind in the Willows*. A giant cockroach, three inches long, entered the tarantula's neatly cleared forecourt, an area West calls the arena, and the spider began almost in slow motion to turn. Tarantulas sometimes stretch out strands of silk like a doormat to amplify any disturbance and announce the arrival of an intruder. Like other spiders they also have extremely fine sensory hairs on their legs. These hairs, called trichobothria, are set in pits with nerve endings on all sides, to locate the source of even the slightest vibration. The tarantula stepped out from its burrow, then lifted two front legs to touch the cockroach gently, almost affectionately.

"It's as if she tastes it, to determine what it is," West whispered.

Then, in a blur, the spider latched its feet onto the roach's far side, flipped it onto its back, and planted fangs in the relatively soft membrane of the underside, near the head. It dragged its victim into the burrow. The roach twitched briefly, then went still. The spider's fangs continued to rise and fall, pumping in venom. We could hear the spider's fangs and serrated teeth begin to click like lobster picks.

Spiders cannot eat solid food. Instead, they pump digestive fluids into their prey. Then they suck up the liquids. Another night we watched a tarantula gradually open a gaping red hole in the belly of a small bat. West nudged the spider, which was perched on the trunk of a palm tree, into a better viewing position. "They're very single-minded about food," West said, when the spider made no attempt to escape. The spider was supporting its own weight and the bat's on a sheer vertical patch of glossy green bark. We got close enough to study its plush footpads with a magnifying loupe. Tarantulas can move nimbly on vertical surfaces because each hair on their feet branches out into hundreds of tiny bristles. "If you were to look at this bark under a scanning electron microscope," said West, "it would appear like giant cracks and craters. So it would be easy for those hairs to find a place to hold on." When an insect annoyed it, the tarantula lifted a leg and shook it like a dog, as if oblivious to the normal laws of gravity.

With the bat clutched underneath, the spider began to rotate. Dewy strands of silk emerged from the spinnerets at its hind end and wrapped around the bat's leathery ears and over its eyes, which had started to ooze.

"As the tissues dissolve, the limbs will come apart," West explained, "and the silk holds it in a neat package." The bat carcass lifted and fell with the slow pumping of the fangs. "At the end of the night the only thing left will be the wings, the bones, and some hair in a big pellet mixed with silk."

The tarantula's abilities as a predator partly account for its gruesome reputation. In Southeast Asia one tarantula species is known as the earth tiger, for the speed with which it lunges from its burrow. Some tree-dwelling species eat young birds in the nest, according to the imaginative reports of early explorers; hence the name bird spider. In Central America tarantulas are called horse spiders because of the mistaken idea that their bite can cause a horse's hoof to fall off.

But the wildest mythology of the tarantula as archfiend is a product of Hollywood science fiction. In the 1955 film *Tarantula*, for instance, a desert town faces a hundred-foot-tall, cattle-eating, house-crushing tarantula. Clint Eastwood plays an Air Force pilot who saves the town from hairy doom by dropping napalm on a spider "more terrifying than any horror known to man."

The sorry truth is that tarantulas are mere animals, vulnerable, like other predators, to the natural order. One afternoon West called us over to see one of the spiders he had collected. She was lying on her back as if dead. Then, with an eerie, trance-like motion, her body began to swell and contract. A tiny split appeared on her flanks, where her eight legs were socketed into the edge of the carapace.

All spiders have an external skeleton, which they must shed as often as four times a year when they are growing. To tear apart its old exterior, the spider forces blood out of its bulbous abdomen and, like Popeye flexing his muscles, pumps it over and over into its extremities and into the area under the carapace.

West pointed to the silken mat she had prepared. "That's to prevent ants and centipedes from attacking her while she's in such a vulnerable position. Normally she would be underground, and the mouth of the burrow would be silked to keep out predators."

The tarantula was almost finished with her molt. Her top and bottom had spread apart like a biscuit rising in the oven. She began to draw out her new limbs, shrugging off the old skin. "See the bend in that new tibia, how soft it is?" said West. "It's just like rubber. There. Everything is loose. She's got her legs out." The spider and her shed skin, on which she now lay, looked like complete duplicates, except that where the old exterior was shabby, she now wore a glossy gray velvet coat.

"It's one of the most energy-consuming things they do," said West, who sat to one side like an intern in a maternity ward, attentive and a little tired, conscious that the patient was doing the real work. "Sometimes if she doesn't get enough nutrients, she won't have the energy to untangle herself, and she'll die, half in, half out, trapped in her own skin."

A tarantula can be an irresistibly rich source of protein. Among their known predators are certain species of storks, owls, lizards, and snakes. But the most impressive are huge *Pepsis* wasps called tarantula hawks. Not long after we returned from Peru, I headed out to Arizona to see what tarantulas are up against.

As in the science fiction film, tarantulas roamed the desert. But they were small and gentle enough that I could cradle them in my palm without risk. Most were males, out wandering at dusk and dawn in a desperate search for a willing mate. Oblivious to the mundane business of eating, they had shriveled away to little more than legs and sex drive. The wasps generally ignored them, preferring to hunt down the more robust female tarantulas in their burrows. The aptly named tarantula hawk is about two inches long, with veiny, rust-colored wings and a metallic blue-black body. Its lanky, articulated legs end in hooked claws, for grappling with the tarantula. The stinger at the end of the female's abdomen can be up to a third of an inch long, and a government entomologist who is a connoisseur of insect stings told me that it is as impressive as it looks. "The *Pepsis* wasp sting," he said, as if savoring the memory, "is kind of . . . profound. It's not like things that make you swear and say bad things about somebody's mother. These things, when you get stung, you might as well lie down and scream. Why not? It takes your attention off the pain."

Patrolling among the saguaro and mesquite, the wasp finds a tarantula burrow and teases the guard silk at the entrance, possibly imitating a male tarantula's opening serenade. If that fails, the wasp will actually enter the burrow to draw out its prey. The first time I saw this happen, the tarantula erupted out of her burrow and reared back in the classic posture of attack: front legs up for the strike, pedipalps elbowed back, fangs flicked out, a blaze of orange hair visible just underneath like a gaping maw. The spider reminded me of some silent-movie sorcerer, body bent back in a malevolent curve, arms arched high overhead as if to sling forth bolts of evil magic.

The wasp's bold strategy is to slip directly under the venomous fangs and plant its stinger in the tarantula's soft tissue. The effect on the tarantula is immediate paralysis. The wasp then drags it off to bury as a macabre nursery for its offspring, laying a single glistening white egg on the victim before covering it. When the egg hatches, the wasp larva will dine on the living tarantula, avoiding the vital organs at first so its immobilized food supply will remain fresh for a month or more.

The path from fear of tarantulas to sympathy and even affection may be a peculiar one, but I'd found in my own family that it was surprisingly profound. My children had dubbed our six-inch Chilean rose hair Queen Mary, and my wife, who is generally dismayed by the creatures with whom I associate on the job, cooed over the tarantula from the start. Queen Mary was, in truth, the perfect pet—she ate only crickets and never bit the mailman. These are traits that have begun to make tarantulas increasingly popular as pets—so much so that officials have had to regulate international trade in Mexican redknee tarantulas, a showy spider, caught in the wild. In 1993 a California man was convicted of smuggling 600 of them, with an estimated street value of $100,000, into the United States.

But Queen Mary's value was far subtler than that. She had warm eyes, yes, but eight of them, in a tufted tubercle at the front of the carapace. I began to think, a little smugly, that the relationship of dog and master staring into each other's eyes was just another narcissistic mammal thing. A tarantula's strange and placid life was a way of seeing into another world. Watching Queen Mary bound us to her as if with a silken knot.

I didn't realize how strong the bond had become until it became necessary for my family to pack the spider in a deli container and ship her to me overnight in the field, for purposes of research. When I phoned home the next night, the first words I heard, in an anxious tone I myself seldom elicit even when I am out in some godforsaken corner of the planet, were: "How's Mary?"

She was fine. But the scary image of tarantulas is everywhere, as if, in the heart of our unnatural cities, we still need the thrill of ancient fears. At the end of our time in Peru, Rick West and the rest of our gang of Vikings had piled into a pickup truck to visit a tarantula collector on a dirt road 30 miles outside Iquitos. At about 28 miles, the truck died in a geyser of steam from the radiator. We hiked the rest of the way in, turning off onto a swampy trail. Clouds began to darken the sky, and distant thunder resonated beneath the sonar pinging of a frog, and the high *tu-who* of a rail. We met a woman short several teeth who was carrying a string of small fish and eating wild grapes. It was another 20 minutes, she said, to Nilo, the collector. We heard the roar of rain nearing, and the winds began to blow up among the trees.

Nilo turned out to be a friendly, enterprising man in his mid-20s. He lived with his wife and three children in a thatched hut, next to a small farm plot. He eked out a living by gathering tarantulas for a dealer back in the city, and he led us out into the downpour to demonstrate his technique. In one hand he balanced a machete by the blade. In the other he carried a stick with a sharpened ice pick at one end.

It took him about ten minutes to excavate the first tarantula burrow, hacking out the clay with angled slices. When the tarantula was finally cornered at the bottom, it made a desperate lunge, and Nilo gigged it through the carapace. He held the tarantula up for display, and it wriggled on the spearpoint, its milky blue blood leaking from the wound. He would sell it in the city for about a dollar, with fifty or a hundred other tarantulas killed in the same way and preserved in alcohol.

Our truck would not start again, and we spent that night in and around it with assorted live tarantulas, which seemed utterly innocuous by now, and a live coral snake in a clear plastic bag, which took some getting used to. All night people woke up from their bad dreams to ask, "*¿Dónde está el naca naca?*" or "Where's the damned coral snake?" We tied the bag to the handle over the passenger door, where the entomologist found the direct eye contact disconcerting, then tucked it into the glove compartment, until someone concluded that the glove compartment probably had not been designed to be snake-tight. Then we heaved it with considerable relief onto the muddy road outside, until it occurred to us that we might now step on it in the course of our nocturnal wanderings.

Three days later, when we finally got to the airport, entrepreneurs were selling souvenirs to other tourists in line. A man named Lucho came up to offer me tarantulas at ten dollars apiece, pinned out in handsome glass boxes. I thought about buying one. It was the perfect image of the tarantula embedded in our genetic memory, the monster whose bite meant certain death. But the preservative had destroyed the natural colors, and the spiders, tarted up like Halloween knickknacks, all looked greasy and dog-eared. I had seen how lovely they could be in real life.

"Thank you, no," I said, and to a stranger in line, I added, "Tarantulas are kind of boring, don't you think?"

SEPTEMBER 1996

OUTWITTING
A THREE-TOED SLOTH

DAVID ATTENBOROUGH

J ack looked up into the tangle.

"Is there something up there, or is it my imagination?" he asked softly.

I could see nothing. Jack pointed. At last I spotted a round gray shape dangling from a liana. It was a sloth.

Few creatures are more improbable than the sloth, which spends its life in a permanent state of slow motion, hanging upside down in tall forest trees. It moves so slowly there was no risk that this one would career off and be lost. I was elected to climb the tree and fetch it down.

The dangling creepers provided an abundance of holds. The sloth saw me coming, and in a slow-motion frenzy began climbing "hand over hand" up its liana. I overhauled it 40 feet above the ground.

About the size of a sheep dog, the sloth hung bottom up and stared at me with an expression of ineffable sadness on its furry face. Slowly it opened its mouth, exposing black enamelless teeth, and did its best to frighten me with it loudest noise—a faint bronchial wheeze.

I stretched out my hand, and the creature made a ponderous pass at me with a hairy foreleg. I drew back and it blinked mildly, as if surprised that it had failed to connect.

Its two attempts at slow-motion defense unsuccessful, the sloth now concentrated on clinging firmly to its perch. Holding on with one hand, I reached over with the other and tried to unhook the animal. As I pried loose the scimitar-sharp claws of one foot and began work on the next, the sloth, very sensibly and with maddening deliberation, replace its loosened foot. Never did I get more than one leg free at a time. I continued for five minutes in this way, not helped by the witty suggestions that Jack and Charles shouted up to me. Plainly, this one-handed struggle could go on forever.

Then I had an idea. Close by me hung a thin, crinkled liana, a vine the Indians call "granny's backbone." I called down to Jack to cut it loose near the ground. Then I pulled up the severed end and held it near the sloth.

The animal was so determined to grasp anything within reach that, as I unfastened each of its legs, it clutched at the loose liana. When all four feet were transferred, I gently lowered away. The sloth, clinging obligingly to the liana, slowly descended into Jack's arms. I clambered down.

There are two kinds of sloths in South America, the two-toed and three-toed. Our captive was the smaller three-toed species. We would have to release it, Jack said mournfully, for its main diet is the leaves of the cecropia tree, plentiful in Guiana but unobtainable in London.

FROM "ANIMAL SAFARI TO BRITISH GUIANA," JUNE 1957

"I THINK SHE'S GOT IT!"

RIGHT IN AMONG THE APES

Jane Goodall

I am often asked, "Do chimpanzees have a language?" They do not, of course, have a language that can be compared with our own, but they do have a tremendous variety of calls, each one induced by a different emotion.

The calls range from the rather low-pitched "hoo" of greeting, and the series of low grunts that is heard when a chimpanzee begins to feed on some desirable food, to the loud, excited calls and screams which occur when two groups meet.

One call, given in defiance of a possible predator, or when a chimpanzee, for some reason, is angry at the approach of another, can be described as a loud "wraaaah." This is a single syllable, several times repeated, and is one of the most savage and spine-chilling sounds of the African forest.

Another characteristic call is a series of hoots, the breath drawn in audibly after each hoot, and ending with three or four roars. This is the cry of a male chimpanzee as he crosses a ridge. It seems to be an announcement to any other chimpanzees that may be in the valley below: "Here I come."

These calls, while they are not a language in our sense of the word, are understood by other chimpanzees and certainly form a means of communication.

In addition, chimpanzees communicate by touch or gesture. A mother touches her young one when she is about to move away, or taps on the trunk when she wants it to come down from a tree. When a chimpanzee is anxious for a share of some delicacy, he begs, holding out his hand palm up, exactly as we do. He may pat the branch beside him if he wants a companion to join him there. When two animals are grooming each other and one feels that it is his turn to be groomed, he often reaches out and gives his companion a poke.

Once, when three males were all grooming one another, I saw a female going round poking at each of them in turn. But she was completely ignored—and so sat down sadly and groomed herself!

There are also many gestures of greeting and friendship. Sometimes when two friends meet after a separation, they fling their arms around each other in a delighted embrace.

Despite this fairly well-developed system of communication, a chimpanzee suddenly confronted with danger gives no alarm call to warn his companions, but simply runs off silently.

This was the way the apes initially reacted to my presence, but after a few months fear gave place to curiosity. Curiosity, in turn, changed to defiance. Then, instead of running away or peering suspiciously at me, some of the chimpanzees would climb into the trees and rock the branches, glaring at me in silence.

Those silent "displays," as modern scientific zoologists call them, were still tinged by fear, and it was many months before the chimpanzees were sufficiently unafraid to react with real aggression. It happened for the first time when I was following a group in thick forest. The chimpanzees had stopped calling when they heard my approach, and I paused to listen, unsure of their whereabouts.

A branch snapped in the undergrowth right beside me, and then I saw a juvenile sitting silently in a tree almost overhead, with two females nearby. I was right in among the apes. I sat down. Then I heard a low "huh" from a tangle of lianas to my right, but I could see nothing. Then came another "huh" behind me, and another in front.

For about 10 minutes these uneasy calls continued. Occasionally I made out a dark shape in the undergrowth, or saw a black hand clutching a liana, or a pair of eyes glaring from beneath black, beetling brows.

The calls grew louder, and all at once a tremendous bedlam broke out—loud, savage yells that raised the hair on the back of my neck. I saw six large males, and they became more and more excited, shaking branches and snapping off twigs. One climbed a small sapling right beside me and, all his hair standing on end, swayed the tree backward and forward until it seemed he must land on top of me. Then, quite suddenly, the display was over and the males began to feed quietly beside the females and youngsters.

FROM "MY LIFE AMONG WILD CHIMPANZEES," AUGUST 1963

LEARNING THE LANGUAGE
DIAN FOSSEY

Its beginning is still vivid in my mind—a misty morning in February as I walk up a slippery elephant tract of mud that serves as the main trail between the nearest Rwanda village and my gorilla observation camp at 10,000 feet on Mount Visoke. Behind me, porters carry a child's playpen, its top boarded over. From the playpen comes a wailing which grows louder and more piteous with each step we take. It sounds distressingly like the cry of a human baby.

The chilling fog swirls a tag game in and out of the great trees; yet the faces of the porters drip sweat after the four hours of hard climbing since leaving the Land-Rover at the base of the mountain. Camp is indeed a welcome sight, and the three Africans who comprise my staff come running out to greet us.

The previous day I had sent them a frantic SOS asking them to convert one of the two rooms of my cabin into a forest. To ruin a room by bringing in trees, vines, and other foliage had seemed to them sheer nonsense, but they were used to my strange requests.

"*Chumba tayari*," they now call, telling me the room is all ready. Then, with many screams and orders in Kinyarwanda, Rwanda's national language, they wedge the playpen through the doors of the cabin and deposit it amid the trees that spout between the floor boards.

Now I pry off the top boards of the playpen and stand back. Two little hands appear from the inside of the box to grip the edges, and slowly the baby pulls himself up. His large brown eyes gaze about the room that is to be his home for the next 68 days. They blink at the sight of familiar mountain vegetation left behind so unwillingly when he was captured almost a month previously.

Then the small black bundle leaps into a pile of nesting material. Hands beat upon the foliage in excitement. But enough of that, there's a tree to climb! Up he goes, hand over hand, until he reaches the ceiling—certainly an unusual way for a tree to end!

Eventually he sits down to peer longingly through the window that faces the slopes of Mount Visoke just a few hundred yards away, and there he finally cries himself to sleep in pathetic body-wracking sobs. Coco, my first infant gorilla charge, is "at home."

In a week's time Coco, a male about 16 months old, was joined by Pucker Puss, a 2-year-old female full of complexes and inhibitions. However, by the time Pucker arrived at camp, Coco was beyond enjoying her company. He was as near death as an animal can be without dying.

Both gorillas had been captured by Rwandese park guards and tribesmen for a zoo in a European city—despite the fact that international conservation authorities have declared the mountain gorilla a rare species, its numbers so limited that survival is a concern. Though I deplored the capture, I volunteered to take care of them until they were shipped away.

Coco had spent 26 days in a wire cage that allowed him no room to stand or sit up. His diet had consisted of alien foods and no liquids, but he had accepted bananas readily and so had managed to survive.

Pucker Puss had refused to eat at all. She was terribly thin and weak, and shared with Coco an intense fear of humans.

The following few weeks were spent in getting acquainted with the young gorillas, giving them medication around the clock, and introducing new foods and formulas. Ever so slowly, they learned to trust me.

Those were trying days, and to make matters worse, the cook quit when I asked him to help out with formula preparation and bottle sterilization. He informed me in Swahili, "I am a cook for Europeans, not animals." The other men were also on the verge of leaving—what with constant demands for fresh foods from the forest and the removal of even fresher dung from the room.

I had to give up my field work temporarily, although in the end my field studies were supplemented and speeded by what I learned from my young charges. This was true especially after they recovered their health sufficiently to be taken out into the surrounding forest.

These excursions provided a unique opportunity for observing feeding habits, grooming, and vocalizations at close range in their natural habitat. It was fascinating to watch the intricate maneuverings of the animals as they searched for worms and beetles in tree trunks or groomed themselves for minute flecks of dead skin.

Then, all too soon, the infants were demanded for their trip to the zoo. Their last excursion into the forest was a maudlin one on my part, but happily the babies did not know they would never see their mountain home again.

Two days after Coco and Pucker left, I resumed my field work. But after more than a two-month absence from my wild gorilla groups, I was uncertain of my reception.

Thus far in my studies I had watched nine groups, each numbering from 5 to 19 members. The average was 13. Of these nine, I had chosen four for close-up observation.

One dominant male, or silverback (so called because the hair across the male gorilla's back turns silver with age), reigns without question within each group. The subordinate males serve as sentries and guards.

The gorillas I contacted on my first day back in the field were headed by Rafiki, a wise old silverback. Armed with some new vocalizations learned from Coco and Pucker, I approached the group, feeling like a stranger. Would I have to win their acceptance all over again?

"*Naoom, naoom, naoom,*" I croaked, first in the deep tones of Coco, then in the higher-pitched voice of Pucker. (This particular sound, I had learned, apparently meant, "Food is served. Come and get it!") The reaction was something to behold. Rafiki came up to me with an expression that seemed to say, "Come on, now. You can't fool me!" They had not forgotten me.

FROM "MAKING FRIENDS WITH MOUNTAIN GORILLAS,"

JANUARY 1970

"SIR, THE TIGER!"

M. D. CHATURVEDI

I had shot a cattle-stealing tiger in the forests of Uttar Pradesh in northern India. Now, determined to put it out of its misery and to end forever its marauding career, I was trailing the wounded beast.

"Sir," said my mahout from his perch above our elephant's ears, "search however much you like, your tiger is just not in this jungle."

The words had scarcely left his lips when the tiger landed on the elephant's forehead, so close that the mahout could have whacked it on the skull with his goad. He did not, however. With an enviable grasp of the obvious he declared:

"Sir, the tiger!"

It was an impossible shot. I had a far better chance of killing my elephant than the tiger. Feeling nevertheless that some sort of action was called for, I raised my rifle and fired into the air.

With a convulsive leap the tiger disembarked and evaporated into the jungle. The next morning we found him by the Sarda Canal, dead. His previous bullet wounds had finally brought him to earth.

In my 30-odd years of living and working with elephants as an officer of the Indian Forest Service, I have more than once had to share my mount with a tiger. But on such occasions I have been almost as afraid of my elephant as of our uninvited guest.

For even the staunchest elephant, with a tiger clawing at its flanks, will bolt. And when a four-ton steam roller like that decamps, a rider may well prefer to jump off and take his chances with a mere cat. To a frightened, fleeing elephant, obstacles mean nothing, and neither does the party on its back. If a thorny overhanging branch happens to delete its passengers—well, so much the better for a speedy getaway.

FROM "THE ELEPHANT AND I," OCTOBER 1957

"GRIZZ"—OF MEN
AND THE GREAT BEAR

Douglas H. Chadwick

I'm out my cabin door early most spring mornings and into Montana's Glacier National Park, moving through first light, spruce, and snow patches. Soon I'm crouched at the edge of a meadow. Coyotes are hunting ground squirrels. Deer and elk are nearby too, glancing over at the coyotes—and at the grizzlies. As the night's frost turns to dew, the great bears graze on the same tender grass and sedge shoots as the hoofed animals.

When a grizzly moves, its silver-tipped fur shimmers and changes color, as if arcs of power were rippling off it. This is the one the Blackfoot Indians called Real Bear—omnivorous, dexterous, highly adaptable, highly intelligent, huge, aggressive, smashingly strong, capable of sprinting at a deerlike 35 miles an hour and living as long as 30 years, and once codominant with man across the western half of North America.

Few encounters with grizzlies are planned. They're sudden—like the time when I was just below the spine of a ridge among fallen rock slabs. Gnarled firs, barely waist tall, gave off the sweet sharp smell of the high country. The bear stepped out from behind a boulder. It had a ring of pale fur circling its chest and muscle-humped shoulders. I shrank back; it caught my movement. I stood exposed. The beast surged toward me and reared up to work over my scent with a head twice the size of mine. And it stripped away every illusion that separated me from nature. Then it left, as grizzlies almost always do.

It's different, hidden here by the spring meadows, watching some rangy boar do a slow rumba, scratching his back on a tree. Or a sow holding her toes, rocking on her backside while her cubs walk on two legs, wrestling and making bear talk. But they can still scare me wild. For two years I followed my fascination with these giants, traveling to their home ground in Alaska and across their shrinking habitat in the lower 48. Does America, I wondered, still have room for the grizzly?

Tens of thousands of the great bears lived south of Canada as late as 1850. Only 600 to 900 remain there now. They have been listed as threatened with extinction since 1975. Standing sheeplike, shoulder to shoulder, the current lower 48 grizzly flock wouldn't cover half an acre. Being grizzlies, however, they roam some 12 million acres in rugged pieces of Montana, Wyoming, Washington, and Idaho. And they still roam our imagination at will; it is part of their natural habitat.

More than a dozen subspecies of the brown bear, *Ursus arctos*, are spread across Eurasia from Spain to Siberia and as far south as India. Two more subspecies make their home in the New World: *Ursus arctos middendorffi*, which takes in only the brown bears of Alaska's Kodiak, Afognak, and Shuyak island cluster, all commonly called Kodiaks; and *U. a. horribilis*, which includes all the other brown bears of North America. As most modern taxonomists see it, grizzlies of the continent's interior and the big brown bears, or brownies, of Alaska's mainland coast are simply different ecotypes within the subspecies *horribilis*; they gradually blend into one another. Many simply call them all grizzlies.

A colossal brown bear might go 1,800 pounds. Most weigh about 1,000. Many grizzlies in the lower 48 reach only 200 to 600 pounds as adults. Much of their diet is vegetarian; animal protein comes from insects, fish, rodents, and carrion. Their reputation as a fearsome predator is overcooked.

The grizzly, in truth, is just a big opportunist. During Indian times these bears ate beached whale carcasses in California and straggling bison in Kansas. When white men herded slow, tame things into its domain, the grizzly ate some of them too. The livestock industry led the way in exterminating lower 48 grizzlies everywhere but in the heart of the mountains by 1900. A two-year-old shot in Arizona's highlands in 1935 was the last grizzly ever taken from the Southwest. Yet in 1964, and again in 1967, a grizzly was found along Mexico's Sierra del Nido range in the state of Chihuahua. Each was killed.

Do any live on? Early in 1983, at a lonesome rancho near Chihuahua's 9,423-foot Nido (Nest) Mountain, I listened to a young vaquero describe the bear he had seen several months earlier. Was it a grizzly? "*Si, el oso plateado*—Yes, the silvery bear."

"On a 1980 survey I too saw a bear here that *might* have been a grizzly," said José Treviño, a biologist for Mexico's federal wildlife agency, as we led packhorses toward the Sierra del Nido's crest. Most likely the large droppings we found in grassy canyons shaded by oak and pine were all from black bears, *Ursus americanus*. But, just possibly, some silvered bear watched us shake our heads and pass on. Rumors of *el oso plateado* also keep trickling out of the high, vast Sierra Madre range to the west.

Colorado's silvertips, with the Rockies at their backs, held out fairly long—until the early 1950s, accounts showed. Grizzlies don't read accounts. Almost three decades later, in 1979, one was killed in the San Juan Mountains. Colorado was the stomping ground of Old Mose, a damn-your-fences, turn-of-the-century outlaw grizz who ended up with a higher price on his head than some human bad guys. He had stomped about 800 head of stock and five of the men who tried to cash him in, or so the legend goes.

Bears, it seems, are what they are and also what we make them out to be. In Heber City, Utah, I found animal trainer Doug Seus romping in the backyard creek with his friend Bart, a ten-year-old, 1,300-pound Kodiak. Years ago, two of Doug's deer keeled over dead of shock when Bart strolled by their pen.

"I train black bears, wolves, and cougars for film work too. My grizzlies and Kodiaks are the hardest to tame, but the easiest to train; generally you only have to teach them something once. They can also be the most affectionate," says Doug, who goes riding on the backs of grizzlies.

In the wild the southernmost proven grizzly range at the moment is within the greater Yellowstone ecosystem. Its 5.5 million acres amount to more than 30 percent of the occupied grizzly habitat left in the lower 48, and at its core lies our oldest national park and best known bear sanctuary—2.2 million acres in extent. In the early 1970s researchers began warning that at the rate grizzlies were dwindling in Yellowstone, they might vanish by the end of the century.

Like millions of other Americans, I saw my first grizzly in Yellowstone. I was a child then. Years later I returned in autumn and was hiking through Firehole Valley when I saw a bulky shape move in the sage about a hundred yards off. Real bear! I still knew almost nothing about them.

The day was clear, chill in the shadows, soft where the sunlight reached. Canada geese and then a line of swans drifted overhead like steam from the geysers. The grizzly lay amid green leaves and yellow grasses, rolling onto its back from time to time, waving its legs lazily in the air. It was beginning to look to me like a bear from a childhood storybook—almost cuddly. Eventually I grew so relaxed that my attention wandered, and I never noticed it get up. It moved behind a clump of brush and started digging. By the time I shifted to a better viewpoint with my binoculars, it had uncovered the carcass of a bison, which it must have cached earlier beneath dirt and twigs, and was ripping off gobbets of flesh.

Now ravens wheeled overhead. The grizzly pulled back and circled the carcass once, enormously alert. I could see an old scar across its blood-wetted muzzle. Abruptly the bear lifted the bison's body and dragged it into the trees. Twice the grizzly somehow broke into a brisk trot with that half-ton prize in its teeth.

As I shouldered my pack, I froze. Another grizzly was crossing the sage, following its nose in the direction the first had gone. Moments later roars stormed over the valley, scattering the ravens. I saw a snarl of bodies through the trees. Walloping blows were exchanged with the speed of a shiver, branches snapped amid more roaring. Then nothing. Silence. I walked light on my toes for two days afterward, still aquiver with amazement and humility, still alive in every fiber.

Not all of Yellowstone is especially good grizzly country. It is merely where grizzlies are allowed to exist. The park itself is a lofty plateau on the Continental Divide, snowbound nearly two-thirds of the year. Lodgepole pine forests offering scant grizzly food take up more than half the land. The mountainous national forest areas surrounding the park actually have a better variety of habitat, but just beyond lies people country. Yellowstone's bears, therefore, have been cut off from other grizzly populations for more than 50 years.

Grizzlies were easy to see in the park in years past, because three out of every four bears had learned to come looking for the handouts humans provided. Until 1941 bleacher seats were set up at garbage dumps for grizzly viewing. But following the 1967 deaths of two Glacier campers from grizzlies used to garbage, Yellowstone began to shut its dumps, hoping to force the bears back to a natural life.

Many grizzlies dispersed to park campgrounds and garbage sources outside the park. More than 180 ended up dead—many, along with scores of black bears, at the hands of park staff. Park biologists insisted the bears were thriving.

One can stand with one foot in Yellowstone Park and the other in the fast-growing town of West Yellowstone, where there were 140 trash Dumpsters and more than a hundred garbage cans available for picking the night I visited. A team of wildlife managers tried to trap grizzlies dining in the town. There were bears in backyards, in Laundromats, and on motel porches. "This is fantastic!" one man told me. "We spent a week in the park and never saw a single bear."

Yellowstone grizzlies don't have names—they have numbers. Some are famous. Grizzly Number 60, whom I met briefly, was one of several Yellowstone grizzlies wearing a radio collar or ear tags for study. A modest-size sow with a rich brown silvered coat, she was captured and relocated several times from various garbage sites outside the park. She returned from afar yet again and was trapped with her twin yearling cubs, filching scraps from the West Yellowstone airport Dumpster. This time she was condemned to death as an incorrigible garbage junkie. Phone calls to the governor from sympathetic humans and a 1,500-signature petition resulted in her sentence being commuted to life imprisonment at a Kansas zoo. One of her cubs died in a fall from a cage slung under a helicopter while being airlifted to the backcountry.

There is a sort of wild-card factor in the meetings between man and bear that throws all calculations and studies to the wind. Number 15, a chocolate-colored boar, grew up around West Yellowstone and nearby Hebgen Lake. Yellowstone authorities kept thorough records on Number 15. By the end of June 1983 he weighed about 435 pounds. He had been losing weight all winter in his den and all spring. He was 12 years old.

Number 15 was anything but aggressive. When he encountered people, it was the bear who turned tail and ran. One evening he ambled into the Forest Service Rainbow Point Campground near West Yellowstone and, before he was captured and destroyed, devoured almost half of a young man from Wisconsin. The people whose garbage had attracted him to a subdivision and a ranch in the same vicinity during the previous 36 hours are still at large.

Before the park shut its dumps, the greater Yellowstone ecosystem probably held around 300 grizzled bears. Now, 18 years later, it holds perhaps 200, and possibly 30 of them are breeding females—grizzlies being difficult to count, these are approximate figures only. Sows are maturing later, giving birth for the first time at age six instead of five, and producing fewer cubs per litter—an average of 1.9 instead of 2.2—at longer intervals than before.

And grizzlies already had one of the lowest reproductive rates of any mammal in North America.

How much longer can Yellowstone's grizzlies survive when in some years their death rate from human causes alone exceeds their birthrate? The Forest Service continues to lease grazing rights in critical grizzly range adjoining the park, though with a condition unprecedented in the history of the West: Move the livestock, not the bears, if a conflict occurs. Grizzly sport hunting ended around the park when the bear was declared threatened, but black bear hunters blast grizzled bears by mistake. Poachers take a toll. A grizzly hide and head can net thousands of dollars. Gallbladders fetch outrageous prices in the Oriental medicine and aphrodisiac market. Front claws, made into jewelry, go for $100 or more.

The not-so-grim news is that as people learn not to tempt bears by leaving garbage around, the bears that are left show signs of becoming self-sufficient. "They're hunting and scavenging more big game, especially elk," says study-team leader Dick Knight. "Some grizzlies also seem to be staying around in park areas closed to hiking and camping." Those reserved areas—refuges within a refuge—now amount to at least one-tenth of Yellowstone National Park.

Perhaps we won't lose the grizzly altogether. Perhaps we'll just change it into something else. Take a remnant population, especially a small, isolated, inbreeding one. Keep blowing away the big, the bold, the conspicuous. And out of the shallow gene pool climbs "a scaled-down version, meek and mild. A grizzly in name only. Maybe that's the only kind our society is willing to live with," speculates lower 48 recovery coordinator Chris Servheen. The end creature may be a U. S. version of the shy, smallish European brown bear, reduced to isolated groups in mountain forests.

In Alaska's St. Elias Mountains big brown bears still live like bears. Here I found glaciers, nearly half the size of Yellowstone National Park, crevassed with blue lights and streaked with mountain scrapings, growling down out of the clouds, and I followed triple-palm-width *horribilis* tracks up onto the ice from the wolf-tracked banks of the Alsek River. Rafting through this northern end of Glacier Bay National Park and Preserve as the earth all around me was being freshly ground into grandeur, I could sense the Ice Age forces that molded the brown bear—and also the polar bear, *Ursus maritimus*, which evolved from the brown bear late in the glacial epoch. The two types are so genetically similar that they have mated and produced fertile hybrids in a zoo.

On Admiralty Island, at the mouth of a salmon-spawning stream edged with salmonberries, I climbed into a tree blind. Night came, and with it a phosphorescent high tide. Seals went glowing by the shore. As the long fish milled upstream, a brownie plunged downstream into them, green fire exploding from its paws, trying to catch underwater skyrockets. Morning brought bald eagles fishing in tides of mist.

In Katmai National Park and Preserve on the Alaska Peninsula as many as three dozen brownies fish a mile-long spawning river between two lakes near Brooks Camp. Around 5,000 people visit Brooks Camp annually, and many try their luck fly-fishing the same stretch of water. Now and then a brownie, having learned to tell when a fisherman has got a strike, will lope over to grab the catch.

On an impulse I plunged into a pool to see how hard it would be to pin a salmon with my own paws. I remembered to look behind me. Not soon enough. A sow and two cubs were between me and the bank, coming closer. The cubs looked skittish. But their mother studiously ignored me, avoiding eye contact as she splashed slowly by ten feet away, a dark island of power in the current. "Though still loners, these bears become more tolerant of each other when they gather to share an abundant food supply," Katmai's resource management specialist, Kathy Jope, told me, "and that tolerance seems to extend to us."

Yet even salmon-feasting brownies can be tempted by our food. And if sooner or later, despite strict precautions, someone does leave out, say, a pack with tasty contents, the usual problem arises. It's no trick for a bear to figure out that a good way to get more such packs is to keep lumbering toward folks until they drop them.

Except sometimes it's a setup. The instant the bear tears into the pack, Katmai rangers pepper its rump with rubber bullets from far enough away that the pellets sting hard without breaking the skin. The rangers may fire a couple of cracker shells—earsplitting shotgun charges that explode in midair—for added effect. Aggressive fish thieves get the same treatment. And human-*horribilis* détente is restored by making use of the same capacity for rapid learning that got the animal into trouble in the first place. Since 1963 Brooks Camp has had to remove only three bears. The sole injury to humans involved a sleeping camper with bacon grease on his britches. He suffered a nip on the rear end.

With that in mind I arrived in Denali (Mount McKinley) National Park and Preserve, which had just been grizzled by the first August snowstorm. A combination of diverse bear forage and sweeping tundra vistas make Denali probably the surest place in the National Park System for visitors to see grizzlies. But Denali's wide-open contours also mean that prudent campers lack tall trees in which to hang their grub. As hiking became more popular, more wild grizzlies were finding snacks at campsites and learning to look for groceries around people.

One grizzly was rummaging through a favorite soapberry patch when it found people camped there and claimed their cuisine. I trotted uphill through the soapberry brush to find ranger-biologist Joe Van Horn awaiting the bear's return. After a food rip-off report these days, rangers may set up a mock camp, complete with tent and packs.

"Then," said Joe, "we try to reeducate the bear by peppering it with plastic or rubber bullets." By tranquilizing the camp raiders and putting radios on them, rangers can follow up and see how well the lesson takes.

The underlying problem is being hit with a novel solution too: a portable food container for backpackers, made of grizzly-proof plastic. (Well, proof so far against all but one 1,400-pounder, tested at a zoo.)

The real grizzly stronghold lies in the northern Continental Divide ecosystem, consisting of Glacier National Park, the Great Bear, Bob Marshall, Scapegoat, and Mission Mountains Wildernesses, and surrounding national forest, private, and Indian tribal lands. Its 5.7 million acres, all in Montana, are home to as many as 600 grizzlies. The lower 48's only sure resident wolves outside the Great Lakes region live here too.

Like other grizzly ranges, this ecosystem is managed by a hodgepodge of bureaucracies with varying goals. And it confronts every species of development from hot pursuit of petroleum to subdivision of bear homes for vacation houses. The mountains reverberate with familiar "Who'll use it—who'll lose it" hollering matches.

Not long ago Montana's legislators decided to let schoolchildren choose the official state animal by ballot. Participation teaches citizenship, all agreed. Guess who won in a landslide? Not too surprising in a state where Grizzly Bars, Grizz Groceries, and the like seem to thrive at every intersection. Nevertheless, a politician who worried that the kids' choice might "inflame more support for the grizzly to the detriment of our economic interests" offered an amendment to switch the honor of being state critter to the elk. Five hundred children descended on the capitol. Grizz, and citizenship, prevailed.

When the wild iris bloomed, I was camping and riding and generally moseying along the Rocky Mountain Front, where the Great Divide meets the Great Plains in a roll of big winds east of the Bob Marshall Wilderness. The first grizz story I heard concerned a full-grown female that was last seen fleeing across a swampy meadow from a gang of charging cows.

Some grizzlies travel as far as 20 miles away from the mountains, out onto the prairie. By radiotracking in 24-hour sessions, state game researcher Keith Aune has found them ambling along, right next to livestock and scattered residences, usually at night. By day they stick to the brush along streams.

In order to put the threat from grizzlies in perspective, consider that the estimated 40,000 to 60,000 brown bears remaining in all North America annually destroy only a few hundred domesticated animals and since 1900 have killed just 14 persons in the lower 48.

In the North Fork of the Flathead River Valley, near British Columbia's border with Glacier Park, Canadian biologist Bruce McLellan and I located the boar he called Jake. Six years old and, at 220 pounds, far short of being your fabled ton of gut-grinding grizzly, little Jake lazed in an emerald tangle of alder on an avalanche slope, probably eating glacier lily bulbs or the succulent stems of cow parsnip. Downhill within easy rifle range, snarling and screeching, a pack of chain saws and bulldozers was busy taking a subalpine forest away to town. Why would any wild grizzly hang around?

I have seen grizzlies that ignored nearby helicopters and those that fled in apparent panic. And once, when a chopper came yowl-whomping over a rise, I saw a large silvertip charge straight for the huge hovering machine. The aircraft lifted up and hurtled on by. The people in it may never even have seen the bear. But it was there in a rage, up on its hind legs, arms out, indomitable, bellowing as if challenging the intruder to return and do battle. It might have won.

Magazine illustrators and taxidermists notwithstanding, brown bears almost never attack by stalking forward on their hind legs. Nor do they curl their lips far back like a snarling mastiff. Or crush victims in bear hugs. No— they come on all fours like a landslide, ears pinned back, lips out, their mouths forming an O-OOAGGH! Few have ever witnessed the reality.

In 1983, 2.2 million people—three times the population of Montana, 11,000 humans per grizzly—passed through Glacier. Two were slightly injured by bears. One of them was ranger Jerry DeSanto, who surprised a sow and cubs at close quarters and started up a tree. Mother bear caught his foot and pulled. He left skin all along the bark, he was hugging the trunk so hard. But now she had him down under her. "Play dead?" Jerry mused. "I suppose that's sound advice. But I just naturally started cussing her and punching her head." The grizzly fled.

"Nowadays, when some guy comes in hollering, `Ranger, you've got to destroy that bear; it came at my Aunt Martha!' we ask a lot of questions and evaluate both the bear's behavior and the people's," former Glacier ranger Terry Penttila told me. "It often turns out that dear Aunt Martha was crawling up behind the bear with her Instamatic camera. We call grizzlies unpredictable. I get the feeling they're studying us, trying to figure out what the heck *we're* going to do next."

Late in autumn I visited a troubled young grizzly in prison—an old concrete cellblock at the Fort Missoula lab of University of Montana biologist Charles Jonkel. This boar had been caught in the North Fork of the Flathead Valley swiping food left out by one of my neighbors. He had been transplanted, then caught again. Now, twice a day, a researcher appeared in front of his cage, goading him to charge. If he did, the boar was sprayed with a noxious substance—red pepper, on the morning I watched. On other days it might be skunk scent, or a concoction sent by Wyoming inventor Frank Child, whose sprays have repelled several grizzlies from a guest lodge and nearby campground in the Absaroka Range backcountry.

"By testing bears' reactions to different repellents here, we can select the most effective ones for future experiments in the field," explained wildlife researcher Marty Smith. "The tests also add up to a strong dose of negative, or aversive, conditioning. The idea is to counteract any positive association that a problem bear has made between humans and food."

After conditioning, this particular bear-school graduate was paroled to the high backcountry of the Mission Range. He was shot in June 1984 while raiding chickens at a cabin in the Swan River Valley.

A month later Doug Dunbar walked toward a resting 650-pound boar in a remote section of Yellowstone, purposely trying to disturb it. Doug belonged to a scientific team that hoped to gain a better picture of how grizzlies respond to people hiking and camping in the backcountry. The team acted as guinea pigs, performing those activities close to radio-collared bears. They discovered that grizzlies typically left and kept moving away for a mile or more after being disturbed. But not always.

"Once we went a lot closer than we meant to," Doug began. "The bear rushed down a hill at us, huffing as he came. We didn't have a gun, but I was carrying a spray can of red pepper. I got him in the face with a stream of it when he was 15 feet away or so. It slowed him down, and he crashed into some branches. He recovered after thrashing around and took me to the ground. Then he gave me a sort of light bite on the stomach. In the meantime I'm yelling and emptying the spray can right in his face. Nose. Eyes. He broke off and ran, shaking and rubbing his head."

Ten days after that a different bear caused Yellowstone Park's fifth fatality from grizzlies since 1872. The victim, Brigitta Fredenhagen, was from Switzerland; she had camped alone in the backcountry.

From the standpoint of improving human safety, further research on grizzlies may prove invaluable. How much more research is the answer to grizzly survival, I wondered. To save a beast that represents an old fierce untouchable majesty, we keep subjecting it to new indignities, tinkering, prodding, and prying.

Such temporizing has already taken its toll. In 1985 at least four female grizzlies were destroyed by people in the Yellowstone ecosystem, where scientists say the population can afford the loss of, at most, one breeding female a year. Are we willing to accept nature as it is, or only as it suits us? We may never find formulas to fit all grizzlies. As I discovered, they are, above all, rugged individuals with different personalities, different knowledge learned over a long lifetime, and a startling range of moods.

When all's said and done, wilderness remains the great bear's truest strength and refuge—a place where it can be itself, a place for giants. For all we understand, the grizzly is nature's way of reminding us to leave room for her to keep working wonders.

Where our last frontiers remain good enough for the grizzly, they will be good enough for all the other wild things that need homes and space and a little respect. And they will be good enough, big enough, wild enough, free enough for us.

FEBRUARY 1986

COUNTING BEAVERS

PETER NEWMAN

If the Hudson's Bay Company prospered by shrewdness and guile, it
was born out of a sort of romance—the passionate union of *Castor
canadensis*, the New World beaver, and European fashion. Before the
popularization of the umbrella, beaver-felt hats provided an elegant way to
keep dry, but there was much more to the fashion than mere practicality. It
was more mania than swank. Men and women in the 18th and early 19th
centuries could instantly be placed within the social structure according to
their hats: The precise technique used in doffing a beaver expressed minute
shadings of deference; meticulous etiquette prevailed about how the headpieces were worn and the sweeping gesture with which they were removed.

So valuable did the beaver headpieces become that they were willed by
fathers to eldest sons. By 1854, when the fashion in beaver hats had already
passed its height, 509,000 pelts had been auctioned off in London alone, and
Hudson's Bay Company accountants calculated that from 1853 to 1877 they
had sold three million skins.

By the winter of 1984-85, Donald McGiverin, the gregarious Scot who has
headed the company in its best and its worst years, was having private as
well as public troubles. His weekend hideaway at Palgrave, Ontario, was
being overrun by beavers. The governor of an empire built on beaver pelts saw
no poetry in this. "The little buggers keep eating away at my only apple tree,"
he complained. He has defended his domain with every available weapon,
including dynamite to bust the dams and steel plates around gnawed trunks.
But the beavers will not leave the governor in peace. Sometimes, late at night
while reading in bed, trying to find solace from the brutal competition of the
marketplace, McGiverin thinks he hears a tree falling.

FROM "CANADA'S FUR-TRADING EMPIRE," AUGUST 1987

INTO THE PAST

DINOSAURS OF THE GOBI

DONOVAN WEBSTER

We are traveling, 28 of us, through a 500,000-square-mile waste-land the size of five Wyomings. We're 12 people fewer than the most famous exploration of the Gobi in modern history: the 1922 to 1930 peregrinations of Roy Chapman Andrews, of the American Museum of Natural History, the first Western scientist to study this part of the world. Yet our expedition's size—and the expense of transporting us to one of the least populated spots on earth—is a well-spent gamble. Our expe-dition co-leaders, Michael Novacek and Mark Norell, also of the American Museum, and their host and colleague, Demberelyn Dashzeveg of the Mongolian Academy of Sciences, know the address of one of the best fossil sites ever found.

Accidentally discovered in July 1993 by Dashzeveg, Novacek, Norell, paleontologist Jim Clark, and several colleagues, the site—called Ukhaa Tolgod—is a basin that extends five miles, ringed by a series of auburn spires. The place is home to the seemingly impossible: eroded cliffs peppered with complete skeletons of 80-million-year-old dinosaurs, mammals, and lizards from the late Cretaceous period.

"The late Cretaceous was when mammals, dinosaurs, and birds were evolving together," Novacek says. "Seeing common ancestors, identifying shared skeletal features of different species at their roots, that's exciting. It helps us trace the origins of modern life."

The first time Ukhaa made news was in 1993, when Norell stumbled across a fossil embryo of the oviraptor group—carnivorous, ostrich-like dinosaurs that walked on their hind legs and had curved claws, beaks, and crests on their skulls. The fossil was still cloaked in bits of shattered eggshell.

The 1993 expedition also extracted the fossil specimen of a mature eight-foot-long *Oviraptor* that had been buried while sitting on a nest full of eggs.

It demonstrates that dinosaurs had parenting behaviors like birds, which care for their young.

Novacek and his colleagues have also discovered hundreds of perfectly preserved skulls and skeletons of lizards and tiny mammals.

"We don't know why all these species chose this one locality," Novacek says. "We think it was a breeding and nesting ground at the edge of a spring or marsh. All we know is that late Cretaceous species lived and bred here in great profusion; then they were buried quickly by sandstorms or collapsing dunes. Sometimes, in the way their skeletons are oriented—forelimbs out and pushing—we see evidence they may have struggled against the sand as they died, like skiers covered by avalanches."

It's sunrise, the morning after a ferocious sandstorm, and we're camped on a wide promontory overlooking a broad dry-wash basin. The 6,800-foot peaks of the Gilvent Uul range stand purple in the morning light.

We're the only human presence visible on this desert expanse, and we resemble a small city. Twenty-two yellow dome tents barnacle the pebbled sand. Canvas safari chairs and stacks of aluminum food lockers encircle a woodstove kitchen.

We heft our rucksacks and spread across the dry wash in groups of two or three as we begin the mile walk toward the twin peaks we call the camel's humps. After 20 minutes we arrive at a natural amphitheater that is far larger than it appeared from our campsite. Its floor is spread with house-size rills that abut tall cliffs of red sandstone.

I follow Luis Chiappe, an Argentine paleornithologist from the museum, up the cliff walls. Eighty feet above the desert floor he moves slowly along a steep pitch, searching the loose sandstone for clues.

"You want to find little fragments of white, little bits of bone," he says. "Then you follow that crumbled bone uphill—and often you will get a fossil specimen."

The amphitheater begins to echo with voices. "Got something here," somebody shouts. "Over here too," someone else yells.

"Here's one," comes a voice from the opposite side. It's Norell. "Looks like *Oviraptor*. Specimen seems to go into the hillside."

In three or four minutes of searching it's obvious a new layer of fossils has been exposed by eroding winds, snows, and rains during the past year—and it holds dozens, if not hundreds, of new fossil finds.

On the cliffside Chiappe and I move forward, a measured step at a time. Chiappe points toward the ground. "Here's a piece of bone," he says. "It probably slid down the hill."

He looks up the slope, takes an uphill step—and there it is. Like a crumbly white shelf, the pale line of a fossil skeleton sticks out from the eroded hillside.

Chiappe unzips his rucksack and extracts a soft-bristled brush and a vial of glue with an eyedropper top. He brushes the fossil, then drops little beads of glue across the bone. "We do this so the specimen won't disintegrate," he says. Producing a steel dental tool, he begins to pick away the sandstone.

Fifteen minutes later Chiappe has exposed the forelimbs and spinal column of an immature, six-foot-long *Oviraptor*. "It's a well-articulated specimen," Chiappe says, smiling. "That means its bones and joints are still arranged as they were in life, and they appear to be complete."

Chiappe marks the fossil's location with a strip of toilet paper and moves on. We spot another exposed fossil a few yards ahead—and another and another. We mark each location before descending to the desert floor.

All around us I hear shouts of other discoveries. Within an hour we've found 30 fossils, including whole skeletons of ten *Oviraptor* and a number of rabbit-size mammals.

Novacek hums a snatch of the song "Isn't It Romantic?" then breaks into another grin. He turns in a circle, taking in the dry wash and the loop of red stone walls, which are now festooned with white strips of toilet paper.

"Something terrible happened to these poor animals," Novacek says. "Which is very good for us. We thrive on carnage."

A hundred years ago, no one considered Mongolia the center of the fossil world. Back then the skeletons being unearthed in the arid American West were what held paleontologists' thrall. That changed, however, in 1922, the year Roy Chapman Andrews and his fleet of Dodge motorcars rolled into the Gobi.

A prototype for Indiana Jones who dressed in jodhpurs and a felt hat, Andrews hadn't gone to Asia for dinosaurs. Instead he hoped to find the fossil origins of humans, a goal he never achieved. His findings, which he chronicled in the remarkable book *The New Conquest of Central Asia* and in the June 1933 issue of NATIONAL GEOGRAPHIC, included discovery of the first *Oviraptor* (Latin for "egg stealer," because it was discovered on top of a nest of eggs) and the first complete skull of a hog-size species with an elaborate head shield and parrot beak named *Protoceratops andrewsi*. The Gobi fossil beds are still the only places where skulls of mammals of the late Cretaceous period are commonly found.

Frustrated by Communist political pressures, Andrews ended his Gobi explorations in 1930. In the next six decades paleontologists from the Soviet Union and Poland pushed deeper into the Gobi, regularly coming out with astonishing results.

Most notable, and now on display at the Mongolian Museum of Natural History in Ulaanbaatar, is a find known as the fighting dinosaurs. Excavated in 1971 by a joint Polish-Mongolian expedition about 80 miles north of Ukhaa, the specimen is two complete skeletons of *Velociraptor* and *Protoceratops* locked in mortal combat. The six-foot-long *Velociraptor*, a smaller version of the two-legged pack hunters from the movie *Jurassic Park*, is bearing down on the hog-size *Protoceratops*. The *Velociraptor* is using its short forelimbs to grasp the *Protoceratops*'s goring snout, while beneath the proto's belly the hooked talons of the raptor's hind claws prepare to slash its opponent open.

More than 70 million years after death, the combatants' frantic energy seems to kick dust in the air.

It's five days after our original search at Ukhaa, and teams have broken up to begin preparing specimens for excavation. Norell and I stroll in a rocky, sun-blasted basin nicknamed Xanadu. It's where Norell—a 37-year-old whose dark sunglasses, rock-star haircut, and full beard suggest an outlaw biker more than the American Museum's associate curator of paleontology—found the *Oviraptor* embryo in 1993. The next year he spotted a circular nest near the spot where he'd found the embryo, but time prevented him from removing the nest.

Now, after ten months of back-burner worry in his cluttered museum lab, he's hoping to see how the snows and winds of the long Mongolian winter have treated it.

As we prospect for fossil eggs, Norell explains the cladistic system of biological taxonomy. Also called phylogenetic systematics, cladistics defines links between living and extinct species by comparing shared physical features that represent evolutionary advances.

German entomologist Willi Hennig, who developed this methodology 40 years ago, exhaustively collated lists of hundreds of anatomical features—such as joint architecture—to create family trees of living and extinct animals. During the past two decades dinosaurs have been added to these trees, linking, for example, the thin-walled bones, hip-joint sockets, and arm, shoulder, and skull features shared by some dinosaurs and modern birds.

"We're using fossil evidence to link different species," Norell says. "But that doesn't mean we understand evolution. When a new fossil comes along and upsets our theories, well, we adapt. That's how we learn."

Norell points to a flattened portion of the hillside. "There's where I found the embryo," he says, his head turning to scan for the nest. "So the specimen should be right about . . . there it is."

Partly covered by a dried, leggy weed, a perfect ring of nine dark orbs rises slightly from the ground. Most of the eggs seem to have been broken open by weathering and are filled with red sand, but some are still buried, making it hard to know whether they're intact and might contain embryos, something that won't be seen until the specimen is returned to New York and stripped of its rock casing. Norell drops to his belly, his face only inches above the nest. "This is great," he says as he starts to scrape the soil. "Oh yeah. Look at this, look at this!"

He pauses for a moment and sits up.

"It's a dromaeosaur nest," he says, invoking the dinosaur group that includes *Velociraptor.* "We've got some infant specimens here too. Look." Norell lifts a tiny twig of fossil bone. "That's the proximal end of a femur, a leg bone." He lifts a half-inch-long, v-shaped piece. "Here's the tip of a jaw."

Because he's conversant in skeletal comparisons—layered on a lifetime of studying fossil and contemporary skeletons—Norell can identify what animal the fossils came from, even by the scant evidence these bones provide.

"How do I know it's a dromaeosaur?" he asks, repeating my question. "These little grooved indentations are sites where muscles attached to the bone. These occur in the same place in all dromaeosaurs."

Because some dinosaur evolutionary trees are more fleshed out than others, the museum's team has let some of the more well-known specimens—such as *Protoceratops* and the four-legged, armor-bodied *Ankylosaurus*—go unexamined. Instead the team has collected specimens of Cretaceous mammals, lizards, and theropods. Theropods are a diverse group of dinosaurs that all stem from a three-toed, meat-eating, upright ancestor. They encompass everything from the gigantic *Tyrannosaurus rex* to today's tiniest hummingbirds.

"It's not that we won't pull a perfect proto if we find one and have room on the truck," Norell says, scrunching over the nest, "but we're collecting mammals and theropods first. I'm mostly concerned with theropods, since there's good evidence that they evolved into birds. They have the same wrists as modern birds, many of the same skull structures, and the same eye placement as modern birds."

He scrapes and brushes, scrapes and brushes. Gusts of wind throw sand and dust into his face and hair, but he doesn't seem to notice. He begins to apply the glue.

Finally he sits back up, a huge smile crossing his face. He takes a strip of orange surveyor's tape and marks the spot by knotting the tape to the nearby weed. He reaches into his bag and removes a Rambo-style knife, which he uses to trench around the nest. When a shallow gutter is cut, he gently spreads his fingers across the nest's surface. "We've just transcended the world of dinosaur bones and entered the world of behavior," he says.

He explains: "There's a nice, round configuration to the eggs. This gives clues to nesting behavior. The eggs didn't get this way by accident—the parent arranged them. If we find other nests with this configuration, well, we can begin to believe egg arrangement is a behavior."

"Some things about dinosaurs we'll never know," he says. "Like what color were they? What sounds did they make? So at times like these, when we find evidence that might show how they lived, we're ecstatic."

Norell reaches out, caressing the nest like an ancient masterpiece. He chuckles. "You'll be reading about this for years."

Time at Ukhaa has slowly melted together. Days are blistering hot, and with each new morning the rhythms of modern life are cooked from our memories, further blanketed by an all-consuming fascination with things Cretaceous. Within weeks wristwatch-based timekeeping has been erased. In its place is a daily succession of gritty work stratified by zones of rising heat.

We wake around seven, with the sky purple and the high-desert air at 40°F. By 3 p.m., after eating lunches of canned tuna and saltines, washed down with sun-hot canteen water, the temperature often exceeds 100°. Still, the afternoon's 110° peak generally doesn't arrive until after five—and it's often accompanied by a 40- to 50-mile-an-hour wind.

The gale results from solar energy on the desert floor, which heats the air and makes it rise. The slightly cooler air off the Gilvent Uul rolls downhill and takes its place—making working, cooking, or doing just about anything fall secondary to merely surviving two hours of flying, searing sand.

It's these afternoon winds that generally cue expedition members to leave Ukhaa's roasting pan for camp. Usually by seven or eight most people have returned to their tents to write field notes and take a quick nap followed by a ten o'clock dinner. Around the campfire we often make a guessing game of time:

"How long have we been at Ukhaa?" I ask.

"Eight days?" someone ventures.

I check my notebook. "Sixteen days," I say.

"When do you think the last dinosaurs walked this place?" I ask.

Mark Norell pipes in. "Dinosaurs are still here—only now they're called birds."

It's strangely comforting, this paleontologist's long view. There seems nothing but days upon days upon days, and in the desert sameness it feels as if we've been here for all of them. Events of last week and millions of years ago merge into an infinite river called time. Yet inside this withering heat, numbing sameness, and sunburned science, the expedition has also been marked by milestones.

On day 8, for instance, after the whole team spent two exhausting days chipping dense stone from a mystery fossil discovered on day 1, it's determined the specimen was already eroded away—only a scrap of tail remains. Because hopes were so high, our entire camp is pitched into a depression. Novacek and Norell—who've been putting in 14-hour days with pickaxes, hammers, and chisels—both silently walk off.

"We've had so many great finds here," Novacek finally says, "that we talked ourselves into believing this one was a given."

Five days later Amy Davidson, one of the fossil preparators for the museum, takes me out to Xanadu to show how fossils are transported home. Walking up a jeep path in a rare drizzling rain, she spots the orange tape that marks the find.

"It's a lizard," she says, removing the surface sand with a brush. "This won't take too long."

After clearing the specimen, she begins trenching around the fossil's red rock.

At the museum the 39-year-old Davidson is the person who takes the rocks we've been collecting and painstakingly reveals the skeletons inside. A professional sculptor before becoming a preparator, she enjoys working with fossils more than creating art.

"Sculpture was too hard emotionally," she says. "Now I get to work the same way—but I know this stone already has a sculpture inside it. It's very satisfying, without all the uncertainty."

In another minute Davidson carefully undercuts the five-inch fossil until it stands like a balanced rock on a small stone pillar. Then she covers the top of the stone with wet toilet paper and gauze soaked in plaster of paris. "This is jacketing," she says. "We want a tight, hard-plaster skin over the specimen to keep it from damage on the trip home."

Soon Davidson snaps the rock from its pedestal and quickly jackets its underside. Once the bottom dries, she cradles the 80-million-year-old lizard into the safety of her rucksack.

Davidson says that she tries to personally jacket as many fossils as she can so she knows what to expect in the museum. "I love working on specimens in the lab," she says. "Sometimes as I remove a jacket, I'll be surrounded by tools and lights and steel, and I get these little puffs of desert smell. That makes me smile. Eighty million years after these things died, they've traveled halfway around the world and landed on my clean little lab table. I become the first person to see them."

When the sandstorm hit, the *Oviraptor* leaned into the hillside to cover a clutch of eggs. Now, some 80 million years later, it is still there, 15 stories up a cliff wall.

The days have slipped by. And now, with only a short time left at Ukhaa, Norell, Novacek, Andy Taylor, the team's mechanic, and I are preparing the largest fossil we'll take this summer: a mature *Oviraptor*, perhaps 12 feet long. Leaning precariously with the pitch of the wall, we've worked on the specimen into the night until it sits on its stone pedestal.

This morning we begin the slow process of undercutting an area roughly the size of a pool table. We work slowly, with steel files and pronged tools. Then: success. "Got an egg here," Norell says, after hours of lying on the sand, gently scraping the specimen's underside.

We all stand to examine the egg. A pale oval encased by stone, it lies eight inches beneath the rock's surface. It's official. We've got the fourth nesting *Oviraptor* the world has ever seen.

Another one—unearthed almost directly across from us on a neighboring butte—is currently on display at the American Museum of Natural History in New York.

I saw it a month before we left for Mongolia, and except that time and death had flattened the scene, the nest looked like that of an oversize bird. The dinosaur was squatting low, over a circle of roughly 20 eggs, as if it had been either warming the eggs or shading them from the sun.

Now Novacek uses his index finger to follow the vertebrae of this new specimen, noting how the long-necked head curves back on the body, like a nesting bird. Locking his hands and lifting his elbows to the height of his shoulders, Novacek squats low, showing Andy Taylor and me how the *Oviraptor* shielded its eggs from the blowing sand.

He relaxes and gently picks at the stone near the specimen's edge. As bits of sandstone flip away, Novacek doesn't seem surprised as he uncovers the hooked, four-inch claw of the *Oviraptor*'s forelimb, which glows white against red rock.

Standing on the cliffside, Novacek compares this specimen to the one back in the museum. "Look at that," he says. "They both have the same nesting posture. I don't know what it means, but it's intriguing."

Then, like a kid with a toy, he kneels close to the specimen and starts counting visible eggs. The tally rises to 15.

As Novacek and Norell begin jacketing the fossil, Taylor and I move along the wall of the canyon in search of another specimen.

Just ahead we find it: another long strip of exposed bone, bits crumbling down the hillside in a white trail. We begin to dig. And, slowly, yet another *Oviraptor* begins to materialize. First we find its hip bones, then we unearth a forelimb claw.

"Hey, Mark, check this out!" shouts Taylor.

"I think you may have found another nester," Norell exclaims when he sees our dinosaur.

Taylor and I slap high fives. Then everyone realizes we won't be able to excavate our specimen. There's just not enough time.

We dig for another few hours before Novacek comes over. "Great find," he says. "Looks like there might be a mass-death assemblage at this level. It's amazing." Novacek stares into Ukhaa's depths. "We'll come back for this one next year," he says.

He instructs us to cover our specimen with bubble wrap and plastic, topping it with a camouflage layer of Ukhaa's red stone so no one else will find it.

Still feeling the flush of our first discovery, Taylor and I are crushed.

Wait until next year? But, hey, hold on! Might there be more nesting specimens here? Might this level hold a whole rookery? What would that say about this place? About dinosaur behavior?

Novacek, however, is adamant: The expedition has to be back in Ulaanbaatar in ten days, and we have a scouting trip deeper into the Gobi yet to go, plus a punishing, three-day drive out.

So, reluctantly, Taylor and I do as Novacek asks, regularly glancing toward the white jacket that now encases the other nesting *Oviraptor*. Tomorrow it will require the whole team and a complex rope-and-pulley system to trundle that 600-pound monster down 150 feet of cliff and onto a waiting truck.

But for now, at sunset, all I can think about is what I'm leaving behind.

JULY 1996

THE GRAVE
BENEATH ST. PETER'S

JAMES FALLOWS

T he historical explanation for the Vatican's importance in Roman Catholicism lies deep beneath St. Peter's Basilica, where it remained hidden for more than 1,500 years. I had a chance to see what lies beneath the basilica in the company of the Reverend Daniel Pater, an irrepressible 32-year-old priest from Ohio. Shining his large spelunker's flashlight, he led the way, explaining that the "new" St. Peter's (consecrated in 1626) is the second basilica to stand on this site on Vatican hill. The first was built in the early fourth century A.D. by Emperor Constantine.

"The question is, why did he build it here?" Father Pater said. At the time, the quarter of Rome called Trastevere, which included the area where the Vatican now stands, was a sparsely settled outskirt. Alongside a road thought to be the Via Cornelia was a Roman necropolis of aboveground burial houses and a Roman circus at least a thousand feet long, somewhat smaller than the famous Circus Maximus.

"With the circus, there was a reasonably flat building area," Father Pater said. "But that's not where Constantine put his basilica." He rummaged in his knapsack for a schematic drawing and spread it in front of me. "Instead, he built it into the slope of the hill. You have to ask yourself, why there? They had to move a million cubic feet of dirt to get a level building surface.

"Not to keep you in suspense," continued Father Pater—only to pause interminably as he refolded his drawing—"the answer seems to be that there was something in this particular place that dictated the location of the basilica. That something seems to have been Saint Peter's grave."

According to Catholic tradition, it was in the nearby circus that Simon Peter was crucified upside down around A.D. 65 during a wave of brutal anti-Christian persecution under Emperor Nero, after the burning of Rome. Peter's body was taken by Christians to the nearby burial ground, and later, among the sarcophagi and elegant redbrick mausoleums, it was secretly venerated.

"That's what we will see," Father Pater said. "The foundation of the church."

For the faithful there had always been sufficient evidence that Peter's grave did in fact lie beneath the altar of the basilica, since before the time of Constantine this had been the Roman Church's belief. But archaeological evidence for this proposition did not begin to emerge until the middle of this century. The crucial step was taken in 1939, soon after the death of Pope Pius XI.

The old Pope had expressed a desire to be buried as close as possible to the tomb of Pope Pius X. The new Pope, the austere Roman aristocrat Eugenio Pacelli, Pius XII, approved a plan of renovation in the grottoes beneath the basilica, where many previous popes had been interred, to make room for Pius XI's tomb and create another chapel. But almost as soon as the workers began digging, they broke through to ancient, concealed layers. Eventually Pius XII ordered a thorough excavation of the area underneath the altar, so as to determine with full scientific rigor whether there was any evidence of Peter's grave.

For the next ten years, through warfare, occupation, and liberation—and always in secrecy—the painstaking work went on.

As Father Pater led the way into the excavations, we moved simultaneously downward into the earth and back in time. First we passed ponderous foundation walls of Constantine's old St. Peter's, eight or nine feet thick and so massive that they still bear part of the weight of the new basilica. Stopping every few feet, Father Pater pointed out how closely the architects of the new St. Peter's had copied the placement of the old basilica's nave and the location of the altar.

We kept moving down, through increasingly cramped and twisting stone passages, until we reached the ancient Roman necropolis, much of its masonry so well preserved that it might have been built two, rather than 2,000, years ago. Father Pater led the way down a narrow street, beaming his flashlight into the doorway of each burial house to reveal square masonry chambers 10 to 15 feet on a side, decorated with frescoes and mosaics.

"Notice how the ceilings have been broken off," he said. "Constantine's builders did that, packing the necropolis with dirt to create a firm base. That explains why it's so well preserved."

Some of the rooms still contained magnificent funeral urns or marble sarcophagi—which Constantine's men, obeying the Roman prohibition against desecrating graves, had left in place. In many chambers, once brilliant frescoes had begun fading toward invisibility; they had withstood centuries of burial but were rapidly losing their battle against the constantly changing humidity of the air. Father Pater motioned me into one chamber where the decorations seemed especially faint. I started to back out, but he pushed me back in and directed his beam upward. There, with some glass pieces missing but the remainder in brilliant, unfaded condition, was the famous mosaic known as "Christ Helios"—the earliest such depiction of Jesus, in a pose reminiscent of Apollo, the Greco-Roman sun god.

In a further twisting progression through stone-sided passageways, Pater led on toward our goal: the site, directly under the altar of Constantine's basilica, where Christians in the second century had built a modest shrine, seemingly marking the site as a holy place for Peter.

The contention that the shrine marked Peter's actual grave arose from two lines of reasoning and research. One, conducted by an Italian scholar named Margherita Guarducci, involved an exhaustive and, in the view of her critics, imaginative interpretation of the graffiti that covered some walls in the zone known to archaeologists as Area P. Much of the writing sounded Christian themes; moreover, a chunk of plaster from a partition known as the Red Wall bore Greek words that Dr. Guarducci read as saying *Petros eni*, which could have meant "Peter is within."

The other evidence was forensic. The excavators' hopes had soared when they found a cache of bones beneath the Red Wall, only to be dashed when, in an examination that began in 1956, the bones proved to come from goats, cows, horses, sheep, and several human beings. It was not until the early 1960s that another group of bones was discovered—bones that had been taken from a repository near the Red Wall and then unaccountably dumped in a storeroom. These bones, by happy contrast, seemed to come from one individual—a man, of robust build, who had died at an age between 60 and 70. The description fit the traditional profile of Saint Peter. There were only fragments of skull—a happy sign for the faithful, since the skull of Saint Peter has long been the holiest relic of the church of St. John Lateran.

In the summer of 1968 Pope Paul VI made the startling public announcement: Bones had been found and, as far as he was concerned, they belonged to St. Peter. That same year the bones were reinterred, along with those of a mouse, according to some accounts, that sometime in the past 1,800 years had found its way into the repository and perished there, ignorant of the glory it had found.

No one has scientifically established that Peter was crucified in Nero's circus, or that the bones beneath the altar were indisputably his. But at a minimum, it is arguable that within a century or two of Christ's death, Christians in Rome believed that their shrine marked Peter's holy place, and probably his grave, and that Constantine located his basilica where he did in an effort to venerate the shrine. If a plumb line were dropped from the dome of St. Peter's, through the present high altar, through the altar erected in the seventh century above the ancient shrine to Peter, through the Niche of the Pallia that encloses the shrine, and on into the Roman necropolis, it would come to rest within mere inches of . . . someone's grave.

FROM "VATICAN CITY," DECEMBER 1985

THE READER OF BONES

RICK GORE

Alas, poor Portia. Her skull was smashed, her pelvis crushed, and now Sara Bisel was playing what seemed like a grisly game of pick-up-sticks with her bones. Yet I felt oddly elated to see sunlight striking Portia's battered bones and to watch flies buzz about her for the first time in nearly 2,000 years.

"Portia had a great fall. I'd bet she was flung from up in the town," said Bisel as she worked. "She clearly landed on her face from some distance. There are roof tiles beneath her. Her thigh bone was thrust up to her clavicle. I don't know if I can put her together again, but I'll learn a lot about her.

"I'll determine her height by measuring one of her long bones. The state of her pelvis will tell her age and how many babies, if any, she had. I might even tell you whether she was pretty, but her face is shattered. Her bones should reveal whether she was well nourished, whether she had any of a number of diseases, and whether she had to work hard for a living. And she's just one person. There's a whole town here!"

Wet earth moistened by the copious groundwater that flows down Vesuvius, has sealed and preserved Herculaneum. Kept continuously wet and protected from the air and climatic changes, many perishable items of everyday life remained intact, albeit often charred. Whole pieces of furniture—beds, cupboards, tables, and chairs—along with fishnets and such foodstuffs as cereals, bread loaves, eggs, vegetables, and even chicken bones, were unearthed much as they were when abruptly abandoned.

The wet earth was also what kept Herculaneum's skeletons in such good condition. For as the victims decayed, the conserving mud compressed about the bones, rather than leaving mere hollows as at higher and drier and ash-covered Pompeii.

Three months [later] Sara Bisel [is] well into her analysis of the skeletons

—the skulls, tibias, fibulas, and other osteal remnants of twenty men, eight women, and nine children—each in its own yellow box and lined up against a wall in her laboratory. The first 12 are the so-called household in flight.

"In that chamber there were three adult males and four females," Dr. Bisel tells me. "I estimate the men were 35, 31, and 25, and the women 42, 38, 16, and 14. There were five children, but I can't tell people's sex before they reach puberty. The three-year-old was wearing gold-and-pearl earrings. The five-year-old had cavities and an abscess. There were also a nine- and a ten-year-old; the latter had an iron house key near him, along with a seven-month-old baby.

"The baby was probably upper class," she continues. "It wore jewelry and was being cradled by the 14-year-old, who I suspect was a slave. I say that because there are scars on the upper shafts of her humeri, where the pectoralis major joins the bone. That means she used those muscles for heavier work than she should have."

Dr. Bisel picks up the girl's skull. "See these grooves on her teeth? They indicate that she didn't get enough to eat when she was about 11 months old. She almost died either from illness or starvation. She was a very good-looking girl. That probably complicated her life if she was a slave."

Another seven months pass, and Dr. Bisel has now analyzed the bones of 45 adults and 10 children. "Except for the slaves, these people are very healthy," she says. "There are a few signs of anemia. They had enough to eat. Many of the presumed slaves, however, appear to have been dreadfully overworked."

She rummages through the bones in yellow box number 27. "This man we call the Helmsman, because he was found next to the boat. He was about 46 and probably a slave. He did not have good treatment, good food, good anything. I don't think anyone who had any choice would look like this. A free man would stop when his body hurt as much as this man's must have."

Dr. Bisel picks out his upper arm bones. "See these large crests on the bones? That's where the deltoid muscles attach. They indicate he did heavy labor.

"It seems safe to say this guy did not have *la dolce vita*," she says, while digging out a piece of the Helmsman's spine. "Six of his middle thoracic vertebrae are fused. You can see the strain put on his arms and back."

She leads me to another box, number 46. "This is my Pretty Lady," she says, picking up a skull. "Just look at her profile and that delicate nose. In your mind's eye, spread a little flesh over these bones. She was lovely! I think she was a middle-class housewife. The way she used her arm muscles makes me suspect she was a weaver."

Next Dr. Bisel goes to a skull most dentists would like to exhibit. It belongs to the celebrated, bejeweled Ring Lady.

"The Ring Lady was a relatively tall, well-nourished woman of about 45," Dr. Bisel explains, skull in hand. "Her teeth had no cavities or abscesses. These people didn't use sugar. *But* she did have periodontal disease. Look!"

She points to numerous little pits on the bone along the Ring Lady's gum line. "This is why you floss every day."

I ask about Portia, the first skeleton Bisel had unearthed. "Portia was about 48, certainly *not* good-looking," she replies. "She had extreme buck teeth. Also, certain of her pelvic bones show rather unusual and unexpected changes. I do not like to make accusations across 2,000 years, but Portia's pelvic bones resemble those I once saw from a modern prostitute."

A less speculative finding is an extremely high, probably pathological, level of lead in Portia's bones.

Scholars have long debated, often furiously, whether lead poisoning could have been widespread among the Romans. Lead can cause brain damage. It has been suggested that the mad emperors Nero and Caligula suffered from lead poisoning. Now Dr. Bisel's chemical analysis of 45 skeletons shows that Portia and one other person had lead levels high enough to have certainly caused them some problems. Six more people had significantly elevated levels.

The most plausible way these people would have ingested lead is via wine. Grape juice was often boiled down in lead vessels to make the thick syrup used to sweeten some wines. Stirring the boiling syrup would have scraped lead from the pots. Thus, heavy drinkers risked heavy lead intake.

"This is the first hard evidence that the Romans may indeed have had trouble with excess lead," says Dr. Bisel. "In no way does it indicate that lead poisoning brought about the fall of the Roman Empire, but it does raise many questions that cannot yet be answered."

From "The Dead Do Tell Tales at Vesuvius," May 1984

I FOUND THE BONES
OF THE *BOUNTY*

LUIS MARDEN

The course was WNW. The breeze had fallen during the night, and just before dawn the ship had almost completely lost way in the water. Her sails hung loose from the yards. Cordage slatted against the masts, the blocks creaked, and the chuckle of water at the bows died to a whisper.

Eight bells struck. Fletcher Christian, acting mate of His Majesty's Armed Vessel *Bounty*, came on deck to relieve the watch. The ship's commander, Lieutenant William Bligh, was asleep in his cabin below.

"I am now unhappily to relate one of the most atrocious acts of Piracy ever committed," Bligh later wrote. "Just before sun-rising, Mr. Christian, with the master at arms, gunner's mate, and Thomas Burket, seaman, came into my cabbin while I was asleep, and seizing me, tied my hands with a cord behind my back and threatened me with instant death, if I spoke or made the least noise: I, however, called so loud as to alarm everyone; but they had already secured the officers who were not of their party.... Christian had only a cutlass in his hand the others had muskets and bayonets. I was hauled out of bed and forced on deck in my shirt....

"Christian ... then said—'Come captain Bligh, your officers and men are now in the boat, and you must go with them; if you attempt to make the least resistance you will instantly be put to death:' and without any further ceremony, holding me by the cord that tied my hands, with a tribe of armed ruffians about me, I was forced over the side.... A few pieces of pork were now thrown to us, and some cloaths, also ... cutlasses.... We were at length cast adrift in the open ocean."

So, on April 28, 1789, began one of the greatest sea stories of all time: the mutiny in the *Bounty*.

That story, with its incredible amalgam of adventure, violence, and mystery, has long fascinated me. While on assignment in the Fiji Islands some years ago, I was astonished to find in the museum at Suva some lengths of worm-eaten planking held together by copper fastenings, marked "Rudder of H. M. S. *Bounty*." The curator told me the rudder had been fished up from six fathoms of water at Pitcairn in 1933.

Two things surprised me: first, that there had still been visible remains of the old vessel as recently as that; and second, that they lay in such shallow water.

Here was a chance to combine my interest in submarine photography with a story for the NATIONAL GEOGRAPHIC on the Pitcairn colony. I did not know whether any traces of the burned *Bounty* still remained on the sea bed, or, if they did, whether I could find them, but I wanted very much to try.

Last winter I sailed for Pitcairn from Panama on the New Zealand Shipping Company's *Rangitoto*. Ten days out from Panama we raised the island. It lay low on the horizon, a slate-colored smudge against the bright gold of the westering sun.

We had still more than an hour's steaming to reach the island, as Pitcairn's 1,100-foot height is visible from 45 miles away.

"You're in luck," Capt. C. R. Pilcher said at my elbow. "We've got a calm sea. You'll have no trouble getting ashore."

The captain handed me his binoculars. Through them I could see three small boats rising and falling on the long Pacific swells.

The island rose slowly out of the sea and gradually took on the shape of a crouching lion rimmed with the white of breaking seas. The boats waited until we stopped; then they shipped their long oars and pulled for our dangling Jacob's ladders. From the bridge I stared curiously down for my first look at the Pitcairn Islanders.

Every upturned face wore a smile, and some people were waving and calling to friends on board. With practiced maneuvers the boats were warped alongside, and almost instantly the Pitcairners began swarming up the ladders, with the women in the lead.

The first men to reach the deck lowered lines to the boat and began to haul up palm-frond baskets full of trade goods—fresh fruits, wood carvings, baskets. The women wore loose cotton dresses and the men were in shirts and dungarees. All were barefoot.

A tall, broad-shouldered man came up the companion ladder. He wore a high-crowned palm-leaf hat and, as he smiled, his white teeth looked dazzling in a handsome tanned face. He held out his hand to the captain. This was Parkin Christian, 73-year-old great-great-grandson of Fletcher Christian and chief magistrate of Pitcairn Island.

"Welcome to Pitcairn," he said (he pronounced it Peet-kern), when the captain had introduced me. "Hope you enjoy your stay."

The features of the Pitcairners, both men and women, were more strongly European than I had expected. They were tanned and brown skinned, but most were no darker than sunburned, brown-haired Englishmen. The women looked more Polynesian than the men.

The *Rangitoto* stayed only an hour; then I said goodbye to my shipboard acquaintances and climbed down the swaying Jacob's ladder. When the last islander had taken his place in the boats, the ladders were pulled aboard the *Rangitoto* and someone called out, "A song for Captain Pilcher and the ship!"

A man began to sing, one by one the others joined in, and then 70 voices of men and women rose in clear harmony, singing the hymn "In the Sweet Bye and Bye."

The sun had set behind the rocky heights of Pitcairn and blood-red streaks, like rents in a blast furnace, slashed across the darkening sky.

A dozen hands raised the mast, made fast the shrouds, and hoisted our jib and gaff-rigged mainsail.

"H'ist hah shrodes higher!" called the captain, and the men hauled on the shrouds to tauten them.

As we drove toward the island, with the lee rail well down, my neighbor on the crowded thwart said: "It's darking."

The man thumped a crate of my air tanks.

"I heardsay you gwen dive in Bounty Bay."

I admitted it.

"Man," he said, "you gwen be dead as hatchet!"

In the half light I could see a line of white breakers ahead. Stark against the sky a pinnacle of rock rose 700 feet—Ship Landing Point. At its base lay the rocky cove called Bounty Bay.

At the captain's shouted "Down sail!" the canvas came down with a rush, and the mast was unstepped. We waited just outside the surf while the captain, holding a long steering sweep, scanned the breakers ahead. The 14 rowers lay on their oars, not even turning their heads, until a particularly high wave lifted us and then let us slide down its back.

"Pull ahead!" cried the captain, and the long oars bent as they dipped in unison. We shot forward as a big sea rose under our stern. The men pulled like demons, keeping just ahead of the roller. At express-train speed we rushed past three black rocks on the port hand, entered a narrow channel of calmer water, then slowed and gently bumped against a sloping grid of logs and planks.

Several men from our boat jumped into the waist-deep water and started to hand crates and bundles ashore. One presented his broad back to me, said "Ready, mate?" and then carried me pickaback in to the landing. Above us the escarpment rose 250 feet to The Edge, beyond which the houses of the village began. Figures passing before the gas lanterns threw long shadows on the white boats. The unloading went forward rapidly, and a pile of mailbags, sacks, boxes, and crates grew on the shore.

When the last boat was stored, everybody, including the women, picked up a sack, a box, or a bundle, and we started up the trail. The heavier boxes and mailbags would go up tomorrow by telpher, or cableway.

Someone asked, "Where's ah man gwen stay long fa me?"

I introduced myself to Fred Christian, at whose home I was to live. Fred is six feet five inches tall, with a broad brown face, curling gray hair, and a gentle smile.

Tom, Fred's 21-year-old son, also shook my hand.

The steep trail is cut into the side of an escarpment. Bare feet take the best grip, and my rubber-soled shoes slipped and skidded. I began to pant, and the women, most of whom carried far more than I, looked at me with friendly amusement.

I saw the lights of houses on both sides. We passed under the aerial roots of a big banyan tree and Fred said, "We home now."

A house of gray, unpainted weatherboards rested on big foundation stones and shone with light.

Flora Christian took my hand at the door.

"I hope you be happy here," she said.

"Thank you, Mrs. Christian." I replied.

"I'm Flora."

"Yes," Tom said with a grin, "we all use our Christian names here."

Of the island's 153 souls, 55 are surnamed Christian; there are only half a dozen surnames on the whole island. To avoid confusion, no two Pitcairners have the same given name.

"Come have a bit o' supper," Flora said, leading us to a porch furnished with a long oilcloth-covered table. Fred bowed his head and said grace.

I had known before coming to Pitcairn that almost everyone on the island was a member of the Seventh-day Adventist Church. All the Adventists of my acquaintance are vegetarians. So I was surprised when Flora placed before me a big platter of steaming corned beef, along with heaped plates of island vegetables.

Fred is an elder of the church, and I asked him about Adventists eating meat.

"O-a, we always eat meat on Peet-kern; church don't forbid it," he said. "We eat bully beef, salt beef, and fresh goat meat."

This license does not extend to pork, however, as Adventists strictly obey the Mosaic injunction against eating the flesh of pigs. This seems a strange prohibition for a people who are half Polynesian, for throughout the South Pacific pork—*pua'a*—is always the center of any feast. Pigs rooted and ran free on the island from the time the mutineers brought them until John Tay, a missionary from the United States, converted the islanders to Seventh-day Adventism in 1886. Since then not a squeal has been heard on Pitcairn.

Another Biblical prohibition restricts the island diet still further.

"And whatsoever hath not fins and scales ye may not eat; it is unclean unto you."

Adventists interpret this to mean large, visible scales, so that smooth-skinned fish are forbidden, as are shellfish.

In early accounts of life on Pitcairn I had read of parties going down the steep cliff face called The Rope to gather shellfish on the rocks below. So far as I could learn, these are a kind of whelk or winkle. I asked Fred if he had ever sampled them, and he replied with a twinkle, "O-a, I used to *like* them, when I was a heathen."

No one knows the exact date on which the *Bounty* arrived at Pitcairn Island, but it was in the first days of 1790. Having landed all the stores, plants, and livestock, the ship's crew stripped her, ran her ashore, and burned her on January 23, 1790.

Christian divided all the land into nine portions among his fellow seamen and himself, leaving none for the Polynesian men. Their resentment smoldered; later it was to burst violently into flame.

Through succeeding generations the land of Pitcairn has been so subdivided through inheritance that by the time I arrived on the island some people owned only four feet of ground. Others are completely landless.

Even individual trees have owners, but no one objects if anyone who is hungry picks an orange or a coconut.

"All right you pick coc'nut," Fred Christian said, "so long you eat it under the tree. Cahn't cahly it away."

I had left northern winter behind when I crossed the Equator, and now in mid-December it was high summer on Pitcairn. Sea breezes keep the temperature pleasant most of the time on this subtropical island. There is usually plenty of rain—fortunately, because the island depends on it for its water supply. The houses have corrugated iron roofs from which the rain runs through gutters and spouts into concrete tanks.

The top of Pitcairn consists of an undulating savanna, set here and there with gray-trunked pandanus trees and thickets of dark-green rose apple. The highest point, 1,100 feet, is on a ridge above Palva Valley, west of the island's center. The early voyagers all described Pitcairn as being heavily wooded, but now axes and goats have rendered it nearly treeless, as far as big timber is concerned.

As [Fred and his son Tom and I] walked along a path skirting a cliff that dropped almost sheer to the foaming surf, I could see bearded billy goats and their bleating nannies skipping down cliff faces.

Pitcairn is only 2 miles long by about a mile wide, and after 167 years of habitation every prominent rock, cove, or cliff has acquired a name.

I had seen one point on the southwest coast of the island marked "Oh Dear" on the map and I asked Fred how it got its name.

"Well, native man wading 'long shore there drop his *malu* (from Tahitian *maro*, loincloth] in water. You know that's all they wear, and he look down and say 'Oh dear!'"

Another point offshore on the west side bears the designation "Headache."

"One man gwen fishin' 'long that place when his boy say: 'Let's go back, my head hurts!' Before he get him back, he dead."

The old accounts speak of "clouds of sea birds," but today one sees only occasional frigate birds swooping and gliding on their tapered high-aspect-ratio wings, opening and shutting their black scissor tails, and pairs of snow-white terns fluttering in graceful arcs against the dark-green foliage of the valleys.

In our walk I saw only one species of land bird, a warbler with erectile head feathers, that chirped and hopped busily among the rose apple trees. Pitcairners call them sparrows, doubtless because they reminded the English sailors of their own little town bird.

We slipped and skidded down a steep trail that plunged toward Adamstown. Near the bottom we met a man wheeling a barrow.

"You bin firewood?" Fred asked.

"Ee-yeh. Pick some plun [banana] too."

From one of the houses just below came the high, shrieking laughter of a woman, a sound as Polynesian as baked pig.

We met Flora coming down from the hill at the trail that debouched at Fred's door. "Bin up planting taty [potatoes]," she called. "Yawly invited long fa us go birthday party."

I had a quick bath in half an oil drum filled with heated rain water, dressed, took a flashlight and joined the family going up the hill.

About 50 people were seated at two long tables made of planks laid on trestles. Piled high on the tables were unbelievable quantities of food: big platters of boiled goat meat, corned beef stewed in coconut milk, chicken, boiled fish, pilhi (made of yams, plantains, bananas, or pumpkin), maize, loaves of freshly baked white bread, mounds of peas and beans, hills of butter, arrowroot, and pineapple pudding, avocados, rock melons (canteloupe), mangoes, and watermelons. Here and there stood pitchers of "drink," a sweet, red liquid made by steeping strawberries in sugar water.

And of course, baked breadfruit.

The Pitcairners are amazing trenchermen. I thought I could hold my own at table, but I was forced to yield to professionals. Fred urged me to have some more beef in coconut milk.

"Coc'nut milk make even sawdust taste good," he said.

Len Brown watched the fish he had helped catch disappear.

"My, dem soon scoff up hem fish; want one he piece, tak' whole platter."

At length even Fred, the master of us all, had to stop. The host looked anxiously at Fred's stilled knife and fork and asked,

"Can I bring you anything?"

"Yes," murmured Fred, "bring me another stomach." He smiled beatifically and added, "I always say Fletcher Christian find a good place to hide."

I could barely croak my admiration to Jessie Clark, who laughed and said, "We have only one meal a day on Pitcairn: start in morning and end at night."

After the party Chester Young told me that the old island dishes are disappearing.

"Have you ever tasted humpus-bumpus?" he asked. "Eddie? China-in-the-milk? Potta?"

Flora told me about Eddie, bananas cooked in coconut milk.

"It's not Eddie the name," she said, "but they put it that way. Eddie—that's Lucy's husband—he like it, so that's why they call it for him."

On Pitcairn today there are only three of the original surnames: Christian, Young, and McCoy. The forebears of the Browns migrated from New Zealand; the original Warrens and Roy Clark came from the United States.

The reason there are no representatives of other mutineer surnames is that in 1856 the British Government, fearing overcrowding on Pitcairn, moved the colony to Norfolk Island, east of Australia. After a few years, some of the people grew homesick and returned. These were the nucleus of today's colony.

Floyd McCoy is the only representative of his family on Pitcairn. From the age of 14 Floyd has been a close student of the island's history, and today he has the best collection of books on the subject on Pitcairn.

Floyd is also inspector of police, but he has very little to do in that line, for there is no serious crime on Pitcairn.

"Our chief offense," said Floyd, "is false report, and there is not too much of that." In other words, gossip—the bane of any small, isolated community.

Floyd is the custodian of two *Bounty* relics, an ax and an anvil. When he visited Norfolk Island, Floyd wanted to bring back the *Bounty*'s copper kettle, but his relatives there would not part with it.

The kettle is of particular interest to the McCoys because back in the mutineer days William McCoy had used it to distill alcohol from the roots of the *ti* plant.

This happened in April of 1798, but long before that date the dark cloud of violence had settled over Pitcairn. The little colony had lived in peace for about two years after the burning of the *Bounty* in 1790. Then the wife of John Williams, one of the mutineers, died in a fall from a cliff.

Williams took the wife of one of the Tahitians, who banded together to take revenge. Over the next few years there followed a series of bloody battles and violent deaths. Fletcher Christian was shot to death as he worked in his field; William McCoy threw himself into the sea after drinking too much of his home-distilled alcohol.

Nine years after the *Bounty* landed, all the Tahitian men were dead, and only two mutineers, Alexander Smith, seaman, and midshipman Edward Young, were still alive.

Young died of asthma a year later, leaving Alexander Smith the only man on Pitcairn, patriarch of a flock of women and children.

When Capt. Mayhew Folger in the ship *Topaz* of Boston called at Pitcairn to look for seals in February of 1808, he was astonished to see a canoe put out to sea from what he thought was an uninhabited island. In the canoe were three young men, bearing presents of fruit and a pig.

The youths took the captain ashore to meet their "father Aleck" Smith.

Captain Folger wrote to the Admiralty telling of his discovery—the first news the outside world had heard of the whereabouts of Christian and his companions. Oddly enough, he and one of his officers aboard the *Topaz* gave three different accounts of Fletcher Christian's death, all based on conversations with Adams. One version said Christian was shot by the Tahitians; another that he died a natural death; still another that he threw himself from the cliffs and was dashed to death on the rocks below, the last perhaps confusing Christian's death with that of McCoy.

Why should Adams have told two or three different versions of Christian's end? Could it be that he did it to conceal the fact that Christian had escaped from Pitcairn and returned to England?

In the years 1808 and 1809 rumors were current in the Lake District of England, Christian's birthplace, that Fletcher Christian had returned to that part of England. At about that time Capt. Peter Heywood, late midshipman of the *Bounty,* who had been tried for mutiny, found guilty, and then pardoned by the King, was walking in Fore Street, Plymouth. He noticed walking ahead of him a man who reminded him strongly of Fletcher Christian. The stranger, hearing footsteps behind him, turned round, looked at Heywood and instantly ran off.

Some students of the *Bounty*'s history have speculated on the possibility that Fletcher Christian returned to England. C. S. Wilkinson, in his book *The Wake of the Bounty,* even suggests that it was Christian who inspired Samuel Taylor Coleridge to write *The Ancient Mariner.*

Fred had told me that his grandfather Thursday October Christian (son of the original Thursday October Christian, Fletcher's first born) had pointed out a spot next to a big pandanus tree where Fletcher Christian had been shot while he worked in his garden, and buried by the women who found him.

I persuaded Fred, Tom, Len, and young Fletcher to go up the hill with me to dig at the place, to see if we could find any trace of a body. It was a blazing hot day, and my friends trudged along without enthusiasm. They carried "muttocks" for the digging.

On a hillside waist high in grass Fred pointed to the spot, and the young men set to work. When they had dug a hole about two feet deep, the three gravediggers threw down their mattocks and disappeared into the grass. In five minutes they returned carrying a big watermelon and some pineapples. We sat in the scant shade and cut up the fruit. Pitcairn pineapples are the best tasting in the world, I make no doubt. The juice runs from them in a continuous stream when you bite into them, and the flavor must be tasted to be believed.

It was too hot for much exertion. Half-heartedly the boys dug down to about four feet. Then Fred said:

"I doan' think them black wimmens bury him—or if they do, they doan' have time to bury him deep. So cahn't be here."

We picked up the tools and walked down the hill. I still do not know whether Fletcher Christian is buried on Pitcairn or in England.

I had always thought of Pitcairn Island as remote, and so it is; yet I was surprised to find how often ships visit the place. Last year, for example, there were more than 60 calls. In practice, one can count on seeing a ship about every 10 days.

Usually they stay about an hour, though some stop longer. Of one who generally stops only half an hour, Flora would say:

"O-a, he a hurry-up captain."

Islanders are hard hit when too many ships call on Saturday, the Adventist Sabbath, because their religious principles will not permit them to trade then. In 1956, 14 ships came on Saturdays. The people still go out to the ship and give some fruit away, but they will not buy or sell on that day.

One of my chief objectives in coming to Pitcairn had been to find, if possible, the resting place of the *Bounty*. I questioned the islanders about any visible remains. Everybody knew that a clutch of iron ballast bars lay in the surf, almost on shore, but no one could tell me anything of the actual ship.

"It-sa gone," they all said. "Nothing left."

Everyone knew, of course, that she had gone down in Bounty Bay. The question was, exactly where?

I soon found in going over the area with a waterglass, and later in diving to the bottom, that no "wreck," as such, remained. The burning, the fishing up of timbers more than a century ago, and, above all, the relentless pounding of the Pacific combers had demolished the *Bounty*. The most one could hope to find would be metal fittings.

One night at Fred's house Parkin Christian told me how he found the *Bounty*'s rudder.

It was 1933. Parkin and Robert Young had been fishing, and they were paddling their canoe toward shore. At the entrance to Bounty Bay, in 40 feet of water over a sand bank at the foot of weed-covered rock, they stopped. Parkin got his waterglass over the side and scanned the bottom.

"These nanway [a kind of fish]," said Parkin, "they lived there, and I try to look for fish. The gudgeon is laying on top of the sand right out, and I start to sing out:

"'There's the *Bounty*'s gudgeon!'

"Then I catch myself, I say, 'Oh, what a fool; I know I can get it for myself.'

"We come ashore. I pull my canoe up and start for home. I come get a line and sinkers and off I go again. I don' want even my wife to know where I'm goin'.

"I get it up first time; it come only so high, then it slip off. It stand right up on bottom; so I let the noose down and it go right down as though I put a hat on my head, and up he come.

"A chap don't see what I take out of my boat. He ask me did I catch any fish; I say I get one."

The gudgeon (it actually turned out to be a rudder strap and pintle) had at first slipped from Parkin's noose; it struck the bottom and uncovered some planks and timbers. It was the *Bounty*'s rudder. Parkin returned the next day to fish up the rudder, but it was heavy and he needed help; so he could no longer keep his find a secret.

We may picture the mutineers on January 23, 1790—Christian well aware that all signs of habitation on Pitcairn must be destroyed, the others torn between the fear of discovery and the knowledge that by destroying the ship they would forever cut themselves off from the world they knew.

All agreed at last, and everything useful in the Bounty was taken ashore: top hamper, timber, all the metal that could be drawn, sails, compasses, chronometer, glass from the great cabin windows, sheet lead for musket balls, forge, muskets, cutlasses, hand tools, pitch, earthenware, guns.

In my mind's eye, I see the *Bounty* anchored in eight fathoms well outside the semicircle of Bounty Bay. One calm day cable was paid out, and she was worked into the bay and run aground. Following seas must have slammed her rudder from side to side with shuddering crashes until it snapped off, and, with a final lift under her stern, the sea-worn little vessel struck hard upon the shore.

Then they set fire to her. Once she was alight, she must have made a stout blaze, with her sun-dried timbers and pitched seams.

I can see her blazing away, and hear the crackling of the flames. The little band huddles silently on shore, watching the flames eat away their last hope of seeing England again.

Lady Diana Belcher, in her book on the mutiny, speaks of the arrival at Pitcairn in 1841 of "H. M. S. *Curaçoa*" (*Curaçao?*) under Capt. Jenkin Jones. She writes:

"Captain Jones, having ascertained the spot where the *Bounty* had been sunk, succeeded, with some difficulty, in raising the charred hull, and found that such had been the solidity of her timbers, that her 'heart of oak' had survived the power of fire and water, and the effects of submersion for half a century."

It seems difficult to believe that a vessel not equipped with special salvage and lifting devices could have raised the "charred hull" of the *Bounty*. No doubt Captain Jones did bring to the surface some sizable timbers of the old ship. In any case, so far as I can ascertain, nothing more was seen of her until Parkin Christian grappled the rudder to the surface in 1933.

Len said to me one day: "I can show you one copper bar. My father first see it 'bout 15 years ago. I dive down to it and touch it, but it's stuck to the bottom."

This was the first word I had had of anything definite that might mark the site; so on the first calm day we got Len's canoe and paddled out to the place where Len had seen the copper bar.

Fifty yards offshore Len stopped paddling and turned to take bearings. He sighted over one shoulder at the soaring rock spire of Ship Landing Point, then looked up at The Edge.

"She right here," he said.

I lifted the waterglass over the side and pressed its glass bottom into the heaving sea.

"See it?" Len asked.

I shook my head. Len peered over my shoulder and pointed. Deep in a fissure I saw a short, gray-green bar, too straight to be a natural growth.

Little yellow wrasses flickered unconcernedly over it, indifferent to the encrusted fragment of history.

I shrugged into the harness of my Aqua-Lung, put on rubber flippers and face mask, and fell backward, diver-fashion, into the sea.

Turning over, I flutter-kicked my way down into the miniature valley, past flowerlike small corals, until my hand closed on the bar. It was cemented firmly to the bottom.

Directly above, Len's face peered through the disk of the waterglass. I made a hammering motion. The face disappeared, and a hammer and cold chisel were slowly lowered to me on a cord.

I stood on my head in the cleft in which the bar lay. Down there my head and shoulders were in comparative calm, but every few seconds the surge would slam into me and my wildly kicking feet were then powerless to hold me vertical. Helplessly I would crash against the coral fingers that clung to the rock and feel the stings that meant the sharp fingers were scoring crimson lines on my legs.

For a quarter of an hour I chipped away around the sides of the two-inch-thick bar. When I had cut a trench in the limestone bottom all the way around it, I inserted a steel rod, heaved, and the bar came away.

In the boat we turned the bar over and over. It tapered slightly to a rounded and eroded point and the upper end was irregular; it was evidently a pintle that had broken off from the rudder strap which held it. I think this is the second of four pintles shown on the Admiralty plan.

Parkin had pointed out from The Edge the spot where he recovered the rudder; that was only a dozen yards from the rocky embrasure that held the pintle we recovered, but though Len, Tom, and I searched the area minutely in the calm days that followed, we found no other trace of the *Bounty*. Obviously, the main body of the vessel lay elsewhere.

"I think," I said to Len, "that as the ship drove ashore, the following seas broke off her rudder. The pintle dropped in the sand, and the *Bounty* drove aground some distance beyond. What do you think?"

"Sound reasonable," said Len.

We talked it over. The thing is relatively simple, we thought: The *Bounty* was 100 feet long; the ballast bars are over there in the surf: the rudder and pintles were found out there; all we have to do is draw an imaginary line between the two places, cruise along this line on the bottom, and we are bound to find some trace of the ship.

Cruise we did; every day of reasonable calm we filled the air cylinders and dived. We nearly plowed furrows with our chins in the bottom. But we found nothing.

Then, late one afternoon nearly six weeks after my arrival on Pitcairn, I took Chester Young out to show him how diving was done. By this time we were losing hope, but we paddled out to near where we had found the pintle.

Len helped me on with my Aqua-Lung, and I dived first. While waiting for Len, I took my bearings on the big rock under which the pintle had lain and cruised slowly over the animate carpet of undulating seaweed, scrutinizing the cove bottom closely. Big jacks swam round me, watching curiously. On a bed of weed I saw a crescent-shaped object. Thrusting my face closer, I saw it was an oarlock. Unlike the standard U-shaped oarlock, this one had one arm markedly longer than the other, forming a tilted crescent that looked strikingly like a new moon or the symbol of Islam.

As I watched, 14 Moorish Idols, bizarrely shaped black-and-yellow reef fish, swam in echelon over the crescent—Moorish fish maneuvering over a Moorish crescent. Fantastic coincidence that only the sea can produce!

Then I came unexpectedly on a long, sandy trench. The end nearest me was covered with white limestone secreted by calcareous algae—lithothamnion, a stone-making plant—and I could see little squiggles in the surface, a curious marking that resembled nothing so much as petrified worms.

I thrust my face closer, almost touching the bottom. My heart gave a jump. The squiggles were encrusted sheathing nails, *Bounty* nails—dozens of them. I looked up for Len. He was just above me, staring questioningly. I reached up my hand for his, pumped it violently, and pointed. He looked up grinning and nodding, and we shook hands again.

We had found the resting place of the *Bounty*.

Beyond, two other trenches stretched toward the spot where the ballast bars lay in the yeasty surf. I had been searching too far to the eastward. Apparently, prevailing winds and currents had veered the ship as she went ashore. The bow had pivoted on the shore, and the stern had swung round to the west.

I began to chip away at the layer of nails. At each blow of the hammer a puff of black "smoke" arose—carbonized wood of the *Bounty*, still clinging to metal fastenings. It was extremely difficult to hold a position on the bottom. Ever and again, the sea would bowl us over completely or carry us shoreward sprawling on our backs.

Near the nails I came on a long bolt, partly uncovered. I carefully chipped down both sides until it came free. Swinging up to the bobbing canoe, I thrust the bolt over the side.

Len and I saw enough to convince us that we had found the line of the keel, or at least one of the main strakes of the hull, though we saw no planks or ribs. Everything was covered by a hard, limy growth.

As we dug deeper, we came upon fragments of the copper with which the *Bounty* had been sheathed, in good condition and almost an eighth of an inch thick. Deeper digging should bring up larger pieces of the ship.

That night I polished and buffed a copper sheathing nail until it shone like gold. A piece of the original *Bounty!* The burnished gold surface caught the light with a mesmerizing effect. As I stared and dreamed, I seemed to see the shipyard at Deptford, with the *Bounty* on the stocks and the shipwrights swarming over her. I heard the ringing hammer blows, the "chink, chink" of the caulking irons, and the "chid, chid, chid" of the adzes paring away the solid English oak. I smelled the winy odor of new timbers oozing sap in the hot sun, the resinous smell of pitch, and the clean astringent scent of Stockholm tar in the rigging.

As I worked, the noisy electric light plants were turned off and a hush fell over Adamstown, for it was the eve of the Sabbath.

By the soft yellow light of kerosene lamps, Fred's family gathered for prayers. Fred's shock of curly gray hair shone like a halo in the lamplight. The light and shadow lay on the bowed heads of the little group with the bold chiaroscuro of a Rembrandt.

After prayers I watched Flora scrutinize the bronze oarlock in the beam of an electric torch.

"I look for the broad arrow," she said, referring to the symbol struck into all large fittings of the Royal Navy in the 18th century, "but I doan' find it." She handed the heavy metal crescent to me. I snapped on my flashlight, and the three strokes of the broad arrow leaped out at me.

"That's it, all right," said Fred. "She's from the *Bone-ty*." I thought back. This could only have come from the *Bounty*'s cutter, for the launch had been cast adrift with Bligh and his loyal men in it.

I once asked Parkin why he thought his ancestor had mutinied. He replied, "Because he was an honest man and Bligh call him a thief; say he steal some coc'nuts."

This is the standard story, but it is difficult to determine in the case of the mutiny in the *Bounty* which of the two chief actors—Bligh or Christian—has been treated unjustly by history. Volumes, literally, have been published on both sides of the story.

What then, was the real cause of the mutiny? As usually happens in real life as opposed to fiction, neither side of the question is all black or all white.

Fletcher Christian left no written record, but *Bounty* crewman James Morrison recorded in his journal that when Bligh was ordered by Christian into the boat, he "begged of Mr. Christian to desist, saying 'I'll pawn my honour, I'll give my bond, Mr. Christian, never to think of this if you'll desist'; . . . to which Mr. Christian replyd 'No, Captain Bligh. if you had any honour, things had not come to this. . . . I have been in hell for this fortnight passed and am determined to bear it no longer, and you know Mr. Cole that I have been used like a dog the whole voyage.' "

There is no doubt that Bligh had a caustic tongue and an irascible nature. He drove his men and was impatient with inefficiency. But the records show that he used the cat-o'-nine-tails less than many other commanders of his day, and that he was solicitous of the welfare of his men. In dirty weather off Cape Horn, he kept a fire going below and even gave up his own cabin to the men who had wet berths. Most remarkable, he brought them through the long voyage without a single case of scurvy.

Christian seems to have been oversensitive—today he would be called neurotic—and given to a feeling of persecution. Like Bligh, he had a quick temper. It seems evident that the unpremeditated mutiny arose from a sudden impulse on the part of Christian, who smarted under Bligh's hazing, but that the opportunity was quickly welcomed by the rest as a chance to return to an island paradise.

I have walked on the black sand beach of Matavai and looked across the green thunder of the surf to the anchorage of Wallis, Cook, Bougainville, and Bligh. Whatever may have been the song the sirens sang, I am certain in my own mind that it must have been in the Tahitian tongue.

DECEMBER 1957

THE FIELD ITSELF

SHELBY FOOTE

The great Battle of Shiloh was over, with both armies in their original camps: one at Corinth, the other at Pittsburg Landing.

But not in the same numbers. In the war's bloodiest encounter to that time, 23,741 of the 100,000 troops engaged had been killed or wounded or were missing; close to 11,000 Confederates and just over 13,000 Federals. Casualties came to roughly 24 percent—the same as at Waterloo, nearly fifty years before. Yet Waterloo had marked the end of something, whereas Shiloh was more of a beginning, with other Waterloos to follow. From Shiloh on, Grant said later, "I gave up all idea of saving the Union except by complete conquest."

What remains is the field itself, those six square miles of green, evocative landscape stretching back from the Tennessee River bluff—Shiloh and the memory it evokes of those who fought here, with courage as immeasurable as the suffering. Cock an ear some calm day in the woods or fields or on the grass-carpeted lip of that tall bluff, and you may hear, behind the stillness, the cries of battle mingling the deep-throated Union roar with the weird halloo of the Rebel yell, the boom of guns and the rattle of musketry, fading to give way at last to the groans of the wounded, blue and gray, and the singing of the bone saws.

All this is there for those who know how to listen for it. One of the great satisfactions a historian, professional or amateur, derives from his work, provided he has done it truthfully and well, comes after he has put the work behind him. Once he has studied and written of an event in relation to the ground on which it happened, that scrap of earth belongs to him forever. To some extent he even feels he owns it. In that sense, Shiloh can be yours too, if you want it.

FROM "ECHOES OF SHILOH," JULY 1979

WHO DID HE THINK HE WAS?

WILLIE MORRIS

Here was a man, the writer Elizabeth Spencer says, "one of us, right over here at Oxford, shocking us and exposing us to people elsewhere with story after story, drawn from the South's own private skeleton closet . . . the hushed-up family secret, the nice girl who wound up in the Memphis whorehouse, the suicides, the idiot brother kept at home, the miserable poverty and ignorance of the poor whites . . . the revenge shootings, the occasional lynchings, the real life of the blacks. What was this man trying to do?"

William Faulkner was born September 1897, died July 1962. In the years since his death, there has been in his hometown the inevitable softening, a singular amalgam of emotions involving pride, puzzlement, fear, mystery, forgiveness, and—in some quarters—a most begrudging acceptance. Some in the town say that Oxford did not really begin to look upon him seriously until MGM arrived in 1949 to film *Intruder in the Dust*, affording the local citizens the multifold titillations of Hollywood, bit parts for homegrown characters, and outside money. The Nobel Prize, with the films and photographs of Count No-Count beside the King of Sweden, must have had almost as salubrious an effect. "The vast majority today realize he's the biggest drawing card this town's got, even if they've only read a book or two," Evans Harrington surmises.

Prominently inscribed today on an outside wall of the Ole Miss library are the words from his Nobel Prize address: "I decline to accept the end of man. . . . I believe that man will not merely endure: he will prevail." In August 1987 there was a ceremony in Oxford to celebrate the U. S. Postal Service's issuing a commemorative Faulkner stamp. There was considerable irony in this too.

Yet one can still perceive an old, smoldering animosity, the remembrance of a long-ago slight from him, a buried enmity, a pent-up bitterness never reconciled: You could walk by him on the square and say hello, and he would look right through you, although the next day he might stop for an amiable conversation. He doctored his book manuscripts at the last moment, changed his words and characters in afterthought to make as much money as possible, lied and cheated for money. Had not his own daughter said in a television documentary that he once told her in his drunkenness that no one ever remembered Shakespeare's child? Who did he think he *was*? One aged town father still says William Faulkner did not like him because he thought him a Snopes. "Well," he says, across the years, "I didn't like *him* either."

Every summer Ole Miss sponsors a week-long Faulkner conference, which usually comes right after the Ole Miss cheerleaders clinic and draws a large group of Americans and foreigners. The cultural hazard for visiting scholars can be unusual.

A Frenchman engaged in a monograph on Christian existentialist symbolism in the later works was taken on a tour of the countryside. "I was fascinated by your peasants!" he exclaimed. Years ago an Italian woman who had known Hemingway was taken to the old Carter-Tate house, a ruined unpainted shell with broken windows and vines ensnarling the porch. "Such marvelous decadence!" she said. "If you just had a *preservative* for all this decadence!"

One recent summer I myself was having a literary talk at a cocktail party with an obliging Russian gentleman. I asked if there were many Snopeses in the Soviet Union. "There are none," he replied sharply. "Under the Soviet system it is impossible to have Snopeses."

Dean Faulkner Wells and her husband, Larry, live in Miss Maud's house, a block south of the square. Her father, Dean, was the youngest of the four [Faulkner] brothers. He was an avid hunter and fisherman and played second base and outfield for Ole Miss. The bond between William and Dean was exceptionally close. William let him use his airplane, a Waco cabin cruiser, and paid for his flying lessons. When all four brothers were flying, their mother would laugh and say, "I don't have a son on earth."

At 28, shortly before his daughter Dean was born, Dean died in a crash in an adjoining county. William wrote the inscription for his tombstone in the old Faulkner plot in St. Peter's Cemetery, the same words as on Lieut. John Sartoris's stone in *Sartoris:* "I bare him on Eagles' Wings and brought him unto me." In his horrendous grief he moved for a time into his mother's house to help look after Dean's young widow, Louise, who was five months pregnant. During this painful time he wrote part of *Absalom, Absalom!* on the dining room table, around which some of the Faulkner family and I often gather for holiday feasts. He took care of young Dean, who was less a niece than a daughter.

Mayor Leslie would deliver a package of medicine from his drugstore to Faulkner's mother's house and find Faulkner sitting in a green glider on the front porch. "Mr. Leslie, if you have a few minutes, let's pass the time," he would say, and they would talk about what was going on in town, which interested him considerably.

He would say to Louise, "Always have fifty dollars in the bank. You can meet any situation." Dean remembers the ghost stories he told the children of the family and the neighborhood, particularly the one about the doomed Judith, who he claimed threw herself to her death off the balcony of the Sheegog-Bailey house (which he bought and named Rowan Oak) after having been jilted by her Yankee beau. He would take his niece to the Charlie Chan movies at the Lyric Theater on Saturday nights, and as they walked home he would ask her, "Dean, did you like what Number One Son did?" and they would discuss the action in earnest detail. No one was to interrupt him when he was writing, but Dean burst in one afternoon and shouted: "Pappy, I've got the best news! An Ole Miss girl has just been named Miss America!" He pulled himself up from his table, took his pipe from his mouth, and said: "Well, Missy, at last somebody's put Mississippi on the map."

FROM "FAULKNER'S MISSISSIPPI," MARCH 1989

AGENTS OF CAPITALISM

NICOLE DUPLAIX

In the hospital in Oshakati [Namibia] I leaned over 11-year-old Monica Sherugeleni and smiled. Shyly she lifted her arm to show me a swelling the size of my palm in her armpit. Warm and firm to the touch, it was a bubo, the symptomatic growth that gives the name to bubonic plague.

"Cases number in the hundreds, and the season isn't over yet," said Maj. Neels de Villiers, head of South Africa's 58 doctors on the scene. "Young children, two to three years old, usually recover. Older patients sometimes develop septicemia or meningitis, and these may die. But our mortality rate is only 4 percent, lower than yours in the States."

Accomplices of plague, fleas evolved as highly specialized bloodsucking parasites at least 60 million years ago, probably living on prehistoric mammals. Their ancestors may have had wings, but these would have tangled in the host's fur. Jumping provided an alternative means of reaching a passing host or evading enemies. Gradually muscles and tendons were modified to help power the formidable hind legs that make the flea a star performer, a true insect Olympian.

Fleas of various species can
- jump 150 times their own length—vertically or horizontally—equivalent to a man jumping nearly a thousand feet;
- survive months without feeding;
- accelerate 50 times faster than the space shuttle;
- withstand enormous pressure—the secret to surviving the scratchings and bitings of the flea-ridden;
- remain frozen for a year, then revive.

In the 17th century when the Dutchman Anton van Leeuwenhoek was perfecting the microscope, he chose the flea as a subject for scrutiny. His observations aroused such interest that the microscope became known as the "flea glass." To great merriment Leeuwenhoek discovered that these minute parasites had parasites of their own.

Plague may have originated among burrowing rodents of central Africa and central Asia. When plague broke out in a rodent population—quickly reducing the numbers—rodents from neighboring colonies moved in, picked up the infected fleas, and spread the disease.

When plague entered the human population, the consequences were catastrophic. The first outbreak may have been a scourge that struck the Philistines in the 12th century B.C.; the Old Testament account mentions "mice that mar the land."

Later three plague epidemics—so vast they were called pandemics— ravaged the world. The first struck in A.D. 541, swirling around the Mediterranean in a deadly maelstrom for more than two centuries, killing as many as 40 million people and weakening the Byzantine Empire.

The second pandemic came in the 14th century, when lucrative trade routes opened across Asia. Caravans and ships brought more than silk and jewels. In October 1347 vessels sailed into Messina, Sicily, with crews dying from a mysterious disease. No one noticed that shipboard rats were also ill.

The next five years were so devastating that they became known as the time of the Black Death. By 1352, plague had killed 25 million people in Europe alone. A common belief that plague was caused by "corrupt vapors" gave birth to the macabre doggerel that children still recite today:

Ring around the rosies,
A pocket full of posies,
Achoo! Achoo!
We all fall down.

Rosies were the pink rash associated with plague; posies were the nosegays carried to perfume the corrupt vapors. Sneezing was brought on by feverish chills; then all fall down, dead.

As the sweeping scythe of plague turned bustling towns into sepulchers and emptied the countryside, it reshaped European society. With few serfs left to till the land, survivors could negotiate for wages with landlords. The breakdown of manorialism and the evolution of an economy based on money sowed seeds of capitalism.

FROM "FLEAS: THE LETHAL LEAPERS," MAY 1988

DARK AND BLOODY GROUND

MOSCOW: THE NEW REVOLUTION

DAVID REMNICK

It was the summer of 1991. The Soviet regime was crumbling like week-old bread, and my wife and I were scheduled to fly home to New York for the last time, ending a nearly four-year stint in Moscow—mine for the *Washington Post*, hers for the *New York Times*. The flight was scheduled for August 18, a Sunday. A few days before, I had interviewed Aleksandr Yakovlev, who had been Mikhail Gorbachev's closest aide throughout the *perestroika* years. The "forces of revenge" within the party and the KGB, he said, were preparing a putsch.

The next day, at a party with some Russian friends on the Moscow River, we talked about Yakovlev's prediction. My friends and I agreed—a coup seemed far-fetched. The Soviet Union, after all, was no banana republic.

"But I will tell you one thing," I said, in the plummy tone of one rehearsing his valedictory. "Check out Moscow in a few years, and there will be shopping malls everywhere."

"You've gone nuts," said my friend Sergei. "Oh, you're right!" Sergei's wife, Masha, said mockingly. "Downtown will look just like Fifth Avenue. Be sure to visit!"

So that was the consensus: no coup, no shopping malls. The world would change, to be sure, but Moscow could forget about Sears, much less Saks Fifth Avenue. A couple of days later the first prediction went sour. There were tanks parked not a hundred yards from my front door on Kutuzovsky Prospekt. The coup was on. (It was over three days later.)

Less earth-shattering to historians, perhaps, is the fact that the second prediction—"the shopping malls vision," as my friends dubbed it on the spot—came true far more quickly than I had imagined. Capitalism may be creeping only slowly and erratically into provincial cities like Tambov, Stavropol, and Vologda, but in Moscow the signs of money are now every-where: advertisements, billboards, finishing schools, neon, Nikes, and, by God, shopping malls. To visit Moscow in the five years since the collapse of communism and the Soviet state is to be thunderstruck on a daily basis. Only the weather is more or less the same as it was.

Not long ago, on one of many trips to Moscow since the Soviet collapse, I met a woman named Larissa Pavlova. She was a teacher who now sold old clothes evenings and weekends to supplement her family's income. Countless thousands of Muscovites work second and third jobs to get by in a world of higher prices, greater appetites, and disappearing social guarantees. "Moscow is filled with what our good Comrade Lenin called contradictions," she said. "The rich get richer and the rest of us tread water or drown. I work much harder than I did in the old days, and sometimes that makes it hard to remem-ber what we've gained. Freedom is sweet, but it's also a heavy, heavy load."

In this new Moscow, money talks and nobody walks. If you have cash (or a credit card), you can taste it all: lobsters flown in from Maine, salmon from Scotland, caviar from Azerbaijan, lamb from Auckland, pineapple from Hawaii. Visitors to Moscow in the seventies remember well the dreary ritual of eating at restaurants offering shoelike "cutlets" and bonelike "chicken tabaca." Now there is every cuisine imaginable—even Russian, if you look hard enough. One night at a Chinese place not far from my old apartment, I asked for hot-and-sour soup but was informed by the waiter that this was a northern Sichuan restaurant, not southern, and would I consider one of a dozen other soups?

More than 60 percent of foreign investment in Russia is in Moscow. The banks, the businesses, the political actors, the cultural and intellectual insti-tutions, the information and communications nexus, the trends in fashion, language, and popular culture—all of it is centered in the capital. In some provincial cities a single natural resource can transform the lives of the top layer of the population—oil in north-central Russia, nickel in Norilsk, diamonds in Yakutia—but the deepest transformations are in Moscow, which, with nearly nine million people, is among the world's biggest cities.

"I suppose I'm a patriot," Masha Lipman, a journalist friend of mine, told me, "but to tell you the truth, there are times when I feel as if Moscow is an entirely separate country, and I don't mind a bit."

If you have money in Moscow, you might live in a gated mansion outside town and send your kids to boarding school in the Alps; you also might meet your end in a contract hit, blown to smithereens by a car bomb ignited by state-of-the-art remote control. If you have money in Moscow, you might be invited to a party at a Mexican restaurant (as I was) and meet a young television executive who will tell you, deadpan, "When I was a diplomat in Rangoon, I was bringing socialism to Burma. Now I'm the guy who brought *Santa Barbara* to Russia!" If you have money in Moscow, you might slap down several thousand dollars to join a private club; the highlight of the evening at one now defunct establishment was a rat race, featuring real rats sprinting through a neon-lit maze. (The race did not begin until a dwarf dressed as an 18th-century page rang the bell.) The owner of a nightclub called the Silver Century is planning to open a new club near Lubyanka Square within firing distance of the old KGB headquarters. He has announced a fervent desire to have party games. He said he would hold mock arrests and serve dishes like "Brains of the enemy of the people." Outside one club I talked to a guard named Vasya, a wiry and ancient man, who told me, "When I was a boy, we used to hunt down rich people and jail them. Now we guard them. For money."

Everyone is looking for a taste of "the sweet life." Hundreds of women in Moscow have quit their low-paying jobs as teachers, doctors, and engineers and have taken to selling cosmetics for Avon, for Mary Kay. (A pink Cadillac in modern Moscow would not be out of place: there are now dealers for Porsche, Mercedes-Benz, Saab, and BMW.) The Communist Party newspaper, *Pravda*, is dying, but a newer version called *Pravda Pyat (Pravda Five)* has started publication in search of the more "left leaning" souls of Generation X. Venerable literary monthlies like *Novy Mir (New World)* hang on, mostly thanks to the largesse of American financier George Soros, but a former Maoist from the Netherlands, Derk Sauer, is making a fortune with Russian editions of *Cosmopolitan* and *Playboy*. On Marshal Rybalko Street a producer named Aleksei Karakulov runs a school for children who want to become supermodels. In today's Moscow the pouty mug of Claudia Schiffer is nearly as ubiquitous as Lenin's once was.

Since the collapse of the old regime and the rise of Yuri Luzhkov, Moscow's popular and all-powerful mayor, there has been an attempt through the manipulation of symbols in Moscow to prove to Russians and the world that the country has reentered the flow of history. City Hall has a special office in charge of renaming streets or, better to say, re-renaming. Kirov Street is Meat Traders Street again. The process of re-renaming is so widespread that no one knows where anyone is going anymore—a fairly apt metaphor for just about anything in post-Soviet Russia.

In his otherwise thin and unrevealing book, *Moscow, We Are Your Children*, Mayor Luzhkov tries to paint an alternative vision of the city's past. Using photographs, paintings, drawings, and old maps, Luzhkov describes a Moscow as glorious as Rome, a city rich with commerce, character, and architecture. Just as Stalin was determined to create a new Moscow by destroying remnants of the pre-Soviet past, Luzhkov is determined to create a new Moscow by rebuilding many of those same places. Russian workers and workers hired from abroad have in just a few years rebuilt or restored the National Hotel, Resurrection Gate at the entrance to Red Square, the Tretyakov Gallery, the Moscow Zoo, Gorky Park, and dozens of other sites.

The story of the construction, destruction, and reconstruction of the Cathedral of Christ the Savior is magic realism, Russian style. After the defeat of Napoleon in 1812, Alexander I signed an edict ordering that there be a contest among architects to design a cathedral commemorating the great victory of the Russian people and the people's gratitude to God for the preservation of Russia. The cathedral took decades to build, but when it was finally consecrated in 1883, it was, if not the most beautiful of churches, certainly the most ambitious. There were five gold domes, the highest of which was as high as a 30-story building. There were 14 bells in four separate belfries—their combined weight was 65 tons.

It was looted and dynamited at Stalin's order in 1931. Stalin's intention was to replace the Cathedral of Christ the Savior (a symbol, for him, of the archaic) with the Palace of Soviets, an edifice so enormous that it would tower over the greatest symbol of modernity at the time, the Empire State Building. For Moscow this building would embody the permanence and the genius of the regime. It would be its Pyramids of Giza, its cathedral at Chartres. Stalin approved a design that was, in fact, 115 feet higher than the Empire State Building, and the statue of Lenin he envisioned at the top would be so huge that it would be twice the size of the Statue of Liberty— Lenin's index finger alone would measure 15 feet.

Stalin's design came to the most banal of ends. The foundation soon became an enormous and stagnant pool. What was delayed by water would soon be put off indefinitely by world war. For years the Palace of Soviets remained nothing more than a reeking sump surrounded by a wooden fence. After Stalin's death his successor, Nikita Khrushchev, decided to convert the construction site into what it had been for years. He ordered the construction of an outdoor heated swimming pool—"the biggest in the world."

The new post-Soviet masters of Moscow are, in their way, no less pretentious, no less interested in aggrandizement, than the old masters. All cities are the result of the vanities and the haphazard tastes of their masters. Moscow could do worse than have a mayor who wants, at once, to rebuild the old and give free rein to the new. The cathedral project will cost 300 million dollars at the very lowest estimate and will result in a near-exact copy of the original. Building began on Orthodox Christmas, January 7, 1995, and the exterior should be completed this year, the 850th anniversary of the city.

The rapid transition from communism, a system in which all were, as Joseph Brodsky, the Nobel Prize-winning poet, put it, "equal in poverty," to one in which the world is almost oppressively filled with opportunity and unfairness, has been delicious for the lucky few and a shock to nearly everyone else. It takes cunning, flexibility, privilege, and youth to make one's way in the new world. Suddenly an outwardly classless society has fractured into classes of radically different experiences and levels of wealth, and the result has been a Moscow filled with resentment, confusion, and jealousy. These emotions are the fuel of modern Russian politics. During the 1996 election campaign I met an older couple who told me they lived on a diet of oatmeal and bread and not much else. They were voting Communist, they told me, because "this brave new world is so cruel."

Even the intellectuals who dreamed for decades of an open society now feel a sense of disillusion. "Before the fall there was a uniformity to life," my friend playwright Aleksandr Gelman told me. "Everyone was more or less equal. Everyone lived more or less okay, or equally badly, but no one was rich. Everyone dreamed about freedom, and this united them. People could recognize each other, who they were, with just a couple of words. This created a certain ambience, a quality of human relations. It wasn't always wonderful, but it was familiar. Suddenly lots of artists and composers and writers began to live quite badly. There was no government support. Their lifestyle changed. They didn't become opponents of democratic reform, exactly, but discontent grew. And so now freedom is associated not with joy entirely but with a depressed state."

In Moscow especially, but in other big cities as well, political jokes have given way to jokes about the new rich—the New Russians. The gibes are what any American or Briton would recognize as nouveau riche jokes. One New Russian says to another, "I just bought the most fantastic tie in Paris. It cost $300!" "Oh really?" says the other proudly. "I just bought the same tie for $400!"

I heard about the owner of a health club in Moscow who was desperate for new members because so many of the old members had been rubbed out in mob hits. It sounded like the beginning of a joke, a fable. But it was told to me as true. The mob is a vivid presence in everyday life. Mobsters run protection rackets, car-heist rings, import-export scams; on a "higher" plane they bribe government officials for trade licenses, state contracts, and sweet deals on the privatization of one enormous industry or another. Mobsters are as present as the snows. There are certain hotels, certain restaurants and nightclubs, where one would have to be a blithe spirit indeed to go without a prayer and a bulletproof vest.

And yet, for most people, it is the pervasive ethic of mobsterism that is even more painful. While it's unlikely that an ordinary person or even a foreign tourist will find himself in the midst of a mafia *razborka*—a showdown—there is every chance that dishonesty will visit. With the fall of the old regime, law enforcement is weaker and suggestible. It seems that nearly every time I've gone to Moscow lately the police pull me over, or the friend I am driving with, and charge us with some bogus violation. Their goal is to extract a bribe: $20, $50, more. It seems the price goes up all the time. When I asked a city official about this, he looked at me with pity and said, "What do you expect from a fellow who earns a hundred dollars a month? Honesty? You try it."

Ironically, one of the most skeptical voices about the vibrant and chaotic culture of the new Moscow is that of the man who initiated the city's freedom in the first place. Mikhail Gorbachev retains a priggish—call it Leninist-puritanical—view of consumer society, of wealth. In general he longs for the Moscow that he first saw as a young man come from the provinces to university. "I think that a lot of what's happening is inappropriate," he told me one morning at his office. "It's the immorality I regret the most. Those who led this democratic process led a purge of everything that had been accumulated in this society for decades. They twisted everything in knots. Those who campaigned against privileges now build themselves gigantic palaces. They snatched up property. They have been like pigs at the trough. I am shocked by this. And for the Russians, this excess of American advertising—well, it's not all negative, but there is so much excess. In the first years after 1991, television was flooded with American and foreign movies."

Unlike most Muscovites, I admire Gorbachev, but it is easy to see that he is, in many ways, a man of his generation. He is missing the complexity of what is really out there on the streets and in the clubs. One memorable night not long ago I went with some friends to a nightclub called Pilot that was filled not with mobsters or obnoxious nouveaux riches, but rather with kids in their teens and twenties, students and young professionals, out for a good time. The rock bands on stage played a mix of American and British pop and new Russian songs; somehow the language of Pushkin extended a hand to Chuck Berry. Everyone danced. Everyone ate and drank. And no one got shot. The night, which lasted until breakfast, was at once normal, cosmopolitan, and Russian.

For younger people, like Leonid Parfyonov, the television commentator, it is natural that Moscow has become an international city and, at the same time, is distinctly Russian.

"That initial inferiority complex is gone, and now there's a kind of sense of wholeness," Parfyonov told me over lunch at a restaurant called Twin Pigs. "People now think, 'Okay, so they live well in the West. And we can visit when we want. But we like it here in Moscow better. We're a tougher people, and life here is interesting now. We'll spend New Year's Eve watching a Grundig television and drinking Swedish vodka and eating American salmon and French cheeses. But we'll sing our songs. Russian songs. That is who we are now in Moscow. We are a city of *everywhere*.'"

APRIL 1997

UNRETOUCHED PHOTOGRAPHS

Jon Thompson

When I visited the apartment where Vladimir Ilyich Lenin lived and worked during his five years in the Kremlin, security was extra strict—documents scrutinized on the way in and out, a soft-shoe man at almost every turn, even an escort to the toilet. The reason: President Gorbachev's office is nearby.

Once inside the Council of Ministers building, I was led along elegant creaky-floored corridors covered with government-style crimson carpeting, past offices posted with the occupants' names. It was impossible to keep track of where I was at any given moment. None of the passages meet at right angles, and to make it worse the corridor windows open on an inner court-yard shaped, ironically, rather like a pentagon. I had been in Russia long enough to wonder whether this 18th-century labyrinth was part of a master plan to disorient visitors.

My scholarly guide at Lenin's apartment-and-office suite, Liudmila Kunetskaya, disarmed me with her courtesy and frankness. "Lenin and his wife were both of the nobility," she told me, with the enthusiasm of one who loves a familiar subject. "His wife, Nadezhda Krupskaya, was a hopeless cook . . . they had a servant . . . Lenin's sister smoked . . . Lenin himself enjoyed hunting, went to bed late and got up late . . . he and his wife slept in separate rooms . . . he had a command of seven foreign languages—French, German, English, Italian, Czech, Polish, and Swedish, plus a knowledge of Latin and Greek."

Lenin was one of many false names he used to confuse the tsar's secret police. His family name was Ulyanov. Lenin and his wife shared their apartment with his unmarried sister, Maria, and the rooms still preserve something of the family's presence. The piano scores copied out in a neat hand bear witness to their musical interests. "Vladimir Ilyich sang baritone, and the women played the piano," Liudmila told me. The oilcloth on the kitchen table, the chipped plates, cheap bentwood chairs, scattered belongings, and personal photographs give the feeling of a real, if Spartan, home. Books were Lenin's passion, and his rooms house some 8,000 volumes in several languages. His own phenomenal output of some ten million words was for the most part published posthumously.

A photograph taken by Lenin's sister shows him near the end of his life, age 53, sitting in a wheelchair after a stroke that paralyzed his right side. A lot of interest surrounds Lenin's ethnic origins, and I thought that it might be possible to discover something by examining unretouched photographs. I was intrigued to observe that Lenin, descended through his father from Mongol Kalmyk forebears, had the epicanthic fold—the extra fold of smooth skin covering the upper eyelid. This feature is not always visible in his official likenesses.

For a firsthand account of life in the Ulyanov family I turned to Lenin's niece, Olga Dmitrievna, a sprightly, bespectacled teacher of physical chemistry at Moscow University, now in her 50s. On a bitterly cold morning she took me to see the house in Cavalier's Row where she had lived with her parents until the 1950s, a short street where the Palace of Amusements and the Palace of Congresses are located. She reminisced about the wonderful time she had as a little girl in the Kremlin. She went everywhere, played in the old buildings, rode a pony in the Secret Garden, and from time to time came upon her uncle's bloody-handed successor, Joseph Stalin, walking in the grounds. "As a child I saw him as a kindly man," Olga says.

Lenin's family, told that the people wanted to see him as he was in life, agreed to the display of his corpse. His wife may have expressed their real sentiments when she wrote to *Pravda:* "Do not allow your mourning for Ilyich to take the form of external reverence for his person." Lenin was, of course, a militant atheist, so it is a great irony that he became the focus of a quasi-religious official cult. Its hallowed images, orthodox texts, and joyous festivals parody the trappings of the religion that he so vigorously suppressed.

The cult's principal relic is Lenin's corpse, exhibited in a glass case in a squat red granite building. Kremlin Commandant Gen. Gennadii Bashkin, whose regiment of guards provides the sentries, told me that since 1924 more than 110 million people have visited the tomb. In 1941, as the German army approached Moscow, Lenin's body was secretly removed and taken to Siberia for safekeeping. His posthumous condition is remarkably good, his beard still red and his skin radiant. His pickled brain—sectioned and preserved in paraffin—resides in the Institute of Neurosurgery.

Stalin's corpse once lay alongside Lenin's, but Nikita Khrushchev had it moved out in 1961. Cary Wolinsky wanted to photograph Stalin's grave, but permission was refused.

FROM "INSIDE THE KREMLIN," JANUARY 1990

A DIFFERENT CODE

ROSS TERRILL

"They're going to shoot!" The voice was disembodied, hidden somewhere in a surging crowd of thousands. We turned and fled as one, bumping into one another to escape the People's Liberation Army, which now opened fire near Tiananmen Square in Beijing. People fell, buses burned, and the air was thick with curses.

It was June 4, 1989. For the first time since the revolution of 1949, Chinese troops were shooting at citizens in Beijing's streets.

"Tell the world our government has gone mad," a woman shouted to me.

Another woman rushed around crying out in despair: "Our students, our students! What are they doing to our students!"

Through coils of smoke I made out the giant portrait of Mao Zedong that hangs in Tiananmen and also the tall white Goddess of Democracy erected by the students—symbols of divergent philosophies of how to order society.

By morning Tiananmen Square was full of tanks. Hundreds of young people were dead—students, workers, small businessmen, and a few soldiers. Over the next weeks thousands more were jailed, and for every one person put in prison, a hundred more were harassed, and a thousand were scared into silence. "If you make a remark about the price of tomatoes," a shopper said, "a neighbor might consider that a political complaint and tell the police."

The army's attack brought one of those sudden, violent changes in direction that have punctuated Communist China's four decades of history. For seven weeks before the massacre, students in more than 80 cities and towns, backed by millions of their countrymen, had captured the world's attention by calling for democracy in China. During the months and weeks leading up to the massacre, I sensed the exhilarating change in the air, a cry for individualism that triggered the student movement. I found young

Chinese speaking as never before—about politics, religion, modern music, and freedom.

With the massacre, top leader Deng Xiaoping, who had opened China to Western ideas and initiated bold economic changes, dashed young hopes with an angry no to political reform and freedom of the mind. For the moment hope was gone, at least inside China. No one could foresee a better tomorrow, so people gave up trying, even caring. People were scared of the government, and the government was scared of the people, as evidenced by a grim joke making the rounds in Beijing:

Two young police officers, Jiang and Tan, were standing on duty at Tiananmen Square. In a quiet moment Jiang asked Tan what he really thought about June 4. "Aw, I don't know, really," replied Tan cautiously, "what do *you* think?" Jiang: "Just about the same as you think, I guess." Tan: "Look, Jiang, if you think about June 4 what I think, I'm going to have to turn you in."

A year after the massacre I traveled widely to see how the young had been coping and to hear how they view the future—for the young will control China's future. Of the 1.1 billion Chinese, nearly two-thirds, some 750 million, are under 35 years old. I interviewed young Chinese in parks and shops and darkened bars, in public baths and train stations, in university dorms and hotel rooms. I was surprised to find that while young people are cautious in talking, their dreams have not been destroyed by the June 4 shootings, just tucked behind a curtain of discretion. To protect some of those quoted here from official reprisals, I have used pseudonyms to conceal their identities.

A generation is waiting—for Deng Xiaoping and his generation to pass on, for the verdict on June 4 to be reversed, for a suffocating Chineseness to be replaced by a sense of China as one nation among others in a crowded world, for communism to collapse and for democracy to rise in its place. "This period of waiting," said one friend, a social scientist in Beijing, "is not dying, and not living."

On the campuses a sullen tranquillity reigns. Many student leaders from 1989 are in prison, banished to the countryside, or in exile. At top schools the freshman class is required to undergo a period of military training. "If they teach them to shoot," said a teacher of political science I met at Beijing University, "next time around the students will win."

Across town at a school of communications, I listened as Zhao Yulan, a journalism student, recalled how a classmate of hers, depressed at the atmosphere of recrimination and brainwashing on campus after the massacre, leaped to her death from the 12th floor of a building. "Such a pity she took it all so seriously," said Zhao.

"The part I like best in *Tom Sawyer*," a recent graduate told me in Beijing, "was when he runs away." This 27-year-old, who left his village at 12 to attend school in a town, was reflecting the escapism and independent spirit I found among many of his contemporaries. In the southern city of Guangzhou I met two young men, Feng and Yang, who are so disaffected that they keep their watches on Hong Kong time. In Beijing I discovered young Chinese, alienated by the government-controlled press and hungry to read something different, snapping up love stories, martial-arts books, and fantastic ancient tales from a tiny roadside stall in a dusty industrial neighborhood.

In the days just after June 4, Lin Mu, a Beijing official, began to chain-smoke. "These are our drugs," said Lin as he held up a cigarette, smoke clouding his eyes. A few days after the massacre, with occasional gunshots still rattling down the capital's streets, I listened as Lin described the tragedy. "For the first time in my life I saw a man die. The left side of his face was blown away by a bullet." I asked Lin if he threw any rocks. "Not exactly," he replied softly. "But I used a metal bar—the sort a cook uses to mix a large pot." I looked across at Lin. His face tensed. "I hit a soldier on the head." A silence stretched between us, and then Lin went on: "He had just shot that man."

"Did the soldier die?"

"I only wounded him," Lin replied, almost whispering.

"In China," said Zhu Yasheng, "there is nothing you can believe in." It was the day after Tiananmen, and this 16-year-old student was explaining why he had recently become a Catholic, the first in a family with strong ties to the Communist Party. He flashed a smile conveying both innocence and passion as we sat in the cathedral just west of Tiananmen Square. Shortly before, he had marched in a pro-democracy demonstration with other young Christians behind a banner reading, "The Lord Loves You, Long Live Democracy."

When I returned to China a year later, I heard that my young friend had joined the military. Surprised, I went to the family's home to inquire. Yasheng's father, a party member and master chef for senior government leaders, tried to reassure me: "Yasheng is fine," said Mr. Zhu. "He is at an air force base south of Beijing. The discipline is good for him. You see, Yasheng's grades were poor, and his middle school thought some time in the military would have a good effect on him."

The elder Zhu could not have been nicer—though perhaps he could have been more candid. Yasheng had told me his grades were excellent, and I knew how much the arrest of a classmate for the crime of "attacking a soldier" on June 4 had upset him.

In Yasheng's room Mr. Zhu proudly showed me books and photos of school and family outings. There was no sign of Yasheng's Catholicism. Where was the Bible he had asked me to send him from Boston?

I asked Mr. Zhu if his son kept up his religious observances. "When he visits Beijing, he does," the father replied, "but he can't at the air force base." I got to the point. "Did the school send Yasheng into the military as a punishment for his participation in the democracy movement," I asked, "and to try to knock Christianity out of him?"

"No, no, no," said Mr. Zhu with a broad smile. "It was his low grades."

Later I showed a Chinese friend the address that Mr. Zhu gave me for his son. "Strange," the friend said, looking at the Chinese characters. "It's an invalid address. The code is for Xuan Wu District, here in central Beijing, where I live. The air force base at Nanyuan is to the south and has a different code."

Months later I have not heard from my young friend, and I suspect that he did not willingly join the air force.

FROM "CHINA'S YOUTH WAIT FOR TOMORROW," JULY 1991

MUJAHIDIN

DEBRA DENKER

The sun is nearly on the edge of the sharp, snow-covered peaks and ridges that mark the far limits of the valley when Mustafa stops and points to a cluster of nondescript mud buildings on a hilltop about a kilometer away. The fort at Ali Khel appears deserted, but inside are Afghan government soldiers and some Soviet officers. Mustafa tells me to stay behind the wall, out of direct line of sight and fire. "Every night the *mujahidin* attack the post," he says. "We will be in a rain of bullets. Do you want to go with us?"

After dark we make our way to the house of a man loyal to my friends' party. Mustafa is relieved that the man's family has not yet left for exile in Pakistan. At night, he says only half jokingly, mujahidin factions are less trustful of one another.

A couple of hours later the attack on the government post begins, and Bahram Jan leads me up the stairs to the square tower with a picture-window view of fiery parabolas of tracer bullets arcing from the mountain-sides toward the mud fort. The fighting goes on for hours in the frosty night, the mujahidin firing Kalashnikov automatic rifles and a heavy machine gun or two at the solid walls of the fort, the enemy post answering with machine guns, mortar fire, and occasional flares. The 120 rounds issued to each of my escorts will not last the night, and some must be conserved for the journey back to Pakistan. They cannot aim for victory, only for harassment.

Over the past five years 325 million dollars in covert U. S. aid has reportedly been channeled to the mujahidin, mostly in the form of smuggled Soviet-made small arms, along with a few antitank missiles and SAM-7 antiaircraft missiles. But there are questions as to how much of this aid has actually arrived inside Afghanistan. Commander Abdullah of Helmand Province said with more passion than realism: "We fight tanks with

Kalashnikovs. Nowhere else in the world do they do this. Send us antiaircraft guns, and the mujahidin, with the help of God, would get the Russians out within one year." Certainly there are few effective antiaircraft weapons. The surface-to-air missiles are notoriously unreliable. When asked about the SAM-7, Ishaq Gailani grimaced. He and other mujahidin representatives would prefer portable, lightweight British or Swedish missiles.

At 3 a.m. we leave the battle behind and by the light of a crescent moon file silently up a riverbed that cleaves the rugged mountains. At dawn the Muslim call to prayer sounds from the village, now well behind us. The gunfire, which had continued unabated, stops. The mujahidin, and perhaps the government soldiers inside the walls of the fort, are now at prayer.

In this narrow, uncultivated valley some of Afghanistan's internal refugees have built crude houses of earth, wood, and stone. They live on what they have salvaged from their fields or imported from nearby Pakistan. It is still early when the roar of the first jet fills the sky. Though it is high overhead, we scatter, hiding under scrawny pine trees, covering our heads and bodies with *pattu*, camel-colored blankets that blend with the earth tones of the land. The noise of bombing echoes through the brown and snow-whitened hills. Beside me, Mustafa's face is grim and set.

FROM "ALONG AFGHANISTAN'S WAR-TORN FRONTIER," JUNE 1985

LIVING WITH THE
MONSTER—CHORNOBYL

MIKE EDWARDS

Near the end of a half-mile-long hallway connecting the four reactors of the Chornobyl Nuclear Power Plant, graph bars and squiggles flash on a monitor. Only a few yards away rises the concrete-and-steel sarcophagus sheathing the remains of reactor No. 4, which blew up on April 26, 1986. An estimated 180 tons of uranium fuel remains in the rubble, scattered or fused with melted concrete and steel. Ten tons of radioactive dust coats everything.

Sensors relay information from the debris: neutron activity, radiation, temperature. In the monitoring room the situation report appears on the screen in traffic-signal colors. As I watched, the display was green. If the debris warms up, the monitor shows orange. "If all the indicators turn red, it's dangerous," shift chief Anatoly Tasenko said. "It happens sometimes." He added this nonchalantly, wanting me to know he's a pro.

At condition red, engineers turn on sprinklers, spraying a boron solution that reduces neutron activity and thus the release of radiation. So far, it works.

In fact, Western as well as Ukrainian scientists believe the rubble probably can't reach a critical state—can't explode. But no one knows for sure what's going on within the ruins of the worst nuclear accident in history.

A new study suggests that the explosion threw out 100 million curies of dangerous radionuclides, such as cesium 137—twice as much as previous estimates. The World Health Organization reckons that 4.9 million people in Ukraine, Belarus, and Russia were affected. But the consequences, though obviously tragic in some aspects, remain unclear.

What is clear at Chornobyl, monitor Tasenko's nonchalance notwithstanding, is that the monster is far from tamed.

One major concern of the engineers and physicists watching No. 4 is the sarcophagus itself. Hastily erected after the accident, the 24-story-high shell is leaky and structurally unsound; conceivably it could topple in an earthquake or extreme winds. The reactor building walls, explosion damaged, are unstable too. And the 2,000-ton reactor lid leans on rubble. "If it fell, it could shake everything loose," said physicist Vadim Hrischenko.

In particular, it would shake loose the radioactive dust, which is increasing as the rubble breaks down. A violent upheaval would spread the dust over the countryside—though not so widely as the initial accident, which also contaminated parts of Western Europe.

Finally, experts know that still-working reactors Nos. 1 and 3 are unsafe. No. 2 was shut down after a fire in 1991; its companions continue to run because Ukraine's energy shortage is so dire.

The Chornobyl power complex, 65 miles northwest of Kiev, the Ukrainian capital, is ground zero in a fenced 40-mile-wide circle. Cleared of its 116,000 residents, it is called the Zone of Estrangement.

My first look inside the zone was upon a landscape that fit the dolorous name. Barn doors hung open and rampant birches grew in flower beds once splashed with hollyhocks. But a few miles farther inside, the zone seemed not so estranged. Despite low-level radiation the 800-year-old city of Chornobyl lives. Its 50,000 inhabitants were evacuated, but in their place have arrived about 6,000 people—guards, drivers, safety technicians, and enough miscellaneous bureaucrats to administer a city of Chornobyl's original size. Featherbedding, a familiar Soviet labor practice, also prevails at the power station, where engineers admit that the workforce—5,600—is twice as large as needed.

Some workers relish zone jobs because the tasks are challenging, and some, surely, for the recklessness of it all. I put my driver, Sasha, in the latter category when he told me, "I've got boar steaks in my refrigerator." To dine on Chornobyl pig is to dine on cesium and other radionuclides that concentrate at the top of the food chain. But most people work here because, as one woman said, "We've got to work somewhere." In economically crippled Ukraine the choices are few.

The bloated payrolls are one more burden for the Ukrainian government, already pressed by Chornobyl-related expenses such as health care for victims and early retirement pensions for the "liquidators," the hundreds of thousands who cleaned up and raised No. 4's shelter. In all, Chornobyl's aftermath consumes 15 percent of Ukraine's budget.

Beyond Chornobyl city, which is nine miles from ground zero, I passed through a checkpoint with changing rooms. Workers issued me a gauze mask that would filter radioactive particles, plus shoes, pants, jacket, and gloves, so that my own clothes wouldn't take contamination home.

Soon I stood 300 yards from the sarcophagus, listening to the agitated buzz of my radiation meter. If I stayed about two months, I'd receive the five rem of radiation permitted yearly for a U.S. nuclear worker. Many Chornobyl workers have received far more; to hold down the cumulative dose, most work only two weeks in a month.

The sarcophagus is the highest structure on this flat landscape, a sore thumb rising gunmetal gray at one end of the long concrete building that houses reactors and turbines. Perhaps it stands out, too, because the land-scape has been thoroughly scalped. Cleanup workers not only trucked away contaminated soil for burial in some 800 sites around the zone but even knocked down and interred nearby pine forests killed by radiation.

I came upon a reminder of the desperate cleanup effort—a motor pool posted off-limits with red-and-yellow radiation signs. Armored personnel carriers bore slabs of lead that had helped protect their passengers. From tanks poked not cannon but cranes for lifting "hot" debris. Thousands of tons of such equipment still await burial, one more task in an onerous chain reaction triggered by the accident.

In the power station I was admitted to the control room of reactor No. 3, where white-smocked engineers watched a wall of gauges. It is virtually identical to the control room of No. 4, where other operators triggered the 1986 disaster while reducing reactor power. The operators and their supervisors were blamed, and five went to jail. Two others were among the 32 workers who died.

After the collapse of the Soviet Union, exonerating truths emerged. The graphite-core reactor had, as suspected, serious design flaws. And manuals made no mention of its ironic instability at low power.

Now the rules prohibit operators from dipping below one-quarter power. Some safety improvements have been made—but not enough, contend Western experts, who to no avail have recommended backup water systems for cooling and such fire-protection measures as steel doors.

"It's ridiculous that the reactors are still operating," Valentin Kupniy, deputy zone administrator, acknowledged. His hands are tied on that; it's a decision for the Ukrainian government, which last spring announced its determination to shut down Chornobyl—but not until other ways are found to meet the national energy shortage.

One day in the zone, I met some "partisans." That's the name given to such people as Nikolai Pavlenko, one of 700 evacuees who have come home. Wrinkled and 71, Nikolai resides in the log house that he built as a young man in the village of Opachychi, 15 miles from ground zero.

Removed to a town many miles distant, he and his wife, Katia, came back three years later. "Everybody wants his own home," Nikolai said simply, as if the matter needed no further explanation. Zone officials have treated the partisans tolerantly, knowing that their families had dwelled for centuries in these now collapsing villages.

Nikolai grows potatoes and cabbages and fishes the streams. "When I need something, I just sort of help myself," he said, nodding toward the empty houses. Radiation? "We don't feel anything," he said.

On the outskirts of Kiev, in a former tuberculosis sanatorium converted to a hospital for Chornobyl children, I met a "firefly." That's the name thoughtless kids apply to evacuees such as 15-year-old Roman, as if they might glow from radiation.

"I have dizzy spells and headaches," Roman told me. And: "My heart hurts."

"It is stress," Dr. Evgenia Stepanova, the chief pediatrician, said later. "He feels his heart racing. He can't run or play sports."

Dr. Stepanova intended to calm Roman's racing heart with tender care, rest, and a nutritious diet. It's about all the hospital can offer. His father has ulcers, his mother headaches.

According to rumors circulating in Kiev, 5,000, even 10,000 Ukrainians have died from various ailments somehow connected with the accident. But because records were carelessly gathered or may not exist, the medical arithmetic can't be summed. Cautious researchers say only: "We don't know how many died."

One of the most tragic consequences evident thus far is a large increase in thyroid cancer in children. In Ukraine, Belarus, and Russia this once extremely rare condition totals more than 300 cases. What other afflictions radiation exposure will bring is a matter of debate. Estimates of the future number of cancer cases range from 5,000 to 20 times that.

I beheld one consequence in a Kiev laboratory under the microscope of Dr. Maria Pilinskaya: chromosomes, magnified a thousand times, broken and mangled. "It is serious," she said. "It indicates risk of leukemia or other cancers."

She discovered this chromosome damage in blood samples from children in seven towns *outside* the zone. All the towns had been sprinkled with radiation, but because the quantity was presumed not to be serious, people were not evacuated. It is impossible to say how many people are so affected. Dr. Pilinskaya could sample only 25 to 30 children per town; most of them were seriously damaged.

For now, according to Western as well as Ukrainian investigators, stress such as afflicts Roman is a more serious concern than cancer or chromosome damage. The psychological and social problems stemming from disrupted lives and radiation phobia lead to real diseases, several researchers told me, including chronic bronchitis, digestive-system problems, and hypertension, and may compromise the immune system. This may explain why, as is reported to be the case, the death rate among irradiated people is far higher than average. By one estimate, 70 percent higher, which indeed would translate into thousands of deaths.

No town I saw was so full of stress—and aching hearts—as Narodychi, whose whitewashed houses stand 45 miles west of ground zero. "Our parents and grandparents built these houses with their own hands," a nurse said. "Let the house be little, but it was ours. It will never be the same anywhere else."

Narodychi is one of the many towns beyond the zone where the local fallout was not considered serious. Then thyroid disorders appeared in children, and Dr. Pilinskaya detected chromosome damage.

So, finally Narodychi was emptying. On a somber winter day I came on a family loading furniture on a truck. "There's no future here," said a woman bringing out dishes. "There's no food to buy, and it's not safe to eat anything you grow."

Across the way, an old man named Sasha, pouring generously from his flask of *samohon*—moonshine—said defiantly: "The only place I'm going is the cemetery."

No one received greater doses of radiation than the first of the liquidators, the Chornobyl cleanup army that may have numbered as many as 750,000 workers. Some got more than 200 rem, enough, physicians say, to cause acute radiation sickness, a breakdown of body systems characterized by nausea, vomiting, and diarrhea. Survivors face an increased risk of cancer.

Other liquidators got little radiation but nevertheless presumed that they were terribly afflicted. In a group of Russian cleanup workers tracked by researchers, stress led to suicides and alcohol abuse. "Everybody told them that because of radiation they couldn't have a normal sex life," a doctor said. "It's a case of bad information causing death."

At Eastertide, tradition demands that Ukrainians visit their forebears. So back to the zone, with government permission, just for a day, came busloads of villagers who had been scattered far and wide—people of communities atomized, in more ways than one.

In the hillside cemetery in Opachychi, shawled babushkas placed tokens of remembrance—decorated eggs and Easter cakes—among the crosses. Families sat upon the graves, the traditional communion. They ate chicken and drank samohon, greeted friends and cousins, cursed the atom, and wept.

In late afternoon thunder rumbled and raindrops drilled the earth. The people looked about wistfully, policed the trash, and streamed down from the hill that holds their fathers and mothers. And their hearts.

AUGUST 1994

"NICHEVO"

TAD SZULC

The May sun is hot in the military cemetery, deserted except for two very young and very sunburned Soviet Army privates. The soldiers crouch in front of the tombstones of comrades who fell in this southwest corner of Poland nearly 45 years ago, in the battle against Nazi armies at Wrocław. Time and weather have dulled the Cyrillic inscriptions on the graves, but the troopers are remedying that, meticulously applying fresh gold paint to each headstone.

It is a final act of decency, a rite of farewell to the tens of thousands who died here, for under an accord with the new democratic government of Poland, the Soviets have agreed to withdraw all troops in the early 1990s.

"When do you go?" I ask one of the young soldiers.

"Oh, I'm not sure when we leave."

"What do you know about these graves?" I inquire.

"*Nichevo,*" he says. "Nothing." He turns to his work again. I am startled by his response, but then I remember that these soldiers were born more than 20 years after the war. I find myself feeling a little sorry for them. Ignored by Poles and cut off from home, they face even worse conditions when they return to the Soviet Union, where their colleagues are being housed in tents and abandoned factories. I sense their alienation, recall their vacant stares, see their rumpled uniforms, and wonder: Is this the great Soviet Army we so feared?

The sun fades, a breeze rustles the shadowy oaks, and the moment is gone. But I know that I have just seen the end of an era. After four decades on Polish soil, the Russians were really going.

FROM "DISPATCHES FROM EASTERN EUROPE," MARCH 1991

CORREGIDOR REVISITED

WILLIAM GRAVES

Nearly half a century has passed now, and some of the images tend to blur. Other images remain sharp and clear, such as a summer day in 1941 when my stepfather and I and an old family friend playfully saluted my mother on the porch of our house in Manila. My mother's camera recorded the scene of a 14-year-old standing proudly beside his stepfather with the friend, Admiral Thomas C. Hart of the U.S. Navy.

Within months war would replace such pleasant scenes with darker images—of the same porch converted to a temporary first aid station; of city streets littered with the bodies of bombing victims; of an island fortress named Corregidor, besieged and dying, yet with a grace and courage that were to become legend.

I saw Corregidor for the first time on Christmas Eve of 1941 in notable company—General Douglas MacArthur and his wife and son; President Manuel Quezon of the Philippines with his family; my mother and my stepfather, Francis B. Sayre, then U.S. High Commissioner to the Philippines.

We were all refugees together from the lightning Japanese invasion of the Philippines that had followed the attack on Pearl Harbor far to the east of us. Within two weeks Japanese invaders had seized much of the main Philippine island of Luzon, threatened Manila with imminent capture, and were driving American and Filipino troops toward a last-ditch defense on the peninsula of Bataan.

On that bleak Christmas Eve our group reached Corregidor by PT boat—one of the craft that would later carry MacArthur and his family on their last-minute escape from the island. Since the outbreak of war I had kept a journal in a school notebook that I still have. My principal entry for that voyage to Corregidor concerns neither General MacArthur nor the war, but a memorable PT boat commander who singled out a 14-year-old passenger for a special honor:

The captain was a swell guy and he let me sit in the cockpit with him while the others sat on deck.

I was to find many other swell guys ashore on the Rock, as Corregidor was popularly known. Despite the image of a fortress honeycombed with tunnels, Corregidor had only a few: The major complex was Malinta Tunnel, which housed MacArthur's headquarters, a thousand-bed hospital, and a smaller Navy command tunnel. With other civilians we were housed in Malinta Tunnel, though MacArthur, Quezon, and my stepfather were also provided with former officers' quarters on a nearby hill overlooking Bataan.

There were nearly 15,000 Americans and Filipinos on Corregidor and three smaller fortresses in Manila Bay. Following our arrival, we found the garrison on Corregidor readying the island for an attack that was certain to come. It came on December 29, and though my diary suffers from all the sins of a teenage journalist, it nonetheless gives a sense of the horror that was to become everyday routine on Corregidor:

DEC. 29. I don't think anybody on Corregidor will ever go to hell, because we had our share of it today. We all went up to the house and about noon some bombers came over. We watched while our anti-aircraft blowed them all to hell, and that ain't no lie. That was the best piece of shootin I've seen since the war began. They were right inside the formation. We could see the planes being thrown around when the shells exploded. One plane was hit and it broke formation. It must have landed outside of the bay a little ways. After that we got into the car and got down to the tunnel. A little while later they started bombing Topside [the high point of the island]. They were using a bunch of dive bombers and down in the tunnel we felt big vibrations. . . . The air raid ended about 2:15 and during the whole time they were bringing in the wounded and dying. One fellow they carried in [had] no feet, just bloody stumps. The wounded guys are the worst part of war. Almost 50% of the injuries have been limbs blown off by shrapnel. 16 guys died after they got here and they're still out in the hall. One guy was a friend of mine. Just before the raid he offered to take me for a ride in his little Crosmobile. His name was Lt. Kysor. Swell guy. Well, now we know what an honest-to-God air raid is like.

It was merely the opening round. Later entries in the diary record days magically free of losses and others with casualties on both sides:

DEC. 30. Few warnings during the day. No casualties! . . .
JAN. 4 [1942]. This morning five Japs came over and 3 went back. That's damn good shootin. This afternoon 9 Japs came over and 4 went back. That's a damn sight better shootin. There were. . . . 3 direct hits on the cold storage plant. Storage plant still ok. A 300 lb. bomb hit within 20 yards of us. Jesus, what a concussion it made.

Raids on Corregidor steadily intensified. Eventually, after weeks of saturation bombing following the first attack, the island was said to have an impressive average of one bomb crater for every 25 square yards of territory. In early February the Japanese added artillery fire to the bombing raids, using batteries on the Cavite shore of Manila Bay. Overnight I became an expert on artillery fire:

Shelling continued this morning until 12:10 and is likely to continue until the batteries (Jap) are wiped out, which we hope will not be long. Shells have an eerie scream or whistle, but if you hear the whistle it means the shell has gone by and it won't hit you. The whistle of the shell is the most frightening thing about a shelling. This firing is not so effective. It is merely a nuisance. It has only killed one and wounded 4 so far.

In fact, the Japanese batteries were never wiped out, and the day would come when Corregidor was hammered incessantly from nearly all sides. Yet the noose tightened slowly, first upon Bataan and ultimately on Corregidor. For most of February I made few entries in my journal, possibly because even disaster can become routine. Still I recall several events during that crucial month that foreshadowed the final outcome.

Soon after we arrived on Corregidor, the garrison went on reduced rations, substituting two meals a day in place of three. By then nearly all meals came out of a can. The island's prewar supply officer must have loved Vienna sausage and sauerkraut, for I can recall the odious taste of both nearly every day. Then during a memorable bombing attack the Japanese scored a fatal near-miss on one of Corregidor's few surviving mules. Dinner the next afternoon was a unique occasion, featuring tough but unmistakably fresh meat.

There was the curious nightly sensation of listening to our intensely personal, and losing, war as described by radio commentators broadcasting by shortwave from the United States. The news was always good: Valiant American and Filipino forces on Bataan were invariably slaughtering Japanese attackers by the thousands or counterattacking with equal results.

Of course, we knew different. From daily visits by troops between Bataan and Corregidor we knew that in fact our forces were ravaged by disease, near-starvation, and lack of supplies and were holding on only through incomparable spirit.

General MacArthur at that time was a puzzle to us, and possibly even to himself. Along with the glowing reports of success on Bataan, the newscasters portrayed MacArthur as a hero of almost superhuman proportions, one whose insight, wisdom, and courage were more than a match for the Japanese.

MacArthur's courage was unquestionable, as those of us who lived with him daily could testify. But for the rest of it, as a Marine rifleman friend of mine put it: "He's just the guy in charge—and not a bad one at that."

Ironically, though we scoffed at the distorted newscasts, we clung to homemade rumors of our own. The most persistent one was the report of a hundred-mile-long convoy that had left, or was on the point of leaving, San Francisco to lift the siege of Bataan. A moment's thought would have revealed the absurdity of such a report. But at the time no one wanted to think, to reason—for to do so was to abandon all hope.

By late February it was obvious that Corregidor was no place for civilians. They took up needed space, consumed precious food, and were a burden on those who had more urgent things to do.

Toward the end of the month President Franklin D. Roosevelt secretly radioed my stepfather to leave Corregidor by whatever means possible. There were three means left, all of them hazardous—PT boat, amphibious aircraft, and submarine. General MacArthur and my stepfather talked it over and made a choice. I learned of it several days later:

FEB. 23. Tonight, after supper, when it was time to go up to the house, I noticed that Mom and Dad were packing some stuff up. This was getting to be a habit. We'd stay in a place just so long and then out would come the suitcases, so I knew we were going somewhere. Naturally, I had to be the one person out of 15,000 on the Rock that couldn't be trusted to know.

In fact, barely a handful of people on Corregidor knew of our planned departure. After dark that night General MacArthur and some of his staff saw us off via a converted yacht that took us to the Bataan shore and anchored till the moon had set. Then the ship headed for the mouth of Manila Bay to rendezvous with a submarine, U.S.S. *Swordfish*. By then I had been told of the plan and of our destination—the United States, via Australia. No one aboard the yacht was more eager for the first view of the submarine:

> We stopped and waited so the sub could come alongside. About half an hour later, we saw a huge black thing (we found out later it was 310 ft. long) just to the right of us and about 300 yrds. forward. In 10 minutes we were on the sub's deck and then we got on the bridge and went down into the conning tower and from there into the main control room. Finally I reached the forward torpedo room, where I was going to live for 16 days. I was pretty tired so I went to sleep. When I woke up, it was about 6:30 and we were traveling underwater. We always traveled that way, on surface at night and under during the day. It's hot as h—l down there when you're submerged.

There was no alternative to the travel routine, for the seas around us were totally controlled by the Japanese, and to run on the surface in broad daylight was suicidal. With ten passengers aboard, five of them women, the 87-man crew of *Swordfish* was ordered to head straight for Australia and to attack no targets on the way. Unfortunately, our enemy had no such orders:

> MAR. 3. Tonight at 10:15 we got a . . . taste of excitement. We were in the ward room (cruising on surface) when suddenly the general alarm went off, all water-tight doors were closed and we dove immediately. We went way down and all fans, motors, everything was shut off and we had to sit still saying nothing. The reason for all this was that a Jap destroyer had been sighted cutting across the moon's path coming full on toward us. . . . We stayed down about ½ an hour, and then the captain ordered us up to 60 ft. to take a look around. The destroyer wasn't in sight, so we proceeded on for the rest of the night on surface.

Until that point I had always considered the submarine service the most glamorous branch of the military. But after one or two similar brushes with Japanese surface ships, I developed serious second thoughts.

On our eighth day under way we crossed over, or rather beneath, the Equator. *Swordfish*'s crew singled me out for a mock trial before one of the engineers dressed as Neptune. A list of my crimes was presented, including the shameful offense of "bubble dancing"—erratic handling of the submarine's bow diving planes, which I had been carefully taught to operate.

I was sentenced to swab the control room deck with a damp handkerchief and to serve coffee to the duty watch. The adult passengers were merely presented with forms signed by the captain certifying that they had crossed the Equator. My journal entry that night was scathing:

> Today we crossed the line, and old Neptune came aboard and initiated me. (I was the only one that got a real initiation, while the others fixed themselves up some fancy certificates but they didn't get the works.)

Though the Japanese controlled the seas south of the Philippines, we managed to slip through the net and reached Fremantle, Australia, on March 11, 1942, after a voyage of 16 days and some 3,000 miles. On that same day, we learned, MacArthur and his family had begun their escape from Corregidor by PT boat.

Less than a month later, on April 9, American and Filipino forces surrendered on Bataan. Corregidor hung on grimly for another month, then fell on May 6.

For nearly three years the island remained in Japanese hands and was liberated at last by the American 503rd Parachute Regimental Combat Team in March 1945. Though I returned to Manila that summer with the U.S. Navy's amphibious forces, I never was able to visit Corregidor. Finally in March 1985—43 years after our escape aboard *Swordfish*—I revisited Corregidor with a group of American veterans who had taken part in the island's defense and its surrender to the Japanese.

I was prepared for the devastation but not for the air of neglect. Like Bataan, Corregidor is a symbol to Americans and Filipinos alike of a tragic but gallant chapter in the history of their countries. Yet Corregidor today is one vast untended jungle that chokes the island's shattered defenses, obliterates paths and roadways, and invades the crumbled remains of buildings like tropical growth in a once great Maya metropolis.

Worse yet, the massive batteries that had defended Corregidor—the

12-inch mortars, the long-range and disappearing guns—are being illegally dismantled by scrap dealers and sold ashore as junk. "The disappearing guns," laments Jim Black, a world authority on the history of Corregidor, "are doing just that—disappearing."

With Jim's help I located the site of our former house near Malinta Tunnel together with that of the MacArthur house next door. All that remain of either building is crumbled concrete steps and the reinforced concrete posts on which the structures rested.

During my stay on Corregidor I was astonished to note several busloads of Japanese sightseers. "Quite a few make the trip from Japan," Jim Black remarked. "Many are descendants of Japanese casualties. After all," he added grimly, "out of some 5,200 Japanese defenders in 1945, 5,160 either perished or committed suicide."

Curiously, the American veterans I was accompanying showed little animosity toward the Japanese, though the latter's studied courtesy reminded one American of his days as a prisoner on Corregidor. "The first thing you learned about Japanese guards," recalled Bill Delich, a retired Army sergeant, "was to back off whenever they smiled."

The U.S. government's own Pacific War Memorial has fallen into disrepair. I visited it one afternoon at Topside and noted cracks in the walls bearing the names of various Pacific campaigns and a memorial pool long since run dry beneath the central monument dome. Yet the spirit of the memorial remains implicit in the lines engraved on one of the walls and dedicated to all Allied dead of the Pacific:

Sleep, my sons...
Sleep in the silent depths of the sea,
Or in your bed of hallowed sod
Until you hear at dawn
The low, clear reveille of God.

JULY 1986

FIRE FIGHT IN THE SOLOMONS

2ND LT. DAVID DOUGLAS DUNCAN, USMCR

As usual, the rain limited all visibility to a few feet. As usual, the Japs waited until the downpour was at its worst, then slipped through the watery screen to the attack.

Cloaked in ferns from head to waist, faces blackened with charcoal, and leaning quietly against tree trunks, the Fijians became part of the jungle in the half-light and the rain. Cool and casual, they placed each shot with terrific speed, but utmost care.

One Fijian soldier was pulling grenade pins with his teeth and hurling the bombs with a mighty shout into Jap faces. His grenades blew Japs and jungle to kingdom come.

A gigantic, six-foot-four mortar man, braced with legs apart and exposed to enemy fire, was slamming bomb after bomb into his gun and firing it from the waist. The shocks twisted his body, but his feet never moved.

Cpl. Malakai Mo stayed always at my side with his Tommy gun. When my grenades were gone, he gave me some of his.

Cpl. Malakai tapped on his Tommy and, catching my eye, pointed to a grenade thrower calmly tying up a hole in his dungarees. Slugs had shot away the seat of his pants!

Those were the Fijians. Gentle but fearless, thinking of a stranger before protecting themselves, standing alone on a hilltop in a foreign land, fighting for their lives.

FROM "FIJI PATROL ON BOUGAINVILLE," JANUARY 1945

SOMETHING GREAT, SOMETHING AMERICAN

ARTHUR ZICH

Kamechiyo Takahashi, 94, of San Mateo, California, recalls her own family circumstance on the eve of World War II: "We'd saved a goodly amount over the years to build a home of our own. Then, when it looked as if war was imminent, Mr. Takahashi said he thought we should take the money and go back to Japan. But our two sons said, 'Wait! We're Americans! Our world is here.' So we built our house and moved into it in the fall of 1941." Just a few weeks later Mrs. Takahashi, busy in the kitchen, heard a radio blaring in the living room. "I couldn't understand the English," she recalls. "All I could hear was the announcer shouting." It was Sunday, December 7.

"Just visualize that day! The Pacific Fleet, our first line of defense, was all but sunk! Our second line was the West Coast, where the heaviest concentration of Japanese and people of Japanese descent resided. And we were getting it straight from the horse's mouth—from intercepted cable traffic out of Tokyo, which we code-named MAGIC—that the Japanese were setting up an espionage-sabotage network on the coast. There was only one thing to do, and that was move those people out of there!"

The speaker is New York lawyer John J. McCloy, 91, Assistant Secretary of War under President Franklin D. Roosevelt.

"Earl Warren, the attorney general out there in California [afterward Chief Justice of the United States], had been pleading with the White House: 'For God's sake! Move the Japanese!'

"The President called Francis Biddle, the Attorney General, into his office.

"'Francis,' the President said, 'are you in favor of this move?'

"'Oh yes, Mr. President,' said Biddle. 'But I want to see it carried out *humanely.*'

"'That's exactly what I want to do,' the President said. 'You help draw the order'—and right then and there, Biddle did. The President went on: 'And I want the Army to carry it out!'

"When he heard of the plan, Chief of Staff General George Marshall pleaded: 'Please, Mr. President, we've got our hands full.'

"'No,' said the President. 'No civilian agency can do this. I want the Army to take it on.'

"We were faced with what Mr. Churchill called the 'bloody dilemmas.' I said, 'We're going to have litigation about this, but we better go ahead and do it. We don't know where their next attack is coming from.' I didn't give a damn whether they were citizens or not."

Scholars have questioned the necessity of President Roosevelt's action, pointing out that the Office of Naval Intelligence, the Federal Bureau of Investigation, and President Roosevelt's own special investigator all assured Washington that there was no evidence of espionage or sabotage by Japanese Americans. Dr. Peter Irons, associate professor of political science at the University of California, San Diego, who conducted an exhaustive study of 2,000-plus MAGIC messages, concludes: "The MAGIC cables do not implicate Japanese Americans in any sabotage or espionage activity. They provide no substantiation for concern on the President's part about the loyalty of Japanese Americans on the West Coast."

"We're charged with wanting to get rid of the Japs for selfish reasons," said the secretary of California's Grower-Shipper Vegetable Association in the *Saturday Evening Post* in May 1942. "We do."

Declared U.S. Congressman John Rankin of Mississippi: "This is a race war." But whatever else is said, ultimate responsibility was the President's. As McCloy states: "Franklin Roosevelt was the only man in the world who could sign that order relocating those people. And he signed it." Reflected Attorney General Biddle in his memoirs: "The Constitution has never greatly bothered any wartime President."

On the West Coast, FBI agents and local police rounded up more than 2,000 suspected security risks: Japanese-language and martial-arts teachers, Buddhist priests, community leaders. Among the targets were picture bride Yuki Torigoe and her husband, who ran a small watch-repair and gun shop in Watsonville, California: "That very morning they took Mr. Torigoe away. I didn't see him again for nearly a year." Eventually, nearly 120,000 American citizens and alien residents of Japanese ancestry were uprooted from

West Coast homes, farms, and businesses and herded, most of them, into assembly centers in racetracks and fairgrounds. Later they were transported to ten desolate concentration camps—the term used by President Roosevelt himself.

The President's order had little effect on Hawaii. Fewer than 2,000 Japanese were taken into custody. Hawaii's 158,000 Japanese represented 37 percent of the population and an even higher percentage of the skilled labor force. "Without them," says Franklin Odo, director of ethnic studies at the University of Hawaii at Manoa, "Hawaii simply couldn't have functioned."

A civilian War Relocation Authority (WRA) was established to assist in the evacuation. Its first director, Milton S. Eisenhower, brother of the general, envisioned the agency overseeing a humane resettlement program that would put the uprooted Japanese back to work in public and private jobs throughout the inland states. But the reception Eisenhower received at a meeting with the governors and attorneys general of ten western states on April 7, 1942, convinced him that such a scheme had no hope of realization. Wyoming Governor Nels Smith warned that if Eisenhower's plan were attempted "there would be Japs hanging from every pine tree." Explained Idaho Attorney General Bert Miller: "We want to keep this a white man's country." Eisenhower resigned.

"So," says Yuji Ichioka, "the great fire sale got under way." Evacuation notices, posted on telephone poles, gave some Japanese just two days to dispose of the possessions of a lifetime. A few, like Mary Tsukamoto and her husband, were able to leave homes and property in the care of trusted friends. Most had to deal with bargain hunters and profiteers.

When evacuation day arrived, Norman Mineta, who was then ten and later became a U.S. congressman from San Jose, put on his Cub Scout uniform. At the 1942 commencement exercises of the University of California at Berkeley, the top scholar was absent. Harvey Itano, who recorded four years of straight A's, was in the Sacramento assembly center. Explained university president Robert G. Sproul: "His country has called him elsewhere."

"Like a lot of couples then, we got married just before the evacuation so we wouldn't be separated," remembers Dr. Kazuyuki Takahashi, retired now after 23 years in internal medicine at Oakland's Kaiser Hospital. Adds his wife, Soyo, "We honeymooned at Santa Anita assembly center."

The racetrack, near Pasadena, was converted into a holding area for Japanese Americans, pending construction of permanent concentration camps. At Santa Anita the Takahashis shared a single, manure-speckled horse stall, and one roll of toilet paper a week, with another newlywed couple. "Manure dust kept drifting down from the walls and ceilings," Doctor Takahashi relates. Soyo adds: "We had four wood-frame cots, with straw-filled mattresses, jammed in crosswise with a blanket hanging down the middle for privacy. After a couple of weeks, mushrooms began growing up through the floor."

"Something great and something American may come out of all this," young Kaz wrote in June 1942. "In the meantime we live on from day to day, not unhappily but in a fog of uncertainty about the future."

By September, ten camps had been constructed in the wilds of Arkansas, Arizona, California, Colorado, Idaho, Utah, and Wyoming. California's Manzanar—where the Takahashis were moved in the fall of 1942—was typical: wood-frame, tar-paper barracks, armed guards in sentry towers, barbed wire. Each barracks consisted of four 20-by-20-foot rooms furnished with an oil stove and a bare hanging bulb. There were no closets, Takahashi wrote, "no shelves, no table or chair, not even a nail to hang one's hat." Open showers and latrines offered no privacy.

Five doctors cared for the camp's 10,000 people. Mary Oda lost her father, older brother, and a sister in the scant space of seven months. Tom Watanabe, now of Chicago, lost his wife and twin girls in childbirth. "What haunted me," Watanabe says, "was that for years I didn't know what they did with the bodies."

Two days before Pearl Harbor's first anniversary, Fred Tayama, one of the pro-American leaders of the Japanese American Citizens League (JACL) at Manzanar, was severely beaten. Three pro-Japanese Kibei—American-born citizens educated in Japan—were arrested for the assault. Next day a riot erupted, the worst violence of the evacuation. Two internees were killed by military police, ten others were wounded. "We stayed in our quarters. We were frightened," Dr. Takahashi relates now.

To separate loyal from disloyal individuals and to identify those who might be called up for military service, the government in February 1943 required internees over 16 to fill out a loyalty questionnaire. Question 27 asked Nisei males: "Are you willing to serve in the armed forces of the United States on combat duty, wherever ordered?" Question 28 asked: "Will you swear unqualified allegiance to the United States . . . and forswear any form of allegiance or obedience to the Japanese emperor . . . ?"

Some 9,000 answered the questions "no-no," qualified their answers, or refused to respond at all. All persons giving so-called no-no answers were summarily branded disloyal. Most were eventually removed from their camps and segregated for the duration at Tule Lake, California. But more than 65,000, about 85 percent of the internees who responded, answered "yes-yes," affirming their loyalty. Explains Hawaii's Senator Daniel K. Inouye, who lost an arm in combat and earned the Distinguished Service Cross, America's second highest decoration for bravery: "We were fighting two wars—one against the Axis overseas and another against racism at home."

The 23,000 Nisei who fought for the country of their birth averaged five feet four inches in height and 125 pounds in weight, with M1 rifle and grenades. They wore shirts with 13½-inch necks, pants with 26-inch waists, and size three boots. They won more than 18,000 decorations for bravery, including a Medal of Honor, 52 Distinguished Service Crosses, 560 Silver Stars, 28 with oak-leaf clusters, and no fewer than 9,486 Purple Hearts.

Nisei were barred from enlisting in the Navy and Marines, but 6,000 served as Army military intelligence specialists in the Pacific. They were attached to about 130 units from eight different countries and the armies of China. Their single most valuable exploit, says Shig Kihara, one of the founders of the Army's Japanese-language school at the Presidio in San Francisco, was cracking Operation Z, Japan's strategic plan for the defense of the Philippines and the Marianas. In the opinion of Gen. Charles Willoughby, intelligence chief for Gen. Douglas MacArthur, they shortened the war against Japan by two years.

In Europe, the mainland Nisei's 442nd Regimental Combat Team, combined overseas with the Hawaiian 100th Battalion, took for its motto "Go For Broke." Fighting in Italy and southern France, the 100/442nd emerged for its size and length of service as the most decorated unit in American history—earning eight Presidential Unit Citations and taking 300 percent casualties. Fifth Army Commanding Gen. Mark Clark told them: "The whole United States is proud of you."

Not quite. Having survived three major campaigns, T/Sgt. Shig Doi hitch-hiked back to Auburn, California. With his duffel bag on his shoulder and a Bronze Star on his chest, the diminutive hero topped the crest of a hill and

looked down onto his hometown. Doi still shuts his eyes at the bitter recollection: "Every store on Main Street had a 'No Japs Wanted' sign out front."

Tule Lake, the last of the concentration camps, closed for good in March
1946. At least a third of all Japanese-American truck farmers on the West
Coast found their lands ruined or lost to foreclosure. Japanese neighborhoods everywhere were gone, their rented homes and shops taken over by
war workers who had flooded into the region.

It has been estimated that Japanese-American losses totaled 400 million
dollars—in 1942 dollars. In 1948 Congress appropriated 38 million dollars to
settle claims, but the processing was so snarled that the internees settled for
an average of a dime on the dollar. Mary Oda's mother, a former teacher who
turned to field labor to support herself, carried the ashes of her dead
husband, son, and daughter around in an urn for six years, unable to afford a
proper funeral. She finally settled for $1,800 just to see them buried.

Some injustices were redressed. In 1952 JACL helped win repeal of
California's alien land laws, and Congress granted the Issei's right to citizenship at last. Among those who applied is Michiko Tanaka, now 81. "I have 11
children living and 22 grandchildren, all citizens," she said. "I'm entitled."

Social barriers fell too. Nisei men and women found that traditional
Japanese values had become marketable commodities in America. "The
Japanese work ethic—personal discipline, deference to authority, high
productivity, and emphasis on quality—corresponds to the old Protestant
ethic," explains UCLA sociologist Harry Kitano. "Once these qualities
were ridiculed, despised. Now they dovetail with the needs of the American
marketplace."

The first Japanese-American astronaut, Lt. Col. Ellison Onizuka of the
U.S. Air Force, who died with six other crew members when the space
shuttle *Challenger* exploded last January 28, had dreamed of spaceflight since
boyhood. At 13 he had stood on the black lava shores of the Big Island of
Hawaii and looked up at the night sky, filled with wonder at the flight of
Alan B. Shepard, Jr., America's first man in space. This is how Elli Onizuka
described his own first flight in 1985:

"I looked down as we passed over Hawaii and thought about all the
sacrifices of all the people who helped me along the way. My grandparents,
who were contract laborers; my parents, who did without to send me to
college; my schoolteachers, coaches, and ministers—all the past generations

who pulled together to create the present. Different people, different races, different religions—all working toward a common goal, all one family."

In 1980 Congress established a commission to investigate the facts and circumstances surrounding FDR's Executive Order 9066. For the first time Japanese Americans came forward and publicly recounted their experiences in the camps. Men and women wept as they testified. "After 40 years," says Dr. Kuramoto, "the emotional boil was lanced, and the healing process was begun."

After hearing testimony from some 750 witnesses, the commission concluded that Executive Order 9066 was not justified by military necessity, that "a grave injustice" had been done to those interned, and that the broad historical causes behind the order were "race prejudice, war hysteria, and a failure of political leadership." The commission recommended the appropriation of 1.5 billion dollars as compensation to the victims. "It was a redemption," says Warren Furutani of UCLA's Asian American Studies Center. "The victims weren't guilty—and the Sansei finally found out what their parents had been through."

Their problem now was to find out who they were themselves. Sansei Philip Gotanda, 35, of San Francisco, a prolific young Japanese-American playwright, went to live in rural Japan. "I was wearing the clothes, getting around fine, feeling comfortable," he relates. "And one day, walking down the street, I had a profound experience: I suddenly realized that all the faces I'd been seeing in the movies and on television, all the faces of the people on the street, were Japanese. Everyone looked like me. For the first time in my life, I was anonymous."

Gotanda pauses, as if to let the experience sink in anew. "I think it gave me the vantage point to accept the fact that I am not Japanese," he says. "For better or for worse I am an American."

And what did Gotanda do then?

"I came home," he says with a smile.

FROM "JAPANESE AMERICANS: HOME AT LAST," APRIL 1986

THE ROAD OF HOPE

William S. Ellis

The main route across Mauritania is called the Road of Hope, and it will take you to where birdsongs are never heard.

A hundred miles from Nouakchott there is a settlement beside the road. It is called Tignarg Oasis, but there are no palm trees, no pools of fresh water. And there are few, if any, adult males, for they have all left to seek work in the towns. Some have been gone a long time, having abandoned their wives and children.

At noontime the children of Tignarg Oasis are gathered in the small store, where bottles of warm soda sit in a refrigerator with a motor long silenced. A few packages of biscuits covered with dust are on the shelf, along with some soap and cartons of dried milk. Nothing more than that. A boy with curly hair and pale eyes is there, leaning against the counter. When asked his name, he smiles and says "Abdullah."

His father went off some time ago to the town of Boutilimit, ten miles down the road. "I go to school some days, but mostly I take the donkey to the well to bring back water," he said. I walked the mile or so with him the next time he went to the well to fill the two large cowhide bags that hung suspended from the donkey's back. He carried a stick in his hand, which he used to tap rather than strike the animal when it slowed.

"When I was six, I started to tend the goats and chickens we had," he said, "and when I reached ten, my father let me move the cattle."

The animals had trampled and overgrazed the ground in a wide circle around the 90-foot-deep well until no grass remained. Such have been the mixed blessings of wells and 1,000-foot-deep boreholes sunk in the Sahel. The attraction of the water to the herdsmen and their cattle is strong, but the damage to the land is devastating and, for the most part, irreversible.

Looking out in all directions from the well, there are not more than two or three trees in sight, and yet the boy tells me that he has heard it said that once the wildlife and greenery were plentiful here. With the water bags filled, we started on the walk back to the village, and as we came closer, I could see that a bulldozer was there, pushing the sand off the Road of Hope.

FROM "AFRICA'S SAHEL: THE STRICKEN LAND," AUGUST 1987

HUE: MY CITY, MYSELF

TRAN VAN DINH

The Vietnamese word *minh* can be translated "my body, myself." The people of Hue call their city Hue Minh, as if the stones of its palaces and temples, the waters of the River of Perfumes, and the tombs of its bygone heroes and emperors are the bones, bloodstream, and spirit of this most historic, civil, and beautiful of Vietnamese cities.

"Wherever I go, I always miss Hue," a folk song says. "I miss the cool breeze on the River of Perfumes, I miss the clear moon over the Imperial Screen Mountain."

These poignant words ran through my mind last November when I returned to Hue after more than three decades of absence, and I wondered if the city of the song, the city I remembered so fondly from my earliest years, still existed.

My efforts to contact old schoolmates had failed; communications between Vietnam and the United States, my adopted country, were difficult and slow. I half-expected to find the war-torn city in ruins and its spirit subdued. Would I myself, a son of Hue who had become an American citizen, be welcome in "the place where my placenta was buried and my umbilical cord was cut"?

Hue soon gave me reassuring answers to these troubling questions. On my first morning I visited Dong Ba (Eastern Wave) Market. When the market women heard me speaking English, they asked if I was *Viet kieu* (overseas Vietnamese) and how long I had been away from home. When I answered in the Hue accent—a soft, drawling, almost inaudible way of speaking—one lacquer-toothed woman cried out in happy surprise: "He still speaks like us! He has been away for so many years, and he is still *de thuong*."

This expression means "likable, charming," and in Hue it is a great compliment. After so many years of absence I truly felt that I was home again.

Later, to my delight, I found most monuments and palaces in Dai Noi, the "great interior" of Hue, in recognizable condition. The imperial capital built in the 19th century by the founding emperors of the Nguyen dynasty preserved its alluring beauty and its architectural poetry.

To its people Hue is a poem, but it began in a legend. In 1601 Lord Nguyen Hoang, father of the Nguyen dynasty, visited a rude village on a site now occupied by the Citadel. There, on a hill shaped like a dragon head, a peasant had seen a lady dressed in a red gown and green trousers. She prophesied: "Soon a true king will come here to build a pagoda that will attract and converge all the heavenly forces and energies of the *Long Mach*—Dragon Veins." Thereupon she vanished into the blue heaven.

Lord Nguyen Hoang built a pagoda on the hill and named it Thien Mu (Heavenly Lady). In 1844, under Emperor Thieu Tri, a seven-story tower was added, with each platform dedicated to a different manifestation of Buddha. Thieu Tri also completed all the monuments and palaces started by his grandfather, Gia Long, and by his father, Minh Mang.

When I entered Hue's famous Quoc Hoc (National Studies) School in 1937, the city, with a population of less than 50,000, was seething with underground politics and bursting with aboveground literature and arts. Writers, poets, teachers, students flocked to bookstores and coffee- and teahouses to discuss the latest issue of the liberal reformist paper *Ngay Nay (Today)* or the newest avant-garde novel by one of the authors of the Tu Luc Van Doan (Self-reliance Literary Group). Some used the occasion to whisper a word to a comrade or a colleague about a secret meeting on a sampan on the River of Perfumes.

The "in" place was Lac Son (Mountain of Joy) refreshment kiosk-cum-bookstore at the entrance of Dong Ba Market. Lac Son was our living room, study, library, and kitchen. A young writer—authentic or would-be— might descend on the Mountain of Joy about four in the afternoon after a long siesta. He would then order a cool drink—fresh lemonade was popular in those days—read a magazine or chapters of a book, or hold court for a small group of admirers or patrons.

By six in the evening he would switch from cool drink to black coffee, a necessary preparation for a predinner beer or Pernod. Then he would select his favorite dish from a street vendor—say, *bun bo* (hot peppered pig feet with beef noodles)—and ask Lac Son to "pay for me and put it on my bill."

Ignoring the sign that hung on the door ("Our shop has no money, so please, brothers, do not ask for a loan"), the pretty young cashier would comply. Later she might advance more money if the well-fed writer felt that his feet were too light to bear him safely home. She knew that the owner of Lac Son was a patron of the arts—and she may have guessed, too, that the boss was a member of the outlawed Vietnam Communist Party.

He had much company in Hue. My own school produced such revolutionary alumni as the future president of North Vietnam, Ho Chi Minh (then named Nguyen Tat Thanh); North Vietnamese Prime Minister-to-be Pham Van Dong; Gen. Vo Nguyen Giap, the victor at Dien Bien Phu; and poet laureate To Huu. On the other political side at Quoc Hoc: the future president of South Vietnam, Ngo Dinh Diem.

In 1945 a group of militant nationalist students from another school became outraged when the Japanese occupation army confiscated rice from Vietnamese peasants, an action that led to the death of two million Vietnamese by starvation. The students, several of them my close friends, set up a restaurant in an orchard serving the best sushi in town. Japanese soldiers came in large numbers to eat this Japanese delicacy. One moonless night the students machine-gunned and killed a dozen officers.

Hue has suffered many wounds of war. When I was a child, my mother taught me *Ve That Thu Kinh Do* (*The Song of the Fall of the Capital*), a 3,000-verse poem about the sack of the city by French troops on July 5-7, 1885, in retaliation for a rebellion against the French protectorate:

> *People were crying and wailing,*
> *Children leading mothers, mothers carrying babies.*

On May 10, 1845, Hue had had its first experience of American power when the U.S.S. *Constitution*, commanded by Capt. John (Mad Jack) Percival, sent an armed party ashore to rescue a French bishop named Dominique Lefèbvre, who had been sentenced to death by the imperial court. Percival took several Vietnamese officials hostage in a futile attempt to force Emperor Thieu Tri to release Lefèbvre; then his men opened fire on a crowd of civilians. In 1849 President Zachary Taylor wrote a belated letter of apology to Emperor Thieu Tri concerning the incident; it was received by Emperor Tu Duc, Thieu Tri's successor.

"May your God, and my God, prevent the shedding of any more blood between my people and your people, My Brother," Taylor wrote.

But during the communist Tet offensive of January 31 through February 25, 1968, Hue was the scene of one of the bloodiest of all battles between Vietnamese and Americans. By U.S. count, 5,113 communist troops, 384 South Vietnamese, and 142 Americans died in 26 days of fighting. My youngest brother (the poet Lu Quynh) and one of my nephews, both living in the Citadel, were killed by direct U.S. bomb hits.

According to U.S. estimates, 2,800 civilians were executed by Viet Cong firing squads and were buried in mass graves. The victims included several of my relatives and friends. My questions about this terrible event were answered with saddened silence in Hue, although Nguyen Van Dieu, the director of foreign affairs of the Binh Tri Thien People's Committee, gave me a commemorative history of the battle in which Le Minh, the commander of the communist forces attacking Hue, admitted that his troops had committed atrocities.

"We were unable to control brutal actions by individual soldiers," Le Minh wrote. "The leaders, including myself, must bear the responsibility."

Before this tragedy Tet, the Vietnamese New Year—a movable feast occurring at the new moon between the winter solstice and the spring equinox—was the most joyful of occasions. Tet is everyone's birthday, the holiday of holidays, an occasion to meditate on the past, to enjoy the present, and to contemplate the future. It embodies the entire spectrum of Vietnamese mythology and religion, the whole concept of man and woman and their relationship to the dead and the living and the spirits.

Every year at Tet, wherever I live, I remember the most memorable Tet of my life, that of 1937, the Year of the Buffalo. I was 14 then, on the verge of leaving home to enter Quoc Hoc School. After the end-of-the-year dinner, during which we invited our dead ancestors back to join us for a week of celebration and reunion, my father, a Confucian scholar who had withdrawn from the "dusty world of things which disturb the ears and offend the eyes," cast horoscopes for every member of our family.

Father paid special attention to my horoscope, noting that the star of literary achievement, *Van Xuong,* was shining from the *thien di* (foreign travels) position directly upon my *menh,* or fate. He predicted that I would be a literary man who would enjoy a greater reputation abroad than at home. "You will also spend some years in the army," Father said. "The *Vu Khuc* [military star] is also in the direction of your *than* [physical being]."

A heavy silence followed this pronouncement. I am descended from generations of literary men and civil servants, and in the hierarchy of traditional Vietnamese values the scholar ranks highest and the soldier lowest. My mother grasped my hands and said, "I know, with these long fingers, that you can be only a scholar, never a soldier."

But my father's predictions mostly held true. While I was a student in Hue, politics and patriotism claimed me, and in 1945 I volunteered for service in the Vietminh—the League for the Independence of Vietnam—in the war of liberation against the French. Some prophecies remain to be fulfilled: Although I became an American citizen and have lived abroad for many years, I have never become a famous literary figure.

The day I left Hue last fall, I got up earlier than usual and tiptoed to the balcony of my hotel room to have a farewell look at the sleeping city. A crescent moon, delicate as a girl's eyebrow, glowed above the shadowy blue Imperial Screen Mountain. On the inky surface of the River of Perfumes an almost invisible lone light was moving northward. A hardworking fisherman going out for his first catch? A drunken poet going home on a pleasure sampan? A cool breeze sent ripples across the shining water.

Slowly the thread of the reddish dawn was drawn across the horizon. From afar the bells of Thien Mu were tolling. I thought of home, of my adopted country, the United States of America, a giant across the Pacific Ocean into which the River of Perfumes also flows. How profoundly different our two societies are! In Vietnam a person lives, works, suffers, succeeds, sacrifices not for the self but for the home, the nuclear family, the extended family including the dead and the unborn, for the village, for the nation. These unbreakable strands form the web of relations that define one's place in society.

In the United States every grown-up is on his or her own. The United States is the most open society in the world. It is the greatest show on earth, a huge public theater where everybody speaks out and acts out an intensely individual fate. In the United States one sometimes feels lonely. In Vietnam one is never left alone to be lonely.

Regardless of these differences and despite the grievous wounds of war, I hope that the two countries can live together in peace.

All things seem possible when one is in Hue. Optimism is a tradition there. During the war against the French, because of the scorched-earth policy practiced by both sides, the countryside around Hue was desolated. A poet sighed:

> *There is not even one tree left on the Imperial Screen Mountain:*
> *The lonely bird sleeps on the bare cold earth.*

This note of pessimism and despair by an intellectual was quickly challenged by a *ca dao*—folk song—of the common people:

> *Here is the river, there is the mountain:*
> *They are still the same.*
> *Our land is as beautiful as brocade,*
> *Why then worry, my love?*
> *Right now, we are going to rebuild our future,*
> *To provide a tree for the bird and a sampan*
> *For you to cross the River.*

NOVEMBER 1989

"SOME MISSED THEIR CHANCE"

MAYNARD OWEN WILLIAMS

One of the welcoming committee at the Paris Conference [soon after the end of World War II] was Mme. Bruninghausen de Harven, whose daughter was about to leave for study in the United States.

"I love America," she said. "We French will never forget the understanding and generosity of your General Bradley in letting Leclerc enter Paris first."

"Nor will we," I answered, "forget that before our soldiers entered Paris, your patriots had taken over most of the city."

Concerning this psychological basis for present happiness and national pride, I asked, point-blank:

"By the time Paris was free, how many of its people had done their bit?"

"That is hard to say. Some, of course, missed their chance. I remember when we tore up paving blocks to build a barricade. The first stone came hardest. As the hole spread, more and more stones could be loosened at once. Onlookers suddenly became workers. So, despite inertia, the spirit of liberation spread."

FROM "PARIS LIVES AGAIN," DECEMBER 1946

A MINYAN

MAŁGORZATA NIEZABITOWSKA

Lublin, a "Jewish Oxford," was famed throughout Europe for Talmudic and cabalistic learning. It was an important center of Hebrew printing. One of the first *yeshivas* in Poland was established here early in the 16th century. In 1939 some 40,000 Jews lived in Lublin. More than four decades later I have come to Lublin to find ten, a *minyan*, the number of males aged 13 and above required by Jewish law to form a quorum for prayer.

The doors of the prayerhouse are closed and secured with two padlocks. Matys Zoberman, the *shammes* (sexton) and the leader of the Lublin Jewish community, opens them with some difficulty. He is old and ailing, and these are serious padlocks, rusty and seldom used. Jews gather here for prayers on only the most important holidays. "Rosh Hashanah, Yom Kippur, Simchas Torah, Pesach [Passover], Shavuos"—Zoberman counts them off on his fingers.

The room is vast and almost bare—an old coat rack on one wall, benches falling apart along another. It takes me a moment to pick out the small pulpit, covered with faded material, near the window. A Star of David is embroidered at the top. Nearby stands a long simple table, with shelves full of books behind it. Some have beautiful, richly imprinted bindings, but they lie in disorder, jumbled and dusty. On the other side of the pulpit stands a plain, crooked cabinet. "That is *aron ha kodesh*, the sacred repository," Zoberman explains. "We have two Torahs."

Zoberman lives in Lubartów, 15 miles from Lublin. Before the war Lubartów was a Jewish town, but now only he is left, the last one. He has passed through many camps. He has worked in quarries, in mines, and in munitions factories. He has seen tens of thousands of Jews go to their deaths.

Three years ago, after the death of the previous president, he was elected head of the Jewish community. He did not want the job. "I am a simple man," he explains with an embarrassed smile. "But they asked and insisted. 'You don't have anything else to do,' they said, 'or any family.'

"There's no money, there's no strength, there are no people...." The old man shakes his head in resignation.

"But once?" I ask.

"Ah, once...." His face brightens for a moment. "Fifteen or so years back there were 20 or 30 of us for prayers. We came every Saturday. There was a kosher cafeteria, and Jews lived in the rooms across the hall. Then they left, they died. There were fewer and fewer of us, fewer...."

"How many of you are there today?"

"A handful."

"But do you still have a minyan?"

"For the important holidays, everybody comes. They come from other places, from Włodawa, from Łuków, from Siedlce. And so a minyan somehow gathers."

"Who belongs to your minyan?"

Zoberman, who has been pleasant, even warm until now, suddenly stiffens. For a moment the old man looks at me in silence.

Then he says harshly: "I won't tell you. You can find them on your own."

FROM "REMNANTS: THE LAST JEWS OF POLAND,"
SEPTEMBER 1986

TO HEAL A NATION

JOEL L. SWERDLOW

For these GIs, coming home had not been like John Wayne had promised. They had gone to Vietnam filled with images of John F. Kennedy and Hollywood movies, and they did their duty, even though few of these images matched the muck and the moral confusion they found in Indochina. After 12 months they were put on an air-conditioned airplane with pretty stewardesses, and suddenly the war was over. "Wash up," one returning veteran's mother had said. "Your welcome-home dinner is ready." He looked down at his hands. Mud from Vietnam was still under his fingernails.

No one wanted to hear what the vets had been through. People who saw them in uniform might spit, shout "Murderer," or ask, "How come you were stupid enough to go?" Or, if you'd arrived home blind or missing an arm or a leg, someone might come up and say, "Served you right."

Thus, many vets carried powerful and disturbing feelings that were buried deeper and deeper as the war became old news to other Americans.

For Jan Scruggs—wounded and decorated for bravery when only 19 years old in 1969—the feelings surfaced in March 1979 after he saw *The Deer Hunter*, an emotional movie about combat in Vietnam. "I'm going to build a memorial to all the guys who served in Vietnam," Scruggs told his wife. "It'll have the names of everyone killed."

Scruggs soon afterward presented his dream to a meeting of Vietnam vets. "We'll accept no money from the government," the son of a milkman from rural Maryland said. "Dollars will come in from the American people." You're naive, they told him. The country will never go for it.

At a press conference Scruggs explained that the Vietnam veteran could be honored without taking a position on the war, that the warrior could be separated from the war. He was enthusiastic and not embarrassed to let his feelings show. "The only thing we're worried about," he concluded, "is raising too much money."

Money did start coming in. Five dollars from an unemployed vet. Ten dollars from a young girl in memory of her father. One check came with only a torn piece of paper carrying the name of a dead GI. "All we want is for people to recognize the sacrifices and contributions they made because the country they love told them it was right," one man wrote.

On the CBS Evening News, Roger Mudd reported that the veterans organization whose only concern had been about raising too much money had gathered the grand sum of $144.50.

Later, a comedian on a network program made fun of Scruggs. It was a good joke, and the audience laughed.

Two other Vietnam vets were not laughing. Robert Doubek and John Wheeler, both attorneys in Washington, D.C., had begun working with Scruggs. Calls went out, and Bob Doubek and Jack Wheeler had no difficulty recruiting a group, organized into the nonprofit Vietnam Veterans Memorial Fund, willing to volunteer thousands of hours at no pay.

A *Washington Post* article by Scruggs placed the VVMF's motives clearly on the public record: "If the war was unpopular at home, it was probably liked even less by those whose fate it was to serve in Vietnam. It was a year-long nightmare. Half the men in my company were killed or wounded. . . . A few months before leaving Vietnam I spent four hours of my life 50 feet from a North Vietnamese machine-gun emplacement. A dozen American youths were pinned down; several were wounded. . . . One fellow exposed himself to the enemy gunners and drew their fire. . . . Then came his screams. . . . We knew we were watching the man who had given his life for us die. . . .

"The bitterness I feel when I remember carrying the lifeless bodies of close friends through the mire of Vietnam will probably never subside. I still wonder if anything can be found to bring any purpose to all the suffering and death."

In September, Doubek, Wheeler, and Scruggs met with Senator Charles McC. Mathias, Jr. (R-Md.), whom Scruggs had recruited to their cause, and a National Park Service official, who spread out a map of the Washington metropolitan area.

Mathias put his thumb on the map. "How about this?" he said.

Wheeler and Doubek looked down. Mathias's thumb was on the Mall, right next to the Lincoln Memorial.

The vets formed a National Sponsoring Committee—which included First Lady Rosalynn Carter, former President Gerald Ford, Gen. William Westmoreland, and Senator George McGovern—and mailed out a fundraising appeal signed by Bob Hope. Tens of thousands of dollars came back, but response to the Hope letter mostly showed how much the memorial was needed:

"My son was killed, and I can't bring it up during a party."

"I did not expect a ticker tape parade, but I served my country faithfully."

"I hope the monument will be built in my lifetime."

"For my son, so he can ask the questions I'll never be able to answer."

"Look at the sheer whimsy of it all. They are dead. I am not."

"Anyone who died in that fiasco is a hero in my eyes."

"Our son did not come home to us."

"Those boys, God bless, were given a *rotten* deal."

Not everyone loved the idea. "To me you are a bunch of crying babies," a man wrote. At the meeting of one government agency, a military officer had even asked, in effect, "Why build a memorial to losers?"

The chief source of potential opposition seemed to be the antiwar movement. "Let's not perpetuate the memory of such dishonorable events by erecting monuments to them," one person wrote. A reporter telephoned Scruggs, and from his questions made clear his antiwar views. "You're real egomaniacs," the reporter finally said. "You're building a memorial to yourselves."

Sensitive to the emotional minefield they were entering, Jack Wheeler warned his colleagues to take no political position and to express no opinions on Vietnam-related subjects. The stakes were far greater than simply building a memorial. "We have become," he said, "trustees of a portion of the national heart."

The site next to Lincoln was perfect. To leave site selection in the hands of an official such as the Secretary of the Interior, however, could mean an out-of-the-way location. The only way to get their land near Lincoln was to get Congress to give it directly to them. If the Vietnam Veterans Memorial was to help bind the nation's wounds, what better place could there be?

Hearings before a Senate subcommittee were scheduled for March 12, 1980. Jan Scruggs with a suitcase full of documents justifying the site on the Mall was in his car, and he couldn't find a parking place. He pulled into a parking lot reserved for senators.

"Listen," Scruggs told the guard, "I've got to testify for the Vietnam memorial. Hearings start in seven minutes."

"Third Marines. Two tours," the guard said, motioning Scruggs into a senator's parking slot.

Congress was doing little for Vietnam vets, yet many senators supported the VVMF because it was asking for land and not tax dollars. The VVMF, with little public attention, soon had 95 Senate cosponsors. Scruggs called the remaining five. "We have 99 cosponsors," he told each. "The Associated Press wants to know who the holdout is." Within hours 100 Senators, the entire U.S. Senate, had signed up.

The bill, giving the vets two acres at the foot of Abraham Lincoln, passed the Senate in just seven minutes on April 30, 1980, but procedural difficulties in the House of Representatives delayed final action until after Memorial Day.

The VVMF, however, still held services at the site. About 400 people attended. Couples held hands or hugged children, and former GIs wearing jungle fatigues or ribbons pinned on business suits stood in tight clusters, as though sheer body proximity helped them share their emotions. Jack Wheeler stepped to the microphone. "There's no more sacred part of a person than his or her name," he said. "We have to start remembering real, individual names."

Members of the audience came up, one by one, to say the name of someone they had lost. My son. My husband. My father. My fiancé. My buddy. My brother. My childhood friend. My classmate. We still love them. We remember.

On July 1, 1980, President Jimmy Carter signed the bill into law. The vets had their land. George Washington, Thomas Jefferson, and Abraham Lincoln would have new neighbors: every GI who served in America's most hated war.

The vets spent considerable time arguing about how best to get their design. Jan Scruggs found the whole issue boring. "Let's put the names on the Mall and call it a day," he said. Finally the VVMF decided to recruit a world-class jury that would, in turn, prompt the nation's best designers to submit entries. Any U.S. citizen 18 or older would be eligible to compete. Bob Doubek wrote out the basic philosophy behind the competition: "Because of inequities in the draft system, the brunt of dangerous service fell upon the young, often the socially and economically disadvantaged. [However] the memorial will make no political statement regarding the war or its conduct. It will transcend those issues. The hope is that the creation of the memorial will begin a healing process."

When the March 31, 1981, deadline arrived, the VVMF had received 1,421 entries. One came from a Yale student who had been given a classroom assignment to design a Vietnam veterans memorial. In late November she and three classmates had driven to Washington to examine the site. It was a cold, clear day, and the only other people nearby were a few Frisbee players. After several minutes she decided that the earth should be cut open, with stone exposed in the wound as part of the healing process. She also thought about death. To her, it was an abstract concept. She was 20 years old, and no one close to her had ever died.

Back at school it took less than three weeks to complete her design, which she saw as "visual poetry."

To help draw attention to the memorial, a former infantryman and a former paratrooper walked 818 miles from Jacksonville, Illinois, to Washington. At the Ohio-Indiana border they were joined by a man who said, "My wife and I want to see our son's name on the monument."

On April 26, about 150 people, including vets on crutches and in wheelchairs, joined the walkers as they crossed the Potomac River. "It would have been nice to have a bigger reception for those guys," Scruggs told reporters waiting at the memorial site. "Well, maybe the Americans killed in Vietnam don't mean that much to a lot of people."

The next day the design jury began four days of closed-door deliberations. The proposed memorials came in all shapes, including hovering helicopters, miniature Lincoln Memorials, peace signs, and Army helmets.

After the first day a juror bumped into a friend in a hotel lobby.

"How's it going?" the friend asked.

"Very strange. One design keeps haunting me."

By noon the next day 1,189 submissions had been eliminated. The remaining 232 were placed together for further examination. That evening the juror once again saw his friend. The juror shook his head. "It's still haunting me," he said.

On the third day the jury was down to 39 entries. Number 1,026 generated the most comments: "There's no escape from its power." "A confused age needs a simple solution." "Totally eloquent." "No other place in the world like that." "Looks back to death and forward to life." "Note the reflectiveness."

"Presents both solitude and a challenge." "It's easy to love it."

After 1,026 won unanimously, the jurors voted again just to make sure. 1,026. The next day Doubek looked up number 1,026. They had expected that the winner would be a prominent professional. "Maya Ying Lin." A woman. An Oriental name. Jack Wheeler recognized her address. An undergraduate residence at Yale University.

Press reaction to the design was enthusiastic. The *New York Times* said: "[It] honors these veterans with more poignancy, surely, than most more conventional monuments. . . . This design seems able to capture all of the feelings of ambiguity and anguish that the Vietnam War evoked in this nation."

The Commission of Fine Arts and other government agencies approved Maya Lin's design, and within weeks the American people started to register their opinion. Fund-raising flourished. Another Bob Hope letter—which read, "It is our duty now to show these veterans (who have yet to receive public recognition) that you and I personally care"—brought in daily sacks of mail.

A radiothon at a shopping center was quickly mobbed. Vets and their families stopped by to tell their stories. Former POWs came to plead for funds. Fathers brought in their children to give small change. People signed over Social Security and disability checks. Nonvets came in with grocery bags filled with cash they'd collected at parties. Radiothon organizers had said at 3 p.m. Friday that they'd be happy with $35,000; by 6 p.m. Sunday, they had $250,000. "What *is* going on out there?" a reporter asked Scruggs. He could only answer, "Hooray, America."

Then, on October 13, a Vietnam vet appeared before the Commission of Fine Arts and called Maya Lin's design a "black gash of shame." He had hit a nerve. The design was hard to understand, and journalists propelled anti-memorial accusations—most notably that it was unheroic, unpatriotic, below ground, and death-oriented—into a civil war among vets. VVMF reassurances that the memorial would be exposed to sunlight all day, and that the names as displayed in Maya Lin's design would speak eloquently of sacrifice, commitment, and patriotism, never attracted as much attention as the attacks.

On January 4, 1982, even though more than 650,000 people had contributed more than five million dollars to build Maya Lin's design, a letter from Secretary of the Interior James Watt arrived. The memorial would not get a construction permit and was on hold until further notice.

That night Scruggs went to the site, and walked over to the Lincoln Memorial. Scruggs looked up at Lincoln. Was the dream about to die? The Civil War had been America's bloodiest conflict, and yet the memorial carried no sense of violence. It was nonpolitical. Nothing favored the North or the South. Nothing said that slavery was morally wrong. Or that the Civil War was right. Like Maya Lin's design, it provided a sense of history, it was simple, and it relied on words. People would read Lincoln's Gettysburg Address and Second Inaugural Address, think about the words, stand quietly, and let the feelings flow. They could come away different than when they arrived.

The memorial would be built. Let the American people come with their children. Let the children ask tough questions. Who are these names? What did they do? Why did they die? Did you know them? What does it mean to me?

After several lengthy, emotional meetings, a compromise was reached: A flag and a representational statue would be added, and opponents would withdraw their objections. The sculptor eventually selected, 38-year-old Washingtonian Frederick Hart, had been the highest placing sculptor in the original competition. Hart's selection symbolized how the country was pulling together. The wall and statue would come from a woman too young to have experienced the war and a man who never served in the military and said he had been gassed in an antiwar demonstration.

At 11 a.m. on Monday, March 15, Secretary Watt authorized a permit. As concrete pilings were driven 35 feet into the ground, workmen in Barre, Vermont, used massive, high-speed, diamond-tipped saws to cut 3,000 cubic feet of granite into slices that were polished first by a series of bricks and then by a felt buffer covered with tin oxide, which is finer than talc.

Guided by computer-generated drawings, workers then fabricated the stone, cutting it into about 150 panels, each of them three inches thick, 40 inches wide, and varying in height from ten feet nine inches to 18 inches.

Shipped on specially air-cushioned trucks to Memphis, Tennessee, the stone was cleaned, painted with chemicals, and allowed to dry overnight. It was covered with a photo negative that was an exact stencil of the names in the order in which they would appear on the wall; then it was exposed to light, left for a short time, washed, and gritblasted. Experiment revealed that cutting letters into the stone one-fiftieth of an inch deep made them cast too heavy a shadow. Even a small error could spoil the memorial.

Architect Kent Cooper, hired by the VVMF to develop Maya Lin's design, made the final decisions: To maximize legibility, use very fine grit, do the blasting straight in front, and stand about 18 inches away so the letters will have maximum depth with uniform shadow. The letters would be .53 inches high and .015 inches deep.

Bob Doubek supervised compilation of the names. Many cases were heartbreaking. Veterans had been slowly dying from war-related causes for years. Some of them were in comas. Some had died in training or while on their way to Indochina. At least one former POW had committed suicide shortly after he returned home.

Who should go on the wall? The VVMF could only rely on the Department of Defense: If the Pentagon, acting in accordance with presidential directives specifying Vietnam, Laos, Cambodia, and coastal areas as combat zones, listed an individual as a fatality or as missing in action, his name would be included. Heartbreak notwithstanding, nothing could be done about the rest.

The names were also at the center of a dispute between Maya Lin and the vets. Her design called for names to be listed in the order of the day they died. She argued that this was essential to her design. The wall, she said, would read like an epic Greek poem. Vets could find their story told, and their friends remembered, in the panel that corresponded to their tour of duty. Locating specific names, with the aid of a directory, would be like finding bodies on a battlefield.

Some vets initially disagreed. If nearly 60,000 names were scattered along the wall, anyone looking for a specific name would wander around for hours and leave in frustration. One solution seemed obvious: List everyone in alphabetical order.

But when the vets examined a two-inch-thick Defense Department listing of Vietnam fatalities, their thinking changed. There were over 600 Smiths; 16 people named James Jones had died in Vietnam. Alphabetical listing would make the memorial look like a telephone book engraved in granite, destroying the sense of profound, unique loss each name carried.

The vets admitted Maya Lin was right.

On September 20, 1982, sculptor Frederick Hart pulled back a tarpaulin covering a 14-inch-high model of his statue. "One senses the figures as passing by the tree line and, caught in the presence of the wall, turning to gaze upon it almost as a vision," he told reporters. "There is about them the physical contact and sense of unity that bespeaks the bonds of love and sacrifice that is the nature of men at war. And yet they are each alone."

To the vets, the statue looked true. Boonie hat. Facial expressions. Fatigues. Helmet. Dog tags in a boot. Way of holding weapons. The men were strong, yet vulnerable. Committed, yet confused. Wheeler told reporters that the sons and daughters of men killed in Vietnam would look at the statue and say, "This is my father. I never saw him alive. But he wore those clothes. He carried that weapon. He was young. I see now, and know him better."

As construction of the wall was rushed to meet the deadline set by the upcoming Veterans Day weekend ceremonies, many people simply stood outside the eight-foot construction fence waiting for a glimpse. Construction workers usually let family members and vets inside. An older man found his son's name, and stood there, clear-eyed and staring. But when he recognized nearby names, people his son had mentioned in letters, the man started to sob.

Most people did something unexpected. They touched the stone. Even young children reached up to fathers and uncles they had never known. The touches were gentle, filled with feeling, as if the stone were alive.

A Navy pilot in uniform brought with him a Purple Heart. "It belonged to my brother," he explained. "He and I flew together. I'd like to put it with the concrete that's being poured."

The pilot saluted as the medal disappeared into the wall.

October brought government approval of the statue, as vets and their families from all over the country began streaming into Washington for dedication of the memorial. One vet walked 3,000 miles. Another sold his household appliances for airfare. Groups checked out of VA hospitals. And in the Midwest a couple heard about the upcoming ceremony on TV, finished dinner, cleared the table, got in the car, and started driving.

"It was," reported a newspaper in Beaumont, Texas, "as if they were all drawn by the same ghostly bugle."

For weeks, volunteers had been practicing reading names for a 56-hour vigil during which every name on the wall would be read in a chapel at the National Cathedral in Washington.

The hardest part was preparing not to cry. Pronunciation was also a problem, and a Polish priest, a Spanish teacher, and a rabbi supplied expert advice.

"Rhythmic Spanish names. Tongue-twisting Polish names, guttural German, exotic African, homely Anglo-Saxon names," wrote *Newsweek* editor-in-chief William Broyles, Jr., who served in Vietnam as a Marine infantry lieutenant. "The war was about names, each name a special human being who never came home."

When you lost a son in Vietnam, you did everything you could to never forget anything about him. You made yourself remember conversations and scenes over and over again. You studied family photographs. You climbed to the attic and opened the cedar chest in which he'd stored his things. You touched the American flag that had come home with him.

So much had been taken from you, so you clung to the one thing they could never take away, something that had been with you since the joy of his birth: his name.

The names were read in alphabetical order, from Gerald L. Aadland of Sisseton, South Dakota, to David L. Zywicke of Manitowoc, Wisconsin. Each name was like a bell tolling. As it was read aloud in the chapel, each ripped into the heart, into old wounds that could heal only after they had been reopened.

Time slots when names would be read were announced, so their sound could reach across America to people who loved them.

In Oklahoma, for example, at the exact moment her son's name was being said out loud, a woman stopped feeding her chickens and whispered a prayer.

A Congressional Medal of Honor winner who had volunteered to read names lasted five minutes before he broke down. He read the rest of the names on his knees.

With more than 150,000 people in town for the dedication, Washington's hotels, restaurants, and streets filled with vets. It was, said one happy ex-GI, "one helluva party."

After many beers, a vet said he had won the Medal of Honor but was afraid of how people would react. To the cheers of a crowded bar, he opened his suitcase, took out the medal with its blue ribbon, and put it on for the first time. A man in a wheelchair slowly pushed through another bar that was filled to capacity. At first no one noticed him. Slowly, the noise faded, and then people reached out to touch him. A former medic sat in a corner, crying. He pushed away all who tried to console him. "I should have saved more," he kept saying. "I should have saved more ."

Another ex-medic was walking down the sidewalk when a man grabbed him.

"You remember me?" the man said.

"No," the medic replied.

"Well, I was shot up pretty bad. Take a close look."

"Sorry, brother, I still don't know you."

"Well, I remember *you*, man. You saved my ass. Thanks."

The vets, along with the American public, discovered the wall.

At night, they used matches, cigarette lighters, and torches made from rolled newspapers to find names. Volunteers stayed until dawn passing out flashlights. One father struck match after match, and then said to his wife, in a hushed voice, "There's Billy."

On Saturday, November 13, Vietnam vets marched down Constitution Avenue to the memorial in one of the largest processions the nation's capital had seen since John F. Kennedy's funeral.

Following speeches by dignitaries, the crowd sang "God Bless America," and paused for a moment of silence. "Ladies and gentlemen," Jan Scruggs said, "the Vietnam Veterans Memorial is now dedicated."

The tightly packed mass surged forward, crushing fences erected for crowd control. As thousands of hands strained to touch names, a lone GI climbed to the top of the wall, put a bugle to his lips, and played taps, slowly. Between each note people seemed frozen, stunned by emotion. Nearby, another vet thrust a sign into the ground. "Honor the dead, fight like hell for the living," it said.

All afternoon, all night, the next day and the next and the next for an unbroken stream of months and years, millions of Americans have come and experienced that frozen moment.

The names have a power, a life, all their own. Even on the coldest days, sunlight makes them warm to the touch. Young men put into the earth, rising out of the earth. You can feel their blood flowing again.

Everyone, including those who knew no one who served in Vietnam, seems to touch the stone. Lips say a name over and over, and then stretch up to kiss it. Fingertips trace letters.

Perhaps by touching, people renew their faith in love and in life; or perhaps they better understand sacrifice and sorrow.

"We're with you," they say. "We will never forget."

MAY 1985

UNTIL THE STOLEN
CHILDREN DIE

JOHN J. PUTMAN

With time, memories of Argentina's dirty war [against mostly youthful terrorists and other opponents of the military government in the late 1970s] are fading, civil rights lawyer Ramón Torres Molina told me. "It is known that 10,000 persons disappeared. Some estimate 30,000. Only 20, more or less, have been identified, discovered in a cemetery in La Boca, down by the river." Ramón himself had been jailed for seven years. Ramón survived; other stories are not yet ended. In an old-fashioned office on Avenida Corrientes, a wallboard holds scores of photographs of young women—smiling, some pretty, all now dead, murdered. It is the office of the Grandmothers of the Plaza de Mayo.

Some of the young women in the photographs had small children with them when arrested during the dirty war; others gave birth while in jail. In time the women were killed and their children taken by the jailers or given to friends or sympathizers of the regime.

"They took the child from my daughter five hours after it was born," said Estela Carlotto, chairwoman of the Grandmothers. "She never saw it again. My daughter was killed two months later. They gave me her body, but they never gave me the child, and I am still searching. He would be 15 years old.

"We believe the number of stolen children may be 500. We are determined to find them."

A genetic bank has been established: Relatives of stolen children can have their blood analyzed there and stored for future DNA fingerprinting, to establish that a child belongs to one family and not to another.

"The blood will be kept until the year 2050," said Mrs. Carlotto, "until the last of the stolen children has probably died."

On my last night in Buenos Aires, I went to a tango bar. The dance and songs, invented here in the last century, are popular again; there are scores of clubs going. I chose a club down one of those crumbling little streets in the San Telmo district. It held no more than 40 customers and was so tiny and so jammed that it seemed as if everything took place in your lap.

"I was deceived," a woman sang. "Now I sing tango. I sell caresses, and I sell love to forget the man who deceived me."

The owner and the singer, both portly, danced belly to belly, she sliding around him gracefully, he sweating. The musicians, a pianist and an accordion player, were Uruguayans from across the river. The pianist wore rubber boots; it had rained that day. Members of an engagement party called out for favorite tangos: *"Gira!" "A Media Luz!" "Caminito!"*

Twice a male singer came in from the street, his hair black-dyed and combed back, his head large, the eyes far apart. The writer Jorge Luis Borges had called this city a labyrinth; if so, here was a Minotaur for that labyrinth. The man sang: "You see that everything is a lie. Never expect anyone to help you, never expect a favor." The crowd sang along, nodding.

It was early morning when I left the club. The streets were empty, the taxi moving fast, other clubs still full. In Buenos Aires the night does not end until dawn.

FROM "BUENOS AIRES—MAKING UP FOR LOST TIME,"
DECEMBER 1994

NATURE ITSELF

WAR AND PEACE
IN A CORAL KINGDOM

PETER BENCHLEY

As we dove through 40 feet, then 50, then 60 feet of silty waters that seemed like tepid shampoo, we could see her lying on her side like a mortally wounded bird come to final rest on a coral slope. One of her wings was fractured, one of her engines gone. Had the engine been blown away by fighter fire? Was its loss the cause of her fall from the tropical sky more than 40 years ago?

She was a B-25, a workhorse of World War II in the Pacific, and my imagination did not have far to stretch to see her ready to fight again. Twin .50-caliber machine guns were poised to fire from her shattered nose, their racks of bullets still stacked and ready though yellow now with growths of coral and algae, patched here and there with red gorgonian coral. The radio direction finder was still mounted, bomb-shaped, on the top of the fuselage, though it had become the home of two giant razor clams whose eely mantles recoiled from my touch.

The cockpit escape hatch was open, slid back as it had been on the August day in 1943 when the pilot pancaked his bomber onto the Bismarck Sea in this narrow strait between Wongat Island and mainland New Guinea. I floated into the pilot's seat and pressed my flippered feet against the rudder pedals and wrapped my fingers around the coral-encrusted controls and gazed through the murk at the windshield. I tried to feel what the hapless crew must have felt on that awful day.

One American had died in the crash—the top turret gunner. The captain (The "old man"! How old had he been? Twenty? Twenty-one?) and the rest of the crew had swum to Wongat Island. There the Japanese captured them. They shipped the command pilot to a prison camp on Rabaul. But the fate of the other men is unknown.

Their epitaphs were stark words in dispatches: "Last seen between Bona Bona and Dumpu . . . Lost at sea near Buna . . . Burning out of control over Madang."

I began to have the uncomfortable sensation that I was sitting inside a coffin.

But then a parrot fish darted in front of me and gnawed happily on the coral crust on a machine-gun barrel. Two angelfish fluttered out of the darkness of the bomb bay behind me. A translucent shrimp traversed the rusty face of the altimeter gauge.

I realized then that death had not prevailed here for decades. Almost as soon as the B-25 had died, the sea had begun to give it a new life, and now what had once been an engine of war was a living monument to the endurance of nature. The plane had become a reef, a festive garden home for thousands of creatures.

Purple sea fans grew from the tail rudder and waved in the current's surge; feather-duster worms, anchored to the steel skin of the plane, spread their leafy feeding arms and gleaned plankton from the green mist; crabs scuttled through the deep silt in the belly of the plane, shouldering aside bullets that the shifting sands had polished to mint newness.

I rose from the cockpit and hovered above the plane, and the current eased me up and away. Within seconds contours of the B-25 blurred, and in a minute it was gone, last seen in eerie resurrection from its grave ten fathoms beneath the Bismarck Sea.

We had set out from Madang on the north coast of Papua New Guinea— photographer David Doubilet, Australian naturalists and photographers Ron and Valerie Taylor, and I—in search of the lost and the never-known. The roughly 20,000 square miles of the Bismarck Sea are a contradiction wrapped in a curiosity. In the early years of the war the waters off eastern New Guinea were among the most active, most tumultuous, most violent on the planet. Hundreds of ships and planes were lost; thousands of men died here and in the battles for Guadalcanal in the Solomons and Rabaul on New Britain. And yet as soon as the war was over, the Bismarck Sea was all but forgotten.

The names of its islands (Palitolla, Baluan, Wuvulu) ring with exotic musicality, stirring dreams of fancied paradise—dreams that conveniently ignore the grimmer realities of illiteracy, endemic diseases, and an infant mortality rate so high that many children are not named until they have survived for at least a year.

Much of the area has never been dived by human beings, yet some of it is already being destroyed by men who trade away their natural heritage for dynamite and beer.

For the most part, it remains a sea of Eden, placid, too close to the Equator to be frequently storm torn, populated by animals who have never seen man. But it is also a sea seething with natural violence and sudden dangers, in which some of the inhabitants—thousands of species live in these waters— can kill a man with a single touch, some with a single taste.

Sailing from Madang aboard the Taylors' 57-foot *Reef Explorer*, we crossed the Isumrud Strait and headed north for the volcanic peaks of Bagabag and Karkar. Like many of the islands in the Bismarck Archipelago, Bagabag and Karkar reflect cultural hybridism: Bagabag is the local name for the island, for example, but its two bays are named Christmas and New Year, for the holidays on which English and Dutch explorers first anchored there in the 17th century. The Germans named the sea for their chancellor Otto von Bismarck, when they annexed the islands in 1884.

We dropped anchor in New Year Bay and gazed at the emerald rain forest that soared high into the perpetual cloud cover caused by the heat rising from the dot of land into the sea air. On the shore was a small cluster of thatched huts—the homes of Bagabag's community of copra workers.

Our first dive was in the Isumrud Strait, and for a moment we feared it might be our last. The current raced between the islands at an indomitable 2.5 knots. The only way we could keep from being swept through the strait and into the open sea was to moor ourselves to rocks and crawl along the bottom hand over hand. What was an obstacle for us air-breathing land creatures, however, provided a cornucopia for the reef residents. They did not have to hunt. They hung steady in the strong current and let their food come to them.

As I clung to a pumpkin-size brain coral, I was greeted by a phalanx of huge green parrot fish, creatures three or four feet long that weigh 50 or 60 pounds, each sporting on its forehead what looked like a radar dome. Known as bumpfish or bumphead parrot fish, these megacephalic monsters paid no attention to me but, on some secret signal from one of their number, lowered their heads to the reef and began to eat coral with their horny beaks, sending through the water a sound reminiscent of hobnailed boots on a gravel driveway.

A speckled gray-brown Pacific cuttlefish danced before my mask, its sleepy slit eye making it look like a weary roué. I reached out a hand, expecting it to flee, but it hovered unafraid and permitted me to run a finger along its side—which, as if in indignant comment, changed color instantly to a vivid lavender.

The reef became an explosion of species, a gathering of nature's clans, all of whom came to explore these aliens who had plunged noisily into their neighborhood. Sergeants major and angelfish swarmed around the divers, sensing neither danger nor prey, merely curious.

Three small silvertip sharks rose up the reef face from the violet deep, like a patrol of outriders scouting the borders of their territory. They eyed each diver, as if appraising him as a potential competitor, then moved on. The other reef fish manifested no alarm at the arrival of the sharks and did not scatter or flee, for apparently the sharks had emitted no chemical or electromagnetic advertisements that they had come to feed.

Watching the sharks glide away down the reef, I had the feeling I was being watched. I refocused my eyes onto the brain coral and there saw, peering at me like an impatient hide-and-seek player wondering why he has not been found, a tiny rainbow: a harlequin tusk fish, five or six inches long, with repeating vertical stripes of red, orange, black, and yellow. It looked at me, flicking its pectoral fins just enough to keep it stable, and I looked at it, wondering what kind of cruel joke nature had played on it. Many animals' coloration provides them with camouflage; it seemed to shriek, "Here I am! Eat me!"

I pulled myself closer. The tusk fish shivered once and vanished into the reef. A vast school of iridescent blue fish swooped by, their brilliant yellow tails flashing in the shafts of sunlight that dappled the blue-green water. Valerie told me later that the fish are called fusiliers and that the name probably derives from the blue-and-yellow jackets worn by the fusiliers of some 18th-century colonial power.

"Some fish are very loyal," she said. "Back in the early days I speared a turrin for shark bait. It got off the spear and fluttered down toward a hole in the reef. Another followed it and tried to cover it with its body, to protect it. It flattened itself over the hole where its wounded friend was. But the shark got it. Ron and I swore we'd never spear one of them again."

That evening we dined on New Zealand lamb, and it occurred to me that here we were, anchored atop an endless supply of fresh fish, eating frozen meat transported from 2,000 miles away. I asked Pip Beatty, the statuesque New Zealander who served as the *Reef Explorer*'s cook, which of the local fish she preferred.

"None," she said.

"You don't like any of it?"

"I don't trust any of it. Down on the Barrier Reef we know what has ciguatera and what doesn't. Up here, everything may have it. We had fish once last trip, and the whole crew got hit. Never again."

Ciguatera is a toxin, which can enter the food chain through algae, is then consumed by the small herbivores, then by carnivores, all the way up the chain to the apex predators—you and me. It seems not to affect the fish, but a man who eats a fish carrying ciguatera may suffer—depending on his size, his health, and the amount of fish he eats—everything from flu symptoms to numbness, ferocious itching, violent gastrointestinal cramps, and perhaps even death. Symptoms usually last for several days, but they can then lie dormant and, upon consumption of even a minuscule amount of alcohol, blossom again.

I knew that in the Caribbean the traditional (though unscientific) test for ciguatera in barracuda was to drop a silver coin into the pot with the fish: If the coin tarnished, the fish was ciguatoxic. I asked Valerie if there was any local test.

"Oh yes," she replied. "Here they put the fish out in the sun, and if the flies don't walk on it, they don't eat it."

The lamb was delicious.

From Bagabag Island we sailed to Cape Croisilles and a shipwreck. Local divers believe that the ship was recruited after the war to sweep mines along the Papua New Guinea coast, and broke down one day in 1946. She drifted, helpless, onto the coral cleavers that line the shore. She lies today less than a hundred feet from shore, in 60 to 120 feet of water, a spectral hulk resting upright on the sloping, rocky bottom.

On old maps when describing unknown lands and seas—presumably so as to seem more knowledgeable than they possibly could have been—cartographers would often scrawl, "Here be dragons." On my chart of this area off Madang I scrawled, "Here be villains," for there we found a huge gathering of some of the most venomous fish in any sea.

Lumped together scientifically in the family Scorpaenidae, they are known as scorpionfish, lionfish, and stonefish. Specific locales have dubbed them more dramatically: horrid stonefish, fire scorpionfish, and so on. All have dorsal spines that, when touched, emit a poison virulent enough to cause (at best) discomfort and (at worst) death. The best that can be said about the Scorpaenidae is that they are shy and unaggressive, and many of them are spectacularly visible—with Aubrey Beardsley wings and great flourishing tails.

The worst that can be said about certain varieties—especially about stonefish—is that they are *invisible*. They are called stonefish because, nestled into the rugged contours of the sea bottom where they wait patiently to swallow unwary passersby, they are indistinguishable from mottled rocks.

We had been warned never to wade ashore without wearing heavy-soled shoes, for any misstep, a stagger caused by a breaking wave, could impale a bare foot upon the spines of a buried stonefish.

One day Valerie beckoned me to a small cave on which she was focusing her camera. I peered inside and saw nothing. She pointed again. I peered again. Nothing. I reached out to pull myself deeper into the cave . . . and Valerie struck me on the arm with her camera housing. I looked quizzically at her and saw in her eyes an alarmed assumption that she was dealing here with a varsity lunatic.

Cautiously Valerie pushed her camera housing into the cave and touched the rock I had been about to grab. It quivered, showering sand over its scrofulous-looking body, then arched the venomous spines along its back, opened a gash that must have been its mouth, and gazed our way with a dark and baleful eye.

Rivulets of sweat ran down my forehead and fogged the faceplate of my mask.

The water was so warm that several of us scorned heavy neoprene wet suits and dove instead in light Lycra bodysuits. (I, afflicted with chronic clumsiness and an uncanny ability to encounter the one razor-sharp stone, stinging jellyfish, or flesh-rending coral on an otherwise innocuous reef, persisted in wearing neoprene.) That afternoon four Lycra-clad divers went down to photograph a pair of moray eels Valerie had lured out of a cave and was feeding bits of fish.

The divers encircled the mouth of the cave and lay on the bottom on a carpet of gray anemone—no different, they thought, from the scores of other anemones they had encountered on scores of other bottoms. They photographed until the poor eels were strobe-stunned, then came to the surface.

Within half an hour all four divers were in agony. Their arms and legs itched and burned; their fingers swelled so that their hands resembled catchers' mitts; rashes, sores, lumps, and welts rose on their buttocks and bellies. They washed themselves with alcohol, with ammonia, with antiseptics; they smeared themselves with meat tenderizer and cortisone creams. Nothing helped. They suffered for almost a week.

The anemone had contained virulent nematocysts, which had fired into the divers through their Lycra wet suits, injecting them with poison.

For every creature that inspired fear, however, there were a dozen that filled us only with awe. One day I found David Doubilet poised, as usual, motionless before a patch of reef. His focus was a plate of bright green coral, which was home to two small fish—one bright orange and tiny, the other purple and slightly larger—that were feeding off the plankton-rich soup swept in by the strong current.

The fish were pretty but, to an amateur like me, not particularly thrilling. I shrugged. David pointed to his lips, then up at the surface: He would explain later.

"They're called anthiases," he said when we were back on the boat. "The female's the little orange one, the male's the purple one. They're the ultimate survivors."

"What do you mean?"

"One male services a whole crowd of females. If the male dies or disappears, if he's eaten by something . . . ," he paused for effect, "the dominant female will begin a gradual transformation into a male. She'll become a male and will be able to breed with females."

"Come on. You don't exp—"

"Yes!" David smiled. "Nature protects the colony in a wonderful way."

There are said to be a thousand species of corals here, and as we dove off Crown Island, 70 miles east of Madang in the southern Bismarck Sea, I believed it. We came upon a giant patchwork meadow of hard corals that stretched far beyond the limits of our vision. From above it looked like a multicolored political map of a whimsically gerrymandered state. There were squares of orange and circles of green, triangles of yellow and rectangles of blue, splotches of mustard and brown and red and gray that descended deep to the end of life-giving light.

Growing from the rocks amid the corals, looking like alien flowers, were countless varieties of crinoids—feather stars and brittle stars and animals for which I had no name—of every color in the spectrum, that extended their sticky arms to gather microscopic food from the water and pass it back to the mouth hidden in the cradle of the arms.

From the coral walls hung bizarre beings that could have sprung from the mind of Edgar Allan Poe—miniature human hearts, I concluded (ascidian sea squirts, I would learn), yellow with blue veins, blue with white veins, purple with yellow veins. They pumped like human hearts too, taking in the water of the sea through an aortic tube in the side, gleaning its nutrients somewhere in an interior chamber, and expelling the water from a vent at the top.

After a break for lunch we moved to another reef, no more than 200 yards away, to see if it was a twin of the first or if it had its own peculiar character and characters. We found devastation, as if a secret war had been waged on this reef alone. There were no patches of color, no live corals at all, no fish, no worms, no shrimps, no sea cucumbers. The reef was as dead as Mars.

I surfaced behind the boat and found Valerie sitting on the diving platform.

"What is it?" I asked her. "A blight?"

"Yes, a blight," she answered with a bitter smile. "The Japanese want to log these islands. They have to get permission from each village chief to log his part of the island. The chiefs trade away the logging rights for beer and dynamite—and use the dynamite to blast fish to the surface. They think the reefs go on forever. They don't know that when you kill a reef like this, it takes a generation or more for it to come back."

So isolated are the islands from one another, so isolated are the tribes that share the larger islands from one another, that cautionary tales about the long-term destruction wrought by short-term conveniences like dynamite can take years to circulate.

There are said to be more than 700 linguistic groups in Papua New Guinea, and often the people of one village neither speak nor understand the language spoken in the village over the next hill. Pidgin is the common tongue, the passport between tribes. It is a marvelous mélange of English, Australian slang, onomatopoeia, and local lore. The word "piano," for example, is *Big fella bockus, teeth alla same shark, you hitim he cry out*—a big box, with teeth all the same size, and if you hit it, it makes a noise.

Many signs are written in pidgin and English, and it was fun to translate. The pidgin for "Intoxicated persons will not be admitted" is *Spak man ino kumin* ("spak" is a variation on the Australian "spark" or "sparky," slang for being drunk, so the sentence reads, "Spark man he no come in.")

The people of Papua New Guinea may have to struggle to communicate, but the more we dove the more we marveled at the speed and fluency with which marine animals seemed to send messages to each other.

Scientists are just beginning to comprehend the astonishing sophistication of communication between sea creatures. Of course they have long known that whales and dolphins "talk" among each other fluently and constantly, but the remarkable capacities of the brains of the so-called lower animals, the cold-blooded fishes, have been relatively ignored.

On Whirlwind Reefs, a submerged shoal 80 sea miles east of Crown Island, the unheard babble between and among species was lively, frantic, and, at times, deadly.

An enormous school of jacks, so numerous that they cast a solid shadow on the reef, cruised by overhead, swimming routinely, unhurriedly, neither hunting nor being hunted.

Beyond the jacks, in the deep water over the edge of the wall, a school of perhaps 20 or 30 dogtooth tuna—shining silver bullets—swam in the opposite direction.

The two schools would pass safely, like trucks on a turnpike.

Suddenly, faster than the blink of an eye, the entire school of tuna turned *as one*—the sound underwater of the turn was like a shirt tearing—and charged into the cloud of jacks.

In seconds that attack was over. Puffs of blood and shreds of flesh were the only testimony that remained. The tuna re-formed and continued on their way; the jacks—their numbers reduced by a few—resumed their casual cruise along the reef.

Whirlwind Reefs was entirely under eight or ten fathoms of water and miles from the nearest island, so it was possible that the reef had never been fished and probable that no one had ever dived it.

I lay on the bottom and isolated a six-inch square of reef and sought every creature who lived within its boundaries. Because water magnifies objects by approximately 25 percent, I was able to find even infinitesimal tenants of my 36-square-inch preserve.

A hermit crab, no bigger than a match head, plodded across a piece of coral like a palsied pensioner, dragging one leg after another.

A transparent worm, thin as a credit card, undulated out of the sand, its bow searching for something while its stern waited patiently behind. Within the waving arms of a yellow crinoid were two pinhead-size yellow shrimps, probably unique in the world, for I understood that crinoid dwellers adapted themselves to their environment, never left it, and bred only with themselves.

A quizzical blenny, one inch long, poked its head out of a hole in the coral and eyed me, as irritated as an inconvenienced concierge.

A feather-duster worm fed from the flowing water until, sensing the approach of my finger, it snapped its floral feeding machine back inside its tubular apartment.

A mottled pink crab the size of an American nickel crouched on a prong of staghorn coral and pugnaciously waved its claws at me, like a fighter in the early rounds getting the measure of his opponent.

The current was racing over the reef, and I reached out to grab a piece of coral to steady myself. The coral flinched. I yanked back my hand, horrified that the next sensation I would feel might be the searing pain of a stonefish's venom. But it was just a clam that had closed in alarm at the touch of my hand.

Even at night the flurried activity on Whirlwind Reefs didn't cease; it changed. As I lay in my bunk, I heard through the steel hull of the boat a sound like a campfire crackling: Colonies of shrimps were cracking their claws 50 feet beneath my head.

The *Reef Explorer* employed as interpreter, boat boy, and general factotum a young native of Rabaul named Michael. Michael worked to put his brothers and sisters through school, and his salary was sent directly to the school as a means of evading a nationwide custom known as *wantok*, under which an individual has an obligation to the entire community and anyone who asks for anything must be accommodated. The system worked in primitive subsistence societies in which everyone performed a supportive function. But now that people were going away and returning supplied (magically, apparently) with something called money that could produce exotic goods, it had degenerated.

"Some people don't work," Michael said. "Wait for me come home, they ask my money and I have to give it. A man I know drink all his money. Why not? He take it home, someone ask it from him and *he* drink it."

Whenever we arrived at an inhabited island, Michael would inquire in pidgin if the residents knew of any wrecks nearby—ships or planes from World War II. More than 300 American and Australian planes (and an untold number of Japanese aircraft) are still officially listed as missing.

In the Witu Island group we anchored in the volcanic crater of Narage Island. Before the anchor had hit the black sand bottom, a dozen dugout canoes set out from shore, bringing robust men and happy children who delightedly circled the boat, chattering about the pasty-faced strangers who came to swim under the water and had an endless supply of sweet soft drinks and English biscuits.

While Michael jabbered his questions in pidgin, David and I stood on the bow and gazed at the jungle-matted mountainside that rose from the water's edge. Natural hot springs bubbled up amid the dense growth, sending ribbons of steam into the sapphire sky.

There was a Japanese patrol boat here, Michael reported, across the crater in 25 feet of water. Three of the islanders came aboard and, soda pop in hand, guided us to a spot beneath an overhanging jungle canopy.

The patrol boat lay on the bottom, as if it had been scuttled there and had simply settled into a peaceful slip beneath the sea. But it had collapsed upon itself, its iron rusting to oxide. It was no more suggestive of life than the husk of a horseshoe crab bleaching on a beach. And because corals did not grow there in the lava crater, it was creating no new life. The B-25 off Wongat Island had told tales of the past and offered promise for the future; this barren relic spoke only of death.

That evening we moved to the crater of Garove Island, also in the Witu group. A pristine Roman Catholic church sat atop a jungle hill, and we wanted to see it. The boat put us off on a table rock, and we clambered up a six-inch-wide trail on the sheer face of a rock cliff. Easy enough, in daylight.

But by the time we returned from the church, night had fallen. We had a flashlight, and the lights from the boat 30 or 40 feet below cast a helpful glow on the cliff face. But the trail was tiny, and it seemed to disappear every few feet in the shadows of jungle growth that overhung the cliff.

I shone the light on the path for the others to make their way down to the first turn, then started down myself. I had been standing off the path, and to regain it, I put my foot on what appeared to be a patch of grass or moss. It turned out, instead, to be the topmost branch of a tree growing out of the cliff face way beneath me.

I saw my foot disappear.

I flailed out with my hands and grabbed air.

And then I was falling in darkness.

I struck water, feet first, straight as an Olympic diver, and I felt a rush of relief and gratitude. The light vanished. My glasses vanished. My shirt billowed up around my head. I bobbed to the surface.

Now came the blood, seeping, oozing, coursing down my leg from a cut that exposed the bone, and dripping into the night sea.

Bronwyn Stewart, the ship's nurse, hosed me down, shoved me into the shower, and, when I was clean, washed the seven-inch-long wound with a strong astringent, doused it with antibiotics, and bandaged it.

"Your diving is done," she said.

Bronwyn was right: My diving was over. The wound began to heal nicely, but I wasn't willing to expose it to the organic soup that was the Bismarck Sea, where it might become host to things that would feast on it or burrow into it.

On our last morning in the Witu Islands I awoke early and hobbled topside for a cup of coffee. The sun was just beginning to peek over the horizon when I went outside.

There, perched on the rail like expectant ravens, were half a dozen island children. They stared at me in awed silence, the whites of their shiny eyes as large as quails' eggs. Then one of them whispered something, and another giggled, and a third pointed at my bandaged leg, and a fourth made a saucy "hoo-hoo" noise. Then they all laughed and pointed and whistled and cooed.

I laughed, too, and reached into the galley for a tin of biscuits.

We left the Bismarck Sea on a sparkling day, passing through the Dampier Strait to the west of New Britain. We were escorted by a fleet of dolphins and overseen by a squadron of birds. It was hard not to think of other fleets and other squadrons that had passed this way 40-some years ago.

Their bones lay below us now, lost but not forgotten. Like the crew of the B-25 off Madang, never forgotten.

FROM "GHOSTS OF WAR IN THE SOUTH PACIFIC," APRIL 1988

SHARKS

FEEDING FRENZY
Valerie Taylor

My gleaming armor was my husband Ron's idea, inspired by steel-mesh boning gloves worn by knife-wielding butchers. "That material might work against shark teeth as well," he declared. Codeveloper and friend Jeremiah Sullivan, a marine biologist, found a manufacturer in Massachusetts whose craftsmen welded 150,000 stainless-steel rings into a covering weighing some 15 pounds.

We tested the suit off San Diego, California. Lured by fish baits, several blue sharks circled. Eyeing a mackerel in my hand, one closed in. I snatched back the fish and shoved my arm in the shark's gaping mouth. The jaws slammed shut as the shark tore at my elbow, whipping my arm from side to side. I waited for the blood and pain, but there was none. The mesh had defeated the destructive, sawing motion typical of the blue shark's bite.

The suit worked! But those sharks were six-foot blues, far from the sea's largest. We needed to experiment further to know how it would hold up against other species.

We had our chance while diving in the Coral Sea off Australia. An assistant speared a cod to lure sharks into filming range. Half a dozen six-foot gray reef sharks moved in. With bait in hand I swam into a frenzy of snapping jaws and contorted bodies. The sharks were all around me— torpedo shapes, gray against blue—moving faster than my eye could follow.

Suddenly I felt a blow and heard a terrible grating noise. A shark had grabbed me by the face, ripping away my air hose. I turned toward Ron, unable to see because my mask had flooded. Groping to find my mouthpiece, I surfaced, but was too weak. The weight of the suit dragged me down.

Blackness began to overtake me when Ron jammed the mouthpiece in my face. I gulped air and sank down, unable to move, shaken, bruised—but alive.

Back on the boat we examined four neat tooth punctures in my chin. The teeth had pierced the gap where the hood meets the suit. A tiny tip of tooth remains embedded in my jaw, where it will stay as a reminder of the day a shark bit my face.

FROM "A JAWBREAKER FOR SHARKS," MAY 1981

WHITE DEATH

RICHARD ELLIS

I had come to Spencer Gulf, lying between the horse latitudes and the roaring forties at the bottom of the world, in search of the great white shark—the largest flesh-eating fish and one of the most dangerous predators in the world. Though this shark is not common anywhere, it seems relatively plentiful in South Australian waters, and the sea lion is probably the reason. From the scars often seen on the sea lions, we can deduce that the sharks attack them, and that the sea lions escape—sometimes.

For the most part, white sharks do not eat their human victims. But a young woman, bitten in half and devoured off a public beach at Peake Bay by a great white in 1985, provided recent, tragic evidence that this shark does not play by the rules—even its own.

Why then does the great white attack? For many reasons, some of which are still not clearly understood, sharks are sensitive to smell, sound, movement, electrical impulses, and even the magnetic field of the earth. They can also see a lot better than we thought they could. The shark that killed the woman at Peake Bay may have heard the commotion caused by her shallow-water diving and moved in to investigate. Only then did its other faculties come into play.

That we might observe the sharks in their own habitat, we had brought along shark cages—yellow boxes the size of elevator cars made of welded steel mesh. Actually these are man cages. When the cage is in use underwater, the diver is inside and the shark is outside the mesh. Stacked on the deck of our chartered fishing boat, the *Nenad*, the cages looked substantial enough. But how would it feel to be in one underwater, face-to-face with the shark the Australians call "white death"?

In a sense I already knew the answer to this question. En route to view the sea lions, I had asked our skipper, Rodney Fox, why we were going to Hopkins Island instead of heading straight for Dangerous Reef, where white sharks are often to be found. He replied, "Once you see the sharks, you'll never want to go in the water again."

In light of those words Dangerous Reef seemed aptly named. Following Rodney's instructions, we ladled overboard an odoriferous slumgullion of tuna meat, dried blood, fish oils, and other secret ingredients that he guaranteed to be tantalizing to sharks. We hoped that the bloody slick would be carried by tides and currents to a great white, which would then backtrack on the scent to our boat. Then we would descend in the cages.

Our first shark appeared less than five hours after we dumped the chum into the water, but the sea was too rough for diving. The great fish swam around the *Nenad* for almost two days as we fed it four-pound chunks of horsemeat and an occasional 20-pound tuna to whet its interest. On the morning of the third day the gray skies cleared, and we lowered the cages.

Breathing my air supply much faster than I usually do, I tried to see through clouds of tommy roughs—foot-long fish that were also attracted by our blood-and-offal soup. Then the shark appeared. At first I could make out only a vague shadow that appeared in the green distance, but the phantom soon solidified into a gray, cone-nosed mass of muscle, cleaving its way through the tommies and heading straight for my cage.

The shark came steadily, majestically, irresistibly. Without pausing, with perfect efficiency, it opened its mouth and bit one of the steel flotation tanks attached to the cage. The tank may have been the first inedible object the shark had ever encountered. My scientific objectivity vanished. I was only a couple of feet from the most famous jaws in the world, and they were chewing solidly on the cage in which I cowered, my scuba tank clanking noisily against the mesh as I tried to get as far away as I could from this remorseless man-eater.

After the first shock and terror, an unexpected calm came over me. I looked out through the viewing port—a section of the cage, face-mask-high with no bars at all—and saw only the shark and the cloud of tommies. It was as if I were truly a part of the shark's element, and not a clumsy intruder in a cage.

My breathing slowed to something approximating normal rhythm. I was not frightened now but awed. I saw the shark for what it was—a powerful state-of-the-art predator, as modern as the latest jet fighter, but with an ancestry that can be traced back 300 million years. Another shark appeared out of the gloom and circled our bubbling, artificial world. For the first time during this dive, I looked at my watch. I had been down for more than an hour, mesmerized by the physical grace and terrible power of these silent, slack-jawed eaters of seal and sea lions—and other large animals like me.

FROM "AUSTRALIA'S SOUTHERN SEAS," MARCH 1987

THE POLE AT LAST?

Commander Robert E. Peary's claim to have discovered the North Pole in 1909 has been, from the beginning, the subject of dispute and controversy. Here is Peary's exultant report on his achievement to the National Geographic Society, which had supported him with funds. Later, to the satisfaction of Theodore Roosevelt, who doubted the claim of Peary's rival, Dr. Frederick A. Cook, that he, not Peary, was first to the Pole, the Society backed Peary's version of the event. But on the 100th anniversary of the Geographic, with controversy reignited, the magazine commissioned a more recent conqueror of the Pole, Wally Herbert, to look into the evidence. After examining the record in the light of his own experience, Herbert concluded that Peary's moment of triumph may also have been a moment of doubt, and that Peary probably had not reached the Pole.

"MINE AT LAST!"

ROBERT E. PEARY

It was a fine morning. The wind of the last two days had subsided, and the going was the best and most equable of any I had yet. The floes were large and old, hard and clear, and were surrounded by pressure ridges, some of which were almost stupendous. The biggest of them, however, were easily negotiated, either through some crevice or up some huge brink.

I set a good pace for about ten hours. Twenty-five miles took me well beyond the 88th parallel. While I was building my igloos a long lead [open water] formed by the east and southeast of us at a distance of a few miles.

A few hours' sleep and we were on the trail again. As the going was now practically horizontal, we were unhampered and could travel as long as we pleased and sleep as little as we wished. The weather was fine and the going like that of the previous day, except at the beginning, when, when pickaxes were required. This and a brief stop at another lead cut down our distance. But we had made twenty miles in ten hours and were half way to the 89th parallel.

The ice was grinding audibly in every direction, but no motion was visible. Evidently it was settling back in equilibrium and probably sagging due northward with its release from the wind pressure.

Again there was a few hours' sleep, and we hit the trail before midnight. The weather and going were even better. The surface, except as interrupted by infrequent ridges, was as level as the glacial fringe from Hecla to Columbia and harder.

We marched something over ten hours, the dogs being often on the trot, and made 20 miles. Near the end of the march, we rushed across a lead [i.e. open water or thin ice] 100 yards wide, which buckled under our sledges, and finally broke as the last sledge left it.

We stopped in sight of the 89th parallel, in a temperature of 40 degrees below. Again a scant sleep, and we were on our way once more and across the 89th parallel.

This march duplicated the previous one as to weather and going. The last few hours it was on young ice, and occasionally the dogs were galloping. We made 25 miles or more, the air, the sky, and the bitter wind burning the face till it cracked. It was like the great interior ice cap of Greenland. Even the natives complained of the bitter air. It was as keen as frozen steel.

A little longer sleep than the previous ones had to be taken here as we were all in need of it. Then on again.

Up to this time, with each successive march, our fears of an impossible lead had increased. At every inequality of the ice, I found myself hurrying breathlessly forward, fearing that it marked a lead, and when I arrived at the summit would catch my breath with relief—only to find myself hurrying on in the same way at the next one. But on this march, by some strange shift and feeling, this fear fell from me completely. The weather was thick, but it gave me no uneasiness.

Before I turned in I took an observation, which indicated our position as 89.25. A dense, lifeless pall hung overhead. The horizon was black and the ice beneath was a ghastly, shelly-white, with no relief—a striking contrast to the glimmering, sunlit fields of it over which we had been traveling for the previous four days.

The going was even better and there was scarcely any snow on the hard, granular, last summer's surface of the old floes dotted with the sapphire ice of the previous summer's lakes.

A rise in temperature to 15 below reduced the friction of the sledges and gave the dogs the appearance of having caught the spirit of the party. The more sprightly ones, as they went along with tightly-curled tails, frequently tossed their heads, with short, sharp barks and yelps.

In twelve hours we made 40 miles. There was not a sign of a lead in the march.

I had now made my five marches, and was in time for a hasty noon observation through a temporary break in the clouds, which indicated our position as 89.57. I quote an entry from my journal some hours later:

"The pole at last! The prize of three centuries. My dream and goal for twenty years! Mine at last! I cannot bring myself to realize it. It all seems so simple and commonplace. As Bartlett said when turning back, when speaking of his being in these exclusive regions which no mortal has ever penetrated before, 'It's just like every day.'"

We had reached the goal, but the return was still before us. It was essential that we reach the land before the next spring tide, and we must strain every nerve to do this.

I had a brief talk with my men. From now on, it was to be a big travel, little sleep, and a hustle every minute. We would try, I told them, to double march on the return—that is, to start and cover one of our northward marches, make tea and eat our luncheon in the igloos, then cover another march, eat and sleep a few hours, and repeat this daily. . . .

On April 23 our sledges passed up the vertical edge of the glacier fringe, a little west of Cape Columbia. When the last sledge came up I thought my Eskimos had gone crazy. They yelled and called and danced themselves helpless. As Ooath sat down on his sledge he remarked in Eskimo:

"The Devil is asleep or having trouble with his wife, or we never should have come back so easily."

A few hours later we arrived at Crane City under the bluffs of Cape Columbia, and after putting four pounds of pemmican into each of the faithful dogs to keep them quiet, we had at last our chance to sleep. Never shall I forget that sleep at Cape Columbia. It was sleep, sleep, then turn over and sleep again. We slept gloriously, with never a thought of the morrow.

FROM "THE DISCOVERY OF THE POLE," SEPTEMBER 1909

"I WILL BANK ON PEARY"

THEODORE ROOSEVELT

I was camped on the foothills of Mount Kenia when a special message was sent up by relays of runners to tell me that the Pole had been discovered. But they named the wrong man [Cook]; and, as I had heard something of his alleged mountaineering exploits in Alaska, I declined to send back a message of congratulation. But about a week afterwards I got another message, telling me that Peary had discovered the Pole, and I said, "That is genuine. I will bank on Peary." So I sent out my message of congratulation; and I told the people who were with me then to watch and they would find that the National Geographic Society would look into that business and declare for Peary. I was rarely more pleased than when I found that that was just what the Society had done.

FROM "WILD MAN AND WILD BEAST IN AFRICA," JANUARY 1911

"I DO NOT SUPPOSE THAT WE CAN SWEAR...."

WALLY HERBERT

Henson recalled that after he took over breaking trail, he would not see Peary until the end of each day's march. On April 6 he arrived at the Camp Jesup site 45 minutes ahead of Peary, concluding by dead reckoning that they had covered the full distance. He greeted Peary with: "I think I'm the first man to sit on top of the world."

Was Peary angry because Henson had not stopped to wait for him, an interviewer asked. "Oh, he got hopping mad," Henson replied. "No, he didn't say anything, but I could tell."

Henson wrote that Peary "fastened the flag to a staff and planted it firmly on the top of his igloo." Then, "As prospects for getting a sight of the sun were not good, we turned in and slept."

After Henson had turned in, a break in the clouds enabled Peary, unwitnessed by Henson, to snatch a sun sight at 12:50 p.m. indicating their position at 89° 57'—three miles short of the Pole. But he could *not* know in which direction the Pole lay because he did not know his longitude. To confirm his position, Peary needed to make more observations when the sun reappeared. He reports that he fell into an exhausted sleep for several hours, awoke to write that famous loose-leaf note ("The Pole at last!!!"), then set out to make them.

Now it was Henson's turn to feel hurt, for one of the Eskimos came in and told him that Peary was going the last miles to the Pole without him— without the man who had done more through the years than any other to help him attain it.

At 6 p.m. Columbia meridian time, the sky still overcast, Peary pushed on with his two Eskimos (Egingwah and Seegloo), a light sledge, and a double team of dogs for an estimated ten miles, made observations at Columbia meridian midnight, and returned to Camp Jesup to take another set a 6 a.m. on April 7. He then went another eight miles, at right angles to his previous course, before returning to make his final observations at Camp Jesup at noon.

Henson described Peary's return. "His face was long and serious. He would not speak to me. I quietly learned from the boys accompanying him that he had made observations a few miles further on. 'Well, Mr. Peary,' I spoke up, cheerfully enough, 'we are now at the Pole, are we not?'

" 'I do not suppose that we can swear we are exactly at the Pole.'

" 'Well, I have kept track of the distance and we have made exceptional time,' I replied. 'If we have traveled in the right direction, we are now at the Pole. If we have not traveled in the right direction, then it is your own fault.'" Peary made no reply.

"Feeling that the time had come," Henson continued, "I ungloved my right hand and went forward to congratulate him on the success of our eighteen years of effort, but a gust of wind blew something into his eye . . . and with both hands covering his eyes, he gave us orders to not let him sleep for more than four hours."

FROM "DID PEARY REACH THE POLE?" SEPTEMBER 1988

NOTHING ABOVE US

―――――――

Sir Edmund Hillary
as related to Beverley M. Bowie

We push on. About 400 feet from the South Peak we are brought to a stop: which route? Bourdillon and Evans took the ridge to the left; then, on their way back, came down the broad face. But I think the ridge looks jolly dangerous, with all that loose snow masking the rocks. We decide on the face.

You can't zigzag up a steep slope like this or you'll undercut it and find yourself aboard an avalanche with a one-way ticket to the bottom. So we go straight up. At least, we go up five steps, walking on eggs, and then the whole crust for 10 feet around breaks up and we slide down again three steps. We don't so much climb the face as swim up it.

Halfway, I turn to Tenzing [Norgay] and say: "What do you think of it?"

"I don't like it at all."

"Shall we go on?"

He shrugs. "Just as you wish."

I make a quick decision. In ordinary mountaineering terms, the risk isn't justifiable. I know that. But this is Everest, and on Everest you sometimes have to take the long odds, because the goal is worth it. Or so I try to convince myself.

We go on, and we get a break. A few yards higher up we run into some snow that's packed harder. Chipping steps, we make our way quite rapidly up to the crest. At 9 a.m. we are standing on the South Peak.

We have these advantages over Evans and Bourdillon: Thanks to a higher camp, we're here four hours earlier, and we have more oxygen and more strength left to finish the job. But just how big a job is it? That's something no one can tell us for sure.

To size it up, we scoop out a seat for ourselves just below the South Peak, remove our masks, and study the summit above. The true crown is out of sight, somewhere up above the ridge that turns its blade right in our faces now. It looks a fair cow, all right, as we'd say in New Zealand. Cornices on the right, overhanging a little drop of 10,000 feet to the Kangshung Glacier on Everest's eastern flank; on the left, steep snow sloping to the lip of the big rock wall that looms over the Western Cwm.

We don't need to talk much. It's obvious that our only route lies between the cornices and the cliffs on the left; the joker is the state of the snow. If it's firm, we have a chance. If it's loose and dry, we've come a long way for very little.

I check the oxygen once more. One full bottle left for each of us. That's 800 liters at three liters per minute—about 4½ hours of climbing. Enough? Well, it will have to be.

We put our sets on again, lighter for the discarded bottles. I feel very fit, and keen to get at the problem. We crampon down to the start of the ridge, and I sink my ax blade into the snow of the upward slope. It is everything we could have asked—crystalline and solid and well packed. Two or three whacks chip a step big enough even for our elephantine high-altitude boots, and a good shove buries the ax shaft half its length, making a very decent belay.

I lead off, cutting a 40-foot line of steps, resting, and taking a few turns of the rope around my ax as Tenzing comes up to join me. Then he belays me as I carve another flight. We move along steadily, giving the rickety cornices a fairly wide berth and taking an occasional gander over the rock face on our left. About 7,500 feet below I can just make out the tents of Camp IV, and I flap my arms up and down like an Abominable Scarecrow, with no particular hope that anyone will see me.

Tenzing has begun to drag a little on the rope by now, and his breathing seems more rapid. As we halt on one tiny ledge, I ask:

"How does it go, Tenzing?"

"All right."

I know, however, that like most Sherpas Tenzing has only a vague notion of the way his oxygen set works. He may be getting groggy and not even realize it. So I check his exhaust tube and find the valves almost completely blocked with ice; he's probably been getting no great benefit from his oxygen for some minutes.

I examine my own tube; to my surprise, ice has begun to form here, too, though not enough yet to interrupt my air flow. Obviously, this is something I'll have to keep an eye on for both of us. Fortunately, my habit of doing mental mathematics on our oxygen supply as I plug along, plus the fact that I'm leading the rope, will keep me fairly alert.

We resume the climb, and I cut another line of steps for perhaps half an hour. Then we find ourselves staring at an obstacle we've dreaded ever since we spotted it on the aerial photos and through our binoculars from Thyangboche: a ghastly great rock about 40 feet high, plunked down right across the ridge. No route on it worth talking about. And no way around it except—

Except where the snow cornice on the right, pulling away a little from the rock, has left a thin gap, a kind of chimney.

We look at it with rather mixed emotions. I'm not one of those blokes who says to himself, "I'll get up, come hell or high water." Mountains mean a lot to me, but not that much. I just say to Tenzing:

"Well, we'll give it a good go."

He takes a belay, and I jam my way into the crack. With my back to the cornice, I face the rock and grope for handholds along it, kicking my crampons into the snow behind me and jacking myself upwards. I use everything I have—knees, elbows, shoulders, even the oxygen set on my back—trying to get a purchase and exert some critical leverage.

My tactics depend on one little consideration: that the cornice doesn't peel off. Of course, Tenzing has me belayed on a bit of rock, which provides a certain moral support. But if the snow gives way, and I find myself dangling over the Kangshung Glacier, it isn't going to matter enormously whether Tenzing can hold me for five minutes or fifty.

Foot by foot I hump and wriggle and pull myself up the chimney. The crack is only a rope's length long, but it's a good half hour before I can reach over the ledge at the top and drag myself onto it. I lie there, panting like a gaffed fish, surprised somehow that I've scraped together enough energy to make it. Then I give Tenzing a taut rope and signal him to come along. For the first time the conviction seeps through me that we are really going to go all the way.

I check the oxygen sets again. The flow rates seem all right. Turning to Tenzing, I say: "How do you feel?"

He just grins and waves his hand upward toward the ridge. I lead off once more, cutting steps. My ax work is still pretty rhythmical and relaxed; I've been chipping away for well over an hour, but, so far, I've avoided the kind of tension that can turn up a sore arm.

One flight of steps, then another, and another. We follow the ridge as it curves around to the right, wondering where the top can possibly be, or if it exists at all. I cut around the back of one crag, only to have a higher one stare me in the face. It seems endless.

Tiring, I try to save time on one stretch by skipping the step cutting and relying on my crampons. After a few yards I go back to my ax; the angle is still too steep, too dangerous. The zest we have known at the top of the rock step is draining away. Dully, grimly, I hack a route around still another knob.

Suddenly I realize that the ridge ahead doesn't slope up, but down. I look quickly to my right. There, just above me, is a softly rounded, snow-covered little bump about as big as a haystack.

The summit.

One last question concerns me: is the top itself just a large, delicately poised cornice? If it is, someone else can have the honor of stepping on it.

I cut my way cautiously up the next few feet, probing ahead with my pick. The snow is solid, firmly packed. We stagger up the final stretch. We are there. Nothing above us, a world below.

I feel no great elation at first, just relief and a sense of wonder. Then I turn to Tenzing and shake his hand. Even through the snow glasses, the ice-encrusted mask, the knitted helmet, I can see that happy, flashing smile. He throws his arms around my shoulders, and we thump each other, and there is very little we can say or need to say.

My watch shows 11:30. Two hours and a half it has taken us from the South Peak; five hours from our tent. It seems a bit longer.

FROM "THE CONQUEST OF THE SUMMIT," JULY 1954

The foregoing article is a rare, perhaps unique case of a collaborator sharing a byline on a ghost-written article. The files suggest that Sir Edmund Hillary insisted on it. Before joining the magazine, Beverley Bowie had graduated magna cum laude from Harvard College, parachuted into Bucharest during World War II for the OSS, and written a novel. During a seven-year career as a GEOGRAPHIC writer and editor, he dazzled his colleagues with the brilliance of his writing and the charm of his manner. He died of cancer in 1958 at the age of forty-four, leaving a wife and five young children and a book of poems written during his final illness. The lines below, privately published after Bowie's death, never appeared in the GEOGRAPHIC.

CRITIQUE
BEVERLEY M. BOWIE

She took the verses at a gulp,
Dubious but possibly constructive medicine,
And gagged.

"Very gay, very debonaire, and very false.
Who is this Death you seem to be on such good terms with?
You drop his name about with careful spontaneity,
And yet I do not recollect him as a guest of ours
Nor, as a matter of fact, his advance press-agent,
That rather nasty fellow, Pain.
One thing I'll tell you:
You never met them in *my* company.
It must have been on one of those
Haphazard trips of yours,
To some unfinished corner of the globe
—Anywhere, so long as it's a thousand miles
From home, and with no telephone.

And now you want to go with them again,
These raffish, no-good bums I've never even met . . .
A matter of necessity, you say. Business. An urgent call.
You'd rather stay here with family, with me,
You'd rather revel in my cooking and my bed,

Apply the diaper and blow the flowing nose—
My foot! You mouth your pretty speeches
But go on packing your valise.
No, I know you. You're off again,
It doesn't matter where or
With what unsuitable companions;
The main thing is to go,
And go without me.

I'll tell you one thing more:
If a card comes drifting back,
Postmarked from Hell or Lethe or Death's Other Kingdom,
Or any other such outlandish pleasure spot,
I'll not read it to the children
Nor prop it proudly on the mantelpiece.

I'll stuff it up your effigy."

FROSTBITE

BARRY BISHOP

We had fallen into the same crevasse. Lute and I hang exhausted over our ice axes. I feel what little strength remains in me drain away. My feet, warm and comfortable throughout the entire climb, now begin to freeze. I stamp ponderously in the snow. No help. The pain in my toes sharpens. Then, as it skirts the edge of agony, it dies in a merciful numbness. I recognize the classic sequence of frostbite. Our plight is precarious and we know it. With oxygen all but exhausted, and with Tom's expiring flashlight our sole illumination, we join forces to head down the mountain [Everest].

We feel our way with cramponed feet and ice axes down the knife ridge of snow that Lute and I had ascended 11 hours before. In our weakened condition we can barely tell one side of the ridge from the other. Yet amazingly, while each of us tumbles frequently, no serious mishap mars the descent. At 12:30 on the morning of May 23, we decide to bivouac until dawn.

We plunk down on a sloping outcrop of rock. Our site is nearly 2,000 feet above the highest previous bivouac in history. By this time Lute and I have slipped into a stupefied fatigue. My feet have lost all feeling and the tips of my fingers are following them into numbness. We curl up in our down jackets as best we can. With his frozen fingers, Lute cannot even close his jacket. He wraps it tightly and hopes for the best.

For the next five and a half hours we remain anchored to that rock. Willi and Tom occupy a spot where they can move a bit. Tom struggles out of his crampons. Then, with typical selflessness, Willi removes Tom's overboots, boots, and socks and warms the feet by rubbing them against his own belly.

I lie dazedly on my back, my feet propped up like two antennae. Almost too weary to care, I wonder how badly they are damaged. I try to wriggle my toes. I feel nothing.

Then suddenly the sun is up. Stiff but rested, we treat ourselves to the luxury of waiting until the sun actually touches us on our rocky perch. Warmed, and with renewed optimism, we commence our descent with a few wry jokes.

We reel down the mountain as much by feel as by sight. Lute cannot focus either eye. I can use only my right one. As Lute belays me around a rock corner, I experience a surge of joy. Two figures struggle up to meet us—Dave Dingman and Girmi Dorje, laden with fresh oxygen tanks. The rock still screens them from Lute. I turn to him: "Do you want some oxygen?"

Lute thinks I have finally and unequivocally lost my senses. He just looks at me. Then I add, "Because here's Dave."

During the night Dave and [the Sherpa] Girmi had climbed to 27,600 feet in a futile search for us. Girmi had elected not to use oxygen—a tremendous sacrifice at that altitude, as we well knew—to conserve the precious gas for us.

Willi had already radioed from on top, but now our teammates learn that all four of us have succeeded—and that all four are alive. I strip off my down-filled boots and for the first time examine my frostbitten feet. The toes are dead white, hard, and icy to the touch.

When the last of the expedition moves out of Base Camp, Willi Unsoeld, Lute Jerstad, and I travel on the backs of Sherpas. Four porters spell each other in carrying each man. By the end of the first day, a fierce rivalry springs up between the four carrying me and the four carrying Willi. Every suitable stretch of trail inspires a foot race.

I awaken at 6 o'clock the following morning and note that the sky is overcast. Surely today will bring no helicopter. I close my eyes and drowse. But 25 minutes later, the whirr of chopper blades snaps me rudely into consciousness. The copter has come, weather notwithstanding. I feel a pang of regret. The expedition is breaking up. Never again will we all be together on a mountain.

FROM "HOW WE CLIMBED EVEREST," OCTOBER 1963

AVALANCHE!

BART MCDOWELL

On the northwest face of Peru's tallest mountain, Glacier 511 absorbed the amber warmth of a setting Capricorn sun. The mass of ice was huge. Droplets of melt seeped into its cracked surface, and the water lubricated its cliffy footing. Heat, cold, and gravity were writing a fatal equation. It was 6 p.m., January 10, 1962; violence was still thirteen minutes away.

Beneath the 22,205-foot glacial grandeur of Nevado Huascarán, shepherds hurried to finish the day's chores. Chilled by the shadows of the Cordillera Negra, they drew ponchos about their shoulders and tossed stones at their flocks to herd them home.

In the valley village of Calla, Señora Montoro de Narcisa found she would need more bread for supper. "Watch the baby until I return," she instructed her older daughter. Then she walked briskly toward Ranrahirca, two miles away.

Prosperous townsfolk of Ranrahirca were relaxing. Alberto Méndez, wealthy owner of a trucking line, had a moment ago arrived home tired from Lima; now he was resting in his comfortable house. Over cobbled streets Lamberto Guzmán Tapia, a barrel-chested mountain climber of 26, walked with happy impatience to a large family party. In the schoolyard teenage sisters Lira and Wanda Giraldo gossiped and giggled with passers-by.

Others worked. In a nearby garden 13-year-old Herminia Mejía hurried to dig the last of the day's potatoes. And at the stroke of 6, town electrician Ricardo Olivera arrived at the power station for his vespertine ritual: throwing the switch to give Ranrahirca five nightly hours of electricity. Olivera welcomed a distinguished caller, Ranrahirca Mayor Alfonso Caballero. The mayor, whose house stood across the street, stayed only long enough to say "*buenas noches*" and stroll on.

At 6:13 p.m., two and a half miles overhead, Glacier 511 shuddered. A man in Yungay first thought it was a cloud turning golden in the sunset: "But I saw that the cloud was flying downhill."

The first long fall was quiet and quick. Then the ice mass, equaling the weight of 1,200 navy destroyers combined, crashed wildly into a troughlike gorge. A crushing sound echoed the length of the valley. Then came a roar "like that of ten thousand wild beasts," as one man described it. "Like an earthquake," said another. "I could feel the rumble in the walls of the belly."

Mountain climber Lamberto Guzmán Tapia heard the noise and knew at once what it was. He had just arrived at his aunt's house. Inside some forty guests clapped and sang the happy Peruvian songs called *huaynos*. "*Alud!*" he shouted. "Avalanche!" No one could hear him. They only laughed and clapped all the harder. With a final shout of "Save yourselves!" Lamberto ran up the street; the happy music receded into a hollow thunder of avalanche.

From her potato field little Herminia Mejía heard the fearful sound. In terror, she began to run uphill across garden plots, "even stepping upon the little plants."

Electrician Olivera sprinted down into the center of town, but realized he could never reach his home in time. People were panicking. Scores were running toward the church, a haven for body and spirit. In the crowd Olivera saw Lira and Wanda Giraldo.

"Here!" he called, seizing each by the wrist to pull them toward safety.

Mayor Caballero stood in speechless awe before his adobe house. He tried to call his sister, but the roar obliterated his words.

From its first fall off the cliff, the avalanche had struck an uninhabited slope. Then the whole flotilla-sized ice mass had actually bounced. Surveyors later counted five impact points—an insane zigzag ricocheting from the sides of gorges. The mass, stirring tempests of shrill wind, carved and collected its own debris: topsoil, crushed houses from four mountain villages, flocks of sheep, granite boulders.

As it approached the valley floor, the roaring avalanche flattened to a mere 60 feet in thickness. It slowed to a mile a minute. By this time it had already taken perhaps a thousand human lives. Now the icy, muddy, rocky mass bore down upon some 2,700 people of Ranrahirca and vicinity. In the next few seconds this avalanche would complete one of history's great human disasters.

Yellow dust engulfed the mayor's view and gritted the eyes of electrician Olivera.

"The girls were torn from my hands—by the winds or by a wall of mud, I do not know," said Olivera. "Electric wires had fallen around me. The girls were gone. Somehow, I came free."

The avalanche had now reached the valley bottom, nine miles from its mountain perch, where it crashed into the Santa River, damming it with debris. It was 6:20.

From the hillside, Herminia Mejía saw the Santa River spill out of its banks to seek a new course; her potato patch was flooded.

As the yellow dust sifted to earth, Mayor Caballero stood mute. "I could speak neither an oath nor a prayer."

The Señora de Narcisa would never return to her children. The party at the Guzmán house, the rich Señor Méndez and his fine home, the church and its worshippers—all were gone.

"I regained my senses," said Olivera. "Looking toward the village, I saw only a waste of mud and ice. I was impressed by a profound silence. Realizing that my wife, my children, my parents were all buried under the debris, I suddenly found myself sobbing."

By official estimate, 3,500 people perished.

Travel folders call this area the "Switzerland of Peru." Actually the magnificent peaks here are more than a mile taller than Mont Blanc or the Matterhorn.

This Andean valley is called the Callejón de Huailas, meaning "corridor of greenery." To the west, the Cordillera Negra stands dark and dry; eastward, the Cordillera Blanca is drenched and glazed. On the valley floor, royal palms contrast vividly with the glaciers overhead. Here flows the Santa River, vested in white by the froth of rapids.

From the Pacific coast we had climbed steeply, ears popping; then we faced the vast, vague sweep of high Peruvian flatlands. Below us, at an altitude of 13,451 feet, sprawled snow-fed Lake Conococha, source of the Santa River.

We followed the river down. Our road was laned by eucalyptus trees, stone fences, slanting fields. Foggy clouds hid the mountaintops; a rainstorm overtook us. I dozed, then awakened to find the Callejón again sunny, and its mountain walls both steep and close.

Peruvian soldiers stopped the car near the disaster area. Assured that we were not looters, they waved us on. We passed two fields, then a row of adobe houses—and the road ended in the debris of the avalanche. This was the living fragment of Ranrahirca.

Bulldozers were pushing at loose mud; we left the car and picked our way to a little whitewashed building—the electric power station—and looked out over the ruin.

No one spoke; the scene resembled an Old Testament visitation. White rock and pale mud stretched a mile across the valley. Below us it fanned into a wide and deadly delta. No ice was visible on the surface. Boulders were mortared together by a crusting mud of granite dust; across the rubble spilled small, disoriented brooks of melt.

"How deep is the debris?" I asked a slender youngster standing nearby. He shrugged.

"Thirty feet in spots; 60 in others."

On the rim of the ruin I met César Barrios, subprefect from the provincial capital, Huarás. "Come, I'll take you to the command post," he said, turning with a limp that favored a bandaged leg.

"You are injured?"

"I fell on the ice. Ours was the first party to cross the avalanche debris the morning after the disaster."

"Out on the avalanche, did you find any injured survivors?" I asked.

"Survivors? Of *that*?" He glanced at the wasteland where so many people had been stoned to death. "No. The avalanche either killed a man or spared him—totally." He was right. In the whole disaster, fewer than two dozen people had been hospitalized.

The command post was one tent, one table, and a telephone. Col. Humberto Ampuero Pérez, heading the Ranrahirca operations, held a map sketched by his staff.

"Here was Glacier 511 on Mount Huascarán," he said. "Geologists numbered the glaciers a few years ago."

It was a classic textbook story of an avalanche. Fattened by freak snows ("even the Cordillera Negra had a sprinkling of white"), warmed by unseasonal sunshine, the glacier had broken from its steep, rocky perch.

"Ranrahirca was the largest town destroyed. But—Pacucco, Shacsha, Yanamachico, Chuquibamba, Calla, Huarascucho, Uchucoto." The guttural Quechua sounded a harsh litany.

"Now, see: It reached the Santa River—and dammed it. The water temporarily rose more than 15 feet. Much debris and ice flowed downstream. A few miles down—way off this map—two bridges were wiped out by the flood.

"That is our problem. The towns of Yungay and Caras are isolated. The avalanche cut off the road from the south; floods washed out the bridges in the north."

And how were these isolated towns being supplied? "Airlift. There is a strip in Caras. Of course, this is the season of rain, and the Callejón is narrow. . . ."

A lieutenant approached: "My colonel, the priest has arrived from Carhuás."

"Excuse me," said Colonel Ampuero. "A mass for the dead. I should attend."

Wilted wreaths of gladioli, daisies, and roses adorned an altar against the raw adobe of the mayor's house.

Thin and bent, Mayor Alfonso Caballero squinted toward the altar. Little Herminia Mejía knelt beneath a tree; saved by her work in the potato field, she was now an orphan. The electrician Olivera stood bareheaded in the sun; stapled to his shirt pocket was a small black ribbon for his loss of 27 kins-men.

As the priest intoned the Latin words, some women wept, quietly and without sobbing.

"All of them are stoics," said Dr. Raúl Paredes Tito when we visited his temporary clinic. "We are giving injections, but look—not even one child has cried.

"These shots are for typhoid. With so many dead still undiscovered—and perhaps 10,000 head of livestock decomposing, too—water sources could be corrupted."

Was typhoid the only epidemic he feared?

"Perhaps even typhus. We are spraying DDT throughout the area. And here in the mountains, of course, we might have an outbreak of *verruga*—a dreaded disease."

Verruga is endemic to parts of the Andes. Spread by a sandfly, it produces symptoms like pernicious anemia. It can kill. "We need to be pessimists," said the doctor.

A cry went up: "*Camillas! Stretchers!*"

"Apparently the men have found more of the dead," the doctor explained. "You should see them work, though it is not pleasant."

I followed the stretcher-bearers. "The helicopter pilot sighted many bodies—seven or eight," a soldier explained. The soldier carried a bugle; he would sound a blast if he sighted a human form.

We walked out onto the ruin, stepping carefully from stone to stone, then onto the plasterlike surface of the drying mud. At first the crust was so hard that our feet left no track. Then, quite without warning, I broke through and sank thigh-deep into mire. Here buried ice had melted, making a messy, fragile honeycomb in the debris.

Up ahead of us the stretcher-bearers had now stopped. "They have found nothing," said Augusto with a sigh. "Now they return." He looked out over the pale rubble. "It was such a beautiful town. Every September we had a great feast. Music, lights! People came from far away—very beautiful, very happy."

There were two ways to get to the isolated town of Yungay: walk across the avalanche debris or ride a helicopter. Jack and I tried our luck at Ranrahirca's improvised heliport.

The Peruvian Air Force had flown three little French helicopters up here. Blankets, clothes, food, and refugees had priority. But at midday one spare seat turned up.

"We need aerial photos," I said, shoving Jack aboard. "Meet me in the Yungay plaza."

After our stint with the stretcher-bearers, this walk across the avalanche rubble seemed easy. Soldiers had marked a firm, winding path with white-washed stones; across the rivulets of melt and the oozing mud, army engineers had built footbridges out of wooden scraps from the rubble.

Unreal as the panorama seemed, the avalanche area was alive with activity. A long line of refugees streamed toward me from isolated Yungay. Beyond the path telephone men adjusted a line across the boulders. Near them soldiers gathered samples to test the soil for replanting fields.

[At] Yungay's Santa Inés Colegio, or high school, now a refugee center, a truck, just arrived from the airstrip, was unloading a shipment of bedding. Inside the front patio, a crowd of brightly clad Indians sat on the tiled floor.

"*Padrecito!*" exclaimed an old woman—and rushed up to take my hand affectionately in her own. She had mistaken me for a priest.

"An easy mistake," said a voice in English. "You're an American and so are we."

The voice belonged to Father Frederic Cameron, of Boston. He and four other U.S. priests of the Society of St. James the Apostle had been put in charge of disaster relief by Peruvian President Manuel Prado.

Father Rudolph Masciarelli showed me around the school; 160 of the homeless slept here beneath the blackboards. Those who lived on the

Ranrahirca side of the avalanche had similar facilities there.

"The survivors are called *damnificados*, those who suffered loss. They represent quite a cross-section," said Father Masciarelli.

"We were worried about the food. Indians prefer one diet, the townsfolk another. The same with clothing. We couldn't give ponchos to the prosperous people of the valley or city garments to Indians of the heights—so everyone gets overalls."

Some 400 people were eating lunch here. The kitchen was a smoky patio animated by the chopping of wood and the stirring of sheepshead soup. Señora Olivera supervised the activity while carrying a baby in her arms.

"No, not my own child," she explained. "This is Teodosia Narcisa Montoro—two months old. Her mother died in the avalanche, but her father lives, thanks to God."

From the child's harsh wails, from the way she drew up her tiny feet, even I could see that Teodosia Narcisa Montoro had colic.

"Milk from the bottle does not rest well with her," said Señora Olivera. "She grieves for the breast of her mother."

During the next few days, Jack Fletcher and I shared in the valley's life of mourning and repair. Now and again, in the distance, we heard an insubstantial and windy sound like the falling of a tree. "Another avalanche— a small one," said [our driver] casually.

With the villagers, we looked into the horror-frozen faces of the dead. Most of the bodies were torn beyond recognition, beyond belief. Stretcher-bearers carried the grotesque fragments, the arms, legs, heads. The valley wore a sickly-sweet stench.

Each day the bulldozers progressed. "In a few weeks," one engineer told us, "the road will be restored across the avalanche path."

Then, pushing into the snow-chilled mud near a stream, the tractors encountered bodies partly protected from the full force of the stones. There were several; preserved by the cold, they seemed to be sleeping.

One was a little boy; lying on the man-sized stretcher, he seemed pitifully small.

The morgue superintendent directed the stretcher-bearers to his patio, pointing a hand dusted white with quicklime; lime was his only disinfectant, his only balm for quick burials. He looked closely into the little face. "Call Señor Jiraldo," he ordered. "Tell him it is one of his sons."

We waited. They lifted the body from the stretcher to the floor. Something fell from the child's pocket; I bent to see. It was a Yo-yo.

A crowd entered; in the middle stood a stocky man with a tense, unshaven face.

"The father?" I inquired of the morgue-keeper. The man nodded and remained silent.

Señor Jiraldo bent down to the figure of the boy: "It is my son Homero." He repeated carefully the whole name for the morgue-keeper's records. "Homero Jiraldo Montes. Please bring water."

A woman fetched a pail. Carefully, the father poured water upon the face of his son, washing away the mud in a brusque liturgy of ablution. The man's face showed no emotion, but his voice was hoarse.

"Homero was my youngest," said the father tonelessly. He took the muddy little shirt and began to undress the child. Carefully, he eased the small arm out of the sleeve. The father paused to look at his son's shoulder; it was marked by a purple bruise. The man said nothing; but gently, and only for an instant, he covered the small bruised shoulder with his own square hand.

"Homero was 10 years old," the father said, his voice growing clear. He continued to undress the child, but more quickly now. He lifted the small body to a bed of boxes, and with his own hands sprinkled the lime. The stoic Andean Pietà was finished. The Yo-yo still lay upon the patio floor.

JUNE 1962

ST. HELENS: MOUNTAIN WITH A DEATH WISH

Rowe Findley

First I must tell you that I count it no small wonder to be alive. Looking back on the fateful events preceding Mount St. Helens' terrible eruption last May 18 [1980], I recognize that I —and others—had been drawn into a strange kind of Russian roulette with that volcano in Washington's Cascades. For many weeks the mountain had masked its potential for tragedy with minor eruptions, then seemed to doze. In our efforts to get a close-range account of a significant geologic event, we moved in with the innocence of the uninitiated— until sudden holocaust shadowed us with peril and changed our lives forever. The very beauty of the mountain helped deceive us. It was a mountain in praise of mountains, tower- ing over lesser peaks, its near-perfect cone glistening white in all seasons. Thousands through the years had given it their hearts—climbers, artists, photographers, lovers of beauty's ultimate expression. Some were among the 61 people drawn into its deadly embrace on that shining Sunday morning.

"Vancouver! Vancouver! This is it. . . ." With those words—tinged with excitement rather than panic, hearers said—David Johnston, geologist for the United States Geological Survey, announced the end of calm and the start of cataclysm. Thirty-year-old blond-bearded David was stationed at a USGS camp called Coldwater II, six miles from the mountaintop, to monitor eruptions.

Those words were his last. The eruption he reported was powerful and unexpectedly lateral. Much of its initial blast was nozzled horizontally, fanning out northwest and northeast, its hurricane wave of scalding gases and fire-hot debris traveling at 200 miles an hour. Its force catapulted the geologist and the house trailer that sheltered him off a high ridge and into space above Coldwater Creek. His body has yet to be found.

The start of the eruption has been fixed at 8:32 a.m. Inevitably, the atomic bomb is cited for comparison in magnitude, but the energy computed is that of 500 Hiroshimas. In a quadrant extending roughly west to north, but including a shallower fan to the northeast, 150-foot Douglas firs were uprooted or broken like brittle straws for distances as far as 17 miles from the mountain.

An earthquake registering 5.0 on the Richter scale triggered the collapse of the fractured north side of the volcano, which was perhaps a factor in the devastating horizontal venting that followed. Tobogganing on a cushion of hot gases, the disintegrating north wall and cascades of rock swept down over the North Fork of the Toutle River, burying it under as much as 200 feet of new fill, which spread downstream in a 15-mile-long debris flow. The lateral blast hurled a thick blanket of ash over collapsing trees, tumbled bulldozers and logging trucks, crumpled pickups and station wagons, adding to the hopelessness of rescue efforts.

Soon the nozzling of the eruption turned entirely upward, and a roiling pillar of ash thrust some 12 miles into the Sunday morning sky, flanked by nervous jabs of orange lightning. The pillar plumed eastward into a widening dark cloud that would give Yakima, 85 miles distant, midnight blackness at 9:30 a.m. and would last the day. Much of eastern Washington, northern Idaho, and western Montana would be brought to a halt by the ashfall. Within days the silt from the mountain would reach the Pacific, after causing destructive floods on the Toutle and Cowlitz Rivers and closing the busy Columbia to deep-draft ships. By Wednesday the cloud would reach the Atlantic.

I refer to no notes in setting down these events, because they have cut a deep track in my mind. In fact, my memory unbidden replays sequences unendingly, perhaps because of their awesome magnitude and perhaps because they involve a deep sense of personal loss. I have only to close my eyes and ears to the present, and I see the faces and hear familiar names. . . .

Reid Blackburn. I knew him only a week—the week before the May 18 eruption. At 27 he was a master of cameras and a student of words, a journalism graduate of Linfield College in Oregon and five-year photographer with the Vancouver *Columbian*, a radio technician, a backcountry trekker. He had just the right talents to keep vigil on the volcano and to fire two remote, radio-controlled cameras recording simultaneous images of significant events. For this meaningful project he was on loan from the *Columbian* to the USGS and the National Geographic Society. His post was a mountainside logging-road camp called Coldwater I, eight miles from the crest of Mount St. Helens, three miles farther west than Coldwater II.

Colleagues say that Reid had the incisive eye of the born portrait photographer, capturing a face precisely when the mask falls away to reveal an instant of truth. He was as gifted in filming animals, anticipating the wistful look of a puppy, the trust of a lamb.

Nine months before, Reid had married Fay Mall, a member of the *Columbian*'s office staff, who shared his life's goals and ambitions.

I first met Reid on Sunday, May 11, when I helicoptered to Coldwater I and spent the night there to watch the mountain. I returned the following Wednesday, Thursday, and Friday. The talk ranged from newspapering to backpacking. As we talked on Thursday afternoon, I felt the ground sway like a boat on water. "An earthquake," Reid said without expression. "It's about 4.5." Repeated jolts had calibrated him.

The eight miles that separated Reid from the crater seemed a reasonable margin of safety before May 18. Afterward, with four feet of ash blanketing the camp, and in the knowledge that people twice that far from the mountain had died, I found it hard to think reasonably about margins of safety.

Harry Truman. He was a man who rejected margins of safety. For more than half a century he had lived at the foot of Mount St. Helens on the shores of Spirit Lake. When sheriff's deputies ordered all residents to leave for safety, Harry said no. Harry had raised the adjectival use of profanity to a new high, and in a position statement that demonstrated his art, he told me why he wouldn't leave:

"I'm going to stay right here because, I'll tell you why, my home and my _____ life's here. My wife and I, we both vowed years and years ago that we'd never leave Spirit Lake. We loved it. It's part of me, and I'm part of that _____ mountain. And if it took my place, and I got out of here, I wouldn't live a week anyway; I wouldn't live a day, not a _____ day. By God, my wife went down that _____ road _____ feet first, and that's the way I'm gonna go or I'm not gonna go."

Harry and his wife, Edna, had built a lodge and cabins by the lake, and their resort became a favored retreat for two generations of vacationers.

Three years ago Edna died, and Harry closed the lodge, renting only a few cabins and boats each summer. When a steel gate was placed across the highway, barring outsiders but locking Harry in, he still did not change his mind: "I said block the _____ road, and don't let anyone through till Christmas ten years ago. I'm havin' a hell of a time livin' my life alone. I'm king of all I survey, I got _____ plenty whiskey, I got food enough for 15 years, and I'm settin' high on the _____ hog."

Harry said that he had provisioned an old mine shaft with ample drink and victuals, and many of his friends hope he might yet dig out of such a retreat. But the lack of warning preceding the May 18 eruption makes it all but certain that Harry was caught in or near his beloved lodge, which now lies crushed under thick debris and the raised level of Spirit Lake.

The mountain he elected never to leave rewarded him with an eternal embrace, a cataclysmic burial of a magnitude befitting deity more than man, an extravaganza befitting even Harry's gift for vocal brimstone.

David Johnston. You already know of his fate, but now you must know of his promise. Like Reid Blackburn's credentials for photography, David Johnston's training for geology was impeccable. The University of Illinois awarded him a degree in geology with honors, the University of Washington conferred master's and doctorate, and the National Science Foundation granted him a fellowship.

Better than most observers, David knew the awesome potential of Mount St. Helens. "This mountain is a powder keg, and the fuse is lit," he said, "but we don't know how long the fuse is." Yet he responded to the need for samples from the crater by volunteering to be the sampler.

"He was a marathon runner in excellent condition," explained Lon Stickney, USGS contract helicopter pilot, who had made more landings on the mountain than any other human. "David figured he could get down into the crater and back out again faster than any of his colleagues."

St. Helens became part of my life late last March. I had been working on a prospective NATIONAL GEOGRAPHIC article on the national forests, and the Fuji-like eminence of Mount St. Helens—named for an 18th-century British diplomat—dominated Gifford Pinchot National Forest. On March 21 my friend Gerry Gause of the Forest Service's regional office in Portland phoned me in Washington, D.C., and said that earthquakes were shaking the mountain.

I checked flight schedules and began to read up on Mount St. Helens.

To my hand came an aptly titled USGS paper, "Potential Hazards From Future Eruptions of Mount St. Helens," by Drs. Dwight Crandell and Donal Mullineaux. They said that St. Helens had been the most active of the Cascade volcanoes, and for a quarter century beginning in 1831 had concocted various combinations of steam, ash, mudflows, and lava eruptions. Before the 20th century ended, they predicted, another eruption was likely.

The quakes grew in number and force; the dormant volcano was stretching and stirring. By Wednesday, March 26, I was convinced, and scheduled an early flight Friday. The mountain yawned on Thursday afternoon, venting steam and ash. By the time I arrived Friday morning, intermittent plumes rose two miles above the peak and tinged its northeast slopes sooty gray.

This was the start of a geologic event—the first volcanic eruption in the contiguous 48 states since California's Lassen, another Cascade peak, shut down in 1917 after a three-year run. St. Helens became a siren to geologists, journalists, and the just plain curious who crowded into Portland, Oregon, and into Vancouver, Kelso, and Longview, Washington. Seers competed in foreseeing holocaust, T-shirt vendors had visions of hot sales, and sign makers exhausted plays on the word "ash." Sample: "St. Helens—keep your ash off my lawn." There were some people who irreverently christened the mountain Old Shake and Bake.

The name seemed deserved as late March became April and April slid past with the mountain still not fully awake. A second crater appeared beside the first, then the two merged into a single bowl 1,700 feet across and 850 feet deep. But the eruption level, geologists said, remained "low-energy mode."

Despite such restraint, there was growing suspense for the country roundabout. It was rugged country, still largely remote except by air, its high places inaccessible under snows most of the year. This was a country of lava caves some thought were home to Sasquatch, or Bigfoot, the giant apelike beast of legend and controversy. This was the wild country over which D. B. Cooper parachuted from a hijacked jet in 1971 with $200,000 in cash; he was never found, though a few thousand of his currency was.

Once this was the land of Indian legend, too, including one in which the favors of a beautiful maiden caused a battle between two rival warriors. They hurled fiery rocks at each other and so angered the Great Spirit that he turned the three into Mount St. Helens, Mount Hood, and Mount Adams.

Spirit Lake, the mirror for the beauty of Mount St. Helens, owes its name to Indian stories of the disappearance of canoeists on its waters as strange moanings arose.

What would arise from modern-day St. Helens was of immediate concern last spring. The situation put great pressure on geologists for forecasts, but they lacked experience with volcanoes such as St. Helens, a composite of alternating layers of ash and lava. They worked long hours to place instruments on and around the mountain: seismometers to record quakes, gravity meters to gauge vertical swellings, tiltmeters and laser targets to detect outward bulging. A Dartmouth College team led by Dr. Richard Stoiber flew circles around the peak to sample its hot breath. Increased sulfur dioxide content would signal magma on the move. At the University of Washington, at Portland State, at other area universities, faculty geologists monitored their seismographs and analyzed ash samples from the mountain for any clues to its intentions.

By Saturday, May 10, the pulse was heavier—some quakes approached 5.0 on the Richter scale. Infrared aerial photos showed several hot spots in the crater and on the flanks. Most alarming of all, the mountain's north face was swelling; it had already bulged laterally by some 300 feet and was still distending at a rate of five feet a day. The volcano would not remain on "hold" much longer.

Still, the third-of-a-mile-wide crater looked drowsy enough in the bright sunlight of late Sunday morning, May 11. With Dr. Marvin Beeson, geochemist at Portland State University, photographer David Cupp and I hopped out of a helicopter onto the crater's northeast lip.

Marvin sought ash samples for analysis. Most of the ash was old, ground-up mountain, but new, glassy ash could be collected and, if it proved high in silica, would indicate how explosive the eruption might be.

Our pilot, Kent Wooldridge, Army trained and Vietnam conditioned, made two precautionary passes before coming to a six-inch-high hover. My jump to the volcano's crest reminded me of watching Neil Armstrong's first step on the moon; would I sink into the mixed ash and snow to my knees or to my hips? Gratefully I found that its consistency was like coarse sand; I sank barely to my ankles, and walking was easy.

While Marvin gathered ash from the crater's lip and David documented the scene on film, I looked around at this uncertain new world. Hundreds of feet below, wispy steam breathed gently from the crater's throat. The south side, towering some 500 feet above us and capped by a disintegrating glacier, constantly whispered and rattled with cascading ice and rock.

The dirty snow was pocked with softball-sized holes. With a start I realized that each hole held a rock or ice chunk lately hurled out of the crater. I wondered how good I would be at the volcano's version of dodge ball, I wondered when the next earth tremor was due, and I wondered why Marvin was so slow at spooning samples.

The week between May 11 and 18 now seems to me part of another life. There was the overnight of the 11th at Coldwater I with Reid. There was time that evening to drive down to Harry Truman's lodge.

Harry greeted me cheerily, iced bourbon in hand, a couple of his 16 house cats scampering underfoot. Yes, his birds had come back—the camp robbers and wrens and blackbirds he fed. Most of them had vanished after the March 27 eruption. The raccoons had never left. The three feet of snow that blanketed his grounds had now melted; long winter was over. He and the mountain were still on speaking terms, and it hadn't told him anything to change his mind about staying.

It was a time for looking back across his 84 years, to his boyhood in West Virginia, to his teenage years in Washington State, where his father had moved to work in the timber, to the Los Angeles of the 1920s, where, Harry said, he used a service station as a front to sell bootleg whiskey that he had brought in by boat from Canada. To years when the late Justice William O. Douglas visited his Spirit Lake lodge, and to his World War II meeting with the other Harry Truman when the latter was the U.S. Vice President.

"By God, if we had Harry S. Truman in Washington now, he'd straighten out those _____ in a hurry!"

Harry R. Truman of Spirit Lake (he never told me what the "R." stood for) had found his life troubled since the mountain began to awaken. "I'm gettin' letters, hundreds of _____ letters from all over the _____ country. Some of 'em want to save me—somebody sent me a 'Bible for the hardheaded.' I get marriage proposals—now why would some 18-year-old chick want to marry an old _____ like me. I get dozens of letters from children who worry about me."

The children's letters moved Harry, especially a batch from an entire class at Clear Lake Elementary School, near Salem, Oregon. Harry said he planned ultimately to answer all his mail, but he wished he could visit the kids at Clear Lake. "I'd like to explain to them about me and the mountain."

Harry's wish met with enthusiasm at the school, and so a helicopter was arranged to take him there on Wednesday, May 14. I went along, on what proved to be Harry's last trip away from his beloved Spirit Lake.

No Santa Claus ever had a warmer greeting; the entire student body—104 strong—cheered and unfurled crayoned banners (Harry—We Love You) as the whirlybird eased down on the schoolyard turf. Principal Kate Mathews and teacher Scott Torgeson, whose class had written the letters to Harry, did welcoming honors. Harry, forgoing his usual adjectives, admirably explained how it is to have lived a long, full life, and to have found a piece of the world as dear as life itself. For each child who wrote him, he had a signed postcard showing Spirit Lake and the lodge.

But what would he do if he saw the lava coming for him? "I'd run," Harry said. The earthquakes worried him more than eruptions, he added, and he had endured a few thousand tremors since the volcano had started to stir. How did he keep from being tossed out of bed at night? "I wear spurs to bed," Harry said.

More cheers and waves. The helicopter eases up and out across sun-dappled fields. The jumping-bean cluster of young well-wishers shrinks and swings out of sight. A panorama of lush meadows and woodlands, prosperous towns, and ample rivers slides beneath Harry's attentive gaze. "What a beautiful _____ country we got, boys—what a beautiful country," Harry said.

Good-bye, Harry, and good luck.

Thursday, May 15. That famous Northwest weather trick—now you see it but mostly you don't—plagues efforts to learn what the volcano is doing. A brief glimpse early in the day shows hardly a steam plume; then the clouds drop a curtain. We sit by the chopper at Coldwater I through overtures of alternating cloud and sun, raindrops and rainbows. The curtain over the mountain never lifts.

Friday, May 16. The mountain is playing games with us. An early morning radio message from Coldwater I reports St. Helens in full view. By the time we get aloft, the curtain is closing. By the time we reach the mountain, the mountain can no longer be seen.

Saturday, May 17. All sunshine and no clouds. The mountain drowses on.

The north-face bulge continues—swelling five feet a day; other signs say that nothing is about to happen. No need to keep flying around the sleepy mountain.

Instead, I drive to Cougar, a little timber-industry settlement some 12 miles southwest of the mountain, to see my friends Mort and Sandy Mortensen, who run the Wildwood Inn, a café and bar catering to loggers, fishermen, and whoever else turns up. Lately, business had been hit-and-miss, depending on what the volcano was doing. The town had been evacuated more than once, and there was no business.

I took the time to reassure myself that the Wildwood Inn's new deep fryer was still turning out delectable fried chicken.

And that was the last day of my final week from another life.

Sunday, May 18. First sun finds the mountain still drowsing. Because it is drowsing, I decide not to watch it today, a decision that soon will seem like the quintessence of wisdom. Because it is drowsing, others—campers, hikers, photographers, a few timber cutters—will be drawn in, or at least feel no need to hurry out. Their regrets will soon be compressed into a few terrible seconds before oblivion.

Ten megatons of TNT. More than 5,000 times the amount dropped in the great raid of Dresden, Germany, in 1945. Made up mostly of carbon dioxide and water vapor, innocuous except when under the terrible pressure and heat of a volcano's insides and then suddenly released.

That 5.0 quake does it. The entire mountainside falls as the gases explode out with a roar heard 200 miles away. The incredible blast rolls north, northwest, and northeast at aircraft speeds. In one continuous thunderous sweep, it scythes down giants of the forest, clear-cutting 200 square miles in all. Within three miles of the summit, the trees simply vanish—transported through the air for unknown distances.

Then comes the ash—fiery, hot, blanketing, suffocating—and a hail of boulders and ice. The multichrome, three-dimensional world of trees, hills, and sky becomes a monotone of powdery gray ash, heating downed logs and automobile tires till they smolder and blaze, blotting out horizons and perceptions of depth. Roiling in the wake, the abrasive, searing dust in mere minutes clouds over the same 200 square miles and beyond, falling on the earth by inches and then by feet.

The failed north wall of the mountain has become a massive sled of earth, crashing irresistibly downslope until it banks up against the steep far wall of the North Toutle Valley. This is the moment of burial for Harry Truman and his lodge, as well as for some twenty summer homes at a site called the Village, a mile down the valley.

The eruption's main force now nozzles upward, and the light-eating pillar of ash quickly carries to 30,000 feet, to 40,000, to 50,000, to 60,000. . . . The top curls over and anvils out and flares and streams broadly eastward on the winds.

The shining Sunday morning turns forebodingly gray and to a blackness in which a hand cannot be seen in front of an eye.

In the eerie gray and black, relieved only by jabs of lightning, filled with thunder and abrading winds, a thousand desperate acts of search and salvation are under way.

Psychological shock waves of unbelief quickly roll across the Pacific Northwest. In Vancouver and Portland, in Kelso and Longview, and in a hundred other cities and towns, the towering dark cloud is ominously visible.

A phone call from my friend Ralph Perry of the Vancouver *Columbian* sends me outside to gaze at the spectacle. As soon as I can, I get airborne for a better look, and recoil from accepting what I see.

The whole top of the mountain is gone.

Lofty, near-symmetrical Mount St. Helens is no more. Where it had towered, there now squats an ugly, flat-topped, truncated abomination. From its center rises a broad unremitting explosion of ash, turning blue-gray in the overspreading shadow of its ever widening cloud. In the far deepening gloom, orange lightning flashes like the flicking of serpents' tongues. From the foot of the awesome mountain there spreads a ground-veiling pall.

Somewhere down there lies Coldwater I, above the rushing waters of Coldwater Creek and the valley I had left in verdant beauty only 40 hours before.

JANUARY 1981

THE OTHER OREGON

WILLIAM LEAST HEAT-MOON

This isn't the Oregon of 60 shades of green arising from rain, rain, rain; not here the great seastacks of the Pacific coast, nor Yaquina Bay oysters or sweet geoducks, or espresso at the back of bookshops. This is the Other Oregon, the Big Empty, an immense space shaped, faulted, and deformed by volcanic processes, and, less than 30 million years ago, turned into desert by the massive rain shadow cast by the Cascade Mountains to the west.

I'm standing at the northern end of Bluejoint Lake just below the high, fault-block escarpment of Poker Jim Ridge, a wall of tenebrous basalt broken upward into the light of day by the great shoving of tectonic plates miles beneath. In a time when this rimrock had seen 30,000 fewer autumns, the spot I stand on was 300 feet below the lake surface, evidence of which shows itself on the ancient shoreline cut by waves into the ridge now 20 stories above my head. But, only a couple of generations ago, this lake, and dozens of others to the south, were gone; it was nothing but an unbroken expanse of cracked mud bottom at least 600 feet deep, a lake of memory marking the grave of a Pleistocene lake then big enough to swallow Boston, had Boston been around.

The fascination of this place depends on trying to see what it has been, how it was so different, although everything exists in kinship, in a direct line of descent: Here fire is the father of stone, volcanoes the mothers of valleys, and wind and ice the rods of discipline that shaped their offspring. More than any other American place I know, this desert corner bespeaks change, the subtle ones sometimes a mask for the grand upheavals. Things, even mountains and hundred-mile-long lakes, vanish, come to light, vanish again. South of here huge Goose Lake dried up in the 1920s to reveal the indelible 1845 tracks of the famous Applegate immigrant trail striking right across the dried bottom, punctuated with bits of broken-down wagons, but the lake rose again to conceal history and leave residents waiting for the next uncovering.

Despite their size, some of these residual waters one can wade across, and they are noteworthy because of their shallowness, yet they exist because they once were deep holes of the ancient lake. It's that kind of inversion, that irony of natural process, which marks this place: What was deepest is shallowest, what was fiery flowing magma is rigid mountain, the buried stands high and exposed, and a hundred feet above a mud entombed juniper forest only sagebrush can grow. Time travel is requisite to traverse this desert in any deep sense, and it is the sweep of years that creates the topsy-turviness, the undulations of a nature that appears to writhe through the eons and toss creation bum over teakettle.

This year the Warner Valley, the bottom of the primitive lake, is blue with water and golden with bunch grasses and shrubs, a string of marshiness just waiting for the next chance to return to a small inland sea. In the 1870s a government report designated the basin as swampland, but 15 years later a writer said, "The principal portion of the valley is sterile, barren greasewood desert with only an occasional marsh or salt lake varying the monotony. It would be difficult to imagine a more desolate and God-forsaken region outside of Assyria, Arabia, or the Great Sahara."

FROM "OREGON'S OUTBACK," AUGUST 1997

ISLANDS AT THE EDGE

JENNIFER ACKERMAN

Hurricane Fran came to the barrier islands off North Carolina on Thursday, September 5, 1996. When the storm made landfall on Cape Fear at about 9 p.m., an 12-foot surf overwashed the north end of Topsail Island, damaging nearly every building. Storm waters rushing back from the sound to the sea cut two new inlets, where the tide was still running out in brown roils. Three feet of sand packed the lower streets, topped by bathtubs, vacuum cleaners, chairs, a child's crib, a silver tea set, lightbulbs inexplicably intact, even a bed still perfectly made. People moved about numbly, stopping to stand before the stumps of pilings that once held their homes. A search team of 60 volunteers set out with dogs to sift for bodies in the wreckage.

Though most residents and tourists retreated inland before the storm hit, Fran killed two dozen people and caused more two billion dollars in property damage. It was the sort of storm that points out the folly of getting mixed up with a barrier island made of sand, the stuff on which, as the Bible says (Matthew 7:26), only a foolish man builds.

Orrin Pilkey, a professor of geology at Duke University and director of the Program for the Study of Developed Shorelines, once described Topsail Island to me as "a disaster waiting to happen—low, narrow, and loaded with dangerous development." We were standing on a dune at Shackleford Banks, North Carolina, a barrier island about 50 miles north of Topsail. It was a sunny day in winter. The sea was calm, but strong waves had recently scoured the beaches. Not far from the high-tide line were scarps in the dunes six feet high, miniature cliffs where charged-up surf had gnawed into the island.

I had come to Shackleford with Pilkey to try to understand what was happening—is happening—here and on most other barrier islands of the

Atlantic and Gulf coasts; to understand how a barrier island responds to the energies of wind and wave, to rising sea level, to storms like Fran, responds as if it were alive, with a kind of wit and wisdom of its own.

Shackleford is the last southern link in the string of barrier islands known as the Outer Banks. Roughly nine miles long and half a mile wide, it parallels the short, sudden westward turn of the North Carolina coast. The National Park Service acquired the island in the mid-1980s. No one lives there now. There are no houses, no condominiums, no boardwalks. Just sand and plants, dune and thicket, forest and marsh.

In the lingo of geologists, barrier islands are loosely defined as long, narrow bodies of sand running parallel to the shoreline, and separated from one another by inlets and from the mainland by marsh or lagoon. They protect the mainland from storm and surf. They also shelter marshes, nurseries to hundreds of species of fish and shellfish and habitat for myriad ducks, geese, herons, egrets, ibises, limpkins, bitterns, rails, coots.

Just over 2 percent of the world's coastlines are fronted by barrier island chains, most of them where the coastal plain slopes gently, where sand is abundant and waves supply enough energy to move the sand about. There are barriers off the coasts of China, India, the Netherlands, Australia, and Alaska. A snaking chain of frigid barrier islands threads the shores of Siberia. Islands of black sand rim southeast Iceland. But by far the longest stretch of barrier islands runs more than 2,200 miles along the coast of North America in an irregular chain from New York to Texas. Its links include New York's Fire Island; the islands of the Jersey, Maryland, and Virginia shores; the long, sinuous ribbon of the Outer Banks; the Sea Islands of South Carolina and Georgia; Cape Canaveral and Miami Beach on the Florida coast; the Gulf coast's Isles Dernieres, Galveston Island, and Padre, the world's longest barrier island.

Geologically speaking, most of these islands are young. The Outer Banks are about 5,000 years old. The Chandeleur Islands of Louisiana have existed for less than three millenia. One theory suggests that the barrier islands of the Atlantic and Gulf coasts were born with the rise in sea level that began at the end of the last ice age about 18,000 years ago. At that time the great polar caps had locked up huge amounts of water, and sea level was 400 feet lower than it is today. With the waning of the ice age, the polar caps melted and the sea began to rise at a rate of several feet a century. As it rose, it flooded low areas behind dune ridges on the seaward edge of the continent, leaving behind a chain of above-water sandbars. Along the northeastern coast the rising sea breached long, fingerlike ridges, or spits, that extended from the mainland. As the sea continued to rise, waves overwashed the islands, scouring sand from the front and depositing it in fans on the islands' backsides. Receding in front, accreting in back, the islands maintained their elevation above rising sea level by rolling over themselves, migrating landward up the continental shelf.

Then about 4,500 years ago there came a pause in sea-level rise, which allowed the islands to pause, grow, and widen. It is pure chance that they lie in their present position.

While the catch-all term "barrier island" gives the impression of uniformity, each island is unique, born of intricate combinations of sand supply, wave energy, and tidal range. Along the Georgia coast, where spring tides reach 11 feet and wave energy is low, islands such as Tybee, Sapelo, and St. Simons are relatively short and wide. Along the North Carolina and Florida coasts, a tidal range of only two to three feet with higher wave energy creates longer, narrower islands such as the Outer Banks and Miami Beach. Padre Island, Texas, with a mean tide range of less than two feet, is so long you can feel the climate shift as you move south along its 110-mile length.

Despite their vital differences, the islands within a chain are inextricably linked, explains Pilkey. "They're like the beads of a necklace, sharing the same sand supply, responding to the same body of water, subject to the same forces of change."

The crest of a 30-foot sand hill offers a 360-degree view of Shackleford Banks, where sea oats, sand, and wind have conspired to build elegant, towering dunes. Among the grasses grows an array of intriguing plants—silver-leaf croton, seabeach evening primrose, dune bluestem, seaside spurge, pennywort—which help to anchor the dunes. There are vines of wild bean, China brier, and muscadine grape; shrubs of yaupon, beauty berry, and dwarf sumac, all superbly adapted to shifting sand. On the eastern half of the island lie sand flats and salt marsh; on the western, a wide swath of deep-green maritime forest, where red cedar and live oak clipped by the salt breeze are whittled into harmony with the contours of the rolling dunes. "Plants control the evolution of a barrier island," explains Pilkey, "and the shape of the island in turn determines the variety of plants. It's a beautifully integrated system of physical and biological life."

Pilkey stoops to show me a vestigial copse of smooth, worn stumps emerging from the surf. Sand has cut away the trees' outer growth and left only heartwood, stubborn remnants of a maritime forest that shaded this spot a few hundred years ago. He bends again to retrieve the battered black shell of an oyster—more evidence of rapid geologic change. Oysters live not in waters of full oceanic salinity but in the brackish waters of the sound. "This is a fossil from a marsh that once stood here," he explains. "This beach is where the sound used to be. In a sense, ocean has come to oyster."

At the center of the island Pilkey leads me to a wide swath of sand, littered with shells and wrack. "It takes a humdinger of a storm to push sand into the middle of an island like this," he says. In narrower portions of Shackleford, overwash has swept clear across the island, pushing sand from the beach face over the dunes to the sound side of the island.

Shackleford is rolling over itself, sand moving over sand, over marsh and forest and lagoon. If you could sit stock-still and watch with a remembering eye, the forms of a barrier island would seem momentary, like the shifting flames of a fire. Every inch moves, shaped and reshaped by wind, waves, currents, and storms. The changes brought about by these forces ripple over the islands, dunes rising and falling, beach expanding and contracting, inlets opening and closing, shapes wavering and blowing, dying and being reborn, not in devastation but in constant rearrangement. Barrier islands metamorphose so rapidly that they have been called "amoeba-like," "ecological banana peels," and "high-speed real estate."

"Barrier islands really do act like living things," Pilkey says. "They respond in sensible, even intelligent ways, to the forces of wind and water."

That is, if they are unfettered. Pilkey believes that barrier islands must be allowed to move and change freely or they will be lost forever. He would like people to leave them alone. "But look! here come more crowds, pacing straight for the water, and seemingly bound for a dive," wrote Herman Melville in *Moby Dick*. "Strange! Nothing will content them but the extremest limit of the land."

We are drawn to these islands. The barrier islands I visited as a child rise up in my mind through a meld of sensations: the good crunch of sand under bare feet, the tangy scent of salt, the cries of the gull and plover. In the sea-molded curves and open space of a barrier island is release from harsh lines and cramped spaces. In the blue water and white sand is a sense of things stripped clean, the big tabula rasa. When I climb up over the fat humps of sand dunes at Assateague or Ocracoke or Fire Island, I confront the sea always with the same delighted astonishment. Something in the water's wide spread both fills the mind and empties it. It is all unfathomed magnitude and mystery. Time slips by; the waves slap. The briny surf and shifting sands correspond to a memory as deep as any we possess.

Before World War II, beach houses and resorts covered about 10 percent of barrier islands along the Atlantic and Gulf coasts. In stretches, the islands of New Jersey, Georgia, Florida, and Texas are one great syncytium of condominiums and resorts offering tall promises of rainbow's end and subdivisions with names that memorialize what has been bulldozed into oblivion: Dunes West, Maritime Woods, Sea Meadows. So transformed are many barrier islands that we often pass onto them unaware that they are islands at all.

By the early 1980s, cottages, hotels, and condominiums were swallowing up barrier islands at a rate of 6,000 acres a year, often with the help of government programs. In 1982 the U.S. Congress took measures to slow the burgeoning development by creating the Coastal Barrier Resources Act. The act protects 186 areas—comprising 453,000 acres—of undeveloped barrier islands along the Atlantic and Gulf coasts. Under the law those who build within these areas cannot receive federally subsidized flood insurance or federal funds for bridges, roads, or water and sewer systems. The Coastal Barrier Improvement Act of 1990 added another 700,000 acres to the system. In most of these protected areas coastal development has nearly ceased. Elsewhere, however, you can almost hear the sound of concrete moving like an incoming tide over dunes, marshes, and maritime forests. Thousands of people continue to build houses and businesses.

The morning after Hurricane Fran, I traveled to North Carolina's southeastern barrier islands to survey the damage with two young geologists conducting a study for the Federal Emergency Management Agency. We moved up the islands slowly, counting the number of houses damaged and destroyed and comparing the damage patterns with hazard maps that scientists had compiled from studies of the islands' geologic features. The places that suffered actual damage from Fran closely matched the areas on the maps marked as danger zones: low, narrow stretches of island with few natural dunes and scarce vegetation, areas especially vulnerable to storms.

The last major hurricane to hit this stretch of coast was Hazel in 1954, a powerful storm that annihilated nearly every building on the islands of Long Beach, Holden Beach, and Ocean Isle. During the 40-year lull in significant hurricane activity that followed, beach houses sprouted everywhere, most of them built by people who had never experienced a major storm. By the time Fran struck, so dense was the development on the barrier islands north of Cape Fear that a storm weaker than Hazel inflicted much greater damage.

People have been living on these islands for a long time. Native Americans such as the Massapequa and Shinnecock, the Accomac, and the Hatteras made summer camps on the islands of New York, Virginia, and North Carolina to harvest food from the sea. They fished and clammed, caught turtles and hunted waterfowl. In fall, the huricane season, they abandoned their summer camps for permanent villages on the mainland.

Early European settlers recognized the dangers of barrier islands and largely bypassed their shores for the relative safety of mainland sites. Those who ventured to live on the islands built their houses on the sound side, protected from storm winds and waves by high dunes and vegetation. They took for granted the vicissitudes of the sea and the supremacy of its force. Some islanders learned to remove floorboards from their houses or open the front and back doors during storms so that floodwaters would wash through rather than tear the houses from their foundations.

Well into this century life on barrier islands tended to be frugal, bare boned, and above all isolated, cut off emotionally as much as physically from the mainland. Often there was no electricity, no law enforcement, no doctor. In many communities generations of watery separation fostered and preserved distinct dialects and vernacular language. Some inhabitants of the Sea Islands of Georgia and South Carolina still speak a dialect so rich and metaphorical that visitors need a glossary to follow conversation. Vital to the Sea Islanders' daily lives are words and expressions largely unfamiliar to the modern mainland ear. The dialect of Ocracoke's older inhabitants too is studded with words like *begombed* (to be soiled) or *quamish* (for queasy). Arnold Daniels, a retired commercial fisherman now 87 who can remember the days before bridges connected the mainland with his home of Roanoke Island, North Carolina, has a brogue so strong it seems a sweet transport back in time or overseas: "There's people in my toime never was off the oiland, only by bowt to go fishin'."

Some of the islands of North Carolina are melting away at a rate of two to five feet a year. The shores of Louisiana, with its flat coastal profile, are rapidly fraying, in part because the coastal plain beneath the state is sinking. Louisiana's barrier islands make Shackleford Banks look like bedrock. Timbalier Island is migrating shoreward at a rate of more than ten feet a year.

Barrier islands once went where they pleased. Now we try to bully them into proper conduct. At the coastal metropolis of Ocean City, Maryland, a field of stone groins keeps a wide berth of white sand in front of the big hotels, and two jetties keep open the inlet separating the resort from Assateague Island just to the south. In essence jetties and groins act like dams in the river of sand that moves along the shore. The jetties at Ocean City have stolen sand from Assateague, accelerating the retreat of its shoreline from 5 feet a year to as much as 30. In the past half century the north end of Assateague has somersaulted over itself.

"At least jetties train natural effects," says coastal geologist Robert Thieler. "Seawalls take wave action head on, with disastrous results." Rigid structures of wood, steel, concrete, or stone built parallel to the shoreline, seawalls destroy an island's ability to respond to storm energy by preventing the movement of sand.

Barrier islands deal with the force of storms in ingenious ways. In big storms a great mass of sand disappears from barrier beaches, dragged by waves out to sea, where it collects on offshore sandbars. These act as a break for the powerful waves that follow closely one upon the other. What remains is a flattened surface of coarse, heavy, porous sand that can absorb the beating blue tons of seawater that would destroy concrete in just a few seasons. Eventually sand washes back onto the beach and blows into dunes.

As sea level rises and islands narrow, replenished sand is lost to waves, currents, and storms. In "hotspots" the erosion can occur rapidly. Over the years the Army Corps of Engineers has mounted an ambitious program to combat the powerful marine pilferage along New Jersey's coastline by nourishing the beaches: taking sand from "borrow" areas far offshore and piping it onto beaches. Nourishment programs have restored beaches and protected buildings on barrier islands from New England to the Gulf coast. But only at immense cost, typically a million dollars or more a mile. At Monmouth Beach, the Army Corps of Engineers restored such a stretch of beach in front of three condominiums in 1994 and again last year. Both times storms swept away the sand within hours.

"There's no question that we're in a fight-or-flee situation," says Ken Smith, founder of Coastal Advocates, a lobbying firm for coastal homeowners and businesses. "But I think the benefits of keeping barrier beaches in their place far outweigh the costs. When people go to these beaches, they want hotels. They want restaurants and boardwalks. Most of all they want beaches. If the attraction on a barrier island is beach, and beach protects the amenities that enhance that attraction, what the heck is wrong with spending money to keep the beach?"

"What is wrong is that owners of beachfront property are not paying their fair share," says Stephen J. Leatherman, director of the Laboratory for Coastal Research at the University of Maryland. "Other taxpayers pay the freight for federal flood insurance and beach replenishment. In nourishment projects locals pitch in about 5 percent, state and county taxpayers pay about 30 percent, and the federal government pays the rest. This is a coastal subsidy, no way around that."

One of the few barrier systems not caught in the tug-of-war between beaches and buildings is a chain of islands off the Eastern Shore of Virginia. One summer day, when a reported quarter million people were packing onto the ten miles of beach at Ocean City, Maryland, Barry Truitt flew over the islands of the Nature Conservancy's Virginia Coast Reserve, about 60 miles to the south. On 14 islands stretching for more than 50 miles, Truitt counted a total of 71 people. And that's the most he's seen on any one day in a long time.

A burly man with a salt-and-pepper beard and a deep tan, Truitt was once a sportfisherman. Now he is director of science and stewardship at the Coast Reserve. He has been navigating the winding channels and broad bays of this region for 25 years. That makes him just a "come here" rather than a "been here." Still, if you ask him what something is, he knows. It's the sleek, vibrant green marsh grass, Spartina. It's a gull-billed tern. It's a tricolored heron.

Even as we moor our boat on the far southern tip of Wreck Island, a ripple of agitation spreads across the colony of nesting terns, gulls, and black skimmers. Truitt counts 300, no 400, no, probably close to 600 skimmers and terns. The birds have Wreck Island pretty much to themselves, and the neighboring island and the one next to that, and so on, for dozens of miles to the north and south. To be on these islands is to be surrounded by sand, grass, water, and little else.

This was not always the case. Until well into this century, a sizable population of tough, self-reliant people made a living on these islands. The third biggest town on Virginia's Eastern Shore thrived on Hog Island. In 1900 the town of Broadwater, on the island's bayside, consisted of about 50 houses, two general stores, an elementary school, an ice-cream parlor, and a community center known as the Red Onion, all situated two miles from the sea. But in the early 1920s storms began to take their toll. By 1933 surf lapped at the foundations of the houses. That year a hurricane took 60 feet of the beach in a single bite.

"People did the sensible thing," says Truitt. "They moved." One by one, islanders floated their houses by barge to the mainland towns of Oyster and Willis Wharf. By 1940 the island was virtually abandoned. Where Broadwater flourished, the sea now rolls. Hog Island waggles about, eroding in the south, advancing in the north. "I call it island migration," says Truitt. "It's only erosion if there's a house on it."

Truitt and a team of researchers recently counted 80,000 pairs of nesting birds on the islands of the Virginia Coast Reserve, many of them beach nesters that depend on overwash to maintain their nesting habitat. Without this disturbance, dune grass grows too densely for terns, skimmers, and plovers to make their shallow scrapes in the sand, and the birds must yield their nesting habitat to gulls that favor grassy dunes. When storm waves wash over the island, wiping out the dune system, the islands once again offer habitat for beach nesters.

On our way back to the mainland, late-afternoon light falls in low rays across the islands, illuminating the peaks of shrubs and trees swallowed up by moving dunes. A flock of terns rises in alarm and settles again. The transitory becomes one with the beautiful, and I think again of the barriers hit by Fran, the grief of shattered homes, the ripped and tattered fixings of human life, and beneath it all, the thin strands of sand where motion is everything.

AUGUST 1997

OLD-TIME TALK WE STILL DE TALKEM HERE!

(WE STILL SPEAK GULLAH HERE!)

PATRICIA JONES-JACKSON

Patricia Jones-Jackson's scholarly passion for Gullah took her to the Sea Islands of Georgia and the Carolinas and to West Africa in search of the roots of the hybrid tongue. On June 30, 1986, while on assignment for NATIONAL GEOGRAPHIC, she died, aged 39, of injuries suffered in an automobile crash on Johns Island, South Carolina.

"THE BUZZARD AND THE HAWK"
A Gullah Folktale, as told by Mr. Ted Williams

You know the buzzard always was a—a nice educated animal you know! E take e time—just like he done with the hawk.
Him and the hawk was sitting down on the limb one day, and he said—Him and the hawk had a consolation[consultation].
Say, "I'm very hungry!!!"
The hawk say, "I'm hungry too! Lord—O Lord!
My stomach! I too hungry!"
The buzzard say, "Wait on the Lord—"
And e look up—Nothing for dead—NOTHING, you know
So the buzzard say, "MAN!!!"
The hawk say, "I can't wait no longer!"
So when he look, a little sparrow come along. And—and—and the hawk get up and run at the sparrow and hit a tree *Uh huh!*
And the buzzard sit on he limb and look the hawk, look at the hawk, when he run into tree. The buzzard say, "I tell you wait on the Lord. Now I gone eat you now!"

Many old words and expressions are still in use among the Gullah speakers of the Sea Islands, for example:

---

day clean: *daybreak*
ugly too much: *very ugly*
this side: *this island*
sweetmouth: *flatter*
one day mong all!: *finally!*
long eye: *envy*
small small: *very small*
small small small: *tiny*
I de shell em: *I am shelling them*
I ben shell em: *I shelled them*
I bina shell em: *I have been shelling them*
I ben don shell em: *I shelled them some time ago*

Hundreds of words derived from West African languages occur in Gullah, and some have crossbred with English to become common expressions. Here are a few of them, with the languages from which they may have come:

goober: "peanut" (*Kimbundu*)
gumbo: "okra" (*Tshiluba*)
heh: "yes" (*Vai*)
hoodoo: "bad luck" (*Hausa*)
yambi: "yam" (*Vai*)
chigger: "small flea" (*Wolof*)
nana: "grandmother" (*Twi*)
tote: "to carry" (*Kongo*)
biddy: "small chicken" (*Kongo*)
buckra: "white man" (*Ibo*)

DECEMBER 1987

MONSOONS

PRIIT J. VESILIND

The sea eagle lifted skyward, nearly motionless in a shaft of tropical air rising from the Malabar Coast of India. It was the sixth of June 1983. In the troposphere a thin jet stream began to slip westward. The earth offered its northern half to the sun.

New heat scorched the Tibetan Plateau and the deserts of Rajasthan and Arabia. It was the time of tension and expectation in India, the time before the monsoon that Hindu astrologers call *rohini*, a time of heat and dry winds that send grit and dust clawing across the arid plains of the north. At midday the earth burns under an unrelenting sky, and at night, as Rudyard Kipling wrote, "The dry-eyed Moon in spite glares through the haze and mocks with watery light the torment of the uncomplaining trees."

The monsoon was late. That week near Ahmadnagar, in the state of Maharashtra, several women collapsed and died from heat exhaustion; after eight hours of heavy labor they had to haul drinking water from a distance of three kilometers over wild and hilly terrain, in temperatures hovering at 115°F. A dust storm lashed New Delhi with winds that reached 65 miles an hour and engulfed the city in darkness. Cloud seeders from California were hired by the city of Madras to replenish dwindling reservoirs. And on the central plateau, water was being sold at seven rupees a barrel in the city of Hyderabad. Fistfights erupted at public water taps in front of the waterworks, and office workers wearing expensive wristwatches drove frantically through the streets in their automobiles, searching for their share.

The eagle soared even higher in the updraft as I picked my way along the dark rocks beside the Arabian Sea. The winds shifted with promise, deepening the resonance of the surf, muffling even the crows that cackled and lurched along the seawalls. The water grew choppy, and the black thorns of fishermen's sails scratched the horizon. Surely the time was at hand.

At the weather station at Trivandrum, capital of the state of Kerala, chief meteorologist Julius Joseph thumbed impatiently through the morning's charts and graphs. "Look," he said triumphantly, pointing to a swirl of isobars, "the low-pressure trough has moved directly over us. A slight shift to the north could bring the monsoon."

But when? There was nothing left but to wait, with the rest of India, for that storied monsoon onset that inspired ancient Hindu poets to eloquence.

"The clouds advance like rutting elephants," wrote the fifth-century Indian poet Kalidasa, "enormous and full of rain. They come forward as kings among tumultuous armies; their flags are lightning, the thunder is their drum. . . ."

For this I had traveled four months through the breadth of the monsoon world—from Africa to north China, from the tropical coast of Australia to the lofty Himalayas of Nepal—to this middling coastal city on the southwest tip of India, where the monsoon was awaited by the first of June each year.

But the onset fizzled. The trough retreated south, meekly, and next morning the sea eagle turned a slow adagio in pale skies. The rain was stalled at sea, storming over the Maldive Islands.

So we waited. We waited as the sun stoked the powerful atmospheric engines of heat and water. We waited as the dusty streets of Trivandrum baked in sweat and evil smells. Wandering cattle licked their lips. Julius Joseph studied his charts.

It would come, it would come. But the fortunes of Asian agriculture, and thus the survival of half the world's nearly five billion people, ride on the monsoon's promise. Vital economic decisions await its whims, and politicians stake their careers on its failure or success.

In India the monsoon is predictably unpredictable. It will come, but it can arrive coyly, even gently, teasing with thundershowers. Rains can skip entire regions. It can rain for days, even weeks, until the earth is squirming with life and walls are slippery with mildew. For another week the skies may be clear, but then rain will come again, relentless, finally tedious, until memories of cracked, dry earth and fierce sun fade into wishful thinking.

June 7. In Trivandrum the breeze quickened. Southern India's central weather station in Madras issued a gale warning for fishermen. Julius Joseph was expectant.

"It's a typical monsoon sky today," he said, "all kinds of clouds, at all levels—a chaotic sky. But the wind is mostly from the northeast, the wrong way."

Wind, not rainfall, defines the monsoon for meteorologists—a seasonal wind that shifts direction twice a year. Asia breathes in, then breathes out. The inhalation is the summer, or southwest, monsoon that blows from mid-May through September, bringing heavy rains from tropical oceans into the continent. The winter, or northeast, monsoon is a reverse flow beginning in October, bringing cool, dry, continental air to most of India and China and rain to Indonesia, Australia, and areas with northeast coastlines.

Though the basic physics of monsoons was described 300 years ago, no one has yet pieced together the entire mechanism or fully understood its behavior.

"Imagine a puff of cigarette smoke blown into a room," University of Maryland meteorologist Dr. J. Shukla explained to me. "A second puff will not follow the first; all will be different, totally unpredictable.

June 8. That evening in Trivandrum lightning danced soundlessly on the clouds that lined the southern horizon. From the seawall I scanned for pied-crested cuckoos from Africa, said to fly before the winds. But there were only the crows and the nasal drone of the muezzin's call to prayer, drifting from a Muslim village across the water.

Islam itself rode the winds to the Malabar Coast. Through recorded time Arab dhows have sailed from the Persian Gulf, borne on the monsoons. They raked India for spices, gems, and teak, and scoured the East African coast for frankincense, mangrove, ivory, and slaves. The legendary Arab sailor Sindbad was said to have reached China on the shifting winds. "Monsoon" derives from the Arabic word for season, *mausim.*

Back in mid-May I had been to the African port of Mombasa to see the remnants of the ancient traffic. A modern facility handles Kenya's container-ized shipping there, but wooden dhows still anchor in Old Town, a steamy, intimate warren that sizzles in chocolate, pungent curries, and fried cassava. Masai tribesmen elbow through the alleyways with sleek Hindu merchants, dark sailors from Abu Dhabi, and caramel-colored maidens whose lustrous eyes dance over veils of Muslim silk.

The *Sarina al Aziz* from India had been unloading koko wood, kingfish, and shark fins from Somalia when I arrived, and Mombasa's longshoremen heaved bales of coffee onto the Taysir from Dubai, bound for the Red Sea.

Like their predecessors, the dhows rarely risk the full force of the southwest monsoon, but head north just ahead of it. Supplementary diesel engines help through rough weather.

"Now there are only a few days left," declared port dhow master Mr. Mnabe, a broad-shouldered African given to repeating himself in a loud voice. "Only a few days left. If the dhows do not sail now, they cannot go."

The Kenyan twilight had shone like a pearl, but by next afternoon the southerly winds had strengthened and coalesced; dark clouds pumped across the eastern skies. The Somali jet stream, a major component of the southwest monsoon, had set in.

This powerful, low-level stream of air begins as trade winds in the southern Indian Ocean. Bent right by the Coriolis force generated by the spin of the Earth, the air mass veers off the Kenya Highlands as it crosses the Equator, gathering momentum northeast along the African coast. The seas shift with the wind until a virtual river within the ocean, the Somali Current, rolls 150 kilometers wide toward Arabia.

South of the West African hump in the South Atlantic, and all across the Indian Ocean, other winds pull north as the continents heat. By the end of May the southwest monsoon has usually begun; moist air is pulsating into West Africa, the Indonesian islands, and continental Asia.

In the Far East the monsoon starts earlier than in India and is just as important. The "plum rains," or *meiyu*, of China drench the southern coast around mid-May. In Japan the *baiu* brings rain into the Ryukyus. But on its way north the summer monsoon causes serious floods, loss of life, and extensive damage to China while at the same time nourishing the crops that feed a billion people.

The powerful monsoon rains hammer Burma and the mountains of Thailand, Laos, and Vietnam. They flood the streets of Bangkok, a slowly sinking behemoth where hasty progress has filled in many of the ancient *klongs* that drain the city.

In India the summer monsoon develops in two branches. In the western branch, vortices powerful enough to disable aircraft can form over the Arabian Sea. A deep, humid air mass churns into Sri Lanka and India's Malabar Coast, battering the Western Ghats with prolonged, nourishing rain, which spills into the central plateau. It buffets the coast in waves, moving north, traditionally reaching Bombay by June 10.

In the Bay of Bengal branch, violent thundershowers, the *kal Baisakhis*, wrack Bangladesh and the Indian states of West Bengal and Assam. Tropical depressions push north from the bay, are deflected west by the southern flanks of the Himalayas, and storm across the scorching Gangetic Plain. Cherrapunji, a perennially soggy village on the south slopes of the Khasi Hills, is overwhelmed with one of the highest average yearly rainfalls on earth, 1,142 centimeters (450 inches).

The two branches usually merge over central India by the second week of July. By the end of September the monsoon has played out against the Himalayas.

June 9. At midnight a stifling silence descended. Air conditioners hiccuped to a halt as electric-power rationing reached home consumers in Trivandrum. All power to heavy industrial users had already been severed. Now, movie houses were restricted to one showing a day, neon display lights were out-lawed, and stores were compelled to close by sundown.

Kerala was down to six days of power, its major hydroelectric reservoirs drained to an all-time low. Only the arrival of a healthy monsoon could prevent a total power outage in the state.

Julius Joseph, scientist and adviser, hung up the telephone at the weather station. "That was Mr. Pillai, Kerala's minister of electricity," he said. "He fears a total power breakdown. But I gave him some hope. The monsoon will come any day now."

Across India reservoirs dwindled into puddles as the rains hovered offshore. About half of the nation's electricity is generated by hydropower, and thus by the monsoons. Government officials confessed to newspapers in anxiety that late rains would impede food production, aggravate inflation, and increase prices—and all this in a preelection year. Prime Minister Indira Gandhi, touring in Europe, asked for monsoon forecasts to be added to her daily political briefings.

The state of Karnataka found itself with 900 extra elephants that had migrated from the parched forests of Tamil Nadu, in India's southeast. Summer rain would barely ease the drought in Tamil Nadu, for the state lies in the shadow zone of the southwesterly winds and depends heavily on the winter monsoon for its water.

During that season of the northeast wind, from October to March, the rest of the country stays relatively mild and dry. Surges of winter-monsoon cold from Siberia are shunted off by the high-rising Tibetan Plateau and funneled into eastern Asia.

All of eastern Asia bears the brunt of the winter monsoon. In the middle latitudes, freezing temperatures and bitter wind, not rain, pulse out of Siberia. Frigid, dry air pushes south. Cold cyclones rear over the Gobi desert, gusting in suffocating dust storms called *karaburan*. The winds stream southeastward, growing water heavy and warm over the sea. They curve southwest, bent by the Coriolis force, and probe toward the tropics.

"In the days of the emperors the frozen bodies were stacked like cordwood on the streets of Beijing, waiting to be picked up each morning." I had heard this from Zhao Zhen of the Academy of Meteorological Sciences in Beijing, where I attended a seminar between American and Chinese monsoon experts.

The science is deeply rooted in China. We were each given a collection of weather data, for example, that spanned 500 years. Deep as well is the Chinese love of learning. A wave of newly published books had hit Beijing as part of the liberalization of cultural life, and on the broad boulevards people gathered like moths to sit under streetlamps after dark, simply to read.

By the time surges of monsoonal cold hit the tropics, they have lost most of their chill, but winds can reach 35 to 45 knots, whipping the South China Sea into a frenzy, setting up rainstorms that drench the coasts of Southeast Asia, Borneo, or the Philippines.

For the heavily commercial city-state of Singapore, the condition of the South China Sea affects shipping schedules and work on the forest of offshore oil rigs. "During the strong winter monsoons even fishermen can't go out," Singapore meteorologist Dr. Lim Hock had told me. "Waves up to four meters high sweep the beaches on the east coasts of Malaysia, causing much damage."

Racing toward the Equator, the northerly winds are heated and sucked upward over Indonesia. Rain squalls roll up mountain slopes. Great columns of soaked, heated clouds rise and tower over the islands and northern Australia. Sumatra, Borneo, and most of the northern islands get ample rains from both monsoons, but a marked dry season sears eastern Indonesia in winter. In 1983 the islands of Timor, Sulawesi, and Bali suffered severe drought.

June 10. The summer rains had reached Burma and Malaysia, but only a drizzle trickled over thirsting Trivandrum.

"Most peculiar," said Julius Joseph. "Rarely does this much delay occur."

Since June 1982 the operative word for world weather had been "crazy." Blamed was a tongue of warmer-than-usual sea surface in the eastern Pacific that South Americans call El Niño, The Child, since it occurs around Christmas every four years or so.

El Niño tossed world weather patterns into turmoil. It deflated the 1982-83 monsoon in drought-struck Australia, stifling the November rains that usually pound the northern coast. Only in early March did the thunderheads straggle into Darwin, capital of the Northern Territory. In its normal cycle the territory is a land of either-or. The monsoon heralds the Wet, with a capital W, as distinct from the Dry. And the Wet thunders into Darwin with enthusiasm; in 1974 the city was virtually destroyed by a tropical cyclone, or hurricane.

At the height of the Wet, wild tropical grasses grow eye-high, and the gullies are choked with vegetation. When the rains stop, the land turns tinder dry. Searing winds sweep north from the outback; bushfires crackle across a territory the size of Oregon, out of control by August.

"The more water, the more vegetation—the more vegetation, the more fires," was the neat but chilling synopsis of Mike Rowell, chief officer of the Northern Territory's Bush Fires Council in Darwin.

"The vastness of it all," he had sighed. "We have more country, more fuel on undeveloped land, and fewer people who know how to handle it than any other monsoon region of Australia. The old-timers understand how to live with fire. Our big problem now is the growth of Darwin—and newcomers not always aware of the problems of fire. The result is a highly dangerous situation at least four months of the year."

By the ancient calendar of the Aboriginals it was still *gudjewg*, monsoon time. *Ngalyod*, the rainbow snake, is the creator spirit, Arnhem Land's symbol of the northeast monsoon. It brings the rains and life; it stands as the rainbow after the storm. But man himself, for a grudge or a sense of revenge, also can summon natural forces.

Jimmy Burinyila, an Aboriginal and curator of the local museum, told me how rain is made: "The water snake, yellowbelly, that one is lightning. Now the file snake . . . the file snake you find in fresh water. It can float, and go *tshhhhhhh!* And make the rain. Now a man can make the sound of the snake, and that brings the rain. He will stay home and sleep, and it will start pouring and pouring."

I had asked Luke Taylor, an Australian anthropologist who does research in Maningrida, about the lack of rains this year.

"The people have had a two-month-long ceremony in the bush," he answered. "They were singing the rain away, keeping it from coming, until they were finished. Others were calling from all over the territory by radio, asking them to stop.

"The meteorologists blame pressure troughs, but we know the real story here. It rained for two bloody weeks after the people broke up the ceremony and went home."

June 11. Indians, beseeching gods and meteorologists alike, still waited. Julius Joseph spent his morning comforting politicians and press at Trivandrum. Heavy cumulonimbus clouds had gathered, but the wind still gusted from the northwest. "Two or three more days," he augured.

The state of Kerala, normally water rich, shriveled. The last monsoon and seasonal rains had failed. Tea fields had turned brown; coffee had missed the crucial "blossom showers." Rubber tapping had been suspended. Rice farmers stared bleakly at the packed earth, awaiting the time to plow.

With the new high-yielding rice strains of the green revolution, farmers who irrigate can grow two, even three crops a year. But half of India's arable land depends solely on monsoon rains and a single growing season. For farmers the coming of the monsoon is still life's critical uncertainty.

In the best of years rice farming is a gamble. Will pre-monsoon showers soften the soil in time? When should seedlings be transplanted? If too soon, they will wither; if too late, the crop will die when the rains stop.

But with a growing complex of irrigation schemes, bore wells, and storage tanks, India has become self-sufficient in food for the first time.

In the west Indian state of Maharashtra, farmers have long been tethered to the monsoon stake. In May 1983, however, humble acceptance was not in fashion. In the village of Karjat 500 women marched in protest and staged a hunger strike against the government's water management policies. Niggling rains had cut harvests to subsistence levels, and, with the monsoon unknown weeks away, even drinking water prospects were grim.

I had journeyed through Karjat soon after, on the road from Bombay to Pune, and to the city of Aurangabad. The road knifed through the bluffs of the Western Ghats, where cripples and sadhus, holy men, perched to gather alms from wealthy travelers. Past Pune lay a flat, torrid landscape of thornbushes and mud huts. Villagers sat in the stifling heat as if stunned, and a dry wind sucked moisture from the dying pipal trees that lined the roadside.

Near the village of Koregaon I stopped on a bridge to watch as women hauled water from a well sunk into a broad, snake-dry riverbed. An old farmer in dirty linen approached, stuck out his chest, and saluted stiffly, in the British manner. "I'm a military man," said Dattu Madhu Glonhane.

He wanted to explain the plight of his village. "God doesn't like this place," he said. "There was a solar eclipse and a lunar eclipse here. We don't have enough water for irrigation, just for drinking. But the earth is good. If it rains this year, there will be lots of crops."

"What if the rains don't come?"

"People are going to start looting," he said. "Others are going to starve. If there is no water, it doesn't matter if you have a job or not. So we're living on hope. Even the birds die of thirst. But birds have wings—they can fly away. We are stuck here."

June 12. I was awakened at night by the bold, dry scrape of cockroaches the size of a thumb, scudding across the nightstand.

"We are all praying for rain," said the chambermaid thoughtfully, as she sprayed in the corners next day.

The city grew impatient. Trivandrum's public schools, scheduled to open June 1, remained shut. Not enough water for drinking and sanitation, officials explained.

The monsoon can be poetic in the countryside but hard news for urban India. In Bombay, drinking water was little in evidence as I walked through the center of India's wealthiest metropolis. I remember a six-year-old boy, scrubbing aluminum pans on the sidewalk, who stood for a moment to catch his breath. Then he walked to a carton of empty soda bottles behind a kiosk and raised each to his lips to salvage the dregs.

And I remember the water vendor who pulled a barrel on a wooden cart through a slum district in the city center shouting, "Water, only one rupee!" A thin, shirtless man implored him for a drink. The two argued. The vendor twirled a black mustache like a melodrama villain and waited for the rupee. The thin man licked his lips. The vendor, indifferent, moved on.

"How much do you make a day?" I asked the vendor, hurrying after him.

"Forty pails, forty rupees."

"That's a lot of money," I said, having been told that the average Indian field laborer earns about 15 rupees a day. "How can you charge so much?"

The vendor did not answer; he simply pointed to the cloudless, intimidating sky.

But in the first sustained downpour, life in Bombay sloshes to a halt. Muddy water fills the taps. Many old buildings collapse. Garbage and cattle dung clog drains, turning streets into stinking canals that invite cholera and dysentery. The low-lying slums that surround Bombay like a grimy quilt are swept away. Train service, lifeline of the city, is severed. Where the tracks cross the neighborhood of Parel, I had met with residents who routinely evacuate their families into a nearby factory building when the water invades.

"We know we need the monsoon, but it's a problem for us," P. G. Bhujbal, a local resident, explained. He pointed to a stream of sewage that trickled from an adjacent apartment building, where chickens pecked at grains of floating garbage.

"We are the lowest point in the area," he said. "The gutter water mixes with the rain water and comes into the houses. We put the tables on top of the beds and sit on the tables. The water is chest high sometimes."

"So many years have passed and always the same thing," said William D' Souza, another resident. "But nobody is doing anything for us. The government? They come, they see, they go."

Yet Bombay waits eagerly for the rains, if only through cultural mandate. Children in underwear rush into the streets to rejoice in mud puddles, and prayers of thanks fill the temples. Only when the reservoirs are full does the rain's soggy monotony wear thin.

In the city of Madras, where the northeast monsoon is the culprit, reservoirs had stood nearly empty that May. The beleaguered Madras Metropolitan Water Supply and Sewerage Board had sunk 132 new deep-bore wells. They had initiated a scheme to divert water to the city from the Krishna River, some 400 kilometers away. They had imported water by steam-cleaned railroad tank cars, imposed a tight rationing system, and dispatched fleets of drinking-water trucks daily to plumbing-poor neighborhoods.

Still, Madras suffered. Trees and grass had withered in the parks. Mere walking was a trial through the cloying heat, exhaust fumes, and the constant whine of beggars. A sign scrawled on a concrete wall offered, "Repent! Jesus will give you rain."

In a poor neighborhood a line of determined women had already formed at dusk at their water-rationing station; their aluminum and brass pots were strung like a necklace on the sidewalk.

"They sleep here in order to keep their place in line," a local resident informed me. "It goes on all night."

At the office of the water board, managing director Dewan Mohammed outlined the dilemma: "We have to hold on till October," he said. "All our rivers are dry. You can walk from Madras to Kanniyakumari [on the southern tip of India] without getting your feet wet. There are no snow-clad mountains for us, no perennial rivers. Tamil Nadu is a dry state, dependent totally on the rains.

"This is the third year that the monsoon has faltered; it's a hardship. But it will not fail; the rains will come. They have to come."

The previous October, when the winter rains were expected, violinist Kunnakkudi Vaidyanathan had waded into the Red Hills Reservoir and rendered a 70-minute-long raga as an invocation to the gods. Self-styled "miracle man" Thomas Jacob, a bank clerk from Kerala, had sent out telepathic rainmaking waves. But only a puja, a Hindu prayer ceremony in which a thousand women in red robes sat with a thousand candles and chanted heavenward, had succeeded in bringing brief showers.

At Kapaleeswarar Hindu temple, where the dried-up temple pool had been turned into a cricket field by street urchins, I watched members of the red-robed sect as they chanted: *Om, shakti, Parashakti! Om, shakti, Parashakti!* beseeching their goddess of supreme strength. The gathering joined a growing procession, the men bearing an altar that smoked with purifying camphor and offerings. Musicians struck up a reedy tune, temple bells tinkled, and the procession clanked and chanted down the Madras streets, past wandering cattle, children being lathered at public water taps, and the ubiquitous movie billboards where macho men postured with weapons beside chubby-thighed maidens in distress.

If prayers alone could bring rain, Madras might be sated. But in India even prayer is a matter of form. Said T. V. A. Seshan, a religious philosopher and an editor at the newspaper *Hindu*, "It has to be incanted in a certain way, with a certain inflection, pronunciation, and pitch. The priests can do it. I can't do it."

He chanted unsuccessfully for me in a gravelly voice. "When a number of persons chant in a particular way," he said, "it creates a certain sound vibration that affects the atmosphere and is capable of seeding the clouds. The priests don't know the scientific aspects of it—they only know the sound has to be in this fashion, in this way."

The wind had picked up that evening, blowing the wrong way from the odorous tidal backwater by the century-old Madras Boat Club. Distant lightning flashed like a pale eye winking. The wind touched the neem trees and whispered through the wicker chairs as Madras waited.

June 13. The coast at Trivandrum was lost in haze and drizzle; the air smelled of iodine. The sky was cast in chalk. I sat in the coffee shop and sulked at the crows. In the previous 83 years only four monsoons had arrived here this late.

Yet rains were reported over other parts of Kerala. The city of Cochin, to the north, had showers at night. On the beach the foam was tinged with evidence—yellow-brown silt loosened by rains in upland watersheds.

Some erosion is natural, but too much of India's topsoil has been lost to the sea. Exposed earth, particularly in the mountains, has little chance to hang together in the sustained downpours of the monsoon. The problem is near critical in Nepal, where nearly a third of the forests have been destroyed in the past 30 years. The Himalayas, the spine of Nepal, are still in full geologic thrust, rising half a centimeter a year with the concomitant grind of earthquakes and crumbling rocks. But Nepalese farmers have accelerated the natural process, carving foothills into fields, angling their terraces higher and higher, hacking too many trees into firewood, and leaving goats and cattle to nibble at whatever is left.

Each year more frequent and more powerful landslides sweep the hills. Terraces, fields, livestock, people, and entire villages have been lost, and many families face each monsoon with growing fear. Thousands have already left for the increasingly overcrowded Nepalese lowlands.

June 14. A lone fisherman, his dark body taut like wires and pulleys, worked his catamaran through the surf to the beach at Trivandrum. He unlashed a net bag of silvery *chala*, a sardine-like local fish, as buyers gathered around. His name was Abel Johnson. Such a man should know.

"The monsoon is God's way of providing fish," he said. "When the sea is rough, the water near the shore will be very cold. Fish like cold water, they will come very close, and we will have good tuna, shark, and prawns. And the vastness of the sea will not matter to us."

"But will it come today?" I pressed.

Abel squinted into the horizon where I could see nothing. "It is very hot," he said. "Also the wind is from the west. There was a change in the waves this morning."

Later I heard thunder, and the air was quite still. There was no wind, I realized, for the first time in eight days. And then, at 2:30 p.m., a squall line of gray edged from the southwest. It deepened into a solid wall of clouds that seemed to push the wind before it. The seas leapt into whitecaps, and heavy waves assaulted the shoreline.

Fishermen scrambled to lash their boats to the wooden frames that lined the beach. Palm trees thrashed like gladiators. Darkness covered the earth, and the monsoon, in a churning mass of "rutting elephants," rode majestically into the Malabar Coast.

The grand lottery had begun. The rains picked their way at random—blessing, denying, destroying. They fell, as an Indian proverb says, on one horn of the buffalo but not the other.

The initial burst merely doused Kerala but overwhelmed the state of Gujarat. A vicious cyclonic storm, with winds reaching 115 kilometers an hour, tore roofs off houses in the port of Veraval, and the merchant ship *Har Gange*, en route from Dubai, was reported missing. Overflowing dams left 150 villages stranded in the Junagadh district. Military helicopters were dispatched to drop food and supplies to hundreds perched on rooftops. More than 500 people perished.

Almost overnight, grass appeared and leafless trees sprouted in green. Centipedes and slugs and earthworms gloried in the rich mud. Sowing began for the kharif—the autumn crop—on June 17.

By June 21 hundreds of structures—offices, homes, shanties—had collapsed in Bombay. Floods had made shambles of train schedules, and thousands of telephones were cut off as water seeped into buried cables.

By July 6 many of India's major rivers were in spate, leaving countless victims. The highway between Bombay and Goa was blocked by landslides, and three people were killed by lightning. Exhausted Aurangabad finally got its rains by July 10.

On July 20 the monsoon was revitalized by a powerful cyclone over the

Arabian Sea. The rains reached New Delhi on schedule, making up for lost time, and nourished arid Punjab and the deserts of Rajasthan four days early. Late rain washed over Trivandrum, and Balakrishna Pillai, minister for electricity, upped the movie-house quota to two showings a day.

Bangladesh rejoiced in the annual flooding of its delta, and Burmese mountain tribes hunkered under palm-frond roofs against the deluge. In Thailand Bangkok sank deeper into the mud. In China the Yangtze spilled into the countryside, inundating 70,000 houses and 300 factories in the city of Wuhan. A million Chinese mobilized to fight the waters. Ten thousand marooned peasants were rescued by a boat-and-bridge brigade of the People's Liberation Army.

In Nepal 30 villagers were killed in a wrenching landslide on August 1, in the Baglung district near Pokhara.

On August 11 the Indian government cited a comfortable inventory in the national grain pool, putting the stamp of success on the monsoon. By August 31 only three states—Bihar, parts of Uttar Pradesh, and Himachal Pradesh— were deficient in rains. Even Madras drank deeply, as unusual sweeps of the southwest system held off disaster in Tamil Nadu.

And when the earth again offered its southern half to the sun, and the jet streams had shifted in the troposphere, the rains ebbed and eased out to sea. Asia exhaled.

But in India the monsoon clouds are pregnant with joy. The rain brings the mating cry of the peacock, and darkness the longing of lovers. When the rains come, people run into the street, their arms spread, their grateful tears blending with the sky's benediction. The patter of the rain is like the laughter of young girls, swinging in mango groves and singing a traditional song:

Swing, swing, Rani Raja, till the flowering of the rose.
Swing, swing, Rani Raja, till the flowering of the marigold.
Swing, swing, Rani Raja, till the flowering of the champa.

DECEMBER 1984

THE RAIN IN SPAIN

Mark W. Harrington

El Pueblo Católico, of New San Salvador, prints a number of resolutions promulgated by the principal alcalde of the town and department of Castañas. They are as follows:

"Considering that the Supreme Creator has not behaved well in this province, as in the whole of last year only one shower of rain fell; that in this summer, notwithstanding all the processions, prayers and praises, it has not rained at all, and consequently the crops of Castañas, on which depend the prosperity of the whole department, are entirely ruined, it is decreed:

"Article 1. If within the peremptory period of eight days from the date of this decree rain does not fall abundantly, no one will go to mass or say prayers.

"Article 2. If the drought continues eight days more, the churches and chapels shall be burned, and missals, rosaries, and other objects of devotion will be destroyed.

"Article 3. If, finally, in a third period of eight days it shall not rain, all the priests, friars, nuns, and saints, male and female, will be beheaded. And for the present permission is given for the commission of all sorts of sin, in order that the Supreme Creator may understand with whom he has to deal."

The most remarkable feature of this affair is the fact that four days after these resolutions were passed the heaviest rainfall known for years was precipitated on the burning community.

FROM "WEATHER MAKING ANCIENT AND MODERN,"
APRIL 25, 1894

VALUE
JUDGMENTS

THE PEALES: AMERICA'S FIRST FAMILY OF ART

Otto Friedrich

On the softly lit museum wall, George Washington stands proud or, as Thomas Jefferson once said of him, "easy, erect, and noble." This is not the white-haired patriarch with ill-fitting dentures later celebrated by Gilbert Stuart but rather Charles Willson Peale's portrait of the ruddy and faintly smiling commander in full command, blue sash of office flowing across his ample belly, one hand resting nonchalantly on the muzzle of a cannon.

"Peale and Washington were rather good friends," says our guide through New York's Metropolitan Museum of Art, a slender young woman named Alice Iglehart. She has curly brown hair and wire-rimmed glasses and three silver bracelets on her wrist. "They liked to sit and talk and joke while these paintings were being done, and I think it's evident that Peale was trying to bring out the warmth and humanity of this person, rather than portraying him as someone unapproachable."

This is Peale's replica of a portrait he painted in 1779, at the request of the Supreme Executive Council of Pennsylvania, to commemorate the American victories at Trenton and Princeton. Peale was a natural choice since he had led a nervous company of Philadelphia militiamen through the mud and snow of both battles, while, as he later wrote in his diary, musket balls "whistled their thousand different notes around our heads."

Peale painted Washington from life seven different times. The last of these sittings occurred in 1795, at Peale's studio in Philadelphia. With him were his talented young sons, Raphaelle and Rembrandt, and his brother James. One of Peale's objects then was to help his relatives earn commissions, so they all set up their easels.

James Peale, who had been taught to paint by his more versatile older brother, remained in that brother's shadow, his health impaired by the war. As Alice Iglehart leads her flock to James Peale's rather stiff portrait of Washington, she speaks of it equivocally. "What James was trying to do was brighten the palette," she says. "This is much more vibrant, more energetic—and yet to me not nearly as realistic and captivating as his still lifes."

She thinks better of an equally stiff portrait by Rembrandt Peale, one of some 70 copies he made from a portrait of Washington he painted in 1823, but she has some mild criticisms of that too. "Rembrandt thought of Washington as a godlike figure," she says. "Washington seems to be floating above us, looking away. His face glows in the strong light and heavenly background of pastel clouds."

The reason I'm interested in seeing these portraits of Washington through Alice Iglehart's wire-framed eyes is that she too is part of the Peale clan.

Charles Willson Peale named 10 of his 17 children (11 of them survived to maturity) for famous painters, and so the first of his daughters to grow up alongside Raphaelle, Rembrandt, Titian, and Rubens Peale was one Angelica Kauffmann Peale, named for a gifted Swiss artist who became a protégée of Sir Joshua Reynolds and a founding member of the British Royal Academy.

When Alice Iglehart, a descendent of Angelica Peale, looks at the portrait of Washington on the battlefield, she is admiring the work of her great-great-great-great-grandfather. Having studied art history and applied for work at the Metropolitan Museum, she was so entranced by Peale's works there that she now gives lecture tours on her ancestor.

"I think there's something really magical about his work," she says. "And I'm fascinated by his love of life, and how much he wanted to accomplish. And I wish to God I could have met the man."

It is a very understandable desire, for there is nobody in the remarkable Peale tribe more remarkable than its founding father. Charles Willson Peale was very much a man of his remarkable time and place, of that generation that created the United States of America. He shared with his contemporaries a love of exploration and invention and a sense of unlimited possibilities. He always retained a quality of innocence, of guileless enthusiasm. He painted many of the great men of his day, many of them as friends, and so our sense of how that whole generation looks comes largely through his work—more than a thousand portraits in all.

He not only painted Washington more often than anyone else did, but he also painted his successor in the Presidency, John Adams, who once described Peale as "a tender, soft, affectionate Creature." Peale painted Adams's successor, Jefferson, with whom he later conducted an amiable correspondence on the best methods of plowing and of planting, and also Jefferson's successors, James Madison and James Monroe. He painted the Marquis de Lafayette, with whom he had spent that hard winter at Valley Forge, and Benjamin Franklin, who sent him the carcass of a French Angora cat as one of the first contributions to Peale's museum of natural history in Philadelphia, the first of its kind in America. He painted John Paul Jones and Alexander Hamilton and Thomas Paine. "Ever fond of perpetuating the Remembrance of the Worthies of my time," Peale wrote in 1780, "I conceive it will be a means of exciting an Emulation in our Posterity to deserve the like Attention, and mankind will receive an advantage thereby."

Because he was an ardent liberal—he even became chairman of the radical political group known as the Furious Whigs—Peale had some trouble winning portrait commissions from conservative merchants. So he built, in 1782, America's first skylighted art gallery, adjoining his home at the corner of Philadelphia's Third and Lombard Streets, on the unorthodox theory that art could be appreciated by the common people.

He was sketching some enormous bones of an unknown animal when his brother-in-law Col. Nathaniel Ramsay told him, "Doubtless, there are many men like myself who would prefer seeing such articles of curiosity than any paintings whatever." This remark was the seed from which Peale's famous museum sprang forth. From that moment, Peale decided to collect and show to the public not only fossilized bones but also specimens of all the animals, birds, fish, and insects (not to mention Indian artifacts) that could be found on this largely unexplored continent.

Peale invented everything as he went along. Taxidermy, for example, was a craft that he had to figure out for himself. He failed to preserve Franklin's Angora cat, but when he heard that Lafayette had sent Washington some Chinese pheasants, he asked if he might have them when they died, and these he succeeded in stuffing. (They are still preserved at Harvard.)

He also invented the idea of displaying his creatures in their natural habitats. A visiting clergyman named Manasseh Cutler wrote in 1787 of seeing a pond in the museum containing "a collection of fish with their skins stuffed, Water-fowls—such as the different speecies of Geese, ducks,

Cranes, Herons, etc.; all having the appearance of life, for their skins were admirably preserved."

Founding fathers like Peale do not appear out of nowhere, of course. The first Peale on record as having received a university education in England was Thomas Peale, son of a carpenter, who graduated from Cambridge in 1680, then became a clergyman in Rutlandshire and married the sister of a local landowner named Charles Wilson. Their son Charles followed in the same path, and so did that Charles's son Charles. The youngest Charles did not graduate, but migrated to London to work as a clerk in His Majesty's General Post Office, augmenting his modest salary by embezzlement.

When arrested in 1735, he was found to have stolen 700 pounds. Since this was a capital offense, young Peale was duly sentenced to be hanged, but his sentence was commuted to banishment for life to the American Colonies. Penniless and friendless, Peale sailed to Virginia, found employment as a schoolteacher in Annapolis, Maryland, and encountered there an amiable widow named Margaret Triggs. Scarcely five months after their marriage, she gave birth, on April 15, 1741, to their first son, Charles Willson Peale.

Charles Peale seems to have been an indulgent father. When his son was six, the father wrote to a sister in England: "Charly, who is a . . . manly straight Boy . . . gives me hopes of being a good Genius, being very docile." The exiled Peale died three years later, leaving to his widow and five orphans very little more than a belief that although they had come down in the world, they still had a claim to landed estates in Rutlandshire.

Young Charly had to be apprenticed to a saddlemaker. It can be argued that learning to make saddles was more valuable in 18th-century America than reading Latin at Cambridge. Peale learned how to use his eyes and hands and to invent whatever he needed. When his watch failed him, for example, he taught himself to repair watches.

His relations with people were equally unschooled and straightforward. He was 17 when he met a girl named Rachel Brewer; she was 14. After a respectable number of visits to her home, he bluntly proposed marriage, saying he would give her an hour to make a decision, then ostentatiously pulling out his smoothly functioning watch. She seems to have been struck dumb. "The time expired," Peale later wrote in the grand third-person style of his autobiography. "He must now take his leave of the Family for ever."

Forever, at that age, sometimes lasts only a few months. "On a Summers Evening, walking out for recreation," his account continues, "by chance he spied Miss Brewer." Rachel told him if he had chosen to misinterpret her silence "as a denial, she was not blameable."

They were married in 1762, when he was 20 and she 17. Then babies began arriving, and all too often dying. The first, Margaret Jane, lived 12 days; James Willson, two years; Eleanor also died in infancy; Margaret lived less than a year. Then their fortunes changed. Raphaelle, future master of still-life painting, arrived in 1774, Angelica Kauffmann in 1775.

It is commonplace to say that 18th-century parents accepted such losses with equanimity, but one of Peale's most affecting paintings, "Rachel Weeping," shows his wife, newly recovered from smallpox, grieving over the body of Margaret "This picture," wrote John Adams after Peale had shown it to him, "struck me prodigiously."

More characteristic of Peale's domestic menagerie is a charming painting called "The Peale Family Group," which shows Peale bending teacher-like over his younger brother St. George, who is drawing a picture of their mother. Gathered around the table are James, his sisters Elizabeth and Margaret Jane, Rachel, and a couple of unidentified children, presumably Eleanor and Margaret, the nurse, Peggy Durgan, and the family dog, Argus.

Peale, it seems, was a benign but watchful father. "My opinion," he once wrote to a friend, "is that all youth should be enticed, persuaided, commended to do good. . . . I think those who use Stripes or any other kind of severities are *lazy, base*, and unworthy."

On a shopping trip to Norfolk, Virginia, in 1762, Peale happened to see some paintings—several landscapes and a portrait. "They were miserably done," he later wrote. "Had they been better, perhaps they would not have lead Peale to the Idea of attempting any thing in that way." In that time and place such paintings were not considered anything so forbidding as art, more like a handicraft, a kind of furniture.

Peale tried painting a landscape, then a picture of himself taking apart a clock. Somebody asked him to do a pair of portraits and paid him ten pounds. Peale began to think this new line of work might be more profitable than the saddlery business. He found a professional portraitist named John Hesselius, living near Annapolis, and promised him a saddle in exchange for lessons. Hesselius painted half a face, then showed Peale how to finish it.

Then, at this threshold of a promising new career, everything went wrong. An associate in the saddlery business embezzled all the available money and fled. Peale found himself bankrupt. Threatened with prison for debts of some 600 pounds, he was forced to abandon his pregnant Rachel in 1765 and flee by boat to Boston. There he was encouraged by the portraitist John Singleton Copley, but it was only the intervention of friends and relatives that won a stay from his creditors and let him return home.

These friends went further. They raised a sum of more than 80 pounds to send Peale to London to study with the famous American painter Benjamin West. West not only treated his younger compatriot kindly but painted a handsome portrait of him as well. And Peale finally learned that his family no longer had any valid claim to ancestral estates. When he finally returned to long-suffering Rachel more than two years later, he was fully ready and able to paint his way out of debt.

To make his career, Peale moved in 1776 to Philadelphia, then the biggest city in the Colonies, but he soon found it embroiled in plans for war. The painter acquired a rifle and, in collaboration with astronomer David Rittenhouse, experimented with various mixtures of gunpowder. He also fashioned a telescopic sight that, on first use, blacked his eye.

At 35, he was anything but soldierly. "Peale was a thin, spare, pale-faced man, in appearance totally unfit to endure the fatigues of long marches," he wrote of himself. Yet two months after he joined the Philadelphia militia as a common soldier in August 1776, his fellow soldiers elected him a lieutenant. Peale not only led his company off to war but also cooked for the soldiers and even made them shoes.

When the British evacuated Philadelphia in the spring of 1778, the city was torn between reactionaries and radicals—supporters of the establish-ment and what the establishment decried as "mobocracy." As a longtime Son of Liberty, Peale kept being pushed into the bitterest controversies. He served as an agent for a commission that confiscated property of wealthy Tories judged to have sided with Britain and on another that investigated the profiteering of Washington's close friend Robert Morris (whose portrait Peale nonetheless painted more than once). At one point Peale was even attacked in the street by an unidentified assailant. It all became too much for him. In 1780 he lapsed into what he called "a kind of lethargy," a condition that we might now regard as a nervous breakdown.

"In some of my intervals of reflection I have been a good deal alarmed at my situation," he wrote to a relative in 1783. In one instance he was sitting by the fireside among his family and suddenly tried to think how many children he had, and could not do so; in another he tried to remember whether his mother-in-law was dead or alive, and could not do so.

The great healing event was the end of the war. "It was to me like waking from a dreadful dream," he wrote years later. "My joy was great to know that I could lay me down to rest, without fear of alarm before morning."

Peale celebrated by building a tremendous triumphal arch, all timber, painted cloth, and fireworks. It was to extend nearly 60 feet across Market Street and 40 feet high. It included a laurel-wreathed Washington returning like Cincinnatus to his plow, plus the figures of Justice, Prudence, Temperance, and Fortitude, and Indians building churches. The sad outcome was that Peale's fireworks set the whole construction ablaze. They also set Peale ablaze as he put finishing touches on the arch. He jumped for his life, breaking a rib or two, but managed to put out the fires in his clothes and make his way home.

Such a disaster might discourage a less enthusiastic creator from ever attempting a sequel, but Peale was irrepressible. When Washington later made his stately procession northward to assume the Presidency in New York City in 1789, Peale was waiting in ambush. On the conquering hero's arrival in Philadelphia, he had to pass under yet another triumphal arch, where, when the 15-year-old Angelica Peale pulled a secret cord, a crown of laurel leaves would fall onto the head of the startled President. Contemporary chronicles claim that the surprise worked perfectly; family tradition adds that Washington paused to kiss the cheek of the white-robed Angelica.

That element of showmanship was central to Peale's museum. It must be scientific and serious; it must educate the people in the ways of God and man, but it must also sell tickets.

His collection kept growing. Soon after he moved his museum into the American Philosophical Society's Philosophical Hall in Independence Square in 1794 (and publicly "bid adieu" to painting, recommending that anyone who wanted a portrait should apply to Raphaelle or Rembrandt), he amassed more than 200 stuffed animals, 1,600 birds, 4,000 insects, and 11 cases of minerals. Peale's living menagerie included an elk that wandered loose in Independence Square, a bald eagle so tame that Peale could hold it in his hands, and a cow that had two tails, five legs, and six hooves. Also several pet grizzly bears.

Peale was already 60 when, in June 1801, he saw a newspaper story reporting that a farmer in the Hudson Valley had discovered some more huge bones of the kind that had originally inspired Peale's museum. Taking along Rembrandt, by this time 23, Peale boarded a stagecoach for New York to see what he could learn about the mystery of the "great American incognitum." He made his way to the farm of John Masten, west of Newburgh. "The greater part of the skelleton was here brought together," Peale noted in his diary, "yet many was still wanting."

Peale artfully asked just for permission to sketch the relics lying in Masten's barn. Masten invited the artist to join the family for dinner, during which one of Masten's sons finally blurted out the question of whether Peale would like to buy the mysterious bones instead of just sketching them.

Peale offered two hundred dollars for the bones plus one hundred dollars more for the right to dig up any more that he could unearth. It was only the next day that Peale found his offer accepted. "My heart jumpt with joy," he wrote to his wife. And to President Jefferson: "The grandeur of this Skeleton when compleated, will I hope excite your curiosity so far as to produce me the favour of a visit to the Museum, and that you may enjoy pleasure while contemplating the magnitude of the animal." Jefferson promptly wrote back to offer the use of Navy equipment to pump out the swamps that Peale wanted to explore and a supply of Army tents for shelter.

But Peale had already devised the pump he needed, a tottery triangular structure that lifted a series of buckets out of the 12-foot-deep pond where the bones had been found. This was powered by farmboys and spectators tramping along inside a huge treadmill. On several occasions, heavy rain nearly caused the structure to collapse, but Peale labored on. After more than a month's work he sailed back to Philadelphia with his crates of treasure. It would take him and Rembrandt three more months to fit the bones together. All told, he would spend $2,000, some of it borrowed, to complete the project. When they were finished, however, they had a marvel. It stood 11 feet high at the shoulder and 17 feet 6 inches in length. Its curving tusks reached out 11 feet.

The great American incognitum was the first mastodon skeleton anyone had ever dug up and put together. Peale did not know that; he thought his discovery was akin to the mammoth bones that had been found in Siberia, so he and all Philadelphia called it a mammoth. It was left to Baron Georges

Cuvier, the founder of modern paleontology, to describe and name the mastodon.

Peale advertised his "mammoth" as "the Largest of Terrestrial Beings!" People flocked to see it, paying a stiff 50-cent admission. It became a kind of fad and added a new word to everyday speech.

Peale's wife, Rachel, died in 1790, apparently of tuberculosis, just short of her 46th birthday. For three days Peale refused to let anyone move the body. He sat by her bedside, waiting in vain for some sign of life. Given the social conventions of the day, the 49-year-old widower with six children soon sought out a new wife. He was much taken with a young woman named Elizabeth DePeyster when he heard her sing a new song named "Hush Every Breeze." They were married in the spring of 1791, and more babies began arriving.

The first new son was named Vandyke Peale, but he died in infancy, and from then on, Peale wanted to honor not art but science. The next son, born in 1794, was Charles Linnaeus Peale. When another son arrived in 1795, the first child actually born in Philosophical Hall, Peale wanted to call him Aldrovand, for the 16th-century Italian naturalist Ulisse Aldrovandi. Perhaps persuaded by some kindhearted soul that this would be a heavy burden, Peale carried the baby in his arms into a meeting of the Philosophical Society and asked the assembled savants to decide on a name. They chose to name him for Benjamin Franklin. Pregnant again at 38, with what would have been Peale's 18th child, Elizabeth felt premonitions. "Ah, Charles," she said to Peale, "if I live I shall be a better wife to you than I have ever been."

Elizabeth died in childbirth. A year afterward, Peale married Hannah Moore, a 50-year-old Quaker whom he described as "a cheerful, discreet and good-tempered woman—not giddy or frisky in her movements." Her only fault, he felt, was her habit of taking snuff—"a nauseous stinking weed."

Peale had strong views about healthy living, which, he was convinced, should enable any prudent citizen to last 200 years. He even published, in 1803, "An Epistle to a Friend, on the Means of Preserving Health," advocating such modern concepts as regular exercise and a spare diet, vegetables cooked in steam, no liquor or tobacco, and, above all, "serenity of mind . . . that sweet benevolence of disposition; that love of order . . . [which] are springs of health that flow in all directions." Hannah admired her sprightly husband but would not give up snuff.

Peale had always tried to run his museum as a profit-making operation— indeed, he raised his family on the proceeds—and yet he dreamed of turning it over to the national government, perhaps to be associated with a national university. He thought that President Jefferson might favor the idea, but Jefferson declined. "One of the great questions," he wrote to Peale, "is whether Congress is authorized by the Constitution to apply the public money to any but the purposes specially enumerated in the Constitution." He thought that a majority in Congress would be opposed.

Rebuffed, Peale turned to the Pennsylvania authorities. After threatening to move his museum from Philadelphia to New York or Washington, he petitioned the state government for public support, and the state responded in the summer of 1802 by letting him move his collection into the recently abandoned State House on Independence Square. So Peale's bats and tigers and insects moved into the very building where Washington and his associates had created the Constitution. At 69 Peale was thus able to "retire," just as his friend Jefferson had recently done. The Peale museum devolved upon Rubens Peale, an amiable boy whose eyes had been too weak for him to study painting. He promised his father the same income that the museum had recently been earning, namely $4,000 a year. Imitating Monticello, Peale bought a farm near Germantown, Pennsylvania, consisting of about a hundred acres of land with mill streams and orchards. Two years of hard work transformed the place, and Peale named it Belfield.

"Though an old man I am still but a young gardener," Jefferson wrote from Monticello to Belfield. Peale could match him in inventiveness. He not only used the moldboard plow that he built from plans Jefferson sent him and adopted Jefferson's system of contour plowing (which enabled him to grow corn 13 feet high), but he also made a corn-planting machine and a horse rake and an apple-paring machine and a milk cart that would not spill milk. At 78 he built one of America's first velocipedes, which one of his younger sons said "goes down hill like the very devil."

Rubens, a botanist who played a part in introducing the geranium from France to America, came on visits to supervise the planting of boxwoods, exotic herbs, and berries.

And Belfield still survives, amid offices, winding roads, and the manifestations of La Salle University. The farmhouse is an amiable, stuccoed, three-story structure, approached by a curving stone walk and an unassuming front porch. Today it is the headquarters of Brother Patrick Ellis, the president of La Salle.

Shortly before his father's retirement to the farm, Rembrandt, who had announced that he wanted to be known henceforth only as Rembrandt, without the Peale, went to study in France and added to his considerable success as a portrait painter. Raphaelle, advertising himself as still a Peale, offered discounts: "A NAME! RAPHAELLE PEALE, To make himself eminent, will paint miniatures, for a short time, at Ten Dollars each. . . ." Raphaelle's real passion, though, was still lifes, a category for which there was virtually no market. Rembrandt got as much as one hundred dollars for his portraits; Raphaelle often sold his glowing fruit for less than $40.

If there was a blight on Peale's busy decade of retirement at Belfield, it was his difficult relationship with Raphaelle, this strange and enigmatic character who may have suffered from the constant competition of his gifted younger brother Rembrandt and from his father's frequent praise of his brother.

Raphaelle could not compete; instead, he joked. He liked to paint optical illusions. On one occasion, shortly after acquiring an untrained puppy, he painted and placed on the living-room rug what looked like a newly deposited dropping. His wife angrily insisted that he clean it up, and so with a triumphant flourish he retrieved it. He was not only a skilled mimic but a skilled ventriloquist as well. One of his specialties was to carve a chicken at dinner while making the chicken appear to beg for its life and shriek when the actual carving began. He played the clarinet, flute, mandolin, and guitar. He painted gorgeous still lifes that few people wanted. And he drank. In a parody of his father, he invented things that went largely unused. He built a machine to purify salt water. He even concocted a new theory of the solar system, in which the sun was "an electric body" that cyclically attracted and repelled the earth.

Raphaelle married a pretty Irish girl called Patty McGlathery. Peale, who was not above snobbery when his own children were involved, disapproved. The objects of his disapproval proceeded to have seven children. Peale supported them while Raphaelle wandered and clowned and drank. Peale scolded his prodigal: "If you applied as you ought to do, you would be the first painter in America."

If Raphaelle was a trial to Peale, his younger sons were almost as much so. Charles Linnaeus played the flute and clarinet but apparently disliked working at that or anything else. Peale apprenticed him to a printer, and Lin quickly responded by running away to sea. He brought back a horned lizard from Brazil for the museum, then went to sea again to join in the naval skirmishes of the War of 1812.

The youngest son, Titian Ramsay II (named for an earlier Titian who died at 18), was a gifted naturalist, but he quarreled about Peale's domineering sister-in-law and housekeeper, Rachel Morris; Peale criticized him for being disrespectful and "a silly boy." He and a group set off in 1817 through the swamps of Florida, sketching and catching whatever they could find. Two years later he joined Maj. Stephen H. Long's pioneering expedition, which was officially assigned "to explore the country between the Mississippi and the Rocky Mountains." Starting in Pittsburgh, the explorers chuffed down the Ohio River, then up the Missouri and the Platte. They got as far as Longs Peak, just north of Pikes Peak.

Peale may simply have been getting too old for the stresses of raising children. Even those sons who had modeled themselves on him now looked on their father's ever changing enthusiasms with a certain condescension. Peale was aware of his wanderings. "I am not unconscious that I have misspent much of my time," he wrote to Jefferson in 1815. He turned to Rembrandt for further lessons, and then he began painting landscapes of the countryside around Belfield.

He painted new portraits of his family. He painted Hannah, head-on, in her rather forbidding Quaker bonnet. He also painted Raphaelle, all angry self-control, with a paintbrush in his hand and a still life of apples behind his head. He painted a wonderfully warm portrait of his brother James by lamplight. In 1818, when he was nearly 80, he painted a new generation of political leaders—President Monroe, Secretary of State John Quincy Adams, House Speaker Henry Clay, Gen. Andrew Jackson.

He painted himself. The most famous of these late self-portraits is "The Artist in His Museum" (1822), in which Peale, with an almost demonic gleam of triumph in his eye, holds high a tasseled curtain to reveal tiers and tiers of stuffed birds. "The light I have chosen for my portrait is novel," he wrote to Jefferson. "My back is towards the light, so that here is no direct light except upon my bald pate, the whole face being in a reflected light." It is a haunting picture, with that farseeing look of the very old.

Peale was 80 in the fall of 1821 when, after a brisk spin on his velocipede, he came down with yellow fever. Hannah, who was 66, soon fell ill as well. Peale mistrusted doctors and all their medicines, particularly the popular purgative known as calomel (mercurous chloride). Hannah entrusted herself to the doctor; Peale did not. Peale woke up in the night and sensed a strange silence. "I hoped from the stillness that they had given her an anodyne while the blisters was drawing," he wrote. "No, the stillness was death."

He survived. Tired of farming and of the country, Peale returned to Philadelphia and resumed management of the museum, with Franklin and Titian II as assistants. Rubens later left to start a museum in New York City.

Philadelphia was preparing to fully celebrate the triumphant return of Lafayette, by now nearly 70. Chief Justice William Tilghman, a man with whom Peale had had difficulties, saw to it that Peale's museum was excluded from the itinerary. But Lafayette strayed from that itinerary, strolled into the museum, and encountered "my dear Peale," his comrade at Valley Forge. They fell into each other's arms, and Lafayette insisted that his old friend join the welcoming party and ride in the same coach with him and the frowning Justice Tilghman.

"I am young, and I am old," Peale wrote to a friend at 85. "I am contented, and not contented. I am alone amidst company. . . . I hope to make 100 ladies happy, yet one would be enough. . . . An accomplished, sensible companion, good nature in abundance to forgive all follies . . . are there such to be had?"

A friend told him about a pleasant lady named Mary Stansbury, in her early 50s, a teacher in a New York school for deaf-mutes. He went to call on her, bringing copies of his "Epistle on Health" and his "Essay to Promote Domestic Happiness." Peale proposed to her that she teach him her method for instructing deaf-mutes, and he would give her lessons in painting or, better yet, teach her his newest enthusiasm, the making of false teeth. She protested, saying that she "had no genius," but Peale pressed on. "I told her that I would be her physician, her nurse and her protector," he wrote in his diary, "that it should be my constant care to please her in every way that was in my power."

She consented only to show him her false teeth and to make a mold of her mouth with beeswax so he could provide her with a new set made of porcelain. Peale had been tinkering with false teeth for decades and had made a complete set for himself back in 1809. He experimented with ox teeth and shells, and though the dental possibilities of porcelain were well-known in France, he was one of the first to use it in America. Peale decided that this help to the aged and others was more valuable than "any other work I can do." There was no great demand for his porcelain teeth, since he charged an impressive $150 for a set. And the man who had once planned to live to 200 now began discovering that this would not be easy.

On his return from his visit to Mary Stansbury, the steamboat to New Brunswick ran aground a mile from its destination, and the octogenarian Peale had to totter through the darkness with a heavy trunk on his back. Feeling poorly on his return to Philadelphia, he suspected that his chest pains meant pleurisy, then that he had strained his heart. But he kept working. A month later, in February 1827, he fell unconscious aboard the steamer *Trenton*, bound for New York. In his suitcase was a new set of porcelain teeth for Miss Stansbury.

He was brought back to Philadelphia, but now his energy was ebbing. On February 22 he went to visit his second daughter, Sophonisba, and asked her to wash his hair. While she did so, he fell asleep. Sophy found it hard to awaken him so that he could get home. A doctor came to examine him, and his third daughter, Sybilla, agreed to sit with him through the night. They were alone, late, when Peale suddenly said, "Sybilla, feel my pulse."

"I can't find it, Pa," she said.

He lies now in a long, low grave outside the beautiful old church of St. Peter's, just a few blocks south of Independence Square. "He participated in the Revolutionary struggle for our Independence," the epitaph says. "As an artist, contributed to the history of the country. Was an energetic citizen and in private life Beloved by all who knew him."

The only one of Peale's seven sons buried nearby is Raphaelle, that gifted and afflicted prodigal, who was reduced, in his last days, to writing bits of doggerel for a baker to insert into his cakes. Crippled by gout as well as by alcohol and arsenic (some say from his taxidermy at the museum), he died in 1825, two years before his disappointed father.

DECEMBER 1990

SATURDAY TO MONDAY

MARK GIROUARD

T he Edwardian period was the heyday of the house party, assembled either for long periods in the summer holidays or at Christmas, or for "Saturdays to Mondays" (the expression "weekend" was considered vulgar). The spread of railways, followed by the advent of motorcars in the late 19th century, made it easier to bring guests together. Parties of 30 to 40 were taken for granted in big houses. There were political house parties, as at Hatfield, where the campaigns for the next Parliament session were planned over the dinner table or over cigars in the smoking room; religious house parties, like those given by Lord and Lady Mount Temple at Broadlands (where Lord Mountbatten was later to live), with hymn sings on the lawn; highbrow house parties, at which intellectual paper games were played after dinner; sporting parties, in houses in which everything seemed to be made out of portions of animals, from inkstands made out of horses' hooves to umbrella stands made of elephants' trunks.

Guests assembled for breakfast at nine o'clock and helped themselves to food from long rows of covered silver dishes on hot plates on the sideboard. Women spent the morning in the morning room, men in the library, but both sexes were often outdoors. At shooting house parties women changed from their morning dresses into tweed coats and skirts and went out to join the men for a picnic lunch. The best shots in England in the late Victorian period were Lord de Grey and Lord Walsingham. Lord de Grey once killed 28 pheasants in 60 seconds with a succession of "left-and-rights" from double-barreled shotguns.

After the day's sport, afternoon tea of cucumber sandwiches, hot buttered scones, and cake was served at five, in the drawing room or hall, or outside in the garden in summer. Dinner, normally served at eight, was the one formal event of the day. Guests were summoned to the drawing room by the booming of a gong and proceeded arm in arm into the candle-lit dining room, according to their social rank.

After dinner, charades or paper games were popular, and after the women had gone to bed the men usually changed into elaborately frogged velvet smoking jackets and stayed up into the small hours in the billiard room or smoking room, drinking brandy, smoking cigars, playing cards or billiards, and swapping stories. Some houses went in for practical jokes. I was told of a guest at Wentworth Woodhouse in Yorkshire who was so infuriated by the booby traps in his bedroom that he left. His host, Earl Fitzwilliam, plaintively remarked, "I don't see what he was making a fuss about. I found a Shetland pony in *my* bed."

During the night there was often activity in the dark bedroom passages. Divorce was not respectable in Victorian or Edwardian society, but in many households discreet adultery was taken for granted. Tactful hostesses arranged bedrooms accordingly. Things could go wrong, however. Lord Charles Beresford (a jolly sailor much in demand at house parties) once slipped into what he thought was the right bedroom door and leapt onto the bed with a loud cry of *"Cock-a-doodle-do!"*—only to find the horrified faces of the Bishop of Chester and his wife gazing at him out of the bedclothes.

FROM "THE GREAT GOOD PLACES: ENGLISH COUNTRY HOUSES,"

NOVEMBER 1985

THE INCREDIBLE POTATO

ROBERT E. RHOADES

Among the first Europeans to see the unimposing plant the Indians called *papa* were conquistador Francisco Pizarro and his rowdy band. When they overran Peru in the 1530s, they were unaware of the buried treasure beneath their feet. They rode roughshod over the papa, in hot pursuit of the Inca Atahuallpa and his fabled gold.

Introduced into Europe over the next 50 years, the potato began four centuries of world conquest. The Inca Empire has vanished. Spain's glory is only a memory. King Potato keeps on reigning. Compared to the vast benefits this versatile plant has bestowed on humankind, all the gold of Peru becomes small potatoes.

Today the potato is produced in 130 of the world's 167 independent countries. One year's crop, 291 million tons, is worth 106 billion dollars, more than the value of all the gold and silver the Spanish ever carted out of the New World. The potato is so nutritious that a man in Scandinavia lived healthily for 300 days on only spuds dressed with a bit of margarine. It takes seven pounds of potatoes, about 23, to total 2,500 calories, the approximate adult daily requirement; so eating a spud without rich toppings is no more fattening than eating a pear—the potato itself is 99.9 percent fat free.

An acre of potatoes yields almost as much food as two acres of grain, and when the water that composes about 80 percent of potatoes is squeezed out, they provide annually more edible dry matter than the combined worldwide consumption of fish and meat. Without potatoes meat production would slump and meat prices skyrocket; nearly half the world's crop is fed to livestock.

Potatoes are for more than eating: distilled into vodka and aquavit, processed into starch, paste, and dye, convertible to fuel for our cars. Gangster John Dillinger reportedly carved a pistol from a potato, dyed it with iodine, and escaped from prison. In India a jack-of-all-trades is called *alu*, potato.

The potato yields more nutritious food more quickly on less land and in harsher climates than any such major crops as wheat, corn, or rice. On average it matures faster than any of these staples—in 90 to 120 days, and edible tubers can be harvested after a mere 60 days.

Nutritionists rate the quality of potato protein higher than that of the soybean, and a single spud can supply half the daily vitamin C requirement of an adult, a fact sea captains early guessed at when they carried potatoes to prevent scurvy among their crews. If captain and crew had been cast away on an island with a bushel of potatoes, they could have grown a ton of food within a year and survived. With milk they could have held out indefinitely. A potato crop is as well suited to backyard gardening as it is to large-scale commercial production.

The potato grows from below sea level behind Dutch dikes to almost 14,000 feet up in the chilly Andes and Himalayas, from the Arctic Circle to the Strait of Magellan, and in the scorching deserts of Australia and Africa.

When Henry Ford first got into the automobile business, he predicted the world would soon run out of cheap petroleum. To make alcohol, he ordered potatoes from Europe that were grown for industrial purposes, but the project seemingly went down like an Edsel. The way things are going, it looks like Ford did have a better idea. Researchers have shown that one acre of potatoes can yield 1,200 gallons of ethyl alcohol in a year.

If, like Ford, we choose to import our alcohol potatoes from Europe, there should be plenty. Europe and the Soviet Union grow 75 percent of the world crop. In a good year, the Russians, who call potatoes their "second bread," account for one-third of world production. Poland, with 15 percent, is second, followed by the United States in far third place with 5 percent.

The future of the Soviet potato crop was seriously threatened in an episode in World War II, as shells from Nazi artillery burst into the potato plots of the Pavlovsk experiment station. The last to leave, Abraham Kameraz, senior Soviet scientist, scrambled to gather up pea-size tubers like precious gems. Slinging his potato sack on his back, he struck out on foot toward Leningrad.

In a dark Leningrad basement he was joined by fellow scientists. They garnered every stick of wood, including furniture, for fuel to keep the potatoes from freezing. They stood watches to beat off the hordes of rats that gnawed at the sacks. Collapsing from hunger, the potato protectors would not touch a single tiny tuber. They were guarding a national treasure, defending the South American potatoes crucial to the genetic revitalization of their own varieties, which were no longer disease and weather resistant. They believed that without potatoes, a staple of Soviet life, German victory would be assured.

In the Paucartambo Valley, high in the Peruvian Andes, only village elders remembered that a Soviet expedition had collected wild and cultivated potatoes there almost 50 years before. Most villagers had no idea how important their potatoes had become in other lands. They wondered why foreigners like me came here to learn about potatoes.

Every chance I get I travel high into the Andes to visit old friends in their potato fields. Last year Don Maximo Zárate roped me into helping with his harvest. Like many small mountain farmers, he makes his living from a little llama herd and a few hillside fields of potatoes.

Half a mile across the valley I saw clusters of brightly clothed Peruvian Indians harvesting potatoes on postage-stamp-size fields stuck to a near-perpendicular mountain slope. Struggling along the rows of Don Maximo's equally perpendicular field, I couldn't believe I was unearthing potatoes. The colors of the rainbow and more, many looked like miniature pineapples, some like coral snakes, and others like bright red cherries or purple gumdrops.

On his six acres of tiny scattered fields, Don Maximo cultivates as many as 45 varieties of potatoes, representing four of the eight potato species cultivated by man. In the United States and Canada, 80 percent of the 1.5 million acres of potatoes are planted to only six varieties. By maintaining diversity, Don Maximo knows that in case of disease, frost, drought, or hail at least part of his crop should pull through.

Andean farmers cultivate as many as 3,000 of the 5,000 or so potato varieties, embracing all eight species. Each has a name, often humorous and creative. In their language, Quechua, a long flat potato is called *mishipasinghan* (cat's nose). A knobby, obviously hard-to-prepare kind is *lumchipamundana* (potato makes young bride weep).

"Is this a potato too?" I asked Don Maximo, as I grounded my hoe, brushed away the soil, and held up an odd object. It was black, long, and curved.

"What's wrong, amigo, don't you Americans know potatoes? We have a special name for that one. We call it pig droppings," Don Maximo said with a hearty laugh. "Just look at it."

The potato's genus, *Solanum*, includes more than 2,000 species, of which about 160 are tuber bearing. *Solanum tuberosum* is the common potato known throughout the world. Although wild potatoes are found as far north as Nebraska, no species was cultivated outside South America at the time the Spanish arrived in the New World.

The potato was erroneously reported grown in Virginia in 1597 by John Gerard, the first man to mention the potato in English print. He called it by its Arawak Indian name, *batata*, which actually meant sweet potato.

The potato has not only been misnamed but misunderstood down the centuries. When introduced to Europe, the potato was cursed as an evil food. The Scots refused to eat it because it wasn't mentioned in the Bible. Leprosy, consumption, rickets were attributed to potato eating. Lord Byron wrote of the "sad result of passions and potatoes," reflecting a conviction of the early 19th century that potatoes had unwholesome aphrodisiac effects.

The potato does have villainous relatives. It belongs to the botanical family Solanaceae, which includes such hallucinogenic and narcotic cousins as mandrake and deadly nightshade. These contain alkaloid poisons such as scopolamine and atropine, used to prepare ointments "giving witches the power to fly." Law-abiding Europeans wanted no such truck with the devil, and so shunned the potato, as well as its cousin the tomato, another of the Solanaceae.

In County Galway, 135 years after the potato blight had struck, I walked across a damp field toward a grass-covered knoll. It was a mass grave from the great potato famine of 1845-1851, a reminder of one of Ireland's darkest hours. After the potato was introduced, the Irish population exploded, and by 1845 had passed eight million. That was more than double the present population, and resulted in a density greater than modern-day China's. The average Irish adult ate 9 to 14 pounds of potatoes a day.

And then came an unknown malady, the deadly late blight, a disease caused by a fungus today recognized as *Phytophthora infestans*. After a rainy, cool period in the summer of 1845, plants slumped mysteriously as though struck down by a scorching drought. The harvested tubers as well as those still in the ground rotted, sending an unbearable stench across the countryside.

The Irish, though hardest hit, were not alone. The potato crops failed across Europe, and mass starvation was followed by pestilence. But in Ireland six ghastly years of famine led to a million deaths.

More than a million Irish sought refuge in North America because of the potato famine. Ultimately two of their descendants, named Kennedy and Reagan, rose to the Presidency of the United States. Only East Europeans eat more potatoes per capita than the Irish. Potatoes and marriage, an Irish saying goes, are two things too serious to joke about.

The Netherlands devotes a surprising one-fourth of its arable land to potatoes. The pragmatic Dutch have made potatoes a lucrative export business, worth more than their tulip industry.

The ebullient French, by contrast, have made the potato high art and the key vegetable in their great cuisine. In Dardilly, Raymond Parot, headmaster of the cooking school École Rabelais, requires his students to prepare 60 potato dishes for graduation.

"In almost every French meal, the potato is a companion," Mr. Parot said. He added with a touch of poetry, "It enhances the taste and gives a softness to the meal."

In Limonest, France, I acquired membership in the Académie Parmentier, Grand Ordre du Noble Tubercule, an association of gourmets, restaurateurs, and chefs who honor and promote the *pomme de terre*, apple of the earth.

After my initiation we repaired to a five-hour feast of potato dishes. Between the potato entrée and the potato dessert, I was regaled with the legend of my academy's patron, Antoine-Auguste Parmentier.

When Parmentier was a prisoner of war in Hannover, Germany, in 1757, he reputedly survived only on potatoes. On returning to France, he found his countrymen facing famine but still suspicious of the vegetable that had saved his life.

Parmentier charmed King Louis XVI into granting him a notoriously sterile field near Paris called Les Sablons ("the sands"), where he grew a dandy crop of potatoes. Knowing well the peasant mentality that "forbidden must be good," he asked the king to station royal guards around the field by day and withdraw them at night. The trick worked, and the moonlight harvest by local farmers began. Potatoes soon bloomed all over the country.

Parmentier presented the king with a bouquet of potato blossoms. Queen Marie Antoinette wore one in her hair.

For Benjamin Franklin, then American Commissioner to France,

Parmentier prepared a feast similar to the one I had just enjoyed: nothing but potato dishes. To cap the night, he served liqueurs made from the harvest of Les Sablons. France still remembers her great potato messiah in gourmet dishes prepared *à la Parmentier.*

Following the potato's historic migration from Europe to North America, I headed for New England. Potatoes were first introduced there in 1719 by Scotch-Irish immigrants settling in Londonderry (now Derry), New Hampshire.

My first stop was Aroostook County, Maine, which for 30 years, until 1957, produced more spuds than any state except its own. Now both Idaho and Washington out-produce not only Aroostook but all Maine. With Maine fallen to third in U.S. production, proud Aroostook farmers, many of their practices rooted in the last century, are trying to adapt to America's new food habits. The U.S. has become geared to fast-food outlets and supermarkets. While the rest of the world still uses mainly fresh potatoes, more than half the potatoes Americans eat are processed as frozen French fries, potato chips, and frozen or dehydrated preparations.

In 1980 Americans consumed five billion pounds of French fries and one billion of potato chips. French fries were introduced to the U.S. when Thomas Jefferson, a former ambassador to France, served them in the White House. The potato chip was allegedly invented in 1853. In Saratoga Springs, New York, short-order cook George Crum, an American Indian, got revenge on a customer complaining about Crum's thick fried potatoes. He defiantly prepared a batch of superthin slices and deep fried them. The rest is history. Today potato chips are an industry that yields about three billion dollars a year.

Potato processing is an ancient technique. For at least 2,000 years Peruvian Indians have made a ready-to-serve dehydrated potato product called *chuño* that can be stored for three or four years. The process involves the same dehydration principles used today, alternate freezing and drying to reduce moisture.

When the heaviest frost falls in the Andes, small bitter potatoes are spread on the ground for exposure to the night's cold, and then left to dry in the sun. After several days, villagers gather them into small piles and do a rhythmic potato stomp with their bare feet. The trampling sloughs off the skins and squeezes out the remaining water.

The potatoes are soaked in water for one to three weeks to reduce bitterness, and then redried. The Indians use chuño in soups, stews, and a sweet dessert called *mazamorra*. In prehistoric times chuño was placed in the tombs of the dead as food for their journey to the afterworld.

In Asia and South America I met scientists who are pioneering the commercial growing of potatoes by "true seed," the tiny seeds produced in the potato plant's berry. By this method potatoes can be grown much like grains. A hundred-pound sack of seed will sow more than a thousand acres. By contrast, the universal method used by farmers requires more than a thousand tons of potato tubers to seed the same amount of land. If perfected, the true-seed method could revolutionize potato growing. In China about 25,000 acres are sown to seed.

The most ambitious scientific effort to make the potato a 21st-century solution to the world food crisis is going on at the International Potato Center in Lima, where I work. The entrance to my organization is guarded by a towering representative of a Peruvian harvest god. In each hand he clutches a potato plant. One is healthy, the other drooping with disease. My colleagues face the same problems that confronted this deity more than a thousand years ago: disease, pests, rigors of climate.

Central to the work of the Potato Center is the World Potato Collection, located in our research station at Huancayo, high in the Peruvian Andes. "One potato, two potato, three potato, four!" The jingle of my childhood echoed in my mind when I first saw the bewildering collection. But my count was way off. Stored in this germ-plasm bank are potatoes representing possibly 13,000 different native strains. Few resemble the potatoes known in Europe and America. Potentially, in terms of future food production, they are of inestimable value.

Only a small fraction of the potato's genetic diversity is found outside South America. The rest is in native potatoes with such scientific names as *Solanum andigena*, *S. phureja*, and *S. stenotomum*. They contain genes resistant to diseases like late blight, wart, viruses X and Y, and others of the 265 diseases and pests known to plague the potato. There are even hairy-leafed species that trap insects with a sticky secretion. The center breeds for this genetic material and distributes seed for worldwide testing, generally in developing countries.

Since this is a living collection, 8,000 specimens are planted every year in the center's Andean fields. And, as a safeguard against crop loss, 5,000 have been sent, in the form of seeds, to the National Seed Storage Laboratory at Fort Collins, Colorado.

My colleague in charge of tracking down wild and native potatoes to "bring them back alive" for the World Collection is Peruvian Carlos Ochoa. His expeditions range from Mexico to the southern tip of South America. His prizes are getting harder to find: Most Andean farmers are abandoning their traditional varieties for more modern, higher yielding kinds, and the wild potato's natural habitat is being destroyed by population growth, grazing, and logging.

"Many potato species are on the verge of extinction," Mr. Ochoa lamented. "Others have disappeared forever, and no amount of money will bring them back. If we destroy the genetic reserves of our major food crops like the potato, we could destroy ourselves."

The Incas, though they knew nothing about genes, were aware of how easily their basic food could be endangered. When their ancient kings called representatives from all parts of the empire to the sacred capital of Cuzco, they prayed for potatoes:

> O Creator! Thou who givest life to all things and hast made men that they may live, and multiply. Multiply also the fruits of the earth, the potatoes and other food that thou hast made, that men may not suffer from hunger and misery.

MAY 1982

IL TRIONFO DI GOLA

HOWARD LA FAY

Palermo's sprawling Vucciria, an outdoor market, recalls every Arab suq from Damascus to Algiers. Through narrow streets converging on the Piazza Caracciolo, shoppers swirl and eddy in a polychrome wonderland. On all sides rise mounds of crimson apples, pale-green zucchini, scarlet tomatoes, purple eggplant, tawny oranges. The proprietor of a fruit stand entices clients with a traditional chant: "*Ma chi ciavuru i fravuli frischi!* What a delicious scent of fresh strawberries!"

Another, presiding over a cart of sweaters in dazzling electric hues, calls: "*Robba mercata!* Oh, what cheap things I have!"

The smells! Fugitive scents of rose and carnation as you pass the florists. The aroma of artichokes, string beans, and new potatoes simmering in big pots. Roasting nuts and trays of baked onions. And the clean, piercing odor of lemons.

I buy a lemon—a huge chunk of gold the size of a linebacker's fist—and eat it, as Sicilians do, like an orange. While far from sweet, it is tangy and refreshing.

On all sides vendors offer the snacks so beloved of Sicilians. *Stigghioli*—goat intestines sprinkled with oregano—roast smokily over beds of charcoal. Men with sharp knives and swift fingers chop *purpu 'ugghiutu*, boiled octopus, into manageable morsels and heap them onto moist plates. But the supreme treat afforded by the Vucciria is *vastedda ca' meusa*—slivers of the spleen, liver, lungs, esophagus of veal fried in lard, sprinkled with salt, and served on a roll.

One day, as I left the Vucciria, I heard a new chant. It struck me as somewhat ambiguous: "*Cavuri, i domestici! Su' cchiu' duci d'un peri di porcu!* How savory, this kale! Sweeter than the foot of a pig!"

The high Sicilian regard for good food reaches its zenith in desserts. The

390

island's pastries and ices have no rivals, and the entire populace seems to sample them endlessly. Once, as I drank a cup of espresso in a café, the dazzling display of pastry overwhelmed all scruples. I selected a cake filled with pistachio-flavored cream. For future reference I inquired the name of this confection.

"*Il Trionfo di Gola, signore,*" the clerk replied. Licking my fingers, I reflected how devastatingly appropriate was that name—the Triumph of Gluttony.

FROM "SICILY, WHERE ALL THE SONGS ARE SAD," MARCH 1976

THOSE PROPER
AND OTHER BOSTONIANS

JOSEPH JUDGE

Perhaps it's her prevailing color, the rose madder of old brick in the late sun, that gives to Boston's sons and lovers the impression we all have of her wisdom, her silent understanding of man's affairs, her willingness to put up with us, sinner and saint alike, as when a May day declines in haze and the sound of drums and tambourines fills Brimstone Corner.

People flow through the place. Boston people: stout women with shopping bags; a gang of young blacks releasing laughter like a string a firecrackers; briefcase-toting men with regimental ties; bearded students in faded field jackets considering the scrawled remarks on the public graffiti boards, a bold hand proclaiming "God is dead—Nietzsche," and a fine thin hand just below with the ultimate truth of it: "Nietzsche is dead—God."

The city loves its stereotypes, the talk of beans and scrod, Boston Light and Back Bay Brahmins, Irish pols and Italian contractors, the sacred cod and bluenose culture, and a famous caste of three—the Lowells (somehow confused in the popular mind with Lodges), the Cabots, and God, speaking to one another in that order.

But it is all a mummer's show. Behind those cardboard props Boston has always been a chaos of humanity, today no less than yesterday, and, contrary to accepted doctrine, its ethnic pot has never really melted.

Consider the firstcomer, the now Proper Bostonian, that Anglo-Saxon, well-heeled, educated Protestant, tracing his descent back, back, back. It is a great (and attractive) simplification. The man whose work for the arts and the less privileged best exemplified Boston civic life in recent years was a Jewish businessman from Cleveland, the late Eli Goldston.

But if one *has* to find a Brahmin, I can think of none more engaging than

Mrs. Harriet Ropes Cabot, curator of the Bostonian Society, whose offices occupy the Old State House; outside its windows occurred the "Boston Massacre," and under it runs the subway.

"I certainly wish they would get their trains out of my basement," said Mrs. Cabot as we met in a hall decorated with the society's relics, antiques, prints, and memorabilia: a lantern, for example, that once hung on the Liberty Tree; the black tricornered hat worn by Maj. Thomas Melville, of whom Oliver Wendell Holmes wrote *The Last Leaf.*

A large woman of independent mind, Mrs. Cabot radiates intelligent good-will. When I remarked that she seemed to be connected to a goodly number of Boston Brahmin names, she squinted a bit and replied: "Yes, I suppose that's true. I worked at the Boston Museum of Fine Arts, then on the Adams family papers, now this. I've just been proceeding through institutions."

As we sat in her jam-packed office and chatted, the conversation was punctuated by the subterranean rumbling of the trains. I asked Mrs. Cabot how the old Bostonians were bearing up under modern times.

"The city is not as comfortable for us as it once was," she acknowledged. "But change is good for the people. Why, right after World War II there was nothing left for Boston but to fall into the harbor. If it had not changed, it would be gone. I must admit though that I like Old Boston parties. Some people regard it as *Sa*-ciety, with a big S, you know, old 'cold-roast Boston.' But it is just people who have been around here longer. When I was young the world seemed very much smaller, and we thought we were the only people in it."

Despite the egalitarianism of recent decades, old George Apley, John P. Marquand's fictional hero, still haunts the Boston popular imagination. I settled back one evening with a distinguished PB (Proper Bostonian) who agreed to express his opinions on the condition that he not be named: "Not that I am afraid of expressing an honest opinion, it is just that here everyone is in his proper career line—banking, insurance, medicine—and public statements are for politicians; the briefer the better, too.

"This is a very understated town," he went on. "It likes things to be comfy, cozy. The citadels of privilege, however, have been slowly yielding. The day of the Hopi is passed."

"The Hopi?"

"Yes. A visitor at City Hall once noticed a man of exceptional energy, and was told he was a Hopi.

"'You mean an Indian?' asked the visitor.

"'No,' came the reply, 'An Irish Catholic, but when he goes to bed he hope 'e wakes up as a Boston Brahmin.'"

Boston can be a sultry place on a summer Saturday; most of those with means have fled to Cape Cod, or Martha's Vineyard, or the North Shore, or the Berkshires, leaving a cement-and-steel oven behind. These are the long, hot hours when archaic Fenway Park roars with the clamor of baseball's most exuberant fans.

Many left-behind Bostonians will wander toward the harbor, a tatterdemalion army with coolers and knapsacks and collie dogs and brown bags and tennis rackets and bikes, to board a boat bound for Provincetown.

On more than one summer weekend, you can go all the way to Italy—not by boat but by a short walk into the North End and its old tenement buildings.

There the rhythm of the days is punctuated, as in Italy, by feasts of saints—elaborate, explosive ceremonies that sweep the people up in a torrent of emotion, like the 54th Grand Religious Festival of St. Anthony of Padua Da Montefalcione.

On Endicott Street one August day, I found a statue of St. Anthony reposing in a red and pink and gold sidewalk chapel. People lined up to attach dollar bills to one of the streamers that flowed down from the saint. The club has 13 charter members still alive, all in their eighties. I met one, Amadeo Fortulati, leaning on a white cane along Endicott Street.

"Once," he said in a firm voice, "you had to be a Monty, a man from Montefalcione, to get into the club. Now," he extended his hand, palm open, "we have an Irishman!"

For 43 years, the statue of St. Anthony lived with shoemaker John Piccone and his family. Year in and out the men carried the statue out into the streets, and brought it back home to the shoemaker's house. And the saint gave them the blessing they sought—the security of a united people, an identity in a hard industrial world, a reminder of who they really were.

In those days they often lived two families to a room, and they went out from the North End by way of old Haymarket Square, into a world of roistering Irish and severe Yankees.

"There wasn't no place to go," said Mr. Piccone.

Around one o'clock the statue of the saint was deftly lifted from the sidewalk altar and hoisted onto the stout shoulders of six men to begin its slow procession. Through the streets of the North End, it was preceded by bands wailing in brass, little girls in white dresses, and old ladies bearing candles, grateful for a favor that prayer had rendered. The saint's procession was both tumultuous and triumphant. He paused at individual homes to receive bouquets of money, some lowered on strings and ropes. At some windows, a mother held up a child who kissed the saint's face and wrapped a wreath of dollar bills around it.

Confetti fell as heavy as snow, drifting in the streets, and the bands playing and people shouting almost drowned out an old man with watery eyes who said, "Italy in exile!"

It was 10 o'clock at night before St. Anthony came home to a wildly applauding crowd, a crush of humanity moving as inexorably as a glacier. The saint's impassive face rode atop a huge parka of money, perhaps $20,000 for the coffers of the club.

That Boston appreciates its heritage more than most cities seems clear during a stroll down always beautiful Commonwealth Avenue on a mild early autumn afternoon. It was that critic of cities Lewis Mumford who cast a deciding judgment on the Back Bay. Excluding only the L'Enfant Plan for Washington, he called it "the outstanding achievement in American urban planning for the nineteenth century."

A vast rectangle of commodious old row houses, displaying decades of architectural history as one walks from Arlington Street westward, this former stronghold of the Proper Bostonians has been given over to rooming houses, junior colleges, and a troupe of bearded, blue-denimed young men and women who play guitars, loud and soft, next door to the former home of Henry Higginson, who founded the Boston Symphony.

Stella Trafford, [a Back Bay Neighborhood Association] activist, has had a frantic few years fending off the developers. "There's always a struggle," she said, "but I've lived everywhere, and I wouldn't live anywhere else. My husband has the pleasure of walking down Commonwealth Avenue and across the Public Garden to work."

"By the way," an affable and charming administrator at the Boston Museum of Fine Arts named Diggory Venn said when I was leaving, "meet me for lunch tomorrow at the museum and I will introduce you to Boston's most beautiful woman." And he did.

"I should have mentioned that she is 2,400 years old," Diggory said as we stood before an incomparable head of Aphrodite known as the Bartlett Head. It is perfection of the classical form, and one of the prized objects displayed in the echoing marble galleries of the famed MFA.

"She will tell you something about the old Bostonians," my host went on. "They knew the meaning of noblesse oblige. Mr. Bartlett, who had made his fortune, wanted to do something for the MFA, so he gave it $100,000. They asked him what he wanted done with the money.

"'Please look upon me as though I were dead,' he said, 'and do what you choose.'

"This is what the museum chose," said Diggory, indicating that glorious marble.

Boston has never claimed that it is "the Athens of America," but it has never denied it either. Assuredly it is a mother country of the eastern Establishment. Boston's past hangs upon it like a fine but faded Chesterfield coat, and here and there about the city are scattered remainders of influence and importance in stone and bronze, like family pictures on a mantelpiece. They show a penchant for the reformer, the upright, the righteous of the world. I do not know another town, for example, that displays the figure of an eminent bishop—Phillips Brooks—with the hand of the Lord Jesus resting on his shoulder in approving intimacy. Boston memorializes Mary Dyer, a Quaker who was hanged on the Common because of her obstinate religious beliefs, and not only abolitionist William Lloyd Garrison but reformers Theodore Parker, Wendell Phillips, and Charles Sumner (twice!).

And there are those institutions where people think, and read books, and converse, such as the Lowell Institute, the Boston Art Commission, the Massachusetts Historical Society, the American Academy of Arts and Sciences, and the Boston Athenaeum. Few places on earth are as civilized as the Athenaeum. Nor are many men as civilized as its now-retired librarian, historian Walter Muir Whitehill. Founded in 1807, this privately owned library since 1849 has occupied a fine old once-enlarged building on Beacon Street, not far from the State House. So unassuming was the institution that until 1965, when the building was declared a national historic landmark, the only exterior designation was the address, "10½," painted on the glass panels of the leather-covered doors.

It truly is, as it has been called, a *rus in urbe*, a place where the peace and calm and sunshine of the country flow into the city. Its five floors, each with a distinct character, hold stacks containing more than 460,000 volumes—but it is not the message of the books but the mood of the building that makes the Athenaeum such an uncommonly pleasant place.

Perhaps it's the view over the old Granary Burying Ground, spread with an early snow, animated by squirrels, the old tombstones saying all there is to say about the brevity of life. Perhaps it's the company—men who you feel talk in a whisper even at home. Or the finesse of thought when Mr. Whitehill notes Thomas Crawford's sculptured Adam and Eve, "who, placed without the swinging doors, are looking rather plaintively towards the Delivery Desk." Today, as before, the library is owned by 1,049 proprietors who are, Mr. Whitehill says, "like its founders, sound individualists, not only in their inclination to follow their own tastes but also in their disinclination to mind their neighbor's business."

Of all the books once banned in Boston, James Joyce's *Ulysses* is probably the best known; some of the same language is used today in Boston's two underground newspapers, the *Real Paper* and the *Boston Phoenix*. In a city almost totally dominated by the liberal *Boston Globe*, these two once-ragamuffin journals are strong on women's lib, tough on waffling politicians, not plussed at all by columns advising how to defeat bad landlords or by sizzling sexual personal notices. These two outspoken street-sale papers say they are trying to keep the Establishment honest; at least they keep a lot of it disgusted.

Not much different, I suppose, from the lambasting of Brahmins late in the last century by ambitious Irish pols, in precincts where anti-Establishment views were redeemable at the polls for votes.

When the city's northern expansion was blocked by the existence of towns in that direction, including next-door Cambridge, and movement to the west was blocked by Brookline (and many a Boston mayor has lusted after Brookline's tax base), the city proper fell away to the south, over 12 square miles of residential development that today resembles a vast wooden three-decker tundra—down through the neighborhoods of Roxbury, Dorchester, and Mattapan, relieved only by the occasional green expanse of a park or cemetery. It was this sweep of low- and middle-class wooden housing that the Irish claimed as their own. I traversed this old section of the city, in the murk and gloom of a winter night, on my way to an Irish wake.

The deceased was a very, very old lady. Two equally old women knelt at the casket, keening through black veils that mournful banshee sound that chills the Irish blood. They paused for a moment as I entered, examined their departed friend, and one of them remarked: "She was hell on wheels, all right."

The deceased had come over as a young girl, worked as a maid in the houses of Boston Brahmins, saved every penny she ever made, and every enemy, and had known only struggle and labor. Her first husband, a railroad man, had the misfortune to be struck by a train, an accident that cost him a leg. The story had been around for years that the red-haired spitfire had run him off after that, yelling from the window, "What good's a one-legged man!"

The surviving relatives had assembled in a back room to fight over the will and drink and tell riotous lies. I took one of them aside and asked if the story about the railroad man was true.

"True, lad. In those days, the Irish buried any parcel, arm or leg or hand, that happened to become detached. It was given a proper burial—thinking, you know, that a person wants to walk into paradise with all his parts on. Well now, I went to the hospital where the man was lying there so sad, and he said to me, 'Patrick, me leg.'

"I said to him, holding my hand up, 'The leg's been buried,' and I showed him the receipt from the funeral home, certifying to the proper burial, at a cost of $36.00. He paid me then and there, reaching up behind the pillow for an old black wallet, and he thanked me most heartfully. And my, did we ever have a party with that $36.00!"

"But didn't you have to pay that money to the funeral home?"

"For what? Michael O'Neill worked there and he had come out with the receipt all made out. That's where we had the party, in the back of the funeral home."

"What did you do with the leg?"

"Heaved it in the incinerator, lad! We figured St. Peter would let the poor man through after the life he'd led—leg or no. Why throw good money into the ground?"

They worked on the railroad, and they worked on the docks, and they worked on the police force, and as nurses and servants and hod carriers. They were poor, the children of famine back home. They were illiterate, the offspring of centuries of suppression.

One old Irishman told me, "They had a room over in East Boston, where the boats landed, and a pole in that room, where they tied the poor lads while they put on their first pair of shoes."

The Irish multiplied, turned their numbers into votes, did battle with Lodges and Saltonstalls, and established a rousing political tradition from which sprang the McCormacks and the Kennedys.

Dorchester still has its Irish, within the sound of St. Gregory's bells, along streets named Clancy and O'Connell, where stores like the Green Leaf have shamrocks in the windows and sell Irish imports. The last of them are leaving Roxbury to the blacks.

I fell in with a young policeman, Roxbury bred. "I moved my mother out of here not long ago—to Dorchester. She's only waiting for the day she can go back to Roxbury. But she's 86. . . ."

The South End started life with every expectation of being a better sort of place, but it had bad luck in the depression of 1873.

The fictional George Apley remembered his father, who had moved to the developing South End, going out onto his front porch one morning.

"'Thunderation,' Father said, 'there is a man in his shirtsleeves on those steps.' The next day he sold his house . . . and we moved to Beacon Street."

A lot of his kind went with them, and the South End became and remained "rooming-house Boston." Nevertheless, many of the area's streets that once tried to be elegant are in fact elegant, especially Union Park and Worcester Square. The South End is famous for its large collection of beautiful bowfront Victorian row houses.

Its potential has not escaped the Boston Redevelopment Authority or the speculators catering to young professionals and white collars. From the Prudential Center southward, many of these houses are being gutted and rebuilt.

I stopped by to see Sam Hatchett, a tall well-spoken black who runs the Little City Hall on Blackstone Square. Sam earned a Harvard degree for the price of a few bushels of wheat. In 1836 John Lowell, Jr., left a bequest to pay for adult education, specifying that the fee per course charged by the school be "the value of two bushels of wheat," for convenience considered by the school to be worth about $5. Related fees have raised the cost now to about $30 per course.

"I love languages," Sam said. "I'm learning Chinese. I'm a curiosity, a black man speaking Greek and Chinese. It knocks them out.

"Down here, you've got to talk everything. We've got 10,700 whites, about 9,000 blacks, a little over 6,000 Puerto Ricans, and almost 3,000 Chinese, Koreans, and Japanese, with a few Syrians and Armenians."

People have been steadily leaving the 600-acre region since the start of urban renewal. As the population declined, the value of real estate rose; a house that sold for $10,000 in 1960 now may run as high as $35,000, and up to $90,000 if "rehabbed."

"The city's South End faces the familiar whipsaw of urban renewal," Sam told me, "casting the poor out in a process that rehabilitates the housing for the well-to-do. Pembroke Street, for example, is Puerto Rican south of Tremont Street, and white upper-middle north of it. We call that other side Pembroke *Other*."

I went up to Pembroke Other and Pembroke Nether as well, where I found young Danny Soltren and his wife with their small daughter almost literally holding the fort.

They occupy the third floor of an elderly house. The kitchen windows look out on a devastated landscape of brick piles, blackened, snow-streaked lots filled with rubble, and broken streets.

"You see the building there to the left," Danny said. "It burned last Friday night. They evacuated us at 5 a.m. because the sparks were flying onto our roof here. That building is privately owned. We have had eight fires in the path of the renewal since summer. That is too many for accident. We suspect arson."

Like so many other things in the South End, the event reminded me of Mary Antin, who wrote so movingly in *The Promised Land*: "While the great can speak for themselves . . . the humble are apt to live inarticulate and die unheard."

Boston's future is as difficult to read as that of any other American city, especially with its growing ethnic awareness, its restrictive tax base, its urge to grow and contrary desire not to, and the dwindling amounts of federal money now available for urban problems.

I went one rainy morning over to the Harvard Yard to talk with Hale Champion, now a Harvard vice-president but formerly head of the Boston Redevelopment Authority during times of growth and stress. I found him still full of fight and optimism.

"Boston continues to be a very attractive place, and for the same reasons it always has," he said. "The city's problem is not financial—there is great wealth—but fiscal, how to raise the public revenues and translate them into amenities that keep a city alive and growing.

"I doubt if Boston could take much more of the super-development we had. It was time we paid attention to the neighborhoods and needs of people, to the questions of education and opportunity, to competing in the world and living as a city. Boston has a lot going for it. We still have a chance."

Boston has accepted, sheltered, educated, put up with, put down, and made some kind of citizen out of all of them. As she has for countless others, that warm brick mother of human aspiration, that bearbaiting ring of local politics, that quiet library of the mind and subtle uplifter of the human spirit—that bawd, that fake, that outrageous flirt of a place that makes a man feel so young.

SEPTEMBER 1974

A WELL-SWEPT WALK

DEBORAH FALLOWS

For more than a year I lived with my husband and our two young sons in a neighborhood in Yokohama called Utsukushigaoka, literally "beautiful hills." Our rented house was small but cheerful, with a backyard so tiny our sons trimmed the grass with scissors. Wind gusted up the hills, swirling the leaves off our front walkway. A well-swept walk is a must in suburban Japan, and the wind was a wonderful convenience.

Or so I thought, until the day my kindly neighbor, Mrs. Kamimura, came over to present yet another elaborate dish she'd cooked for us Americans. She casually mentioned that in our absence she had swept the walk. I looked outside—the walk looked the same as usual—and realized with embarrassment that she, not the wind, had been sweeping away the leaves all along.

My neighbor let me know gently and indirectly that she'd been sweeping up after me, but that it was now high time I assumed this chore myself. Because I was a foreigner who could not be expected to know what was expected of me, Kamimura-san had taken it on herself to keep up the standards of the street and also to save face for me. The longer I lived in Japan, the more I realized that Kamimura-san's good deed illustrated a basic truth about Japanese life: the unquestioned and unquestionable duty to do what is expected of you and do it properly.

FROM "JAPANESE WOMEN," APRIL 1990

CALIFORNIA DESERT

BARRY LOPEZ

I t is an hour now since the sun has risen. I've been sitting here, 700 feet up on the crest of a sand dune, watching a soft, vaporous light fill Eureka Valley. The Eureka dunes rise at the southern end of this huge, quiet basin, beneath a jagged line of gray-blue and magenta mountains called the Last Chance Range. The cloudless dawn sky towers, intensifying a feeling of unbounded space.

The mountains that rim this valley, streaked with ocherous beiges and paprika reds, appear barren, but they are full of plants and animals that merely elude the eye. A pocket mouse the size of a walnut. A desert tortoise asleep in its burrow. Evening-snow, a wispy-stemmed plant that remains invisible against the ground until its white flowers open suddenly at nightfall.

A morning fog that earlier clung to the dunes has dissipated. The twittering of sage sparrows on the desert floor below, no longer muffled by the thick air, now drifts up. The air on this fall morning is not moist enough to also bring with it the odor of creosote bush and bur sage from below, but I can trace an unbroken line down the perfect French curve of the dune, out across the broad pastel strokes of the basin and into the mountains. I can get the feel of this land *that* way. The Saline Range, five miles to the west, is as crisp to my eye as the featherstitching of beetle tracks in the sand by my hip. This near and far clarity of the valley tightens up the vastness—the land seems simultaneously remote and immediate.

It is as restful as a calm ocean, seen from the shore dunes.

Eureka Valley sits at the northern edge of the California Desert—technically speaking, those sections of the Mojave and Sonoran Deserts within the state's boundaries. The Mojave is a relatively cool, high desert, where snow falls in winter; the Sonoran, lying at a lower elevation to the south, is drier, hotter, and more extensive than the Mojave. (The Sonoran Desert includes the Colorado Desert, comprising the Imperial and Coachella Valleys, and the much smaller Yuha Desert southwest of the Imperial Valley.) Rainfall in both the high and the low desert is usually short and violent, and so undependable both as to time and place as to seem to have no pattern. Its lack, along with the sun's heat and light and erratic and fitful desert winds, sets a general limit on life here.

The California Desert is less arid, however, than Old World deserts like the Gobi and the Sahara. Also by comparison, the range of its plants and animals, many with a seeming genius for locating or retaining water, is stunning. As is its variety of habitats—hot springs, saline sinks, cool, foliated canyons, sun-blasted bajadas, sand-dune systems, perennial streams, and Joshua tree "forests." After a winter of moderate but well-spaced rains, wildflowers may rise like fragrant breath from the earth—carpets of blue lupines, white primroses, yellow marigolds, and purple sand verbena. In Lanfair Valley in the eastern Mojave blue grama grass, Indian ricegrass, and big galleta grass roll under the press of the wind like Kansas wheat.

The beauty of the California Desert lies more with its exotic character than with its landforms. The very subtle shading of its soils, pale greens fading into lavenders. The thick, velvet darkness of its midnight canyons. The tremulous voice of an elf owl at a fan palm oasis in the stone fastness of the Chuckwalla Mountains. The way saffron light vibrates over the white surface of a playa at sunset. It is a land as open to the eye as the surface of the moon.

It would be strange, of course, if others didn't see the desert differently. For many it is not a place of hushed and intricate beauty, but a dreary stretch of wasteland between Las Vegas and Los Angeles. A vacant lot awaiting development. "There's nothing important out there," a driver told me at the start of the Barstow to Vegas motorcycle race, yelling over the racket of his engine. "We're the ones making something useful out of it, putting this race on."

The desert's usefulness is thought to lie, variously, with its considerable mineral wealth—borates, gypsum, gold—and its strategic reserves of molybdenum, tungsten, and lanthanides. Or with its dependably clear, sunny weather, eminently suited to the testing of missiles and aircraft. Or with its reservoirs of alternative energy—sunlight, wind, and hot groundwater. Or with its capacity to serve as an unfenced recreation area for a burgeoning population eager to escape the congestion and foul air of large cities.

These differing views of how best to use the desert were first brought into sharp focus early in the 1970s—with an explosion in the sale of off-highway vehicles. Interstates 8, 10, and 15 and California 14, the major routes into the desert from the populated coast, were now jammed on Friday nights with motor homes and recreation vehicles. Some pulled trailers full of equipment: gyrocopters, land yachts, ultralights, motocross bikes, and dune buggies. Once lonely places like Jawbone Canyon and Johnson Valley in the western Mojave were suddenly full of noise, dust, and people.

Ostensibly much of the initial disagreement over desert use was between vehicle operators and wilderness advocates, or between desert cattle ranchers and environmentalists. But real differences of opinion were more broad based. People living permanently in small, scattered communities in the desert didn't care for visitors running roughshod over the land on weekends, target shooting at isolated stock tanks and leaving piles of litter behind. Other visitors, those who had long regarded the desert as a sort of shopping mall for ironwood, pet tortoises and tarantulas, arrowheads, and barrel cactus, found themselves at odds with people who felt that public land should now be protected from such illegal poaching. Archaeologists were distraught over an increase in vandalism and theft at historic and prehistoric sites in the desert.

Clearly, an overall plan for managing recreation and other desert activities was needed. In 1976 Congress ordered the Bureau of Land Management (BLM) to come up with one. (Roughly 72 percent of the California Desert's 25 million acres is federally owned.) Four years and more than a hundred public meetings later, a final version of the California Desert Conservation Area Plan was drawn up, and its provisions now constitute a guide for desert managers' decisions. The meaning and intent of the plan in specific instances is still being interpreted, so special interest groups—power companies, ranchers, miners, cross-country motorcycle racers, scientists, educators, and the military—continue to press for interpretations and amendments that will favor their ends.

By all accounts the BLM has done a commendable, even heroic job of ameliorating conflict in putting the plan to work. Few, however, see a bright future ahead. The population of the Los Angeles-San Diego area continues to grow and to make increasing demands on the desert. Vandalism and theft persist. According to the BLM, roughly one-third of the desert's prehistoric sites have been damaged, and about one percent of its prehistoric artifacts disappear each year. "It doesn't take a smart man to see what's wrong," cattleman and longtime resident Gary Overson told me one afternoon at his Kessler Springs Ranch in the eastern Mojave. "But it'll take a smart man to fix it."

In several months of travel and interviews in the desert I met no such Solomon. But the threads of wisdom—what to do to ensure the longevity of this unique part of North America—did become clear. The gist of nearly every thoughtful conversation I had was the same: a need for public education, developing an abiding regard for the land itself, and finding some way— public or private—to come to the aid of the BLM.

Education takes many forms. Mine was seen to in part by a young man named Bruce Bannerman, a biologist at the University of California's study center in the Granite Mountains. The lanky and blond Bannerman and I were walking down a dirt road one brilliantly clear morning, and he made a sweeping gesture to the south and east. "Where else," he beamed, "can you count 26 separate mountain ranges from your front door?" The evidence before us was vivid. Mountain ranges in this part of the Mojave surface whole from the earth, like stone porpoises. The sheer compass of it all makes you exuberant.

"I've smelled the Pacific this far inland once or twice," said Bannerman later, as if to further impress on me the unorthodox scale of the place. I had, in fact, begun to think of the desert itself as an ocean. The glint of sunlight on vast and uniform shields of gray-green vegetation is very like its metallic glare from a rolling sea. The mountain ranges stand on the land like archipelagoes. Cloud shadows drift slowly across the empty basins or across the flanks of salmon-tinted mountains like huge fish. Occasionally the land becomes so extensive the horizon itself becomes nautical—the edge of the earth seems to curve over into space.

Bannerman's destination was Snake Spring, a damp oasis tucked in a crevice of the Granite Mountains. We climbed up to it easily, and sat there in silence amid the trees. Water is so dear over so much of the desert that wherever it flows freely, as here, an atmosphere of serene calm prevails. The cool air fell over my shoulders like a mantle, and I surveyed the hundred square miles of desert basin below me, looking for coyotes and the lineaments of its geology.

"What was that?" I asked, breaking our long silence.

"Red-spotted toad," said Bannerman. "You rarely hear them during the day. It's a night sound."

Before we left the cove—I could not resist shuffling loudly through a thick layer of cottonwood and willow leaves on an incongruous swatch of green desert grasses as we departed—Bannerman showed me a shelter. It was a kind of natural breezeway in the granite where one could sit out of the sun and still watch the desert. I adjusted my sitting position as I was directed and soon found what Bannerman intended I should—my hands came to rest on slick depressions in the rock alongside my hips. Knowing what to look for, I now saw four such pairs of depressions. They were bedrock metates. Centuries ago, perhaps, Indian women had sat here grinding seeds.

Months later, on an August afternoon, I visited an older Indian site. Four of us clambered down a slope of basalt boulders and out onto a dry wash at the bottom of upper Renegade Canyon. My companions, civilians working for the Navy's environmental branch at the China Lake Naval Weapons Center, had brought me to a remarkable location in an area where more prehistoric rock art may be concentrated than in any other place in North America.

I stood transfixed before a wall of dark gray basalt. Pecked into its uneven surface was a bewildering array of images: large deer and mountain sheep, geometric designs in the shapes of shields and atlatls, or spear-throwing sticks, and human figures of different sorts. They were made by hunter-gatherers who apparently specialized in hunting mountain sheep.

What held my gaze was complicated—the sheer number of drawings, the seeming freshness of some of them, etched as they were by the late afternoon light, and how undisturbed the area appeared to be. (The Navy restricts public entry to the site.) I don't think I ever felt the presence of history so acutely—a conservative estimate puts a date of about 1000 B.C. on the oldest of these drawings.

At the southwestern end of the upper canyon, one of the archaeologists showed me an open-air site where these people had once camped. Here was evidence of their cooking fires, a waste midden, and the debitage of their stonework—myriad flakes of obsidian glass gleaming brilliantly in the setting sun. Here, too, were grinding slicks, bedrock metates like the one I had seen near Snake Spring. And odd petroglyphs called cupules—shallow holes the size of Concord grapes, pounded into the rock.

The falling light made it necessary to turn back, but I was most reluctant to leave. I trailed behind the others, walking backward, so that I would not lose eye contact with the scene. It seemed imbued with the power of human history, like the stone walls of Jerusalem.

At what point, exactly, people first moved into the California Desert is a topic of considerable debate among archaeologists. Researchers at the Calico Early Man Site in the central Mojave claim stone tools found there establish man's presence about 200,000 years ago. Dates of 30,000 to 40,000 years before the present have been suggested for cultural materials found at China Lake. But a widely agreed upon date for man's presence in the desert doesn't come until the end of the Pleistocene, some 12,000 years ago.

The desert was a wetter, cooler place then. Paleo-Indians living on the shores of rain-fed lakes subsisted on waterfowl, shellfish, plant foods, and large and small game. Some 5,000 to 7,000 years ago, as the lakes slowly dried up, these cultures gave way to smaller, more nomadic groups that, increasingly, found their food in the drier uplands of the desert. These so-called Archaic traditions endured for several thousand more years, until the ancestors of the tribes known to modern history emerged.

During this same period the modern assemblages of plants and animals scientists today call "Mohave Desertscrub" (creosote bush, Joshua tree, Mojave yucca) and "Sonoran Desertscrub" (creosote bush, burrobrush, saguaro, indigobush) also came into being. At the close of the Wisconsin Ice Age, the only "dry desert" in the area existed around the mouth of the Colorado River. Over millennia, however, many of those plants and animals took advantage of the changing climate to extend their ranges farther north, while the northern plants and animals moved into higher elevations in the desert mountain ranges. Some of the original colonizers of one of the plants that came up from the south—the creosote bush—may, incredibly, still be alive. An individual creosote bush clone growing in Johnson Valley in the central Mojave, for example, has been traced back to an ancestor an estimated 11,700 years old.

The Spanish, intent on establishing an overland route between Mexico and the California coast in the 1700s, were the first Europeans to cross the desert. Mountain men like Jedediah Smith entered the Mojave early in the

19th century and by the 1860s a number of trails and wagon roads had been opened through the territory.

In the 1870s and '80s railroads brought an influx of miners to the region and the first cattle operations started up in the eastern Mojave. The first desert resort hotel at Palm Springs opened in 1886. By 1910, the Imperial, Coachella, and Palo Verde Valleys had been irrigated for farming. In the 1930s agriculture spread northward out of the Los Angeles basin into Antelope and Apple Valleys in the western Mojave, and people began to purchase five-acre "jackrabbit homesteads" there. The aircraft industry followed, attracted by the Mojave's year-round good flying weather. The military then discovered in the desert a perfectly lonely and dry place to train personnel, test weapons, and store matériel. (Military installations now occupy about 3.2 million acres in the desert.)

The Imperial Valley has grown to 470,000 acres and become the nation's winter vegetable garden. Nearly 80,000 people live in the Palm Springs area today, at the foot of the San Jacinto Mountains. And the single-blanket jackass prospector and 20-mule-team borax wagons have become part of the nation's folklore.

In many ways, the record of this history is one of the desert's most engaging dimensions—old mines with names like Queen of the Night, Chief of Sinners, and Pride of the Union. The Army's World War II desert training camps. And remnants of the Plank Road built across the Imperial Sand Dunes in 1915, to shorten the automobile route between El Centro and Yuma. In an effort to preserve this heritage, the BLM has listed such sites among 77 protected areas of critical environmental concern in the desert.

As I followed my companions out of upper Renegade Canyon and away from the petroglyphs that afternoon, I fretted over the vulnerability of the evidence of human history in this region. Although it is not specifically addressed in the desert plan, preserving a sense of the depth and breadth of human history in the desert, both aboriginal and modern, lies at its very foundation. It is this that makes acts of vandalism, such as the flagrant disregard of motorcyclists for intaglios (large, prehistoric ground drawings) in the Yuha Desert so depressing. That and the poor prospects for being able to protect what is left of this heritage in the desert.

It was in the company of BLM rangers that I saw that side of the desert perhaps least familiar to most of us—the intense and sometimes strange use to which it is put. Many people regard the desert as worthless land and expect no interference in their activities out there. Some are completely unaware that they are violating state and federal laws, or that all the desert has been zoned according to the desert plan to control its use. You can no longer trail blaze with a four-wheel drive, build a squatter's vacation cabin, or harvest a truckload of ironwood to sell to Mexican carvers. Miners can no longer bulldoze roads wherever they wish. And someone who has just emptied his sewage tank in the blackbrush may be stunned to learn that a BLM ranger is a federal law-enforcement officer, handing him a federal ticket.

The primary job of BLM rangers is to protect the natural and cultural resources of the desert. An equal part of their work, however, judging from the time I spent with them, is education and public relations—explaining to varmint hunters, rockhounds, exotic-vehicle owners, amateur archaeologists, survivalists, and a million casual tourists that there is a new pattern of public use here.

The day I spent with Jerry Needy, a tall, circumspect ranger working out of Needles, was informative. Needy was familiar with a desert I did not know. As we pulled off U.S. 95 to begin a backroads tour of the Turtle and Old Woman Mountains, he said, matter-of-factly, "I pretty much operate on the theory that everyone out here is armed, or they've got a weapon in the vehicle." Needy once stumbled into a Colorado Desert training camp for Latin American revolutionaries stocked with, among other things, stolen military weapons. On another occasion he ran into a mobile drug-lab operation and two heavily armed men.

As Needy described the number and range of guns he'd seen in use in the desert, I realized how uneasy I had become about them. Virtually every road sign I had seen in the desert was bullet riddled. Some had been hit by so many shotgun blasts they were mangled beyond recognition. It is the intensity rather than the mere fact of this kind of destruction that is finally so unnerving. Over a period of several months, as I stared at the remnants of mining operations and ghost towns like Picacho and Hart, destroyed by explosives, gunfire, and arson, and pulled apart by vehicular winches— people looking for the gold caches of dead prospectors, I was once told—I found myself fighting for perspective. It is a very small part of society that behaves like this, but all of us must confront the dismal evidence of their scorn for the value of human history. To see so much of it is unsettling.

Finding a "release from city tensions" took on new meaning the day I spent with ranger Bill Vernon at Imperial Dunes, a strip of sand hills 45 miles long and five miles wide at the eastern edge of the Imperial Valley. Over the past 13 years nearly 70 people have been killed here, most in recreation-vehicle-related accidents. The number of injuries suffered and the incidents of drinking under age, fistfights, and public nudity are uncounted. Over long holiday weekends, especially on Thanksgiving and Presidents' Day, 40,000 people may visit the area. (The BLM's figure is 792,000 visitor days per year.)

There is a dizzying madness to the wild spectacle at Imperial Dunes, the aimless hurtling of vehicles through clouds of dust, noise, and darkness; but Vernon defends this antic racing, helter-skelter over the sand, night and day, as "legitimate sport." "Seventy-five percent of these folks are hardworking, good people; 10 percent are lowlifes, just incorrigible; 15 percent are running the ragged edge, usually with a few beers," he told me. "But they have as much right to the public lands as anyone else."

Some 200 miles to the north, a much more subdued and better behaved crowd gathers at Dumont Dunes on long weekends. The purpose of coming out to such a place to drive around in the sand is essentially social, one man told me. He and his family spend a total of 30 days a year in the desert. They drive out from Yorba Linda in their motor home, pulling a dune buggy and other recreation vehicles in a huge trailer. He brings his children, and his daughters bring their boyfriends. "The desert," he said, "is the greatest thing that ever happened to my family."

Reckless off-highway vehicle use and incidents of vandalism, because they leave such visible scars, draw an inordinate amount of attention, in the view of some. One four-wheel-drive operator, leading a group across the desert with scrupulous care, shrugged off my discomfort at bullet-riddled signs and vehicle-damaged hillsides. "What about the proliferation of power lines out here? That's *public* vandalism."

Many off-highway vehicle enthusiasts, weary of having to shoulder most of the blame for the visual deterioration of the desert, say it is power development and large-scale mining, as well as ranching operations, military exercises, and agricultural expansion, that are the real culprits. They point a finger at abandoned munitions dumps, overgrazed hillsides, open-pit mines, and noxious fumes at chemical plants.

Their charges are undeniable. In Trona, California, where Kerr-McGee produces chemicals from a brine solution beneath the salt crust of adjacent

Searles Lake, the air was so thick with sulfurous fumes one day that I became nauseated. An area I viewed from a helicopter on another day, in the vicinity of the Cady Mountains, was crosshatched with cattle trails. From the Amboy Road, east of Twentynine Palms Marine Corps Base, one can clearly see heaps of overburden produced by the National Chloride Company and Leslie Salt in their surface operations on Bristol Lake. Outside of compliance with the law, however, there is little more that can be demanded of such operators by a society that insists on their products.

One day, weary of the sight of too many chemical plants, too much cow-burnt land, and, as one executive put it, too much "chloride farming," I made a detour to Big Morongo Canyon. There, at the 3,900-acre Big Morongo Canyon Preserve, I stepped out of the glazing heat into the shade of Fremont cottonwoods and red willows. More than 265 species of birds have been seen at Big Morongo Canyon. Their notes, along with the *kreck-ek* of the Pacific tree frog, fill the air. Along Big Morongo Creek one might see a docile red diamond rattlesnake sunning on flattened bulrushes. I walked the preserve's shaded trails and tried to collect my thoughts about the desert's future.

A weakness in the desert plan, in the view of many, is that while it apportions the desert equitably to different interest groups, and while it strives for a form of management that will ensure the desert's integrity for years to come, its basic operating premise—it directs the BLM to "manage, use, develop, and protect"—is an internal contradiction. Pressured by special interest groups, given a mandate like this, and hampered by a lack of funds and personnel, the BLM must compromise.

Dennis Casebier, a desert historian and longtime observer of conflicts over the desert's use, told me one day that conflict was no longer the central issue. "What's wrong," said Casebier, "is that we have no vision. How do all these different things—four-wheel-drive tours and cattle ranching and geothermal development—relate to each other? BLM can't just make everyone happy. They've got to sit down and decide what they want the desert to look like in 20 years." Which is to say the country itself, the people acting through Congress, must decide what they want the nation's public lands to look like in the future.

I left Morongo Canyon that day, oddly, with a sense of hope about the desert's future. The Bureau of Land Management is staffed with dedicated and thoughtful people. Bill Vernon puts in 18-hour days at Imperial Dunes.

Jerry Needy remembers to bring five gallons of water to an elderly miner isolated at his waterless claim without a vehicle. Ev Hayes, the BLM area manager at Needles, gets out of his truck during a torrential thunderstorm to carry several wandering desert tortoises safely across the road in Ivanpah Valley. In the face of a continuing pattern of budget and personnel cuts they remain hopeful.

A second cheering element is the extent to which private individuals and groups have come to the aid of the desert. Just east of Palm Springs a consortium including the Nature Conservancy, state and federal wildlife agencies, and the BLM has established the 13,000-acre Coachella Valley Preserve, principally to protect the threatened Coachella Valley fringe-toed lizard, an animal highly adapted to life in and on sand dunes, and several palm oases from development. The California Off-Road Vehicle Association has worked with the U.S. Air Force to restore a section of the Plank Road in Imperial Dunes. Business organizations, private and public museums, and hundreds of volunteers have joined to build watering holes for desert bighorn sheep, maintain protected areas for the desert tortoise, and restore vandalized intaglios.

The final source of hope is much harder to define but unmistakable when you encounter it. It is the enthusiasm and thoughtfulness with which many of the desert's year-round residents conduct their lives. These ranchers, yucca harvesters, miners, and even a landscape painter I spoke to all seemed to have one thing in common. They spend a great deal of time out on the land, and they feel it is a privilege to live in this country. Lean and reserved, it has a ring of integrity they admire and seek to imitate.

Death Valley is the scene of yet another, more complex issue—the removal of the wild burro population. Few dispute the fact that a concentration of burros makes it hard for desert bighorn sheep to make a living alongside them. The burros foul water sources and denude the land, exposing it to erosion. The thinking behind their removal, however, is somewhat fuzzy. There are many exotic species in the California Desert—English house sparrows, tumbleweeds, mosquitofish, wild horses—but the boom has been lowered only on the burro.

Gene Nunn, a BLM cowboy in his late 40s with sparkling blue eyes, has been in charge of the burro roundup in Death Valley for several years. "If the moon fell out of the sky," he told me, "and burros were around, they'd be blamed." The burro, reason Nunn and others, is probably not responsible for every one of the adverse environmental impacts he's blamed for in the desert. What's more, the burro never asked to be put there. He was brought in and then abandoned by prospectors to fend for himself—which he's done. There should be a place out there for him, thought Nunn.

I wasn't sympathetic to this argument at first, but after traveling with the cowboys for several days while they worked I felt admiration and sympathy for these small-footed, tough, sleepy-eyed animals. They have neither the allure nor the romance of the wild horse in their favor but they have a kind of dignity, by virtue of their survival in this arid and ungenerous land. It is we, really, who have changed the desert; the burro is just doing what he has always done.

In this context I recalled a bleak stretch of the Mojave east of Lancaster. The native species of grass there have nearly all been driven out, replaced by red bromegrass, cheatgrass, Russian thistle, and several other exotics. The dilapidated For Sale signs of land speculators wobbling in heat waves along the highway make the landscape here seem even drearier. How *will* we manage the desert in the years ahead? Will our wisdom in caring for it show to the same extent as this power we have to rearrange nature? And will there be a culprit as convenient as the burro to blame if it doesn't go right?

One winter evening, on my last trip to the desert, I drove down to Badwater in Death Valley from Furnace Creek and walked out on the playa. This is the lowest spot in the Western Hemisphere, 282 feet below sea level. I walked far out on the salt flat and stood there until the last bit of daylight faded from the western sky and the stars came out. The faint starlight was enough to see by. I could not see my car, but I was not worried. I could see the spine of the Amargosa Range against the indigo sky, and I knew the notch in that ridge below which memory had fixed an image of the car as I walked away.

Far out on the playa I realized these walks had become a habit. I went off arbitrarily, up dry washes and out across the most ordinary-looking bajadas. I let myself be tutored by the land, with the help of a few animal and plant guides and a handful of notes. Without fail I would come on something remarkable—a cactus, for example, called dead cactus, because it always looked that way. I would walk into the sudden red brilliance of a vermilion flycatcher put to flight. Or hear the low-throated booms of moving sand dunes. One day near Iron Mountain I went out across the desert just to stare into the Colorado River Aqueduct. The contrast between the cool, dark water and the sere desert plain all around, nearly white with the savage sunlight of an August afternoon, was extreme. The cavitating sounds of running water, headed for Los Angeles and San Diego, seemed utterly magical.

I remembered, standing there at Badwater, the words of people who lived and worked in the desert. "You're on the edge of a drought all the time," cattle rancher Gary Overson had told me. I thought of what Ken Norris, a legendary professor of biology from the University of California at Santa Cruz, had said to students at the Granite Mountains study center: "The most powerful thing you can do out here is face reality." And I recalled the words of John Van Dyke, a turn-of-the-century desert traveler. What one seeks out here, he wrote, what finally holds you enthralled, is "the weird solitude, the great silence, the grim desolation."

A light wind came across the surface of the playa from the northeast. I squatted down and laid my hands flat on the ground. The surface was cool and gritty. A commons, I was thinking. This fierce land, with its wild flash floods, its resourceful plants and animals, its titanic reserves of quietude, its many shades of purple, its cholla cactus that snare afternoon sunlight and wear it like a cloak, all this is public land. A commons.

I fixed in my mind that point in the pitch darkness where I thought the car might be, and started walking.

JANUARY 1987

A LEAN YEAR

ROBERT M. POOLE

"Nobody really lives off the land these days," said Douglas Blake, up to his shins in snow on a January morning. The temperature was stuck somewhere around zero, and the ice on Grand Lake was frozen four feet thick. But the sun was shining.

Like a few other Labradorians, Douglas still traps animals on occasion, but more as a diversion than a necessity. Blakes have trapped along this lake for generations. Douglas's ancestors did it on snowshoes; we used snowmobiles, driving on the frozen lake, dismounting every few miles to see if anything had wandered into his traps, baited with bits of fish.

"What are you hoping for?" I asked.

"Marten, fox—maybe a lynx." He led me through the frozen brush. "I'd be surprised if we got a lynx. Nobody's seen one around here since the big forest fire in 1985." And even if a lynx turned up, the skin would fetch only $85 or so, down from the $800 range of the 1980s. That was before the recession, and before animal-rights activists made fur unfashionable.

"So why are we out here?"

"Better than being inside," Douglas answered. He was right. The air was sharp, the mountains muffled in snow, the blue sky shining as if newly made. We zoomed along the ice, all alone, bumping over cracks and pressure ridges, checking traps.

"Nothing here," Douglas said from the bushes. "Nope," he said, farther up the lake. Nothing. Nothing. Nothing. Then we found a luckless Canada jay, which had blundered into a marten trap and broken its neck. Back on the machines.

Nothing. Nothing. Nothing. Then wolf tracks. They looked bold and purposeful, heading straight up the shoreline. Douglas, who works as a wildlife officer for the provincial government, guessed that five wolves

416

formed this pack. "Fresh tracks," he said. We followed until one set of tracks peeled off from the others and headed toward shore, straight for the traps. Then the tracks stopped cold, 20 feet short of the traps, and I could picture the big animal sniffing the air, catching the warning scent, doubling back to join the others.

The day ended at twilight, with one dead jay to show for it. Later, thawing by a cast-iron stove in Douglas's one-room cabin, Douglas mopped up the last bit of grouse stew with a hunk of bread. "It's one of those lean years," he said.

FROM "LABRADOR, CANADA'S PLACE APART," OCTOBER 1993

HOW MRS. K. GOT THAT WAY

Boyd Gibbons

The Babylonians and Egyptians found that if they crushed grapes or warmed and moistened grain, the covered mush would bubble and become a drink with a kick. Louis Pasteur discovered that yeasts are single-cell, living fungi and that fermentation is their act of survival. Because alcohol is a toxin, fermentation is self-limiting. Once alcohol concentration reaches about 14 percent, or the sugar runs out, the multiplying yeasts die and fermentation ends. A stronger drink requires distillation.

The origins of distillation are obscure. The Arabs get credit not so much for the process, but for the word. *Al-kohl* is Arabic for finely ground antimony used as eye liner, and it came to mean any exotic essence.

So far as is documented, alcohol was first distilled in the Middle Ages, at a medical school in Salerno, Italy. Considered an important medicine, wine was boiled and the vapors then cooled and condensed to produce a more powerfully concentrated drug. A Spanish scholar gave this ragged brandy the name *aqua vitae*, the water of life.

Distilled alcohol evolved in Russia as *vodka*, in Holland as juniper-flavored *jenever* (the French called it *genièvre*, which the British blunted to *gin*), and passed through charred barrels, peat smoke, and across the Irish Gaelic tongue as *uisce beatha*, or whiskey.

The first Neolithic buzz remains unrecorded. But Solomon Katz, an anthropologist at the University of Pennsylvania, has a persuasive theory that alcohol may have been responsible for the earliest agriculture—to secure a dependable supply of beer.

"Most modern beers are very thin, but ancient beer was a food," says Katz. "Fermentation added needed B vitamins, essential amino acids converted by the yeast. And yeast also deactivated several toxic compounds in the barley, making it more palatable. Beer was better than bread in the sense that it also had alcohol in it."

Historically, people drank alcohol when they could get it: as food, in place of fetid water, as relief from the misery of life, to chase after pleasure—at births, weddings, and festivals. Wine poured down the pagan hatch, Dionysian and Bacchanalian. Alcohol was not only acceptable, it was esteemed, revered. The Old Testament prophets had long issued warnings against excessive drink, Moses proposing death for rebellious, drunken sons. Socrates warned, "If we pour ourselves immense draughts, it will be no longer time before both our bodies and our minds reel."

"The popular mythology of alcohol," wrote Berton Roueché, "is a vast and vehement book. . . . perhaps, the classic text in the illiterature of medicine." A shot of brandy chases the chill. (It actually makes you colder.) The French can't have many alcoholics, because they drink wine. (Not true. They have a high incidence of alcohol-related problems, with twice the rate of death by liver cirrhosis as in the U.S.) Similar defenses are made for beer, yet most alcoholics in Britain are beer drinkers, because beer is still predominantly what the British drink. It's not what you drink; it's how much alcohol goes down your throat.

Alcohol enters the bloodstream through the small intestine and, to some extent, through the stomach. A fraction exits in breath, sweat, and urine. If you eat while you drink, alcohol is absorbed more slowly and with less effect. But on an empty stomach or if carbonated—champagne, whiskey and soda—it moves more rapidly to all vital organs.

Alcohol is chiefly metabolized—chemically deconstructed—in the liver, through which the entire blood supply circulates every four minutes. Enzymes in the liver metabolize alcohol into acetaldehyde, a highly toxic chemical, which is then converted (in the liver and elsewhere) into acetate, and finally into carbon dioxide and water.

The process is slow, roughly three hours for each ounce of pure alcohol. Despite a vigorous folklore, virtually nothing will speed up the liver or sober up the intoxicated. Coffee on top of a toot only produces a wide-awake drunk.

Alcohol is a depressant of the central nervous system. By depressing both inhibitory and excitatory neurons, alcohol can produce in different people (in different settings and with different expectations) the life of the party, the bore, the morose recluse, the fighter, the rake. "It provokes the desire," wrote Shakespeare long before science examined the endocrine system, "but it takes away the performance."

Over time heavy drinking can bring on brain and heart damage, gastritis, pancreatitis, anxiety, malnutrition. It can depress the immune system. Heavy drinkers show a higher incidence of throat cancers (they're often heavy smokers—likely a synergy at work). Depression is more often the result of heavy drinking than its cause. A pregnant woman takes a drink. Within minutes her fetus has the same drink. Alcohol is one of the leading known causes of mental retardation in the Western world. It can damage the vulnerable developing brain and may impair placental function as well.

Mrs. K, age 55, was lying face up on stainless steel. I knew her name because it was printed on her thigh with a felt-tip pen. She was slit open ready for autopsy, the vital organs on a tray at her feet. A wood block was beneath her head, her mouth wide open in a terrible last gasp.

Martti Tenhu, the chief medical examiner for Helsinki and environs, was holding Mrs. K's heart in his hand. "This is the heart of a typical alcoholic, twice the size it should be. I expect she drank a truckload of vodka in her lifetime."

He scissored open the coronary arteries, which supply blood to the heart muscle.

"Smooth as a baby's. Typical of a daily drinker. Alcohol must help somewhat in fighting arteriosclerosis, but the bad effects of heavy drinking overwhelm this good effect. Alcohol is toxic to the heart muscle and the brain. It's very dangerous to say to Finns, 'Take two or three drinks a day, and it will be good for you.' They will take ten or twenty. If you're taking ten drinks a day, you may have smooth arteries, but you're dead at 50."

He snipped open her stomach, the upper end reddishly irritated by her heavy drinking. "That's hemorrhagic gastritis."

"The heart pumps 35 million times a year," Martti said. "This one is so flabby and enlarged from heavy drinking that it wasn't pumping very well, so the blood accumulated in the lungs and caused edema, or excess fluid. It bubbles up like Coca-Cola when you squeeze them." He placed Mrs. K's sodden lungs on the scale—twice the normal weight. He squeezed them and they fizzed.

Nearly one-third of her heart muscle was useless scar tissue, caused by

drinking. "There wasn't enough blood to supply this large heart with sufficient oxygen. These heavy drinkers may get heart arrhythmia a hundred
times during their lives. Then one day, like this lady, they drop dead of
heart attack."

Back home on a Sunday afternoon I assume the autumnal position of
American Guy (supine on couch) to watch football, a sport subdivided by
that quintessential American art form: the warm-buddies beer commercial.

A cynic might see something slightly cock-eyed in these scenes of robustly
handsome yuppies coming off their lobster boats in flannel shirts and teased
mousse hairdos, backlit by the slanting glow of sunset, punching shoulders,
and retiring to the company of incredible-looking women in the coziest tavern on the coast of Maine.

Am I envious? Sure, having never found anything quite like this chummy
tableau. These commercials have captured on one minute of tape all the
romance, the yearnings, the fellowship of alcohol and mankind.

But then life isn't a beer commercial.

FROM "ALCOHOL, THE LEGAL DRUG," FEBRUARY 1992

ALL THAT GLISTERS

PETER T. WHITE

At the Gold Museum in Bogotá, visitors enter darkness that gradually lights up into a dazzle of thousands of gold objects—breastplates, tweezers, nose ornaments, fishhooks—from Indian cultures that flourished before the Spaniards came. Quimbaya, Muisca, Sinú. . . .

A French family ogles a little golden raft with ten small figures and one big one. *Extraordinaire! Fabuleux!* It's a chief smeared with gold dust in ancient ritual. Possibly El Dorado, the Gilded One, says a museum official.

And the Indians? "They had the gold pulled off their noses and their holy burials ransacked and learned to keep quiet about gold." To this day the tribes won't talk about gold. But it is said that up in the snowy mountains, twice a year, at the time of the solstice, Indians still dance with golden masks. . . .

The Gold Museum belongs to the Bank of the Republic and pays well, so it gets hundreds of additions yearly, dug up from graves the Spaniards missed. "Gold is the curse of Colombian archeology," muses the museum man. "If those graves just had pottery, few would bother them. But what we display here fosters pride in the past. It shows that Indians who made such masterpieces were people worthy of respect. So maybe it'll lead to better treatment for the few who are left, maybe save them from extinction."

Burials are *guacas*, pronounced WHA-cas. Men who dig them up are *guaqueros*, and I go with them in the Magdalena region in the north. We search, dig, sweat, find only bones and broken pottery, complain, dig more, and then a gleam, excitement. It's a nose pendant of the Tairona culture, buried hundreds of years ago. Not bad but not big. My companions yearn for a chief or a shaman—a single hand-size chest ornament could pay each of three men the equivalent of eight years' wages!

Gold is still mined in Colombia. Around a bend in the river Telembí, which runs into the Patía that runs into the Pacific, I hear roaring, squealing, clanking. It's a dredge, four stories high. Every two seconds, around the clock, up clanks a bucket with nearly a ton of muck and gravel and maybe three hundredths of an ounce of gold. An engineer says all gold comes from hard rock originally, but nature and time did a lot of work for us, breaking up rock so that gold washes down to settle in riverbeds, so-called alluvial or placer gold.

In a deep channel dug into the rust-colored riverbank, a man with a crowbar pries at a bluish gold-bearing layer. Half a dozen women stand bent over, ankle-deep in water, holding wooden pans heaped with bluish stuff to be washed. It's an ungainly stance, rear up and head down, but they work gracefully with a swift, gentle rocking of the pan, a sweep of the arm to remove a stone or slosh on a little more water. The soil washes away, the heavier gold particles remain.

Along the shallow tributaries, I see here and there a hut and a woman panning and smoking. Why do they keep the burning end of the cigarette *inside* the mouth? "So it won't go out in the rain."

Firecrackers, bells in Barbacoas, the river town. It's the day of the Assumption of the Virgin, and her image, carried through the unpaved streets, is dressed in sumptuous gold. We love her, we love to see her this way, that's the way to praise her, says the mayor, says a beggar. These people are poor. Atop many a dark face of a child the curly black hair has a golden tinge, a sign of malnutrition.

Barbacoas has no newspaper or radio station, so when a new gold purchasing price is telegraphed from the capital, the mayor sends a man with a drum to read an announcement at a dozen street corners. This morning it was 1,182 pesos an ounce. That's $54. Two months ago, 1,080 pesos. Eight months ago, 780.

People come in dugout canoes to sell their fractions of an ounce at an agency of the Bank of the Republic. Others sell to traders who weigh less reliably but pay a little more. The bank agent says less and less is coming in. Is the gold giving out? No, it's not that. A lot is illegally exported to Ecuador. Annual gold production figures show only what was received by the bank—not how much really was produced in Colombia that year.

FROM "GOLD, THE ETERNAL TREASURE," JANUARY 1974

THE BUSINESS OF CHIC

It is 15 minutes past the hour when his show is scheduled to begin, but the guests of Paris *couturier* Yves Saint Laurent are still pouring through the door. Mme François Mitterrand, wife of the president of the republic; Catherine Deneuve, the most beautiful woman in France; and jewelry designer Paloma Picasso, the daughter of the celebrated painter, drift to the gilt ballroom chairs that have been reserved for them in the front row. An American movie star is shown to her seat on the other side of the room.

In homage to Saint Laurent most of the fashionable women up front are wearing several thousand dollars' worth of his creations. Any single part of an original Yves Saint Laurent outfit sewed for the wearer—a skirt, a jacket—costs not less than $3,000. These prices seem fair to his clients, not only for the luxurious fabrics, the matchless workmanship, the perfect fit of the garments themselves, but also for the tradition (Marie Antoinette often exceeded her annual clothing allowance of 120,000 gold livres) and the security of knowing that they look perfect.

Beyond a door framed in grapevines at the far end of the room, Yves Saint Laurent himself waits nervously, surrounded by the wand-like young women who will model his new collection. He makes the final adjustments in feverish silence.

The runway is already lined with photographers, each equipped with several cameras, poised to capture the first moment of glory or disappointment. The world fashion press are poised with notebooks and pencils to record their judgments. Selections from grand opera issue from loudspeakers. At last, after a further 15-minute delay, the first model appears in a sweeping royal blue cape over a bronze suit. The audience breaks into loud applause.

With minor variations this scene is duplicated each July and January in the salons of the other designers of the high-fashion clothes for women that the French call *couture* (literally, "sewing"). The Chambre Syndicale de la Haute Couture defines a couturier as one who has his own *atelier* (workroom) employing not fewer than 20 people and presenting at least 75 designs on at least three models in each collection. *Haute couture*, the name for the product of such ateliers, can be used only by the 22 members of the Chambre Syndicale.

Newcomers do exist. In January 1989 the Italian designer Valentino, who has been showing his ready-to-wear clothes in Paris for 15 years and his couture in Rome for 29 years, presented his first couture collection in Paris. "I have *dreamed* of showing my couture collection here," he told me.

Valentino's earlier work may have made him a rich man, but his Paris couture show was the ultimate endorsement of his craft. The couturier is bound by no creative restrictions, no concern for price, no worry as to who will buy the new styles. Originality is all.

Perhaps, however, couturiers are more aware of their customers than other artists: "When there were beautiful bodies to dress, it was my greatest pleasure to dress them," Mme Vionnet, whose venerable couture house was at its peak in the 1920s and 1930s, said to me 15 years ago, just before she died at 98. "For the others I did my best."

Couture now caters to "the others." In the mid-1970s Saint Laurent became the first designer to move his shows from his fashion house, where couture clothes had always been made, to the more spacious ballroom of one of Paris's grand hotels. Before that, models resembled statues, and the audience stared at them in solemnity and silence—no music ever played, and applause was seldom heard. Except for the irrepressible Coco Chanel, who watched her shows from the top step of the stairway in her famous house in the Rue Cambon, designers stayed behind the scenes.

Even today applause is saved for the most spectacular creations. But sometimes the simplest garment—an impeccable black suit, for example—will inspire a burst of applause. At the Saint Laurent show last July, the audience clapped for the Lesage grape embroideries on some of his creations.

Only once in 23 years of covering the Paris shows do I recall a negative reaction. That was in the early 1970s, when Christian Dior showed leopard-skin coats in his collection, and American editors and photographers hissed this exploitation of an endangered animal species. Coats made of the skins of leopards and other great cats were shown the next season, but never again.

Customers possessed of the sort of figure admired by Mme Vionnet can buy the clothes worn by models in the shows for half price. Most require different sizes, and these are created, one at a time, by the couturier's seamstresses and tailors. It may take as many as six fittings to make sure that the dress is perfectly draped for the body, that the covered snaps are in precisely the right place, that the gold metal chain (at Chanel) anchors the jacket precisely as it should, that the supple silk lining doesn't pull.

Nothing in a house of couture carries a written price. If the customer thinks that the price is too high, she can say so; occasionally it will be adjusted.

It is a brave soul who suggests changing the look of a design. The rare victories of customer over designer are justly celebrated. Gloria Guinness, wife of the heir to a vast Irish fortune, scandalized fitter and *vendeuse* by demanding changes in the late Balenciaga's pyramid-shaped dress. "Gloria, how dare you change one of my designs?" Balenciaga asked her sternly. "I dare because my husband will be paying the bill and will not like the dress precisely as you have designed it," Mrs. Guinness replied spunkily. "You are absolutely right," Balenciaga agreed with a grin. Mrs. Guinness was photographed frequently in the adjusted style.

Gloria Guinness's triumph was perhaps unique, but regular customers do have certain privileges in addition to a seat in the front row. The Duchess of Windsor, who did as much for the French fashion industry in her time as Nancy Reagan did for its U.S. counterpart in our own day, often benefited from a 40 percent discount. Regulars who missed a collection used to be sent sketches, descriptions, and prices. Nowadays fashionable women who can't attend the shows are more likely to order from videos or photographs.

Most women treat their couture purchases like the treasures they are. Deeda Blair, a medical-research consultant from Washington, D.C., who wears some of her Paris dresses for as long as 16 years, donates garments she knows she will never wear again to museums. Ivana Trump, wife of New York tycoon Donald Trump, packs older designs off to her mother in Czechoslovakia. But the late Lorraine Rowan Cooper, wife of former Kentucky Senator John Sherman Cooper, would occasionally use the sturdy wool from a couture skirt to cover an ottoman.

"Couture is necessary and must be preserved, because it is the last refuge of the craftsman," Yves Saint Laurent once told me. "The rich woman must preserve couture. Maybe that is not a law, but it is her duty. Otherwise couture and its crafts will die, and rich women will be responsible for the decline of this art *extraordinaire!*"

Already some of the crafts are dying out. Saint Laurent is finding it increasingly difficult to get high-quality *passementerie* (trimming) to replace the original trim on clothes inspired several years ago by the costumes of the Russian peasants of tsarist times or the raffia used in his African designs. The fine satin and taffeta needed to stitch together the 16 parts of a glove are also becoming scarce.

Designers live not by couture alone, but by the things that couture makes possible in the mass market—fragrances, ready-to-wear clothes for men and women, shoes, scarves, and other items with the designer's brand on them. This business started less than 25 years ago, when Saint Laurent kicked off his ready-to-wear line. Other designers followed, to their immense profit: Such products are estimated to bring in nearly 200 times the 50 million dollars earned each year by couture itself.

Buyers from all over the world flock to the official ready-to-wear shows that take place twice a year in tents set up in the courtyard of the Louvre. There is nothing ladylike or gentlemanly about these crowded, market-driven shows. Rock music blasts, and ten models come down the runway at one time, wearing fantastic outfits. A designer has to be director and producer, or hire someone who is, in order to compete.

Clothes are often exaggerated, over-accessorized to beam the message loud and clear to the professional audience in the back of the tent. The designer's chosen team of hairstylists and makeup artists changes the models' look to suit the designer's choice of image. At least 50 other designers show their clothes in schools, restaurants, theaters—even their apartments. The first American to make it big in the ready-to-wear shows is Patrick Kelly, originally from Mississippi, who like a coach before the big game always engages his models, assistants, and dressers behind the scenes in a brief prayer session before the show begins.

Ready-to-wear may not be genteel, but it's good business for French fashion and good business for France. The French government and fashion industry are attached by a strong and ancient thread. President Mitterrand encouraged establishment of the Musée de la Mode in the Louvre and still worries whether the elevators work properly.

Louis XIV established dress edicts for his court that pushed upwardly mobile nobles to the edge of bankruptcy. Like the modern designers who loaned dresses to Mrs. Reagan, he understood the trickle-down theory of fashion—that if someone in a special position wears something, others will imitate. The Sun King decreed that only noblemen of a high rank could wear silver bullion on their waistcoats. "This created a vast popularity for lumps of silver," says Harold Koda, curator at the Fashion Institute of Technology in New York City.

Traveling aristocrats brought the styles of the French court to other European courts. French ambassadors carried books of swatches and designs as a way to boost the silk and other luxury industries.

Napoleon understood that the French Revolution had virtually destroyed France's silk industry, which was essential to the nation's economy. "I saw you in the same dress two weeks ago," he might say, beginning a conversation with a young noblewoman in the simple cotton dress popular at the time. "Don't you think it would be better to dress more richly, like some of the others who are bedecked in silk and embroidery and lace?" The emperor ordered butlers to keep the fires in the court banked, so that the chill would encourage women to cover themselves with more silk.

One wealthy 19th-century American, a Mrs. Moulton, who had been invited to Napoleon III's court at the Palace of Compiègne, bought 21 dresses from Worth: "Eight day costumes (counting my traveling suit), the green cloth dress for the hunt, which I was told was absolutely necessary, seven ball dresses, five gowns for tea." About such lavish wardrobe expenditures she once grumbled, "Some compliments were paid me, but unfortunately not enough to pay the bill."

Other American women have been at the very center of couture. Early in this century Paris designer Jean Patou decided that his "sporting look" was particularly suitable to the long-legged, athletic American woman. According to Patou's grandnephew, Jean de Mouy, who now runs the house on the Rue Saint-Florentin, Patou went to New York City in 1926 and made a deal with Florenz Ziegfeld to hire showgirls to use in presenting his collection. Today many leading models are Americans.

If all this history and current turmoil tells us anything, it tells us that fashion may change, but it never dies. The healthy overstatement of the ready-to-wear shows reassures us on that score, as people come from all over the world in search of clothes that people will buy in the hope of looking perfect.

At the Claude Montana ready-to-wear show last October, there was a wait of more than an hour and a half from the time the show was scheduled until it finally began. Scattered handclapping gave the first hint that the crowd was restless, and before the show started, the rhythmic pounding of feet seemed to rock the tent. But once the show began with a parade of models in wide-legged pants, see-through blouses, jackets, and coats, the audience cheered and the delay was forgotten.

Even the couturiers seem to be getting into the spirit of the future. "It was your best, your best!" one retailer told a dazed Saint Laurent after a recent show. A member of the press kissed the couturier on both cheeks and said, "It's hard to imagine you could do such a brilliant collection again!" And Saint Laurent agreed, "You are probably right."

But he probably will do it again. As the French say, it is his *métier.*

JULY 1989

THE THRUSH
ON THE ISLAND OF BARRA

ARCHIBALD MACLEISH

By the sea loch Island cattle,
    auctioned off for overseas,
shriek in their frantic pens in the
    late
light and the thrush answers
    them . . .

I am remembering something—
    No,
not remembering: it was told to
    me;
some terrible aching thing that
    I was told of the
old time, of the poor crofters

cleared from the Highland glens,
    from the Hebrides.
The landlords wanted the land for
    sheep, not Gaels.
There were sails on the grey sea
    and voices calling
landward over the surf: the
    thrush answered.

Archie Beg MacDonald told it:
    a man could walk from Northbay
    over Barra

clear to the other side and the
    doors open,
the dogs running in and out of
    the open doors

and the unmilked kine at the
    gates—that moaning:
only the unmilked kine and the
    dogs and afterward
evening and the thrush above the
    thatch.

I am remembering something—
    No,
not remembering. My father's
    father
spoke the tongue—not I—that
    can remember.
Nevertheless I hear the Island
    cattle
shriek in their frantic pens. I hear

the thrush answer them: pure
    song,
perfect indifference
    like the will of God.

MAY 1970

SMALL-TOWN AMERICA

GRIFFIN SMITH, JR.

As I drove through the farming country of northern Missouri, the November night was blanketed with silence. Along my route just two places blazed with light. One was the white frame Christian church in tiny Mooresville, where through clear uncurtained windows I saw a dozen worshipers joined in song. The other was Casey's General Store on the highway outside Hamilton—a quick-stop, gas-and-go chain grocery stocked with videocassettes, open until eleven o'clock for anyone who cared to rent a movie. The old and the new: the small town as we remember it and as it may become.

Small-town life has always held a special place in Americans' affections. "Crime is scarcely heard of," Thomas Jefferson said, enumerating the village virtues of the new republic, "breaches of order rare, and our societies, if not refined, are rational, moral and affectionate at least."

Even more than that other great mythic American experience, the frontier, our memories of small towns are laced with warm nostalgia. "The people who lived in the towns were to each other like members of a great family," Sherwood Anderson wrote fondly about his childhood days before the turn of the century. "A kind of invisible roof beneath which everyone lived spread itself over each town. Beneath the roof boys and girls were born, grew up, quarreled, fought, and formed friendships with their fellows, were introduced into the mysteries of love, married, and became the fathers and mothers of children, grew old, sickened, and died. . . . under the great roof every one knew his neighbor and was known to him."

We remember small towns as places of contentment and stability—of volunteer fire departments and town bands, of gazebos on the main square, of courthouses and barbershops, of horses and hitching posts, of general stores and county fairs and choir practice and moonlight walks; places

431

where people had a sense of common purpose and shared values, and the constable always knew which boys were sneaking cigarettes.

Their very isolation provided a sense of security. "The town waited for you," recalled Henry Seidel Canby. "It was going to be there when you were ready for it. Its life seemed rich enough for any imagination. . . . You belonged—and it was up to your own self to find out how and where. There has been no such certainty in American life since."

There is, of course, another side to the story. A quick cure for excess sentimentality about small towns is to talk to someone who has actually lived in one. They will tell you of the lack of privacy, of the occasional self-righteousness and meanspiritedness, of the urge to conformity that is the dark obverse of values shared. In Edgar Lee Masters' *Spoon River Anthology* (1915), an aspiring actress reflects on the town's failure to understand her dreams. "In all this place of silence," she laments, "There are no kindred spirits." In *Main Street* (1920), Sinclair Lewis looked at fictional Gopher Prairie, Minnesota, and dismissed it as "tediousness made tangible."

Even Thornton Wilder, whose play *Our Town* (1938) is among the most loving portrayals of small-town life, did not lose the chance to poke gentle fun at the irrepressible boosterism. The town historian informs the audience that Grover's Corners lies atop Pleistocene granite. "It's some of the oldest land in the world," he adds. "We're very proud of that."

Grounded in 19th-century ways of life, small-town America reproduced itself across a continent. Examine the counties on a map of the United States, and you will find these basic units of American self-government remarkably uniform in size across the country's eastern half. That is no coincidence; they were commonly drawn just big enough for any farmer in his horse-drawn wagon to reach the county seat and return home in a day—about a 20-mile round-trip. Out West, when the open spaces finally became too great and counties were laid off to larger scale, people devised novel ways to cope with distance; the German settlers in the Texas Hill Country built midget "Sunday houses" in town so that the necessary day-trip to church could be lengthened into two.

For generations small towns were the dependable constants of the American scene. But no longer, or at least not in the old familiar ways. In the 20th century small-town America has been caught in a whirlwind of social and economic change. Statistics tell part of the story. The small town reached its zenith in 1910, when 17.5 percent of Americans lived in communities with populations of less than 10,000; that figure has declined ever since (to 11.2 percent in 1980). By 1940 over half the nation lived in metropolitan areas of more than 50,000.

Farms were the economic reason for being for most small towns, and their numbers diminished by a million between 1960 and 1970 alone. A resurgence of growth in small-town America during the 1970s (when only 460 of the country's 2,400 nonmetropolitan counties lost population) has proved short-lived; about half the nonmetropolitan counties have lost population since 1983. These statistics speak of effects, not causes. Behind them lie deep changes of technology and economics, of mind and attitude. Together they stole not only the small town's purpose but its innocence as well.

People felt the ambivalent lure of the great cities. For some they held the promise of jobs; for others they offered what Michael Lesy calls "an almost heavenly radiance of change and refreshment." In his classic study of late 19th-century Black River Falls, Wisconsin, he found that many who chose to abandon the rigid order of small towns did so to escape responsibility rather than to gain it; they "came to the cities not . . . to get work but to be entertained, not to be masters but to be charges."

Then there was World War I, a sudden opening to the outside world whose impact can be seen most forcefully by simply comparing the contents of a 1914 issue of a small-town newspaper—my Grandfather Smith's *Soliphone* of Paragould, Arkansas, will do—with the contents of that same paper in 1917. In 1914 the news concerns are church suppers and temperance drives and local crops and politics; the advertisements promise goods that are "the best in Greene County." By 1917 the editor is reporting from the front in France and merchants describe their offerings as "the best in the country" or "the world." As a result of the war millions of Americans went for the first time beyond the horizons of their towns; in a real sense they could never quite go home again.

And everywhere there came to be automobiles and paved highways. Together these banished the historic logic of the small town—the day's ride in the wagon—and freed the farmer to shop at lower prices in more distant cities.

Survival has come easiest to those small towns that have devised new purposes for themselves. Places like Forsyth, Missouri, and Mountain Home,

Arkansas, which attract urban retirees, have unexpectedly renewed their lease on life. Others, like Lee's Summit, Missouri, and Georgetown, Texas, which lie within a half-hour radius of metropolitan areas, have enjoyed an influx of commuters who combine small-town living with city jobs.

Fayette, Missouri, a town of 3,500 well off the beaten track in the central hills, surprised me by its vitality. There is a small Methodist college there, but that alone did not seem to account for the sense of pride and polish in the place. I got an explanation from Walter Schroeder, a professor of geography at the University of Missouri in Columbia, 25 miles away. "Fayette is becoming a 'dormitory town' for young professionals who work here," he said. "It's full of gorgeous Victorian houses with ten-foot ceilings—the sort of thing they love. And they can buy them for a song."

Still other small towns, fortunate enough to find themselves beside an interstate highway, make a modest living attending to travelers' needs. For the rest—for the quintessential small towns that framed whole lives from birth, to marriage, to old age and death—the future is far less sure. More than larger cities they have difficulty surviving the economic pressures of hard times. Vulnerable to the collapse of oil prices or the farm-belt drought, they lack the resilience to bounce back.

What matters most is jobs and the will to survive. Chillicothe, Missouri, a farming town of 9,000 people far from any interstate, has both, in proportions great enough to warm the heart. I strolled down Washington Street, past the Ben Bolt Theater, a movie house that was not only still in business but was also fine enough to grace a much larger town; past the courthouse where a carillon given by the Staton Abstract Company was pealing out its morning concert; past the Adams-Baker insurance agency, where passersby did not fail to wave a greeting to the folks inside.

New jobs have come to Chillicothe from a sheet-metal factory, supported by an Industrial Development Corporation and a bond issue. And in a twist that sociologists seem not yet to have fathomed, the new discount store on the highway was explained to me by one young resident not as a threat to local merchants but as a sort of civic status symbol, proof positive that Chillicothe was a successful town. "We have a Wal-Mart," she said proudly. "Hamilton doesn't have a Wal-Mart."

Missouri's Highway 5 bisects the state from north to south. To drive it is to take a snapshot of Missouri small-town life today. Browning, Laclede, Brookfield, Marceline, Keytesville, Glasgow, Fayette, Boonville, Lebanon,

Hartville, Ava, Gainesville: Some are thriving, some are death masks; some are spruced up, others are ulcerated; still others are forested with For Sale signs. Interspersed between them are the ubiquitous rural convenience stores that have in many ways supplanted the old market towns themselves.

Now their fates depend on luck and simple courage. Custodians of a vanishing America, who could fail to wish them well?

Yet what seems gone now, irretrievably so, is the old innocence. When I consider what has changed, it is not the satellite dish or the cable beaming the Super Bowl that comes first to mind; nor the black-and-yellow Neighborhood Crime Watch signs in Boonville ("If I don't call the police, my neighbor will"); nor the Manhattan-style spray-can graffiti splattered on Glasgow's library wall; nor the videocassette stores whose racy films surpass the vividest gossip of a bygone day.

Instead it's the "Sho-Me Shopper," an advertising broadsheet that circulates in more than 30 towns in northern Missouri. Leafing through it, I came upon a feature called "Back to Basics Cooking." Pot roast and homemade bread? No, the Recipe of the Week was angel-hair pasta with snow peas in Chinese sauce, stir-fried in a hot wok.

What would Gopher Prairie think of that?

FEBRUARY 1989

TWO HEARTBEATS

CATHY NEWMAN

In winter I dream of trout. Brook trout with orange fins and lemon yellow bellies. Rainbow trout: all crimson and emerald. The golden trout, brilliant as a newly minted coin. There are about 30 species in the trout family, a lifetime of pursuit.

In winter trout hug the bottom of ice-clad streams. Their metabolism slows in synchrony with the still, white world. They may lunge for a minnow or snow fly, but mainly they wait for spring—like me.

Winter melts. The stream stirs, and so do I. I go to a river I know—a broad coil of green water called the Delaware, which forms part of the border between New York and Pennsylvania. The river tumbles over rock, rushing past slopes clad in laurel and hickory.

Caddis flies emerge from mummy cases in which they snuggled as larvae; they rise from the surface like brown mist. Mayflies float on the current, their wings upright on water like tiny sails. They lift off in silver clouds, mate, and fall back. The air is soft. The water boils with trout.

Which wisp of feather and fur will conjure the trout? Sweeping my hand through the water, I scoop up a fly the size of a rice grain. Its body is apple green, its wings like a tiny crumpled pair of silk stockings.

From my vest I choose its dead ringer, a fly known as a Blue-winged Olive. Behind that next boulder languishes the trout of my winter night's dream, sheltered from the brisk current that propels food past his mouth. Observe his rhythm as he dines. Advance. Snap. Retreat.

With breathless hope I lift my rod and flick the fly upstream. It drifts wide. The next cast—short. The third. . . .

A gray snout breaks the surface. The fly vanishes. A swirl of water in its place. I pause. One heartbeat. Two heartbeats. I raise the rod tip. The line stretches and lifts, touched to life by a flash of gold that darts away from me.

I reel him in. No, I coax him in. One does not rush a trout. It is a delicate dance. I reel in line. Wait. Watch. Reel in again.

Tired, and within reach, he is slipped into the net. Gently, I reach for my trophy. Now I hold him: a foot-long wild brown trout, bright, and so alive—ruby- and black-speckled flanks, a belly of burnished bronze, amber fins. We regard each other eye to eye. Unhooking his lip, I set him free. At first he hardly stirs; fins weakly fan the water. Then, a sudden retreat. He vanishes into dark green water—and memory.

FROM "A PASSION FOR TROUT," APRIL 1996

AFTERWORD

OH! SUSANNA!

Roy Blount, Jr.

What is funny about the NATIONAL GEOGRAPHIC? That is an odd question to explore in the GEOGRAPHIC. I feel certain that Mr. Baird Orey, the person who had more back issues of the magazine than anyone else I knew when I was a boy, never looked for the answer to such a question in them. When the Oreys would have us over for supper, Mr. Orey would go to his shelf packed full of GEOGRAPHICS and look for the issue where he had once read something, all the details of which he couldn't remember.

"I believe you'll find that the natives of Micronesia live on poles," he would work into the conversation, unexpectedly.

"On poles?"

"Poles—I remember. . . ."

He would get up and begin pulling out issues.

"Huts on poles?"

"Not *huts*, so much as—it was in, what year? Look! Here's a two-headed turtle!"

That was the part I liked, when Mr. Orey would start finding things he didn't remember at all.

"This twin-headed turtle," he would read to us aloud, "shows why such freaks, though not uncommon, rarely escape their natural enemies for long: each head controls the two legs on its side."

"Imagine," Mrs. Orey would say.

"Often the right head sounds 'Retreat!' while the left orders an advance. Result: the turtle gets nowhere."

"My stars," Mrs. Orey would say. "Baird. . . ."

". . . has a single blood stream, shell, and lower intestine, most other parts are dual. The heads often fight over food and seldom agree on a common objective."

"Whole families just on poles?" my father would say. He liked to get Mr. Orey going. By that I mean he liked to pin Mr. Orey down.

"I think you'll find," said Mr. Orey, moving on from the turtle reluctantly, "that the family structure there is not at all what we . . . Hazel, which issue was it. . . ?"

"I just don't know, Baird. Don't look for it the whole rest of the evening, now, Hon."

But he would keep sneaking looks over there, and my father would say, "I can't feature how poles would hold them up," and he and Mr. Orey would argue about it without either of them having a clear picture of what they were arguing about. Which certainly wasn't the magazine's fault. Nor was it my father's, as he would not refrain from pointing out. Meanwhile I would be on the floor getting a clear picture of the turtle. I have remembered that turtle for 36 years. I was relieved, recently, to discover that I hadn't made it up. I found it in the library by looking through all the issues that came out in 1951 and '52, when I was ten and eleven.

No one I knew back in Georgia when I was that age had ever, except in the Army, traveled anywhere farther away than Washington, D.C., which is where NATIONAL GEOGRAPHIC staffers start out from. But we all knew of jungle life, fezzes, desert islands, lumberjacks, and igloos, largely from two sources: the GEOGRAPHIC and, in other magazines, cartoons.

The cartoonist got it all from the NATIONAL GEOGRAPHIC. I feel certain that no person working for this magazine has ever actually been boiled in a pot— which is perhaps one reason why it has been the source of so much humor.

The NATIONAL GEOGRAPHIC gives off a sense of security. "These fur-hatted Kirghiz admired the way the author packed a yak with diamond hitch, but disliked his boots (too cold, they said). Quolan Larh, who never heard of the U.S., learned to sing 'Oh! Susanna.'"

If someone named Quolan Larh could learn "Oh! Susanna," I could learn about yaks in good humor. Re-perusing those issues of the early fifties has taken me back to my childhood, which was strange (being childhood) but by no means exotic, at least for its place and time. I was prepared to believe anything, as long as it made sound American sense.

By that I mean, I suppose, made sense to my father. He preferred such information as was found in the July 1951 article about wood. The whole wood picture. "Versatile Wood Waits on Man." (Nothing in it about people living on poles—I checked.) The NATIONAL GEOGRAPHIC wasn't out to shock me, so I could cheerfully accept that in New Guinea natives wore marsupial fur in their ears.

There is something funny about an institution that juxtaposes marsupial fur in foreign ears with the story of wood, but I don't know how to put my finger on it. You might as well ask what is funny about cats, uncles, plumbing, breakfast, lawn mowing, Thanksgiving, Pikes Peak, television sets, or monsters under the bed. In any staple of national life there is bound to be comedy.

You notice I haven't said anything about breasts. Neither did my father or Mr. Orey.

PUBLISHED AS "SPOOFING THE GEOGRAPHIC," SEPTEMBER 1988

A BARKING SNAKE

MARK B. KERR

On the journey from Tumaco I was accompanied by an Englishman named Nelson. The first day out we stopped for the night in this interior channel. The vegetation was dense and thick, and parasitic vines stretched completely across the waterway. Many different kinds of parrots combined with innumerable insects and lizards and a few monkeys to make night hideous; and when a sharp, curious noise like a dog-bark caused my friend to thrust his head from under his leafy canopy to inquire, "What is that noise?" I answered "An equi snake." Nelson dropped back under his ranch, and when he ventured out in the morning remarked, "What an infernal country, when even the snakes bark!"

FROM "A JOURNEY IN ECUADOR," JULY 1896

CHARLES MCCARRY, author of eight critically acclaimed novels and seven other books as well as many articles, short stories and poems in leading magazines, has long been associated with NATIONAL GEOGRAPHIC. As a writer, he contributed articles and books on many subjects, including the official history of the National Geographic Society published in the magazine's 100th anniversary issue in 1988. While Editor-at-Large during the 1980s he brought to the GEOGRAPHIC some of the illustrious authors and gifted newcomers whose work appears in this anthology together with that of distinguished contributors who came before and after.